BECOMING

Metropolitan

"NATIONAL COMMUNITIES ARE NOT THE ONLY KIND."

—ALFRED DÖBLIN, 1925

BECOMING

Metropolitan

URBAN SELFHOOD AND THE MAKING OF
MODERN CRACOW

Nathaniel D. Wood

 NORTHERN

ILLINOIS

UNIVERSITY

PRESS

DeKalb

Published by the Northern Illinois University Press, DeKalb, Illinois   60115

Manufactured in the United States using postconsumer-recycled, acid-free paper.
Design by Julia Fauci

Frontispiece— J.R., "Scene on Market Square," 1912. From the collection of the Friends of Fine Art in Cracow. Photograph by Z. Witek. Used with permission.

Photographs in the photo section are from the Krieger "Cracovian Types" series in the Historical Museum of the City of Cracow, taken by Ignacy Krieger and his son, Natan, 1870–1915. Reprinted with permission.

Library of Congress Cataloging-in-Publication Data
Wood, Nathaniel D.
Becoming metropolitan: urban selfhood and the making of modern Cracow / Nathaniel D. Wood.
     p.   cm.
Includes bibliographical references and index.
ISBN 978-0-87580-422-4 (clothbound : alk. paper)
1. City and town life—Poland—Kraków—History—20th century. 2. Urbaniza-
tion—Poland—Kraków—History—20th century. 3. Kraków (Poland)—Press
coverage—History—20th century. 4. Journalism—Social aspects—Poland—Kraków—
History—20th century. 5. Group identity—Poland—Kraków—History—20th century.
6. Nationalism—Poland—Kraków—History—20th century. 7. Social change—Poland—
Kraków—History—20th century. 8. Sociology, Urban—Poland—Kraków—History—20th
century. 9. Kraków (Poland)—Social life and customs—20th century. 10. Kraków
(Poland)—Social conditions—20th century. I. Title.
HT384.P62K739 2010
943.8'62—dc22
2010005050

Contents

Maps and Figures

Acknowledgments

This book could not have been completed without the assistance of numerous individuals and institutions. My foremost assistant in this regard is Professor Krzysztof Zamorski, the former director of the Jagiellonian University Library in Cracow and a professor of history. For a decade now, from the date of my first pre-dissertation travel grant to the happy conclusion of this book, Krzysztof has been my adviser and advocate in Cracow, a ready source of contacts, sources, and sophisticated suggestions. While in Cracow, I was fortunate to meet, often thanks to Krzysztof's introductions, some of the city's foremost historians, including Jacek Purchla, Jan Małecki, and Irena Homola-Skąpska. All were gracious in sharing sources, texts, and ideas, especially early on. Krystyna Zbijewska (1920–2009), a veteran journalist and Wyspiański scholar, took me on a tour of the Palace of the Press (Pałac Prasy), the former home of *Ilustrowany Kuryer Codzienny* and present home of her newspaper, *Dziennik Polski*. Meanwhile, the cordial and patient staff of the Jagiellonian University Library, the Polish National Archives in Cracow and Spytkowice, the Historical Museum of the City of Cracow, the Czartoryski Library, and the Austrian National Library in Vienna helped me find materials I would have otherwise missed. Their smiles of recognition after a hiatus since my last trip always made me feel welcome. I would also like to thank Lucjan and Ewa Miś for making each stay in Cracow more pleasant and comfortable and Walter Whipple for cultivating my interest in Poland and accompanying me on my first trip to Cracow.

I am profoundly grateful to my graduate adviser at Indiana University, Maria Bucur, whose rigorous courses, intelligent counsel, and steady support were invaluable in directing my development as an historian of East Central Europe. Committee members Owen Johnson, Jeff Wasserstrom, and Larry Wolff (who graciously agreed to serve as an outside reader) offered expert guidance on the dissertation and on how to transform it into a book. Special thanks as well to Dror Wahrman, whose graduate course on the cultural history of industrial society introduced me to the value of exploring filthiness in the city, and Bożena Shallcross, who supervised my translation of articles from the Varsovian weekly *Tygodnik Illustrowany* as a first-year graduate student and whose suggestions on the earliest versions of this project proved so prescient.

My colleagues at the University of Nevada, Reno, where I spent a year as a postdoctoral fellow, were generous and welcoming even though it was clear my stay would only be temporary. A travel grant from UNR enabled a trip to the archives in Cracow that significantly expanded the source base of the manuscript.

At the University of Kansas, I have benefited from unstinting support and guidance. I am grateful for excellent libraries and helpful librarians, who have cheerfully ordered numerous books and microfilm from Poland, and for great students and colleagues.. Special thanks must go to Eve Levin, who has been an ideal colleague and friend, and Anna Cienciala, who has always made me feel welcome and valued. Thanks as well to Jonathan Earle for savvy advice on preparing the manuscript. I am also grateful for support from Paula Courtney of Digital Media Services and the Russian, East European and Eurasian Studies Center in printing and shipping the manuscript.

I am indebted to the anonymous readers at Northern Illinois University Press for their careful, insightful, and timely reading of the manuscript. Keely Stauter-Halsted, Eve Levin, Marie-Alice L'Heureux, and Roshanna Sylvester also read versions of the entire text; I thank them for their critical and positive remarks, all of which were needed. Pieter Judson, Alexander Vari, Scott Palmer, and my fellow junior colleagues in the KU History Department, Katherine Clark, Greg Cushman, Jacob Dorman, Megan Greene, Sheyda Jahanbani, Ernest Jenkins, Liz MacGonagle, Leslie Tuttle, Kim Warren, Jenny Weber, and Lu Yang, have offered advice and critiques on various chapters. I especially wish to thank Leslie for encouraging words on my revised introduction, and Jake for emboldening me to try Google Books. To him I owe my discovery of Ménie Muriel Dowie's *A Girl in the Karpathians*. Patrice Dabrowski, Agata Barzycka, Sean Martin, Markian Prokopovych, Harald Binder, Simon Hadler, Jakub Machek, and Bob Rothstein have offered expert advice on the project. Amy Farranto, J. Alex Schwartz, Julia Fauci, Linda Manning, Susan Bean, Sandra Batalden, and others with Northern Illinois University Press have been patient, professional, and encouraging throughout.

Several grants and fellowships have assisted me in researching, writing, and revising this book. I am extremely grateful for an Indiana University Pre-Dissertation Travel Grant, which inaugurated the project, a Fulbright-Hays Dissertation Research Grant, which enabled the pleasant but laborious process of reading and evaluating thousands of pages of the popular press, and the University of Kansas Faculty General Research Fund Grant allocations #2302018, #2301255, and #2301358, which helped me uncover more materials and expand and revise the manuscript. A Vice-Provost for Research Book Publication Award from the Hall Center for the Humanities at the University of Kansas has significantly improved the book by defraying the costs for maps, indexing, and the inclusion of additional images.

Zbigniew Witek, director of the Society of Friends of Fine Art in Cracow, Zdzisław Pietrzyk, director of the Jagiellonian University Library, and Michał Niezabitowski, director of the Historical Museum of the City of Cracow, have graciously granted permission to print images from their collections. I am also grateful to the *Austrian History Yearbook* and *East Central Europe* for permission to use text and material from my articles, revised segments of which appear in chapters 2, 6, and 7. I have since arrived at somewhat different conclusions from that early *AHY* article; it has been a pleasure re-working and re-thinking the material over the years. I am grateful to Brandon Minster for initial work on maps and to Darin Grauberger and Eric M. Weber of the University of Kansas Cartographic Services for the excellent maps included in the book.

Most of all, I wish to thank my immediate and extended family for years of genuine interest and support, ranging from encouraging conversations to reading my articles, coming to visit during a long stay in Poland, or helping to look after my family when I had to go abroad by myself. My parents, David and Marilyn Wood, and my siblings and their spouses have been constant in their support, as have my wife's family. Hugs and kisses for my dear children, Lydia, Ethan, Elizabeth, and Meredith, for all those times they were willing to close the basement door behind them while Daddy worked, and above all for Erin, who studied Polish, spent a year in Cracow with me and our newborn daughter, and has supported me in every way ever since. I dedicate this book to her.

A Note on Translation

In referring to the principal subject of this text I have chosen to use Cracow throughout instead of Kraków or Krakow, because historically, Cracow is the city's English-language name and therefore affirms its status as a city of international significance. English-language books generally refer to Vienna, Munich, or Warsaw, for example, and not to Wien, München, or Warszawa. Cracow's sister city in Galicia, Lemberg/Lwów/Lvov/L'viv is more problematic. Though one recent historical study of this period asserts that Lviv is the city's recognized English name, other English-language texts concerned with this period just as frequently use Lemberg, in part to stress its Habsburg character. I refer to the city as Lemberg, as this was the city's internationally recognized name when it was under Habsburg dominion, though in quotation Lwów occasionally appears, so as to reflect the Polish perspective. In the epilogue, which refers to the city in 1924, when it was under Polish dominion, I use Lwów.

In the text, where an English translation of a specific term appears, I provide the original Polish parenthetically upon its introduction. For some terms, however, including the titles of newspapers, I have chosen to use the original Polish, including spelling that is no longer proper now but was correct at the time (e.g., *kuryer* instead of *kurier* and *illustrowany/ilustrowany* for *ilustrowany*, which had not yet been standardized). In such cases, English definitions follow parenthetically upon introduction. References in the text use the contemporaneous title of the publication, which for two of the major sources for this study, *Kuryerek Krakowski* and *Nowiny dla wszystkich*, changed shortly after their introduction (to *Kuryer Krakowski* and *Nowiny*, respectively). Endnotes for newspaper articles provide the month in English, for ease in determining when the article appeared. Polish-speaking readers who wish to follow the reference will have no trouble translating the month back to Polish. Personal names appear in their original spelling, with the exception of King Kazimierz III Wielki, who is generally recognized in English as Casimir III the Great, and Franz Josef/Franciszek Józef, who appears as Francis Joseph.

Building names such as St. Mary's Church (Kościół Mariacki) or the Clothiers' Hall (Sukiennice) and toponyms such as the Ring-Park (Planty) or Main Market Square (Rynek Główny) generally appear in English translation. Street names, however, have not been translated, for ease in finding them on a map. In Cracovian municipal government the chief executive was (and still is) called a president, assisted by a first and (beginning in 1905) a second vice president. I have chosen to refer to these municipal leaders as mayors and deputy mayors in the text, except when stating their title (e.g., "Józef Sare was elected II Vice President of Cracow in 1905. As a deputy mayor . . . ."). Unless otherwise specified, all translations from Polish or German are mine.

BECOMING

Metropolitan

Introduction

UNLIKELY METROPOLIS

All Poles look upon Cracow, foreigners and our own study in our city, . . . entire crowds of people come here to see our wonderful memorials of history and art, to be invigorated by the national spirit. Therefore Cracow should look after all the wonderful things that the past has given it with the greatest respect and the most diligent care, and at the same time do as much as it can to contribute to the level of civilization of our nation.

On the other hand, Cracow, having belonged throughout its history to the West, has the obligation to move with the spirit of the times and meet as well as it can the needs, which, for the good of the people, genuine and well-understood progress demands.

—Stanisław Domański, II Vice President of Cracow (1904)[1]

In her 1891 book *A Girl in Trousers; being the history of a young lady's adventures in the Karpathians*, Ménie Muriel Dowie characterized the city of Cracow as "old, tired, and dispirited," "a mass of old buildings" reaching out to embrace the traveler as she steps from the "Ring-platz" into the old city. Cataloging the signs of life around her—women working their market stalls, busy shops, the red-roofed courthouse, and lines of cabs—before rather contradictorily dismissing them as things one has "no time to notice," Dowie focused on the pathos of a city mired in its past. Trumpets blared from church towers, playing what she called "the Hymn of Timeless Sorrow," leaving her overcome with the feeling that the city would never regain its splendor as "a gay capital, a brilliant university town full of princes, of daring, of culture, of wit." Unlike Lemberg, the other large city (and capital) of Austrian Galicia, which had the optimism of "any other big new town," Cracow's day had passed. Even if there were to be a new Polish state, she observed, there would be "no place for aristocratic, high-bred Cracow." As her description of the city continued, Dowie acknowledged that it would be unfair to render Cracow as "moribund," noting that "Austria has erected some very handsome buildings," but she stuck to her impression that "everything modern, everything new, was hopelessly out of tone in Cracow; *progress, which, tho desirable, may be a vulgar thing, would not suit her, and does not seem at home in her streets.*"[2]

In this utterly sentimental vision of Cracow, Dowie was reflecting (and even amplifying) the opinions of her hosts, the gracious Poles who must have facilitated her stay in their city. She was a purveyor of the myth of Cracow as the "Polish Athens"—aptly expressed by deputy mayor Stanisław Domański in his 1904 inaugural address (excerpted in the epigraph)—that saw the city as the cultural capital of a non-existent Polish state,[3] a bastion of Polish art, learning, culture, and national identity to which Poles from all over flocked to revere the historic symbols of the nation. The myth of the "Polish Athens" was not entirely backward-looking—for it did look forward to the creation of a Polish state, much as Athens had served as an early nineteenth-century capital of Hellenism and eventually an independent Greece—but its focus was decidedly on the nation and on the past. And as Dowie rightly read it, the myth sat a bit uncomfortably with the city's modern, urban development, making it seem "a vulgar thing" to, say, install electric streetcar lines in a city whose greatest value was its patrimony of national treasures. Dowie's focus on the city's storied past forced her into a pair of blinders that occluded her view of the urban life all around—the shops, market stalls, and horse-drawn cabs awaiting a client—in order to bask in the melancholy glow of the city's old buildings.

As the twentieth century began, Cracow was under the influence of two major historical forces: the interplay of national and imperial politics and the effects of the Industrial Revolution in the guise of modern urbanization. Each force was vital in shaping the city, but one, the national role of the city as a center of Polish culture and identity, was generally more important to the elites of the day and has since dominated the historiography of the city.[4] Most histories of fin-de-siècle Cracow, particularly those in Polish, have emphasized the city's role as a national repository of high culture, Cracow as the "Polish Athens."[5] This book is about the other force, Cracow's modernization, as seen primarily in the pages of the popular press, and the cultivation of its attendant myth, the myth of modern "European civilization." It emphasizes a shift that began around 1900, as Cracow began to take on the trappings of a modern "great city" (*wielkie miasto, Großstadt*). Rather than reiterate the story of nation-building and national self-identification, in this book we point instead to the significance of Cracow's *city-building* and the development of a more tenuous, but not insignificant source of self-identification, namely, identification with modern urban life.

For all of Dowie's conviction that "progress" would be "a vulgar thing" on Cracow's streets, the city could not escape the forces of modern urbanization. During the first fifteen years of the twentieth century, Cracow's population doubled, its territory grew eightfold, and its appearance and outlook became increasingly modern and metropolitan. In 1916, writing about his native Cracow, Jan Stanisław Bystroń noted, "A characteristic trait of the growth of modern society is the fact that mankind increasingly gathers in great centers. The growth of great cities is a phenomenon inseparable from the capitalist era and entirely symptomatic of the times in which we live."[6] As people poured into the city and its suburban communities, it increasingly made sense to eliminate old boundaries and administrative distinctions so that commerce and urban services could function more efficiently. Urban inhabitants needed effective transportation, paved roads, running water, public safety, and better schools. As Vice President Domański also observed in his speech in 1904, Cracow had "the obligation to move with the spirit of the times" and meet the demands of "progress" for the "good of the people." Even if it was more gratifying to propound the city's uniquely significant national role, as a political leader in an increasingly democratic society, he recognized as well the central importance of modernizing like other European cities.

Memoirists and contemporaries alike recognized Cracow's great changes during this period. In his creative memoir/popular history, *Igraszki z czasem* (Playthings with Time), Stanisław Broniewski wrote that the second decade of the twentieth century was a "watershed period in the life of Cracow, in which it reshaped itself from an old-fashioned little town to a modern city."[7] His contemporary the poet and journalist Mieczysław Smolarski, born in 1888, acknowledged that it was not immediately obvious at first but that, looking back, Cracow of 1910 was "no longer the quiet city of his youth. It had modernized, straightened up, and gotten crowded. At the same time it lost much of its former appearance."[8] A journalist writing for Cracow's most popular daily, *Ilustrowany Kuryer Codzienny* (The Illustrated Daily Courier), described the city's transformation this way:

Until not long ago, Cracow was called a "sleepy hamlet" or more mean-spiritedly, "the dragon's pit." Today our city is repairing that opinion and from an insider's point of view, it's going pretty well.

Cracow has straightened up, tossing out its old tatters . . . and has slipped on European dress, maybe not exactly its size and a little shoddy, but it always presents itself well in [its new attire].[9]

Like Vice President Domański, the paper referred to Cracow's moderniza-tion in terms of its relationship to Europe and the West, but it displayed little respect for the myth of the Polish Athens. Poking fun at one of the city's most adored myths, the story of the dragon mortally outwitted by a clever tailor who stuffed a sheepskin with pitch, the paper called for Cracow to make continued efforts to drape itself in the garb of big cities abroad.[10] The article challenged the nationalist vision of the city in favor of a competing discourse, the myth of modern European civilization.

HISTORICAL BACKGROUND—
NATIONAL AND IMPERIAL POLITICS

No one would dispute the role of nationalism and imperial politics in shaping Cracow's nineteenth-century history. Cracow began the century under the dominion of the Habsburg Empire as a result of the third parti-tion of Poland (1795), in large part due to an uprising organized on its main square by the famous champion of liberty Tadeusz Kościuszko, who was also a veteran of the American Revolutionary War. During the Napoleonic Wars the city joined the Duchy of Warsaw and was then re-annexed by the Habsburgs after Napoleon's defeat. As a beneficiary of the Congress of Vienna, it emerged in 1815 as the Free City of Cracow. In 1846 the Habsburgs took over the city again in response to a Polish nationalist uprising centered in Cracow and a peasant *jacquerie* in the countryside. Twenty years later the city gained autonomy as a result of Polish cooperation with the Habsburg authorities and an empire-wide shift toward communal autonomy.[11] Cracow had won the right to autonomous self-government as an Imperial Royal Free City. A failed uprising in Russian Poland just three years before had encouraged many Poles to take a more conciliatory approach vis-à-vis their imperial masters. The Stanczyks (Stańczycy), a conservative political faction in Cracow, urged cooperation with the Habsburgs in order to focus on local development.[12] Their opponents by the 1880s, the liberal democrats, pushed even more for the city's modernization, while promoting Cracow's role as the center of Polish heritage and culture.

During the last third of the century, Poles from all over, including the surrounding Austrian province of Galicia as well as the other partitioned territories of the Russian and German empires, flocked to the city for patriotic commemorations.[13] Medieval and Renaissance buildings from the city's heyday as the capital of the former Polish-Lithuanian Commonwealth were cleaned up and restored, or updated by patriotic artists such as Stanisław Wyspiański (1869–1907), whose art nouveau stained glass windows of God the Father in the Franciscan Church drew (and continue to draw) thousands of gaping visitors. As in other nationalizing cities, a theater and national museum were built, even though Cracow was not even the capital of Galicia—that honor belonged to Lemberg—and had not been the capital of a Polish state for three centuries.

Poland's erstwhile capital, Warsaw, could not serve as the "Polish Athens" because of strict Russification policies after the Uprising of 1863 and ethnic competition in the city. The Russian authorities sought to create a usable Russian past in Warsaw, while marking the city as their own.[14] And unlike in Cracow, where the Jewish elite tended to cooperate with the Polish elite, in Warsaw so-called Litvaks streaming in from the Pale of Settlement as the city grew tended not to assimilate into Polish cultural life.

Unlike Lemberg, too, where Ukrainian nationalism was ascendant, Cracow had few nationalist conflicts vis-à-vis minorities. Jews were well represented in city government and among the elite; the attitude tended to be cooperative in nature. For this reason, Cracow's nationalists tended not to be as virulent as Polish nationalists in the Russian Empire, where the antisemitic National Democrats (Endecja) grew increasingly popular.[15] The Endecja was weak in Cracow.

The intersection of nationalism and imperial politics clearly had an effect on Cracow's economic and urban development as well. On the negative side, the Habsburgs' treatment of the city as a garrison town after 1846 meant that, thanks to its location at the juncture of the three partitions, new walls were erected around the fortress city at about the same time as Vienna began tearing down its medieval walls to create the famous Ringstrasse. This was a major brake on urban development. Yet on the positive side, as soon as locals began to govern themselves, the Cracovian backwater began to regain some of its former glory. As Jacek Purchla has put it, Cracow's modernization in the late nineteenth century came about largely because it was a "Polish den," a haven for wealthy aristocrats whose beneficence aided in the construction of new buildings as much for the nation as for the city.[16] To be sure, this freedom aided in the city's development, as local administrators had more at stake in developing "their" city. Yet modernity on Cracow's streets was not always under the control of the aristocratic elite. As the city became more populous and more democratic (exemplified by continued population growth and the proclamation of universal manhood suffrage in Austria in 1907), it was no longer sufficient to propound urban development in the name of the nation (*naród*). Rather, as Vice President Domański succinctly acknowledged, Cracow's "obligation" to modernize arose more directly from another set of reasons: Western civilization, the *Zeitgeist*, and "for the good of the people [*lud*]." Cracow's place in European civilization demanded it.

Ethnically or religiously speaking, anyway, not all Cracow's inhabitants had reason to identify with the Polish nation, particularly in some of its narrower definitions. Nearly a third of the population of the city was Jewish, and a smattering of German, Ruthenian, and Czech speakers lived there too (see chapter 1). From the perspective of the city's aristocratic and educated elite, Cracow's modernization was supposed to be rational, aesthetically pleasing, and quintessentially *Polish*. For the tens of thousands of petty urbanites, shopkeepers, clerks, bureaucrats, schoolteachers, pupils, housewives, former villagers, and others, however, national patriotism often mattered less than the practicalities of everyday urban existence. This is not to say that ordinary inhabitants of the city were not nationalists (of whatever stripe), but to remind ourselves that they were also becoming metropolitan. And recognizing one's identity as an urbanite at times amounted to the subordination of national identification. As inhabitants of one of the two islands of civilization (Lemberg and Cracow) in Galicia, the poorest province of the Austro-Hungarian Empire, Cracovians had plenty of motivation to identify themselves with fellow urbanites abroad. The villagers in the countryside may have been in the process of transforming from peasants into Poles (or Ukrainians),[17] but in assessing their "level of civilization," denizens of the city often found their co-nationals quite lacking. As their city both literally and figuratively entered the twentieth century, Cracovians looked to other European cities for models on becoming metropolitan.

URBAN SELFHOOD

While scholarship on nationalism in East Central Europe has typically shown that cities were frequently the vectors for growth of national self-identification, this book demonstrates that even in highly nationalized cities such as Cracow, other forms of identification may have challenged nationalism's presumed hegemony there.[18] For ordinary people throughout the region, nationalism could be seen as ennobling, as the gentry nation expanded to include them in the Polish and Hungarian case, or as primarily peasant peoples such as Romanian and Slovene speakers transformed from farmers into teachers and civil servants. And in many cases, as the late Dennison Rusinow observed, to become urban was to become national: moving to the city often meant learning one's national identity and choosing to embrace it.[19]

For those who remained in the countryside, national self-identification was not always immediately attractive. Many inhabitants of villages and small towns identified with the nation only as it suited them—to the consternation of urban activists, the "guardians of the nation," who sought to protect the nation by convincing those whom they saw as their co-nationals to identify with the nation.[20] Just as Pieter Judson's groundbreaking study of this process in southern Bohemia, South Styria, and the South Tyrol has shown that people did not always see the utility of national self-identification, frequently preferring other, more complex or hybrid, systems, so too this book seeks to show that national self-identification was not as hegemonic or "natural"—even in a city—as was previously thought. Even in Cracow, the site of numerous national commemorations, urban and interurban self-identification had great appeal.

Despite the wishes of nationalist activists, for most urbanites identification with the nation tended to be situational and episodic and frequently less fervent than desired.[21] There is no doubt that national identification became increasingly important in the cities of the empire during this period, but its existence need not rule out strong imperial, municipal, or interurban identifications, as well.[22] As Eric Hobsbawm has observed, "we cannot assume that for most people national identification—when it exists—excludes or is always or ever superior to the remainder of the set of identifications which constitute the social being." National self-identification, Hobsbawm further observes, could flare up or lie dormant, depending on the situation.[23] Historians have shown how events such as a politicized murder of a national activist could contribute to highly symbolic uses of urban space and the assertion of national identity,[24] but in the realm of everyday existence, national identity need not have mattered as much.

For many inhabitants of these rapidly growing agglomerations like Cracow, national identity was not as pervasive as national(ist) narratives of the city might have us think. Such people left fewer records; they were not the architects, city planners, and politicians whose voices are easier to resuscitate. They were less concerned with making their city national than they were with making it safer, more comfortable, more "European." As they became literate and read accounts of urbanites abroad, they became increasingly convinced of the benefits of modern European civilization, even if it meant admitting that they were currently "backward" or a bit behind. As they looked toward the future, it was often Europe and not necessarily the nation that seemed most promising. This is not to say that the sources of identification could not coexist or even cooperate, as they most assuredly did, but to point out that the presumed preeminence of one—the national—deserves rethinking. The nation could help one get to Europe, but European civilization remained the overarching goal. In the absence of commemorations, conflict, or competition for resources, the set of associations connected to modern urban life was generally more relevant than the national.

Even in moments of national-historical commemoration, there is evidence that national patriots felt that their urban co-nationals were insufficiently enthusiastic. During the tremendous celebration surrounding the 500th anniversary of the Battle of Grunwald in July 1910, Cracow's popular illustrated press felt it necessary to print articles justifying the celebration with titles such as "Why we celebrate the Grunwald anniversary." Once the commemorations were under way, the press complained bitterly that only the intelligentsia showed up, the crowds were too small, and far too few people participated in the illumination of their windows as part of the celebration. Those who did, one article groused, had only been enterprising shopkeepers, who took advantage of the opportunity to advertise their wares at night.[25] This is not to say that the celebration had been a failure—as Patrice Dabrowski points out, the Grunwald Commemorations represented the apogee of Polish prewar commemorations in terms of participants and planning[26]—but to acknowledge that committed patriots doubted the support of petty urbanites and were disappointed that those citizens most inclined to play along may have merely sought to profit from their public pronouncements of patriotism.

Depending on the context, the inhabitants of cities—like moderns everywhere—have identified and continue to identify themselves in a number of ways. They may identify with their sense of class, religion, gender, neighborhood, city, ethnic group, nation, or in a larger sense, with modern urban civilization itself. In his masterpiece set in the waning years of the Habsburg Empire, *The Man without Qualities*, Robert Musil observed:

> For the inhabitant of a country has at least nine characters: a professional one, a national one, a civic one, a class one, a geographical one, a sex one, a conscious, an unconscious and perhaps even too a private one; he combines them all in himself, but they dissolve in him, and he is really nothing but a little channel washed out by all these trickling streams, which flow into it and drain out of it again in order to join other little streams filling another

channel. Hence every dweller on earth also has a tenth character, which is nothing more or less than the passive illusion of spaces unfilled. . . . This interior space—which is, it must be admitted, difficult to describe—is of a different shade and shape in Italy from what it is in England, because everything that stands out in relief against it is of a different shade and shape; and yet both here and there it is the same, merely an empty invisible space with reality standing in the middle of it like a little toy brick town, abandoned by the imagination.[27]

As impressive as Musil's grasp of the multiple characters of the modern self may be, it should come as no surprise that an observant inhabitant of the Habsburg Empire and more particularly its metropole, Vienna, would have reason to sense the fragmentation of identity in the modern world. The multi-ethnic, multi-religious complexity of the empire—home to at least twelve major linguistic groups and a large population of Jews whose national and linguistic identity never counted in the censuses, but whose role in the empire was indisputable—invited such observations. Still, even in an age of nationalism and divisiveness, Musil seemed to sense that there was something that all modern selves had in common: that abandoned toy brick town. Perhaps fittingly, then, even though he began with a country, and continued to reify the national differences between spaces such as Italy or England, he ended up with a town. Borders may move across the map and characters fluctuate, flowing in and out like rivulets of the self, but the little brick town remains. As an "imagined community," urban identification has a place in the modern self that may be more stable, intimate, and proximate than identification with the nation, but it has been generally overlooked.[28]

As one of the major story lines of the nineteenth century, the growth of great cities was a phenomenon that captured the interest of contemporaries in Europe, the United States, Latin America, and anywhere else that saw the effects of industrial capitalism in pulling ever greater masses to the metropolis. Contemporaries were obsessed with the sheer immensity of the undertaking and strained to make sense of the astonishing numbers of people and goods that coursed through the city. They also frequently worried about the moral effects of modern urban life. In an age of increasing mastery over the processes of disease and contagion, as an understanding of germ theory and the construction of efficient sewer systems increasingly controlled the vectors of disease, bourgeois writers frequently identified the city as a place of great contagion, where moral depravity could spread as efficiently as the literal diseases that had decimated urban populations for millennia. Meanwhile, identification with the city, the set of psychological, social, and intellectual changes that occurred as citizens adapted to modern urban life, was of great interest to early sociologists like Georg Simmel, who speculated that city life actually altered people's physiological perception, by placing special emphasis on sight over other increasingly disused senses.[29]

Few contemporary scholars have analyzed the process of urban self-identification explicitly. In his 1980 book *City People: The Rise of Modern City Culture in Nineteenth-Century America*, Gunther Barth explored typical sites and sources of urban identity, including the metropolitan press, department store, ball park, and vaudeville house. Barth's study captures much of the process of urban and even interurban acculturation that Cracovians experienced at the beginning of the twentieth century. However, Barth's American exceptionalism does not really allow for such a process to occur in European cities. Claiming that Europeans, "[r]ooted securely in a world ruled by a pantheon of great masters, . . . saw culture as a timeless affair," Barth doubted that Europeans could accept the contingency of modern urban culture that his nineteenth-century American protagonists increasingly embraced.[30] In effect, Barth ascribed an older definition of "culture" (i.e., high culture) to Europeans, while reserving the newer anthropological version of the concept ("city culture") to his subjects. Yet, as this book demonstrates, in Cracow during the first decade and a half of the twentieth century, "old masters" and old dictates were increasingly challenged by the new, and citizens increasingly accepted the contingency that this new inter-urban mass culture provided.

Gábor Gyáni's 2004 book *Identity and the Urban Experience: Fin-de-Siècle Budapest* does not cite Barth but is clearly written with many of the same issues in mind. Gyáni's general method is to use a discrete source or set of sources—a diary, suicide statistics, divorce records, formal complaints about "the hoodlum argot" of the "Budapest language"—to illuminate larger issues (often addressed in European or American scholarship) about modern metropolitan life. Gyáni acknowledges the importance of the daily press but offers no analysis of the press itself as a source of urban self-identification.[31]

Like Barth and Gyáni, I am intrigued by the creation of modern metropolitan identities, particularly in a place where one might not expect to find them. Cracow, like many of the cities of the day, found itself in the midst of a significant transformation from a middling sort of place into a big city. Its inhabitants, in describing and reacting to the world around them, increasingly viewed that world through city eyes, grasping it via metropolitan ways of thinking. They and the city they inhabited were becoming metropolitan.

By "becoming metropolitan," I mean the process of adaptation to modern urban life, in such a way that one was conscious, even if only indirectly, of one's participation in what contemporaries frequently termed "modern urban civilization." It meant choosing to wear modern, or what was typically called "Western," dress. It meant learning to navigate life in the city and, soon enough, recognizing that one's worldview was no longer the same as that of one's family or forebears in the countryside, or even in the city of a generation before.

The word metropolitan, of course, has many meanings. It is the adjectival form of metropolis, which can refer to the seat of a bishopric, the center of an empire, or a capital or large city—the meaning most applicable here. In contemporary Polish, the word *metropolia* has the same meanings as metropolis, though a century ago the word most commonly used to describe a large city was *wielkie miasto* (literally, big/great city). Its adjectival form, *wielkomiejski*, appeared frequently when people sought to describe big-city attributes, from big-city filth (*wielkomiejski brud*) to metropolitan transportation (*komunikacya wielkomiejska*).

In the nineteenth century, according to the generally accepted definition, a "great city" was a city of more than 100,000 inhabitants. Before 1900, Cracow did not quite qualify; by 1910, however, its population had surpassed 150,000. In 1910, after nearly a decade of negotiations and planning, Cracow incorporated many of its surrounding municipalities, becoming *Wielki Kraków*, Greater (Metropolitan) Cracow. In successive years more communities joined Greater Cracow, and in 1915, with the incorporation of the city of Podgórze from the opposite side of the Vistula River, Greater Cracow was complete. Cracow was now the fifth-largest city in the monarchy, yet it was still only one-third the size of Prague and not even one-tenth the size of Vienna, which had a population of more than 2,031,000 in 1910.[32]

Cracow is worthy of our attention, not because it was a teeming industrial center—it was not—but because it was an unlikely metropolis, a relatively conservative, provincial sort of place where, according to cultural elites of the time, national identity and reverence for the past were often more important than urban identity and concern for the future. (As the Cracovian intellectual Wilhelm Feldman somewhat snidely observed at the turn of the century, "Whoever wishes to get to know the Polish soul should seek it in Cracow, conjured up in its stones and pictures, in its melancholy graves and in the handful of its choice spirits. And whoever wishes to get to know the life and future of Poland should really just go to Warsaw, to that city of never-ending youth").[33] If we take the national narrative as central, then our focus turns to the city's monuments and the patriotic commemorations that occurred there, its artists and writers and their lasting significance in the Polish canon, and the role of the city as a backdrop for Joseph Piłsudski's legionnaires in

1914.[34] But if we look to the boulevard press and its readers and writers, who could not have foreseen the results of the Great War and the restoration of Polish statehood in 1918, we begin to see a different city, a city that for all its national charms and idiosyncrasies was also becoming a modern metropolis. And even here, in non-industrial, medium-sized, highly nationalized Cracow, identification with modern urban life was profoundly attractive for the tens of thousands who read the popular daily press. They may have feared the filth and crime associated with life in the great city, but they generally believed in the Enlightenment vision of science and progress that suggested urban life could be better. They were aware of their commonalities with urbanites abroad, and they preferred the amenities of city life—paved roads, running water, electric streetcars, electrification, cafes, theaters, schools, and hospitals—to the general absence of these in the countryside. In daily life at least, the myth of modern European civilization was often more immediate and compelling than the myth of the Polish Athens.

While it may include aspects of national identification, urban self-identification is not necessarily national. As Jeremy King has shown in his sophisticated studies of Budweis/České Budějovice, local urban identities often defy the simple polarities of nationalist agendas, and ethnic differentiation does not ipso facto create distinct nationalities.[35] It helps to speak or read the same language as one's neighbors, but urban speech promiscuously assimilates the jargon of its inhabitants on the local level, and urban life in one city often shares enough in common with life in another to enable a sense of transnational communality. Urbanization and modernization, like urban identification, are also transnational, reinforcing the distance between those who are modern and urban and those who are not. By focusing on Cracow's becoming metropolitan, rather than its process of becoming Polish, this book complicates the often falsely teleological nature of many studies of the city, which see its nineteenth- and early twentieth-century history as an exceptional moment between periods of Polish self-rule.[36] It explores Cracow's relationship with its modern present and future, downplaying, as did the contemporaries featured here, the overwhelming emphasis on the glorious nationalist past in order to revel in the contradictions, the delights, and the terrors of becoming metropolitan.[37]

MODERNITY, PAST AND PRESENT

To focus on Cracow's becoming metropolitan, however, is not to *ignore* its relationship with the past. As in most European cities, modernity in Cracow had to coexist with the physical remnants of the past—whether by destroying, reappropriating, or building around them. *Scena na Rynku* (Scene on Market Square), a painting signed by an artist known only as J.R. and presumably painted in 1912, beautifully illustrates the juxtaposition of present and past in Cracow (see Frontispiece). The painting depicts an evening scene downtown on the "A-B line" of the main square in early summer. Electric street lamps glow above the famous Clothiers' Hall (Sukiennice), which towers resplendent in rose and yellow pastels. Throughout the square a number of stiffly rendered people stroll or interact, while a noble couple rides by in an automobile, driven by a uniformed chauffeur. If the background represents Cracow's connection to the past (with feudal castes of gentry, peasants, Jews, and soldiers in the square keeping to their own), the foreground must represent the city's modern present, with tramlines and an automobile, members of the petite bourgeoisie in modern dress enjoying a stroll, and most prominently, the enterprising street children trying to sell flowers or newspapers. To be sure, this book focuses on the foreground, but to erase the background would be to commit the same error as Ménie Muriel Dowie in her depiction of the city, only in reverse. Cracow's modern present had to compete and coexist with its past, and it is this context that makes its modernization particularly salient.

The concept of modernity has traditionally implied a break with the past, a self-conscious sense of newness or novelty,[38] yet as Lynda Nead has shown, modernity in mid-nineteenth-century London was not merely a break with the past but, rather, a constant state of compromise with it. The construction of new streets, the installation of sewers and railway lines, and the erection of new buildings in the city all required the destruction of existing structures, while all around other remnants of the past remained. Modernity, then, was the experience of constant dialogue between old and new.[39]

Observers of Cracow have long known that the city's modern existence is in perpetual dialogue with its glorious medieval and Renaissance past.[40] Quite often, however, it seems that the past has had the domineering voice. In numerous accounts of their hometown, Cracovian writers have described a city in which the stones speak.[41] A Cracovian journalist asked in 1979 whether Poles and Cracovians in particular were "chorzy na przeszłość," or sick with the past, as one might be sick with the measles.[42] The erudite humorist, essayist, translator, and pediatrician best known during this period for his role as a founder of the cabaret Zielony Balonik (The Green Balloon), Tadeusz Boy-Żeleński (1874–1941), termed the city's fin-de-siècle obsession with relics from its past "*pomnikomania*" (monumania), or a mania for statues or monuments.[43] This book makes an effort to bring out the other side of the dialogue, demonstrating that, for many "ordinary people" and the journalists who wrote for them, preserving the glories of the past was not always as pressing as European-style modernity.

Studies on nationalism and commemoration predominate in this part of the world, and not without reason; the development and maintenance of national identities is a central feature of the region's modern history.[44] Yet Central Europe has also undergone the processes of modernization and urbanization, and relatively few works specifically address the cultural history of urban life for this region.[45] Significantly, the citizens of the rapidly growing lesser cities of Central Europe felt themselves to be part of the urban experience under such scrutiny in the largest cities of the age, and they borrowed a number of tropes and narrative structures in use there. Connected by the train, telegraph, and especially the modern newspaper, urbanites increasingly shared a common culture.

THE POPULAR PRESS AND THE CITY

The principal source of my analysis in this book is a close reading of the entire run of Cracow's first three boulevard newspapers, *Kuryerek Krakowski* (the Little Cracovian Courier, 1902–1904), *Nowiny dla wszystkich* (the News for Everyone, 1903–1913), and *Ilustrowany Kuryer Codzienny* (or *IKC*, the Illustrated Daily Courier), which ran from 1910 until 1939 (my close reading stopped in 1915, with the creation of Greater Cracow), supplemented with evidence from popular literature, memoirs, and archival materials. An analysis of the popular illustrated press offers one of the best cultural-historical portraits of the modernizing city, depicting it in ways that studies of architecture, politics, or urban planning—which tend to rely on the perspective of social elites—generally cannot. More than any other kind of newspaper, the boulevard press described the city on whose streets its papers were sold.[46] Unlike political newspapers, which were more concerned with their party's interpretation of national and international politics, the mass circulation press focused on the news and sensations of the city in its attempt to reach the widest possible audience. In translations of articles and reprints of illustrations from city newspapers across Europe, the popular illustrated press also connected readers to other cities, providing a template through which they could interpret the processes of modernization that took place about them. Potent symbols of the "great city" from abroad, such as filthiness and sexual danger, increasingly appeared in Cracow's popular press as the city grew.[47] Meanwhile, fashions, dance steps, detective stories, and other big-city sensations from Paris, London, New York, Vienna, and Berlin reached a mass audience in Cracow, as elsewhere, via the popular press.

On one level, at least, the success of these papers meant that their readers, average Cracovians, likewise embraced their modern, urban existence. Complaints in the press about the failures of urban amenities such as running water, electric streetcars, and city sanitation reflected citizens' desire for greater comfort and efficiency in the city. Meanwhile, theater reviews, feuilletons, and snippets from the daily chronicle helped readers navigate and enjoy the city. Boulevard newspapers gave readers a common urban vocabulary, shaping the contours of metropolitan conversation. In their daily hodgepodge of news, sensationalism, entertainment, and useful information on the city, newspapers mimicked the "spectacular reality" of urban life.[48]

Popular newspapers both reflected and shaped public opinion—a feature that critics at the time and ever since have lamented. In his seminal study, *The Structural Transformation of the Public Sphere*, Jürgen Habermas points out that, as the mass circulation press arose, it deliberately avoided discussion of political issues, focusing instead on the "'immediate reward news' (comics, corruption, accidents, disasters, sports, recreation, social events, and human interest)" that maximized its sales. As news reports turned into entertaining narratives, he writes, the net effect was to "erase the line between fiction and report."[49] Needless to say, Habermas finds this aspect of the popular press deeply troubling, representing as it does a counterfeit public sphere, "a public sphere in appearance only."[50] And Habermas is not alone in this gloomy assessment of the mass circulation press. The Swiss sociologist and press historian Jean Chalaby contends that the sensationalist press represented the advent of a new discourse that appealed to readers' sentiments instead of to "reality." Chalaby laments that the media, ever since the last third of the nineteenth century, were to blame for increasing rather than diminishing public ignorance.[51]

Yet several scholars of the fin-de-siècle urban popular press, most notably Peter Fritzsche, Vanessa Schwartz, and Roshanna Sylvester, have taken another stance on the "spectacular reality" of the mass circulation press, pointing out that it was popular precisely because it helped explain the world in which it was consumed. Sylvester's study of pre-revolutionary Odessa engagingly explores the creation of urban "types" in the press and the effort to define respectability in a city known for its criminality. For Odessans the stories in the popular press were not just entertaining diversions, they were primers in respectable behavior and a warning of the dangers of the metropolis.[52] Peter Fritzsche argues that the popular press in Berlin functioned as a modernist voice, a multivocal representation of the city that ran counter to conservative, elite interpretations of the urban experience. Newspapers were indispensable guides to the city that helped readers to see themselves as part of a metropolitan public: "[As] readers encountered the city, they became increasingly self-conscious of themselves as a city-wide public," Fritzsche writes. "It was not so much newly kindled nationalist feelings or old-fashioned civic virtues as the pleasures of urban spectatorship that created a tentative, but unmistakable unity in a shifting environment."[53] This is an observation mirrored by Schwartz in her study of "spectacular reality" in fin-de-siècle Paris, which she claims "created a common culture," because citizens had "visual evidence" that a shared metropolitan "world, of which they were a part, existed."[54] In these scholars' accounts, the popular illustrated daily press was so successful, not because it dulled political sensibility and ignored "reality," but because it matched so perfectly the mass culture environment of the big city.

Fritzsche, Schwartz, and Sylvester illuminate the respective metropolitan cultures of the cities they study, something I do in this investigation of Cracow as well. Where this present study differs from theirs, however, is in the fact that, first, unlike Berlin or Paris, or even Odessa, which were among the largest and most modern cities of the day, Cracow was an unlikely metropolis. If readers of the popular press in Cracow, a medium-sized city obsessed with its past and nationalist significance, were also developing metropolitan identities, then this tells us something about the influence of these newspapers and the importance of urban self-identification among people about whom the historiography has generally assumed that only national identification matters. For citizens of middling but modernizing cities like Cracow, discovering and enacting metropolitan identities reinforced their break from a provincial past while affirming their belonging to modern urban civilization.

Second, while other books recognize the importance of the press in promoting local metropolitan identification, none of them really considers how the popular press of this era helped develop *interurban* identification, or a sense of commonality among residents of cities that may have transcended national borders, both literal and metaphysical. Again, because of Cracow's position as a junior partner among the "great cities" of the day, it is instructive in this regard, as well. Cracow's connection to the interurban culture of the time can be seen as evidence of an increasingly global society in the era of the locomotive, telegraph, telephone, and modern newspaper. Even if the city did not experience all of the hyperbolic sensations of a Paris or Berlin, it shared enough urban "common ground" that when its newspaper readers encountered stories from such huge cities, they had a framework through which to comprehend them. Strolling the city streets, sipping coffee in cafés, riding the electric tram, and above all, reading the boulevard press connected Cracovians to modern big-city culture.

In order to understand Cracow's metropolitan transformation, it is necessary to consider its history, population, geography, and demographics more closely. Chapter 1 explores the city's layout and population at the turn of the century, often in comparison to other cities in the empire and region. It demonstrates the demographic and social shifts that made mental shifts, such as identifying with modern urban life, possible. Chapter 2 investigates Cracow's popular press as a simultaneously local and multinational form. This chapter introduces what I call "the interurban matrix," the daily blend of news and sensations from home and abroad that characterized the popular press of the day and helps explain its popularity. The chapter also provides a history of the popular press in Cracow, focusing on the career of Ludwik Szczepański, the innovative editor of *Nowiny dla wszystkich*.

If Szczepański represents a crucial innovator in Cracow's press history, Cracow's mayor Juliusz Leo, described in chapters 3 and 4, is his analogue in city government. The forward-looking and ambitious mayor of the city from 1904 until his death in 1918 was largely responsible for the creation of Greater Cracow. Chapter 3 offers a close analysis of a special series from 1903 to 1904 in *Nowiny dla wszystkich* about the creation of Greater Cracow, illustrating the contentious, but pragmatic, terms of debate surrounding the planned incorporation of the surrounding communities, while offering a rare view of the suburban perspective on incorporation. Chapter 4, meanwhile, demonstrates that despite the rhetorical use of the nationalist trope "Polish Athens" in speeches by politicians like Leo, local citizens and suburbanites understood the incorporation of the surrounding districts not as a national triumph but as the desired "Europeanization" or modernization of their city.

One of the most visible signs of modernity in Cracow was the appearance of electric streetcars and automobiles on its narrow streets. Chapter 5 analyzes images and discourses related to new transportation technologies such as electric streetcars, automobiles, and airplanes. This chapter demonstrates that despite sensationalistic stories about tram accidents, which appeared shortly after the machines were introduced in the city, within a few years the newspapers only complained about the trams' inefficiencies, not their dangerous speed. Although newspapers delighted in the sensational aspect of automobiles and airplanes, they also did much to familiarize readers with the new technologies. In this regard, chapter 5, like the chapters on the creation of Greater Cracow, shows how readers were developing metropolitan attitudes as they effectively "naturalized" the city around them.

Adapting to urban life was not easy, particularly due to the city's association with moral and literal filthiness. Chapter 6 explores images of filth and corruption in the "great city" and the modern desire to control these problems through effective hygiene and policing. It argues that although the newspapers and the citizens who read them clearly manifested discomfort and even fear about becoming a big city, they ultimately embraced their urban existence. Complaints about urban filth, like complaints about the inefficiencies of the trams, should not be taken as evidence of rejection of the metropolis but, rather, as proof that ordinary citizens were committed to city life and believed it could be better. While "great-city filth" may have been frightening, modern urban life was definitely preferable to the mud and boredom of rural life. In differentiating themselves from their co-nationals in the countryside, Cracovians chose to identify with modern metropolitan culture.

The concluding chapter explores the ways that Cracovians, and especially those who were considered most vulnerable to the dangers of the city, were becoming metropolitan, whether in adopting modern fashions, joining or following the successes of local sports clubs, or adopting other urban behaviors such as visiting cafés, attending the theater, and reading the newspaper. The epilogue briefly investigates the persistence of metropolitan identities in the years following the Great War by turning to another outsider's depiction of the city, that of the German writer Alfred Döblin.

Overall this study opens a new way to look at the history of urban culture in East Central Europe by displacing the central importance of nationalism in favor of another source of identification that coexisted with and at times supplanted it. It demonstrates that the grand telos of national development need not be the only story line associated with the region's late nineteenth- and early twentieth-century history, pointing out instead the very real attraction for tens of thousands of ordinary Cracovians of becoming metropolitan.

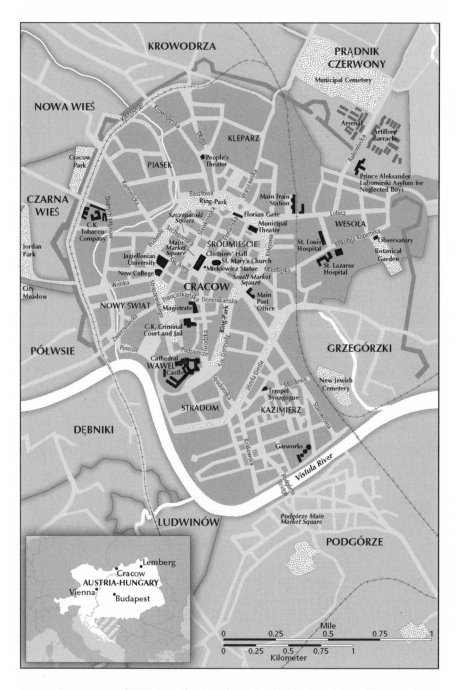

Map 1—**Cracow around 1900.** Note the ring of Austrian fortifications. Most of them would be gone by 1903, as a new line of fortifications was erected further from the city center.

CRACOW AROUND 1900

People, Place, and Prospects

I'm well-born . . . for I was born in Cracow.
—**Kazimierz Marjan Morawski**[1]

with its 50 churches and monasteries, this Cracow-fortress,
this Cracow of bigots and bureaucrats.
—**Ignacy Daszyński**[2]

And yet, God forbid, despite the fact that we have here among
us enlightening institutions and moral institutions, and
we even had a public meeting about prostitution, thefts in
Cracow are as ordinary as a gathering of servants under the
statue of Mickiewicz.
—*Nowiny,* January 11, 1908

On an elbow of the Vistula River running along the edge of the dolomite hills of
the Carpathian plateau, Cracow lies in what is now southern Poland, but in 1900
its location put it in the northwestern corner of the Austrian province of Galicia,
at the narrow center of the two bulging halves of the monarchy embracing the
Kingdom of Hungary. Less than 100 kilometers to the south, the border with
the Slovak territories of Hungary ran along the peaks of the Carpathians. Some
50 kilometers to the west of Cracow lay the German province of Silesia, while 25
kilometers east of the city, the border between Austria-Hungary and the Russian
Empire began to follow the Vistula as it meandered northeast to Sandomierz.
Cracow was a "central place city," with a localized pull clearly affected by this

geopolitical situation.[3] Fully 87 percent of its population in 1900 had been born in Galicia: 40 percent in Cracow itself and 47 percent from outside the city. Less than half of the remaining 13 percent came from Austrian territories, particularly Moravia and Austrian Silesia. Of the nearly seven thousand inhabitants born outside of Austria, the majority were Polish Catholics or Jews from the other historically Polish territories, especially the Polish Kingdom (Królestwo Polskie) in Russian territory.[4]

A newcomer to Cracow in 1900 would have found it a bustling, but dirty and rather provincial, place. On the cusp of a new century, the city was growing rapidly, although it lacked the appearance or feel of a modern metropolis. Churches dominated its skyline, only horse-drawn vehicles and pedestrians moved along its streets, and most people in the city would have been readily recognizable according to rank, religion, and class. The universal and universalizing symbols of modern urban culture—major municipal and commercial buildings, electric streetcars, electric lights, and petty urbanites dressed in ready-made Western attire—were still relatively rare or absent altogether. The city was poised to embrace its modern, capitalist, big-city existence, but in 1900 it bore far more traces of the past than evidences of that modern metropolitan potential.

Still, there would have been much to inspire awe, especially St. Mary's Church (Kościół Mariacki) with its imposing asymmetrical twin towers and the massive Main Market Square (Rynek Główny), among the largest in Europe, with its central adornment, the Clothiers' Hall (Sukiennice), a long two-storied marketplace with airy colonnades flanking each side. There were numerous stately churches, the handsome Municipal Theater (completed less than a decade before), parks full of chestnut and linden trees, fascinating remnants of crenellated medieval walls, the courtyards, auditoria, and academic buildings of one of Central Europe's oldest universities, and of course, the castle and cathedral atop Wawel Hill overlooking the Vistula River. Centuries before, Wawel had been the home of Polish kings, and much of the city's current glory was still due to that fact. But at the time, the castle complex itself was decrepit and surrounded by barracks for the Austrian army.

The city's teeming marketplaces, meanwhile, full of women in colorful scarves and long skirts, ragamuffin street youth, and haggling shoppers, would have attracted attention as much for their stench as for their wares. One memoirist of the city, the daughter of a doctor, recalled that she held her breath every time she had to pass through the markets at Szczepański Square, the entrance to the Clothiers' Hall, or Small Market Square.[5] Meat brought in from the surrounding countryside on dung-splattered carts sat in the open, awaiting the scrutiny of passersby. Municipal running water was as yet unavailable. Housing conditions were generally terrible, expensive, overcrowded, and unsanitary. Cholera outbreaks remained a serious threat (the last had occurred only eight years before), and all segments of the population, but especially the poor, had reason to fear respiratory diseases such as tuberculosis, which was the cause for *half* of all deaths in the suburban districts of the city and a much graver threat than in Berlin, Vienna, or Warsaw. That year in Ludwinów, a proletarian neighborhood on the opposite bank of the river, nearly *every* death was due to tuberculosis or pneumonia.[6]

If the potential immigrant to Cracow was a young woman from a peasant household (as was statistically the most likely case), her destination, no matter what means of transportation she may have used to get to town, would have almost certainly been the new statue of Adam Mickiewicz on the Market Square, in between the Clothiers' Hall and St. Mary's Church. Regardless of whether she knew anything about the great poet-patriot whose remains had been transported from Paris and interred in the crypts at Wawel a decade before, she would have been told by others at home or along the way that this was the place to go to find work as a domestic servant, particularly on the first day of the month. Here, beneath the statue, women from near and far gathered, well into the 1920s, as willing participants in a slightly different sort of meat market, where they would hand over precious references and answer some questions while enduring the scrutinizing gaze of their prospective masters in order to find work and a place to live. According to one resident, the commonest question put to prospective servants at the statue was: "You're not a thief, are you?"[7] "Civilized" Cracovians hated it; even if the servant market's rational location in the central shopping district had arisen entirely to meet their needs, the whole process seemed too open, too naked: a blatant reminder of the poverty of the countryside—and their willingness to exploit it—in the heart of the city. Just as when the socialists gathered in the same spot for parades and strikes, it besmirched the original commemorative purpose for the statue, undercutting the ability to control the meanings of social space.

In the November 15, 1903, issue of *Nowiny dla wszystkich*, in a section entitled "Our reader's little complaints, justified and not," one reader lamented that the Mickiewicz statue had been reduced to a marketplace for servants. Another bemoaned the tendency of meat dealers to handle meat and money with the same hands.[8] While they may have called attention to different problems, both readers were really complaining about the same thing. For them, Cracow was insufficiently civilized, insufficiently modern.

Aware of their common problems at home and the variety of solutions attempted in other cities abroad, *Nowiny*'s readers and writers sought a more modern, "European," city, where the raw vicissitudes of capitalism and rapid industrialization were subjected to the control of scientific rationality, where education, hygiene, sewers, and running water helped stem the ravages of disease, and where paved streets and electric streetcars helped orchestrate the movement of people and goods throughout the metropolis.

And in large part, as the first decade and a half of the twentieth century progressed, they got their wish: Cracow early in the second decade of the twentieth century was a markedly different city from its incarnation in 1900. Most of the historic landmarks were still there, renovated perhaps, and the dirty markets continued to operate, though some of them, such as the one on Small Market Square had been closed by municipal authorities. Yet the city and its citizens had nonetheless changed. They were becoming metropolitan. From 1910 to 1915, little Cracow became "Greater Cracow," a city eight times its former size, as suburban communities and the city of Podgórze joined the city. Running water and electric streetcars were put into use in 1901, electrification occurred in 1905, and by the winter of 1910/1911, "all spheres of society, but especially the clerks" could buy frozen meat shipped all the way from Argentina in their downtown shops.[9] Local farmers and rural landlords felt duly threatened by this direct incursion of the global marketplace, but Cracow's increasingly urbane citizens were glad for the alternate source of inexpensive meat.[10]

Around 1900, spurred by the demands of rapid population growth, insufficient urban services, and desire to emulate the development of large cities within the empire as well as others abroad, Cracovian leaders and many of its inhabitants increasingly recognized the appeal of transforming Cracow into a modern European big city. The social and demographic changes of the two decades before the turn of the century helped make this shift of mentality possible. Following a pattern common in central and southeastern Europe, Cracovians sought to follow the model of other European great cities in the process of transforming their city into a modern metropolis. Thus the "Little Vienna on the Vistula," as Cracow was commonly known, was poised to become a "big city."

Already in 1846, Cracow was the easternmost tip of a railway linking it to the Silesian capital, Breslau, and from there onward to Berlin and Hamburg. Within a year railway lines connected the city to Warsaw and, by 1848, to its new imperial capital, Vienna. For Galician peasants and Jews migrating to North or South America, Cracow was often the last linguistically familiar point on the journey to the oceangoing vessels in Hamburg or, less commonly, Trieste. There were several Cracovian travel agencies that specialized in such journeys, which became much more frequent in the 1890s and at the beginning of the new century. Cracow's privileged citizens would have used the train to get to Paris, the French Riviera, Italy, the Baltic seashore, or more frequently, the mountain resort town of Zakopane, south of the city.[11] By the early twentieth century, one could travel 413 kilometers to Vienna in a mere seven hours on the fast train. The trip to Lemberg would have taken an equal amount of time, though geographically the Galician capital was closer by almost 90 kilometers.[12]

Poles from all over traveled to Cracow to participate in patriotic commemorations, visit sacred sites of Polish nationhood, or attend the university. For German-speaking tourists, Cracow was recognized as a worthy tourist destination; travel guides consistently had much more coverage for Cracow than for the larger city of Lemberg.[13] Two American travelers, Sallie and William Thayer, made Cracow one of only five locations visited on their 1905 tour of Austria (the others were Vienna, Prague, Salzburg, and Bischofshofen). They stayed in the Grand Hotel and placed a mark in their German-language Baedeker next to entries for St. Mary's Church, Wawel Castle, and the statue of Copernicus.[14] Cracovians, and especially the elite, could keep track of notable visitors to their city by scanning the "arrivals" section of the conservative newspaper *Czas* (Time), which published the names of guests in the city's best hotels. But, of course, the largest influx of visitors to the city came from the ranks of the rural proletariat, who came to Cracow seeking work or who passed through the city on their way to and from employment in the West.

NEIGHBORHOODS

To the young woman seeking work in 1900, downtown Cracow (Śródmieście) must have seemed an amazing, variegated place. Of all the city's eight boroughs, the city center was certainly the most diverse, where everyone from aristocrats and professors to beggars and gypsies could easily cross paths. Aristocratic families, including the Potockis, Lubomirskis, and Czartoryskis, had their palaces along the Market Square or its adjacent streets. Lawyers and wealthy businessmen, some of them Jews who had moved downtown in the latter third of the nineteenth century or Polonized Germans and Czechs whose parents had come to the region from Bohemia or Silesia in the first half of the nineteenth century to work in the nearby

Wieliczka salt mines or as imperial bureaucrats and administrators, had their homes and shops downtown as well. The young woman would have seen the privileged alighting from carriages and cabs, middle-class patrons of the horse-drawn trams, and all sorts of people moving through the market square on foot. Dandies and elegantly attired women would have strolled along the A-B line of Main Market Square, from St. Mary's Church toward Szczepańska Street, Szczepański Square, and on to the Ring-Park (Planty), the ring of trees and footpaths that encircled the entire Old Town. (Just that year, on the Planty side of Szczepański Square, the Society of the Friends of Fine Arts building, the official home of Cracow's Secessionist-style movement, was completed.)[15] Orthodox Jews in black gabardine likely attracted her attention, as they moved to and from downtown, mainly along Grodzka and Starowiślna Streets, the major commercial thoroughfares that connected the center of the city with Kazimierz, the primarily Jewish district. Meanwhile, she may have caught the eye of any number of students, with their longish hair and robes. Soldiers, too—some six thousand of them inhabited the garrison town in 1900—likely leered at her as she walked by. The population of Śródmieście had been on the decline since the early 1880s, as citizens chose to live in less crowded neighborhoods outside the city center, and the downtown converted, as in other European metropolises of the day, into an increasingly commercial space.[16]

Sweetshops and restaurants dotted the main square, including Hawełka's and Wentzel's, two of the city's most popular establishments. Jan Fischer, the gregarious businessman, sportsman, and owner of Cracow's first automobile, plied paper products in his much beloved shops on the Market Square.[17] Along Grodzka Street, which seemed to pour from the southern corner of the square toward Wawel and the river, and Floriańska Street, which ran between St. Mary's Church and the part of the Ring-Park nearest the train station, one could buy all sorts of goods, from jewelry and furs to lamps, clothing, books, and medicine. The café and sweetshop popularly known as Jama Michalika (Michalik's Burrow), a gathering place for artists and literati, was located on Floriańska Street in view of St. Florian's Gate, a remnant of the medieval fortifications.[18] Many of the churches, streets, and buildings downtown were named after saints, including St. Michael's Jail, which was connected to the C. K. (Imperial Royal) Criminal Court. The jail was located under a telegraph pole, a detail that came to stand in popular parlance as a metonym for the jail itself, such that Cracovian criminals instead of "going to jail" spent time "under the telegraph."

East of downtown, jutting out from the oval-shaped city like a large cartoon nose was the district of Wesoła, home to the main train station and many of its workers. Proportionately, Wesoła had the smallest population of elderly people, presumably because some of those workers, Austrian Germans or Czechs, chose to retire elsewhere in the empire. The comparative lack of elderly citizens could have also arisen from the fact that so much of the neighborhood itself was new. In 1900, almost one-third of the 310 buildings located in the district were less than a decade old.[19] The main post office, university botanical garden and observatory, and several medical facilities, including the St. Louis (Ludwik) and St. Lazarus Hospitals, were all located in Wesoła. (The latter hospital was a regular stopping place for the city's hundreds of legally registered prostitutes whenever they underwent periodic mandatory checkups for venereal diseases—often on Tuesday and Friday mornings at nine.)[20] Just beyond the northern border of Wesoła, on Rakowiecka Street, was the Prince Aleksander Lubomirski Asylum for the Upbringing of Neglected Boys, a modern building completed in 1893. The asylum was designed by local architects and underwritten by a huge donation of two million francs from Lubomirski, an expatriate aristocrat who lived in Paris.[21] The Arsenal, just across the street from the asylum, was one of several military installations in the vicinity, including the artillery barracks up the street and the imposing four-story Archduke Rudolf Barracks on Warszawska Street.[22] During the first few years of the twentieth century, as the fortifications around the old town were dismantled, even more military installations appeared in this area. Beyond the Arsenal lay the municipal cemetery, built after the graveyards adjacent to churches downtown were leveled for sanitary (and spatial) reasons in the first decade of the nineteenth century.

North and northwest of Śródmieście were the districts of Kleparz and Piasek. Workers, many of them recent migrants, as well as artisans, shopkeepers, and petty bureaucrats predominated in Kleparz, while professors and professionals tended to live in Piasek, which was adjacent to the university. Nearly one-tenth of Piasek's population was entitled to vote, more than in any other neighborhood, particularly because of the large number of educated citizens of the First Curia (Intelligentsia) there, who constituted 6 percent of its total population.[23] Perhaps unsurprisingly, Piasek also had the most servants per capita of any neighborhood in the city in 1900. (Servants constituted 15% of the population in Piasek, 12% downtown, and approximately 10% in all of the other districts, except Kazimierz, where they accounted for only 6%.)[24] Newer multi-story apartment buildings in Piasek, which were more likely to have basement rooms for servants and porters, ran up to the formal borders of the city. Just across the border where the main thoroughfare, Karmelicka Street (so named for the Carmelite cloister it ran alongside), bisected the outer ring road and train tracks was Cracow Park.

For all its academic character, Piasek was also the site of the city's largest business, the Imperial Royal Tobacco Factory on Dolnych Młynów (Lower Mills) Street, with more than a thousand employees, most of them women, the "cygarniczki" (cigar girls) who earned from six to fourteen crowns a week using machinery to roll cigars and cigarettes.[25]

Beneath Piasek lay the rather small Nowy Świat (New World) neighborhood. Jutting out in a narrow strip from its northwestern corner was the City Meadow (Błonia), a field frequently used for fairs, Sokół (Falcon) quasi-military fitness maneuvers, and other entertainments. (This field would be the site of a rather raucous visit by Buffalo Bill's troupe in August 1906.)[26] Locals likened the City Meadow to the Prater in Vienna. The Rudawa, a small tributary to the Vistula, ran along one side of the meadow, and along another (already in the suburb of Czarna Wieś) were Jordan Park and the city racetrack. Jordan Park, named after the physician Dr. Henryk Jordan (1842–1907) who founded it, had exercise equipment for city youth, a summer restaurant that provided free meals for exercising children, a small pond with paddleboats, and busts of famous Poles surrounded by shrubbery and park benches. At the southwestern corner of Nowy Świat was a small train station and one of only three bridges spanning the Vistula. The Dębniki Bridge offered a fine view of Wawel Castle to the right as one passed over into Dębniki, a generally working-class suburb that had grown by 226 percent in the last decade due to overcrowding and overpriced real estate in Cracow. (Cracow's population had grown by 22% in the same period.) Many of the inhabitants of Dębniki, Zakrzówek, and Ludwinów worked in construction, quarries, or tanneries. Day laborers, cab drivers, laundresses, and cygarniczki from these districts would have used the bridge daily to get to work.[27]

The tiny Wawel neighborhood with only 78 inhabitants, most of them members of religious orders affiliated with the cathedral, occupied the hill south of Nowy Świat and the city center. Perched on a large limestone outcropping, it afforded a good view of the city and the suburban neighborhoods across the river. Because of this strategic location, the Austrians had integrated Wawel into the first series of fortifications built in 1848 after their takeover and dissolution of the Free City of Cracow. Rendered somewhat obsolete by a newer ring of fortifications, Wawel was now in a state of disrepair. After years of negotiation, city officials finally managed to gain formal control of the castle complex in 1906. Patriotic Poles had great aspirations for Wawel's restoration, including Stanisław Wyspiański and Władysław Ekielski's grandiose 1905 plan to create a modern "Akropolis" on the site with a parliamentary building, an amphitheater, and an oval track for footraces, but in 1900, even formal Polish control remained in the realm of wishful thinking.

The border between the next two districts, Stradom and Kazimierz, was the old corridor of the Vistula, which had been filled in some twenty years before, thereby greatly improving the sanitary conditions of the area, while more thoroughly incorporating Kazimierz into the city. Cracow's only tree-lined Parisian-style boulevard, Dietl Street, was built atop the corridor. Dietl Street took its name from the city's first mayor after autonomy in 1866, the professor of medicine Józef Dietl (1804–1878), whose farsighted plans to create a more modern and hygienic city continued to guide city growth well after his death. But the impressive boulevard was also a testament to the energy and wealth of Cracow's Jewish commercial and financial elite, many of whom took up residence there once the boulevard was completed. Like many urban revitalization projects of the era, including the remodeling of the Clothiers' Hall in advance of the Józef Ignacy Kraszewski Jubilee in 1879, the construction of Dietl Street was financed largely with Jewish capital.[28] Most inhabitants of Stradom and Kazimierz were Jews or poorer Christians. Stradom was relatively small in size and population, with fewer than 4,500 inhabitants, but had more members of the Third Curia (Artisans and Shopkeepers) than Wesoła, which had three times as many inhabitants. Approximately two-thirds of Stradom's inhabitants were Jewish.

Kazimierz was the heart of the city's Jewish community, having been a home for Jews since its founding in 1335 by King Casimir III the Great (Kazimierz III Wielki), and an explicitly "Jewish Town" ever since King Jan Olbracht expelled the Jews from Cracow in 1495.[29] In 1900, fully one-quarter of Kazimierz's 24,310 inhabitants was Christian, but in the popular imagination it remained a quintessentially Jewish neighborhood. (Christians tended to live in the southern part of the district, near the gasworks and the river.) Synagogues, including the progressive "Tempel" on Miodowa Street, ritual slaughterhouses, cheders, and the Jewish cemetery were located there; mostly concentrated in the historic Jewish Town between Bożego Ciała and Starowiślna Streets, where Jews had been hemmed in for centuries by restrictive laws, tradition, and desire to remain among co-religionists.[30] Polish Christians who did not live there themselves tended to picture Kazimierz as filthy, uncared-for, and ragged.[31] And to be sure parts of it were—due primarily to overcrowding. Housing was so inadequate that people often inhabited attics and hallways, and cholera outbreaks were always most severe in Kazimierz. But there were also several modern apartment buildings in the district, designed by talented native sons such as Józef Sare (1850–1929), who also oversaw the construction of the New College building (Collegium

Novum) for the university in 1881 and who became the deputy mayor of the city in 1905. (Sare's capable service to Cracow, including his oversight of the evacuation of the city in the first year of the Great War, earned him widespread support, even if some Christians may have originally balked when he did not renounce his faith upon assuming office, as many of his Jewish predecessors in the higher ranks of municipal government had done.)[32]

Cracovian Jews largely governed themselves, interacting with Polish politicians in municipal and provincial government. Beginning in 1866, with the granting of self-government to the city, Jews were eligible to serve in municipal government so long as they met the criteria of the curia system, which discriminated in terms of sex, wealth, and education but not religion. The percentage of Jewish municipal elected officials thereafter was rather high, at approximately 20 percent, but not consistent with the percentage of Jews in the population, which was nearly 35 percent in 1869 and 28 percent in 1900.[33] The *kehillah* (Yiddish *kahal*, Polish *gmina*), meanwhile, was the fundamental unit of local government, acting as the representative voice of the Jewish community in interactions with Polish and Austrian authorities. Despite their competition in religious and other matters, progressive and Orthodox Jews in the *kehillah* essentially agreed that the progressives "would act as a liaison with the Polish community while the Orthodox would manage religious matters such as the rabbinate, *mikvah* (ritual bath) and ritual slaughter."[34] Socialist Bundists, Zionists, and Integrationists, led by the lawyer Adolf Gross (1862–1936) and Józef Sare, had begun to complicate the Jewish political scene in Cracow by 1900. Gross's Party of Independent Jews, formed that year, "opposed both the complete assimilation of Jews and their medieval-style segregation in ghettos" and had its greatest electoral success before the war.[35] The Zionists, led by the talented Ozjasz Thon (1870–1936), who collaborated with Theodor Herzl in organizing the First Zionist Congress and served as rabbi of the progressive Tempel from 1897 until his death, more directly advocated for Jewish national aims but did not reject elements of Polish acculturation. Thon conducted his sermons at the Tempel in Polish, for example. Overall, there seems to have been a pattern of increasing Polish acculturation, but not assimilation, as Jewish political and ethnic identity grew stronger.

As for Christian Polish attitudes toward the Jews in Cracow, the Polish historian Andrzej Żbikowski (who remonstrates most of his colleagues for downplaying the Jewish history of the city) concludes the standard attitude was one of ignorance and indifference, but that Cracow was not really an antisemitic city. As in other central European cities of the day, non-Jews connoted Jews with filthiness, dishonesty, and trade, but most of Polish society did not support the various attempts to foment modern antisemitism. The antisemitic newspaper *Głos Narodu* (Voice of the Nation) had a core constituency, but offshoot political parties from the paper never got more than a small percentage of the vote in municipal or parliamentary elections. The socialist paper *Naprzód* was a loyal supporter of Jewish rights and delighted in mocking *Głos Narodu* for its "buy only from Christians" slogan, despite the latter's willingness to run advertisements from Jewish businesses. Those who tended to be most antisemitic, Żbikowski concludes, were the shopkeepers and other business people who competed most directly with Jews in the same trade.[36] Jewish memoirs from this period, meanwhile, often stress the separateness of the two communities. For those who desired to remain apart, Jewish "Kroke" was a city unto itself.

Unlike Budapest, which was neatly bisected by the Danube, Cracow was, in 1900, an exclusively left-bank city, a point not lost on one of its brightest inhabitants, Tadeusz Boy-Żeleński, who lived in Cracow from his student days in the 1890s until after the First World War. Boy-Żeleński, perhaps the preeminent Polish translator of French literature, wrote that prewar Cracow, with its aristocratic, educated, and artistic mien approximated only one-half of the French capital:

> There were quiet, narrow little streets, picturesque nooks, and old churches—it was a left bank, truly impressive, that no other capital would put to shame. But there it ended; for on the right bank of the Seine roars the entire modern, wealthy, populous, teeming, fashionable Paris, while on the right bank of the Vistula was only—Dębniki.[37]

Boy-Żelenski's witty observation, however astute, was a bit unfair. After all, the progressive and prosperous town of Podgórze also lay on the other side of the river, just across from Kazimierz. Boy-Żeleński may not have traveled to Podgórze regularly, but traffic on the Podgórze Bridge was always heavy, despite the tariff levied on the Cracow side.[38] For local Jews whose families and businesses frequently straddled the river, as well as for the increasing number of people, Jews and Christians alike, ranging from day laborers to professors, who worked in Cracow but lived in Podgórze because housing was more affordable there, the bridge was an essential link between the two cities. While they remained legally separate, by the turn of the century Cracow and Podgórze were more closely related than ever before. A horse-drawn tram ran from the Podgórze main market square to Cracow's main train station and back. The electric streetcar "Jedynka" (the number one) took over the same route in early 1901.

Historically a suburb of Kazimierz, Podgórze was chartered an independent town by Joseph II in 1784 as a counterweight to Cracow, which remained outside the territory sheared off by Austria in the first partition of Poland. The Austrian city grew dramatically, especially after 1866 when, under self-government, city leaders elected to make it a free-trade town with attractive tax policies for warehouses, workshops, and factories. Cracow's strong guild structure and traditional thinking, meanwhile, hindered industrial development there, while the army fortifications prevented meaningful expansion of manufacturing in the suburbs north of the river. In 1870, Podgórze's population of 4,000 was only one-twelfth of Cracow's, yet by 1900 its population had soared to almost 18,000, or one-fifth. As much as one-third of the industrial workers in the entire greater Cracow territory worked in Podgórze, and seven of its ten largest factories were situated on the Podgórze side of the Vistula. Because of its more recent vintage, perhaps, Podgórze was a more democratic and equitable city than Cracow. Approximately one-third of its inhabitants were Jewish, yet there was no Jewish ghetto; Christians and Jews lived next to one another throughout the town. And Podgórze's electoral policies were more liberal than those in the city across the river.[39] Podgórze may not have been bustling or fashionable like right-bank Paris, but it was generally more modern, democratic, and industrialized than left-bank Cracow. It had electricity five years before Cracow and was clearly either an engine for greater Cracovian growth or a threat to the royal city's independent strength, depending on one's perspective.

LIVING CONDITIONS AND POPULATION

Life for most inhabitants of the city was cramped, unhygienic, and unhealthy. Because demand for living quarters so clearly exceeded supply, rents in the city were generally more expensive than in Paris or Vienna for comparable apartments, while average incomes were lower.[40] During the half-decade from 1897 to 1902, rents increased on average by 100 percent.[41] About a third of the city's population lived in "poor apartments" composed of a single room with a small kitchen attached, while fully 55 percent lived in "small apartments" of one to three rooms. Less than 10 percent of the population lived in an apartment of more than four rooms.[42] Frequently, the smallest apartments had the most inhabitants; rooms smaller than four square meters could house as many as ten people. Overcrowded, overpriced apartments meant that citizens spent a lot of time in public or semi-public places including the streets, parks, coffeehouses and theaters. Social reformers like Dr. Jordan, who not only oversaw the creation of a park but also organized the construction of workers' barracks in the suburbs, tried to ameliorate these awful living conditions, while other members of the elite lobbied for the creation of a people's theater so that the city's poor could have an inexpensive venue to experience culture.

Poor hygienic conditions contributed to the persistence of communicable diseases like tuberculosis. Many notable Cracovians, including Stanisław Wyspiański and several writers from families of the intelligentsia, lost a parent to tuberculosis.[43] The installation of running water in 1901 had a dramatic effect, but it would take some time before even the better apartments had reliable fresh water. In 1902, only one in every 389 citizens had a bathroom at home; by 1904 this figure had improved to one in every 144![44] In homes without a bathroom, women and children bathed in the kitchen once a week; men would patronize one of Cracow's two public baths.[45]

Sewers had existed in the city since the fourteenth century, undergoing repeated cycles of obsolescence and renovation. In 1813, the senate of the Free City of Cracow issued a decree that all property owners were obligated to build sewers for their buildings that could accommodate the city's plans. By 1866, when autonomous government began, the entire downtown had functioning sewers for rainwater, wastewater, and sewage. Unfortunately, a major destination for the sewers was into the river just below Wawel Castle. In 1880 a concrete sewer system was begun, though by 1900, solid waste removal was still a nightly task, disturbing the peace and befouling the air as carters hauled night-soil along cobblestone streets to pits outside the city. The completion of the municipal water supply in 1901 would make the sewers much more effective.[46]

Cracow remained small—fully half of its buildings were only three stories tall including the ground floor, or two stories by European reckoning—and its total space, not including the City Meadow, was only 5.77km². (At 5.48 km², Podgórze was nearly identical in size.) The major reason for relatively low buildings in Cracow arose from an 1883 law that stipulated the height of multi-storied houses could not exceed the width of the street, with an allowance for a maximum height of fifteen meters on streets of the standard width for new construction, which was twelve meters.[47] Prevented from growing outward by the fortifications and upward by this conservative law, Cracow could not handle the influx of migrants that poured into the city at the turn of the century. Tightly packed, with a population density of 15,827 per square kilometer in 1900, it was more crowded than Lemberg or even Budapest, which was the fastest-growing capital city in Europe at the time.[48] The Lemberg newspaper *Słowo Polskie* (the Polish Word) attested that Cracow was by 1908 the most densely populated city, not only in the

Austrian Empire, "but perhaps even in all of Europe." Cracow's population density of approximately 17,000 people per square kilometer dwarfed
Vienna's figure of 7,000, Berlin's 2,500, and Lemberg's 5,000.[49]

Like Budapest, Prague, and other nationalizing cities in east central
Europe, where multilingual, multi-confessional populations were becoming increasingly consistent with the ascendant national group, Cracow was
becoming increasingly Polish.[50] Unlike in Budapest and Prague, where
German speakers constituted more than half of the population at the beginning of the nineteenth century, Cracow's German-speaking population in
1800 was relatively small, about 7 percent. Still, early nineteenth-century
laws designed to acculturate the city's Jews by requiring them to attend Polish
schools largely failed because too few Jewish youth could speak Polish. For
them, German remained preferable. After a period of Germanization in the
two decades following Austrian annexation in 1846, Polish self-identification
became much more apparent in the last third of the century, under conditions of autonomous government. The shift was apparent in Podgórze as well,
which made the switch from German to Polish as its official language in 1866.
Migrants to Cracow from Bohemia, Moravia, and eastern Galicia during
the first half of the century increasingly identified with Polish culture as the
century progressed. Many of their sons rose to positions of prominence in
the city. Of the six mayors after autonomy, Józef Dietl, Mikołaj Zyblikiewicz,
Ferdynand Weigel, Feliks Szlachtowski, Józef Friedlein, and Juliusz Leo, five
had surnames that bespoke their non-ethnic-Polish origins.[51] The current
mayor in 1900, Józef Friedlein (1831–1917), was a Protestant bookseller
from an established Cracovian family.[52]

Despite the clear Austrian influence in the city, particularly in the guise
of the military, German was not spoken as much as one might expect. "Even
in the K.u.K. Armee, where the officers and subordinate officers were Polish,
only the commands would be issued in German," the novelist Ferdynand
Goetel recalled in his memoirs. "You just didn't hear German on the streets.
It's true that on Sundays and holidays the officers in full dress would parade
along the A-B line chatting with their Viennese coquettes, exiting to go to
the sweet shop Maurizzia, and it's true that the occasional [Cracovian would
come back from a trip to Vienna singing] 'Wien, Wien, nur Du allein . . .'
[but] the imperial-royal sentiments of Cracovian bureaucrats and a good
portion of its inhabitants did not conflict" with local municipal pride and
the widespread use of Polish.[53] Ninety-three percent of the civilian population declared Polish as its everyday language in the 1900 census, with 5.87
percent declaring German. Yiddish was not an option on the Austrian
census forms; most Jews in Cracow would have therefore selected Polish as

their everyday language (and according to one contemporary source, many of the 4,284 Jews who marked German as their first language in the 1900 census had also written Polish and Yiddish in the margin).[54] Czech, Russian, and "other" all registered less than half a percent.[55]

By 1910, the percentage of civilian German speakers had dropped to 1.77, thanks in large part to the incorporation of the overwhelmingly Polish Catholic suburbs (which registered 98% of their population as Polish speakers and 96% as Christian).[56] The percentage of those in Kazimierz and Stradom who declared German as their primary language of everyday use declined in this period, as well, evidence of the increasing linguistic Polonization of the Jewish population there. Still, some Cracovian Jews clearly resented being counted as Polish speakers. Prominent Jewish leaders including Adolf Gross, Józef Sare, and *kehillah* president Samuel Tilles issued proclamations in advance of the December 31, 1910, census that sought to persuade their reluctant co-religionists to mark Polish, despite the obvious inequity of a system that did not allow them to select their true mother tongue. "In comparison with the conditions of 20 years ago, or even 10, everyone who loves the truth must acknowledge that . . . the Polish language reaches ever greater masses of our fellow confessionals and is becoming not only their language of conversation, but even their father and mother tongue," one proclamation read. "Why should we, to our own loss, obscure this truth? Is it only to spite someone?"[57] Despite the overall drop in German speakers, their number rose slightly in Piasek and Kleparz during the first decade of the century, an increase almost certainly attributable to the increasingly metropolitan nature of the city, as managers and businessmen from elsewhere in the monarchy took up residence there.

Plenty of Cracovians were bilingual or even multilingual. Émigrés from Russian Poland, whose numbers always increased in Cracow after unrest there (especially after 1863 and 1905), would have known some Russian. Most Jews spoke Polish in addition to Yiddish (and males also knew Hebrew). Soldiers and bureaucrats knew German. Educated citizens, regardless of confession, spoke German and French and, increasingly, some English. Children learned German in school; students in *gymnasium* studied modern and classical languages as well. Occasional articles in the popular press relied on knowledge of German, as in a humor piece that suggested replacing seemingly "German" parts of Polish words—to ridiculous effect. Bro*war* (brewery) thus became bro*był* (bro+was), para*graf* (paragraph) became para*hrabia* (para+count), and wy*buch* (explosion) became wy*książka* (wy+book).[58] French continued to be the preferred language of exclusion for the aristocracy and upper gentry, though as the city grew connected to the global marketplace, often as a result of migration, working-class citizens increasingly could speak in foreign tongues as well. According to one newspaper chronicle notice from 1908, when a gentleman and his wife plotted their bargaining strategy at a suburban market stall in French, they were startled to hear the vendors use a foreign language of their own. "What are you speaking?" the woman demanded. "English," one of the vendors replied. "Clearly you haven't been to America, ma'am, but we have. You didn't want to speak to us in our language, so we're using one you don't understand."[59]

In 1900, Roman Catholics constituted 70 percent of the total population of Cracow, with Jews making up 28 percent (Greek Catholics, Protestants, Orthodox Christians, and a few unaffiliated persons made up the remainder). The Jewish population of the city had grown much more rapidly throughout the nineteenth century, by a factor of 13 as compared to 3.75 for Christians. Yet the proportion of Jews to Christians in Cracow had begun to decline by the 1890s, as the belated effects of the demographic revolution of decreasing mortality and greater mobility that had rippled across Europe finally began to bear fruit among Galician Catholic peasants.[60] In the period from 1887 to 1905, the total civilian population of the city rose from 66,192 to 94,735, evidence of the massive influx of migrants from the countryside. The number of Jews in Cracow, meanwhile, grew only by 681 from 1890 to 1900.[61] By 1914, Jews constituted only 22.5 percent of the population of Cracow, thanks to the incorporation of the overwhelmingly Christian suburban districts, where many migrants had settled.[62]

Evidence of the demographic revolution in decreasing mortality could be seen in Cracow itself, even if life expectancy remained dreadfully low by today's standards. Over the period 1881–1925, the average life expectancy was not quite 34 years. Of course plenty of Cracovians lived much longer than that, including the occasional centenarian like Juljanna Dobrołęcka, who died in 1901 at the purported age of 116, but high incidences of communicable diseases and high infant mortality torpedoed the overall life expectancy in the city.[63] Still, in comparison to other big cities of the day, Cracow's child mortality from age 0–5 was relatively good. At 37.2 percent of all deaths, it was comparable to Boston (37.1), and better than in Vienna (38.2), Prague (39.4), London (41.2), Copenhagen (42.8), Amsterdam (43.8), Budapest (46.7), Hamburg (47.0), Antwerp (47.6), The Hague (53.7), Magdeburg (54.5), and Berlin, where 57 percent of all deaths were children aged 0–5.[64] (One reason for the low percentage could be the unusually high incidence in Cracow of widows, whose eventual deaths would have altered the age ratio of deaths in the city.) Consistent with patterns of modernization elsewhere, both natality and mortality in Cracow were on the decline by the turn of the century. In 1887, there had been 33.25 births and 26.29 deaths per thousand in Cracow. By 1905 these figures had declined to 27.21 and 18.91, respectively.[65]

One of the classic factors accompanying nineteenth-century demographic revolutions was an increase in illegitimate childbirths as more individuals, isolated from the social control of the local village, gave birth to children out of wedlock. This pattern manifested itself in Cracow, as well. In the early 1880s, at its peak, unwed mothers accounted for two of every five live births in Cracow. By the first few years of the twentieth century, this figure had dropped to slightly more than a third. Nearly *half* of all Jewish births from 1903 to 1905 were illegitimate, though there was much higher incidence among Jews of legitimizing children after the fact.[66]

Demographically, Cracow was a young and feminine city. Despite the large military presence in the garrison city, the number of women in Cracow consistently matched or even outnumbered men overall. Warsaw, Lemberg, Vienna, Prague, and Breslau all had more women than men, but none had as high a disparity as in Cracow.[67] Among the civilian population the disproportionate number of women was quite pronounced: according to the 1900 census, for every 100 civilian men in the city there were 119 women.[68] The disparity arose not from higher birthrates for girls—the rates for boys were slightly higher—but from the influx of teenaged girls and women in their twenties from the countryside who came seeking work as household servants. For every 100 baby girls in Cracow, there were nearly 120 women aged from twenty to thirty, and only 64 between the ages of thirty and forty.[69] At 9.5 percent of the civilian population, Cracow had the largest per capita number of domestic servants in the Habsburg Monarchy, about 2 percent more than any other city.[70] The large number of household servants in Cracow reflected not a burgeoning class of nouveaux riches but, rather, the persistence of a small but powerful cluster of the aristocracy and a large population of shopkeepers, artisans, bureaucrats, and professionals (intelligentsia) who also employed housemaids to maintain status and because they remained affordable.

Yet, as the economist Jan Bystroń noted in 1916, by the twentieth century the proportion of servants in Cracow was on the decline. Bystroń saw this drop not as a sign of "the fall of the resources" of the city but, rather, as evidence of its westernization, as the economy diversified and servants simply became too expensive for many petty urbanites to afford.[71] Women who would have formerly gone into service now had more options for employment, including the tobacco factory and other nascent industries. Indeed, the protagonist of Artur Gruszecki's social novel *Cygarniczka* (1906) chose not to join her servant friends and instead went to work as a "cigar girl." The male author of a series in *Nowiny* from 1909, tellingly entitled "Our Women and Servants," argued that women in Cracow "[did] not know how to count," because it did not make financial sense to keep servants when rent in Cracow cost as much as one-third of one's income and servants cost 30–40 crowns a month to keep. A petty bourgeois wife replied, affirming that she and her fellow Cracovian women knew "how to count very well," because they "[could] not afford foods out of season" and had to "be extremely strategic" with their resources. "We need servants to get everything done, and it's a cost that comes in place of trips to the forest or park as they do in Vienna or nights at the theaters," she wrote. "We simply cannot afford such pleasures and so go without. We from the clerk's sphere (*z sfery urzędniczej*) do plenty of our own housework and shopping, but we still need servants."[72] Clearly, the social necessity of keeping servants outweighed their economic cost, but for many petty bourgeois citizens such conspicuous consumption was becoming increasingly difficult to afford.

PROFESSIONS AND SOCIAL GROUPS

Our imagined woman migrant to Cracow in 1900 would have had to rely on her wits and good fortune to get a job as a housemaid, stay in her mistress's good graces, and avoid the advances of her master or any number of men in the city. As elsewhere, servants were frequently sexually abused, and many worked either clandestinely or legally as prostitutes at some point. Even the English governess of the Wojciech Kossak household, a prominent artist family in Cracow, was arrested for clandestine prostitution.[73] Though perhaps not as flippant as their colleagues in Vienna, who even had a name for the "sweet young girls" from the countryside—*süsse Mädels*—whom they happily exploited, many Cracovians certainly connoted servants with sex.[74] In 1903, a father chose not to take his children to the popular play *Miss Maid* (Panna Służąca) at the People's Theater, because he feared it would be "too scandalous" for his girls and little boy.[75] "Poor Marysia" was a feuilleton in the popular press that told the tale of a 16-year-old servant girl who left service for a few days and then came back asking for her old job. Not surprisingly, her former mistress asked for an explanation. Marysia replied that she had found better-paying work, but her elderly master had molested her.[76] Soldiers frequently flirted with or even assaulted servant girls but apparently never married them, if city marriage statistics from the beginning of the century are to be trusted.[77] Pregnancy and childbirth could cost the housemaid her job, and some women resorted to infanticide. Nearly every report of infanticide in the popular press referred to a servant mother (see chapter 6). In the decade 1895–1904, more than a quarter of the officially recorded homicides in Cracow were of infants.[78]

But servants were not only victims. Domestic servants occasionally retaliated against their masters, exploiting their presumed powerlessness to avoid immediate suspicion. In several cases that attracted the attention of the press, servants who plundered or even murdered their masters were not initial suspects, and their eventual discovery as perpetrators came as a shock.[79] From the perspective of a sympathetic observer of village life in the Carpathians, metropolitan exploitation could go the other way, too, as domestic servants and "common women" in garrison towns often took the pay of simple peasant soldiers in return for their "'affections'" and "a little extra sustenance" while passing along venereal diseases.[80] Domestics exercised their agency in seeking the best opportunities they could (including prostitution) and were not entirely without legal or popular support when they were treated unfairly. In 1903, Ignacy Dattner, a wealthy resident of Karmelicka Street in Piasek, accused his housemaid Teklusia Wiatrówna of having stolen a diamond ring worth 800 crowns. The newspaper was happy to report that "thanks to the cleverness of police agent Malikowski" the "most blameless" woman had been "spared arrest, investigation, and other such pleasantries," when the agent's hunch to have the doorman check the trashbin produced the missing ring. Wiatrówna's only failing was not to have noticed the ring while dutifully sweeping up sometime after it had slipped from her master's finger.[81] Cracow still retained a strong sense of noblesse oblige that obligated the protection of its presumably weakest members, and servant girls frequently fit this category.

Another such group, capable of eliciting both pity and execration, was the bevy of street children who seemed to proliferate as Cracow took on the characteristics of a big city. Neglected children (*zaniedbani dzieci*) and juvenile offenders (*małoletni przystępcy*) aroused great concern, and by the middle of the first decade of the twentieth century had become one of the commonest subjects in the popular press (see chapter 6). Their poverty and increasing brazenness made bourgeois citizens uncomfortable, and as elsewhere during the nineteenth century, numerous charitable institutions arose in an attempt to assist and control them.

Cracow's most privileged saw it as their duty to look after the less fortunate, especially children. Of the twenty-one charity organizations that merited a listing in the city yearbook for 1903, six dealt with children.[82] Typically headed by nobility or religious authorities, the registries of these charities were peppered with honorifics, from "His Excellence" to the almost ubiquitous "Dr." Unsurprisingly, the surname of the Galician viceroy Count Andrzej Potocki was a particularly common sight, especially as it applied to his wife and daughters-in-law. A perfect illustration of the prevalent attitude of beneficence and control can be seen in a series of photographs of the Lubomirski Asylum for the Upbringing of Neglected Boys, which depicts groups of closely shorn boys eating in a roomy cafeteria, diligently laboring in a workshop, shivering bare-chested in Cracow's first indoor swimming pool, exercising to drumbeats, and dutifully kneeling in prayer in their sleeping quarters. In nearly every photograph, adults (teachers and/or nuns) and a prominently mounted crucifix preside over the scene. A plaque in the boys' dormitory exhorts, simply and directly: "*Módl się i pracuj*" (pray and work).[83]

Yet Cracovians also took a certain pride in their street children, or "Antki," as they were called.[84] As Marian Turski recalled, the "generally honest" boys, who were "produced—but not reared—in the suburbs of Cracow," would fish, keep pigeons and rabbits for sale, and peddle matches or newspapers to get by. As resourceful, plucky, and ubiquitous as the pigeons with whom they shared Market Square and its side streets, Cracow's "Antki" even merited a comment in the Baedeker entry on Cracow. According to an Antek anecdote in Baedeker, one evening on the Market Square a boy who appeared no older than eight approached a man for some change. When the man asked the boy why he was out so late, the youngster "replied without hesitation: 'I'd tell you, sir, but my wife is giving birth, and I've got nothing for the midwife.'" The boy got a donation.[85] As elsewhere, Cracovian upper- and middle-class observers simultaneously marveled at street children's cleverness while recoiling at their situation, which had foisted adult concerns upon them prematurely. The joke in Baedeker arose from the sense that the boy rapidly repeated an adult's answer, even though he appeared biologically incapable of fathering a child.

As attitudes in the city modernized, the imperative to control street children increased. Several newspaper articles from 1905 noted the desire to move the boys far from the big city, where they were "schooled in crime," into "reform houses" in the countryside. Still, "the inhabitants of attics and crates"—so-called in an article that noted where street children squatted—generally preferred to be among their own and frequently escaped the workhouses to join comrades in the city.[86]

Cabbies, who were often the fathers of the street children, and the apartment guards who lived in damp rooms below street level likewise elicited feelings of consternation and magnanimity among the city's elite. Looking back on the lost era of deference before the world wars and communism altered her hometown, Eleonora Gajzlerowa fondly recalled the cab drivers from the suburbs, whose rugged tan complexions were marked with deep furrows from the elements and whose bushy sideburns emulated the style of Francis Joseph. She loved riding in the fiacres, especially when the driver would stop and cover the passengers from the rain.[87] Doormen, meanwhile, tended to be less deferential. House guards were clearly necessary in the same way that servants were—as traditional status symbols—but their ubiquity arose as well from city mandates requiring their presence. Not coincidentally there were also more of them per capita in Cracow than in any other city of the empire.[88] In a humorous feuilleton from 1907, a contributor to *Nowiny* observed that his doorman, or rather his "landlord's doorman," had had a crooked red nose, an affection for vodka, "eight children of his own and eight that aren't his own," and an aversion to opening the building for its tenants when it was cold. He hastened to point out that "he also carefully guards the building. There were only five thefts in the whole estate last month."[89] It was said that Cracovians had a paltry nightlife in comparison with their fellow urbanites elsewhere, because their doormen charged so much to let them in after ten o'clock in the evening.

One can imagine why the house guards would have been so grumpy, for they often had the worst living conditions of anyone within city limits. Porters and their families lived and slept in subterranean rooms that often measured no more than four square meters and had condensation dripping down the walls.[90] As the feuilletonist for *Nowiny* observed, "His apartment is underground and only gets sunlight every few years, when they're working on the cellar. So you can understand why he doesn't spend a lot of time there." Still, writing before the first election after the declaration of universal suffrage in 1907, the feuilletonist jokingly remarked that he would vote for his doorman before voting for his landlord, "because Social Democrats stand for progress, and besides you can always talk to your guard. I don't know about my landlord." From the middle-class perspective, doormen may not have opened the gate or cleared trash from their buildings as effectively as they (or the city authorities) would have wished, but they were a familiar face with whom one could always strike up a conversation.

Gajzlerowa also recalled the gypsies encamped on the City Meadow and especially the beggars, who best exemplified the city's poverty and its small-town generosity. Beggars, who were never called beggars but "*dziady*" (grandparents/beggars), as the word "żebrak" (beggar) was thought rude, were a major feature of Old Cracow before the war.[91] Cracovian *dziady* knew their clientele and catered to them as obsequiously as the cab drivers sought to please Gajzlerowa's physician father. In a well-known joke that says much about Cracow's hierarchy at the turn of the century, a beggar at St. Mary's Church was said to call out, "Sir Count, can you spare some change?" and, hearing the reply "I'm not a count," quickly corrected himself, "Ah so, sir professor, . . ."[92] Some beggars were Cracovian institutions, including a long-haired and grizzly bearded blind man who posed for artists and who appears in photographs from the famous Ignacy Krieger atelier. Others, according to Gajzlerowa, included the legless Austrian veteran who saved enough to give his daughter a huge dowry for her wedding and a married couple who worked such prime spots by St. Mary's Church that they could afford to hire a servant to deliver their lunch punctually each day.[93] Such was Cracow—even the beggars had servants!

Of course, these are precisely the kinds of stories that the privileged loved to tell themselves, as reassurances of their benevolence and rightful place in the community. To be sure, there were many charitable institutions, including the justly famous Brother Albert's Shelter for homeless and indigent men, founded by the painter and one-legged veteran of the 1863 uprising Adam Chmielowski, along with guilds and workingmen's associations, and even a system of municipal welfare, including the provision of coal when the winters were most severe.[94] The emperor's 1866 statute to the royal capital city entitled all legal citizens of the city to community assistance in the "instance of poverty, illness, or inability to work, according to proper laws and precedents."[95] But in 1900, more than half of Cracow's inhabitants did not qualify for formal citizenship, largely because they had not lived there for the requisite ten years, and welfare, whether from the city, religious institutions, or private charities, could not erase the fact that the majority of Cracovians remained poor.

Escaping poverty in such circumstances was extremely difficult. Grasping this, many migrants, fresh from the countryside, chose to live in the suburbs where they could continue a semi-rural existence with small vegetable garden plots, and occasionally even livestock. Within the city limits, however, there was little room to practice agriculture. Slightly more than 1 percent of the population in 1900 declared that they earned their living by farming.

In terms of occupation, Cracow was largely a city of bureaucrats, professionals, tradesmen, and artisans. There were many itinerant laborers but few industrial workers and even fewer industrialists, though by the turn of the century the ranks of each group were growing. The average business was small, employing only two to five people. Only eight of the city's nearly three thousand businesses in 1902 had more than one hundred employees.[96] Besides the tobacco factory, the most significant large industries, like the

L. Zieleniewski factory, tended to make farming equipment or building materials—further evidence of the relatively underdeveloped provincial economy. Of the four major categories for which Cracovians could declare their profession on the census (farming, industry, trade, and "individuals in public service, the free professions or without a profession"), the highest figure, 37 percent, was in the final category. Factoring out dependents in all categories, almost twice as many Cracovians belonged to this category as worked in trade or industry.

At the top of this group were aristocrats, followed by the intelligentsia. Lawyers, doctors, administrators, and professors made up the upper echelon of the intelligentsia, followed by a much larger group of civil servants, clerks, teachers, and writers.[97] The upper ranks of the intelligentsia were well-represented in social and philanthropic organizations, municipal government, and the press. Professors enjoyed a privileged position, and public attendance at lectures by some of the most famous professors, including the professor of Polish literature Stanisław Tarnowski, could be quite significant. Cracow had one of only two Polish universities at the time (the other was in Lemberg) and attracted students from beyond the Habsburg Empire. The first women entered the university in 1894; the first female graduate of the medical school, a student of Dr. Jordan, earned her degree in 1906.[98]

Socially, if not numerically, Cracow was dominated by its intelligentsia and by a large core of petty bourgeois citizens, the "clerks' sphere." As in Budapest, many members of the intelligentsia came from the lower ranks of the country gentry. Wealthy in connections, if not in cash, they came to the city and found bureaucratic or administrative positions, many of which were not overly demanding and left plenty of discretionary time for leisure. One inhabitant of the city recalled that her father was the "antithesis of a bureaucrat" and never went to work before ten; a diarist in Budapest from an analogous background seems to have had quite similar working habits.[99] But life in the clerk's sphere, particularly for those on the lower rungs, was not always leisurely. A joke in one of the popular papers entitled "The Lobster" captured the hierarchical world of petty insecurities and groveling for position that was common among bureaucrats. In the story, a man receives a lobster from his brother in the navy, and hoping to curry favor, passes it on to his superior, who then passes it on, until finally someone gives it to a member of parliament. The representative does not have time to eat the lobster and so gives it to a friend. The friend gets very sick from eating it (because it was certainly not fresh by now) and blames the representative. The blame goes all the way back to the poor minor civil servant who got the lobster in the first place. Readers from the clerks' sphere would have chuckled knowingly at the conclusion of the story when the poor fellow realizes that despite his best efforts, "his chances for advancement were shot, for sure."[100]

Noting the tendency for capital cities to attract the "best and brightest," Boy-Żeleński remarked that because Cracow was a capital of sorts this could have held true there too, but in actuality, the best bureaucrats, ministers, and officials regularly moved up the ranks to Lemberg and Vienna, leaving Cracow with a middling bureaucrat mentality.[101] In 1900, there were nearly two thousand people in Vienna who had been born in Cracow, while only 415 people in Cracow had been born in the imperial capital.[102] Cracow may have been a magnet for Poles from Galicia and the other partitioned territories, but it could not compete with the metropole.

Of the nearly 250 doctors listed in the 1908 city annual calendar, most did not list a specialty, but of those who did, physicians of "skin and venereal diseases" and "women's diseases," like Eleonora Gajzlerowa's father, Maksymilian Cercha, were the most common. This squares well with Stefan Zweig's observation that one of the major consequences of the era's reliance on prostitution was a preponderance of physicians for venereal diseases.[103] Until the appearance of "Dr. Ehrlich's 707," a treatment for syphilis that was widely advertised in the newspapers by the end of the first decade of the twentieth century, sex with prostitutes may have been legal, but it remained potentially lethal. In 1907, Cracow's most famous artist and playwright from this period, Stanisław Wyspiański, died in his late thirties from complications due to syphilis contracted in his youth. Those mandatory "sanitary check-ups" and quarantines for sex workers at St. Lazarus Hospital failed to assure their clients' safety from disease (their own safety was of secondary importance to the authorities). While the police kept a classified tally of registered prostitutes, fastidiously noting their address, medical appointments, and movements to and from the city, another list of women professionally tied to reproduction could be made more public.[104] Among the few women whose names appeared in the annual calendar were the city's midwives, who were not quite as numerous as its physicians but whose names and addresses took up nearly two full pages.[105]

More than one-third of all Cracovian households were employed in trade; among Jews the proportion was more than one-half. Petty shopkeepers, grocers, and owners of cafés, restaurants, and taverns made up the majority of this group. There were several wealthy store-owners, including the aforementioned Jan Fischer in the paper business, and Gustaw Gershon Bazes, a Jewish seller of porcelain lamps on Grodzka Street and an influential businessman and politician.

A quarter of the population was employed in manufacturing, including categories ranging from instrument making to carpentry and construction. The largest group among them by far, manufacturers of clothing (cobblers, tailors, and seamstresses), made up one-tenth of the total population and were more or less equally represented among Christians and Jews. These trades frequently had guilds and associations, often divided along religious lines. The prevailing stereotype of the violent shoemaker (which perhaps arose from their use of hammers and the presumed stress of making a living as a petty artisan) abounded in popular culture, fiction, and the press. Occasional news stories of cobblers clobbering their wives, apprentices, or rivals effectively bolstered the stereotype of "the shoemaker's fury."[106] Proportionately there were more tradesmen, professionals, and public servants in Cracow than in Brünn/Brno and Graz, similarly sized towns of the empire, and fewer people employed in industry.[107] The persistence of so many artisans and petty bourgeois citizens in Cracow demonstrates its relative lack of industrialization vis-à-vis the more industrialized cities of the empire, primarily in Silesia and Bohemia, or in Łódź or Warsaw in the neighboring Russian territories.

Other notable social groups in the city included clergy—priests, monks, nuns, and rabbis—and artists and actors. Suffice to say, Cracow in 1900 was highly religious and deeply valued the arts, though dogmas and practices in either domain of the soul were beginning to be challenged. As in Vienna, Cracovians obsessed over the theater, its personnel and repertoire. Even nine-year-olds apparently attended the premiere of Wyspiański's modernist drama *Wesele* (The Wedding) in 1901.[108] Artists and musicians were also highly esteemed. According to Boy-Żeleński, when a young distillery inspector, who also happened to be an amateur musician, asked a young woman to marry him she agreed, but on the condition that he abandon his profession and become a "true artist." The young man left his position, studied diligently, and went to Paris with his bride, suffering a few years of penury before becoming one of Poland's most renowned musicians. Ordinarily, women would tell a young man that as soon as he gives up his art and gains a reliable job they could marry, Boy-Żeleński pointed out with a flourish; in Cracow the reverse was true.[109]

The School of Fine Arts, which had been founded in 1818 in order to train graphic artists, painters, and sculptors, was re-commissioned in 1900 as the Academy of Fine Arts. In the second half of the 1890s, modernism began to take hold among the avant garde, thus challenging the bombast of nineteenth-century historicism and, frankly, the School of Fine Arts' most famous teacher, Jan Matejko (1838–1893). Cracow's best artists, such as the internationally acclaimed Józef Mehoffer (1869–1946) and Stanisław Wyspiański, still took on commissions of church art, though their choices were not always traditional; Wyspiański's riotous art nouveau makeover of the gothic Franciscan Church in Cracow is a case in point. As in Budapest, the modernist movement in Cracow, Młoda Polska (Young Poland), was somewhat limited in its international applicability by its nationalistic tendencies, but its practitioners were deeply conversant in the theories of the day, from Nietzsche to Maeterlinck to Ibsen, as a glance through any issue of their flagship publication, *Życie* (Life), makes clear (see chapter 2).[110]

Religion and religiosity remained a vital part of everyday life in the city in 1900, the fundamental source of identification and cultural practice. Still, by the turn of the century, liberals, socialists, and nationalists challenged the primacy of religion with a new set of beliefs, priorities, and rituals. Most Cracovians found ways to reconcile modern life with religion, as in the case of the progressive Jews of the reform Tempel. Religious festivals such as Carnival, which preceded Lent and inaugurated a fortnight of dancing and balls, or Emaus, which commemorated the resurrection of Jesus as he walked the road to Emmaus but generally meant an opportunity for recreation along the riverbanks, had shed much of their religious overtones and served to mark the passing of the seasons. Other challenges to religious dominance were more direct. Socialists had long railed against Cracow's ultramontane conservativism, as typified by its preponderance of cloisters, clergy, and churches. As early as 1882, Ludwik Waryński blamed the clergy for shamelessly exploiting the poor, while perpetuating social ills such as prostitution and street begging.[111] In the winter of 1910/1911, anti-clerical students at the university protested the opening of a social science division of the School of Theology and the appointment of Father Kazimierz Zimmermann at its head. The students blocked Zimmermann's inaugural lecture and called for the de-coupling of the School of Theology from the university.[112] They were ultimately unsuccessful and public opinion was not on their side, but the days of an unchallenged ultramontane Cracow were definitely over.

POLITICS

Politics in Cracow depended most on the city's position as a loyal Polish stronghold in multinational Austria and the dynamic between Poles and Jews in the modernizing city. In 1900, Cracow was squarely in the hands of the Stańczyk conservative faction, but liberals, socialists, and independent Jews were all beginning to challenge this dominance.[113] The liberal democrats clustered around the newspaper *Nowa Reforma* (founded in 1882) were on the rise in the last decades of the century, and took over the reins of municipal authority from the conservatives shortly before the empire-wide declaration of universal suffrage. Despite their successes against the conservatives, historian Maciej Janowski argues, the liberal democrats failed to adapt to the demands of mass politics in the twentieth century and proved unable to compete with the nationalist parties for popular support, especially in the parliamentary elections of 1912.[114] Within the city, however, the liberal democrats' grip on power remained strong until after the war.

The Social Democrats, led by the unflappable Ignacy Daszyński (1866–1936) from the Wesoła neighborhood, grew increasingly powerful from the turn of the century onward. In May 1902, Daszyński, who had already served two terms in parliament, was chosen as a city councilor in Cracow for the "small business" curia in his district, where he got two-thirds of the vote. "My voters were petty Jewish merchants," Daszyński recalled in his memoirs, "who under the influence of Dr. [Adolf] Gross had nothing against me." As the "only socialist among conservatives and conservative democrats" on the sixty-member city council, Daszyński was nonetheless relatively well accepted.[115] "I brought new life into this rather boring atmosphere of meetings, and they listened to me eagerly, at times even taking up my suggestions. Most frequently they rejected them, often while appropriating their intentions." According to Daszyński, he worked to support city workers, to keep taxes as low as possible, and above all to reform the franchise.

Daszyński recalled that he got along well with President Friedlein but noted that the vanity of Friedlein's successor as mayor, Juliusz Leo, made the newcomer difficult to work with.

> Dr. Juliusz Leo, a Stańczyk, who one night metamorphosed into a conservative democrat, . . . was a talented individual and remarkably well-suited as mayor of Cracow, but his vanity and overweening ambition made him unfair and unlikable. He battled with me from the president's chair, but when he realized—from bitter experience—that socialism in Cracow was not a passing fancy, but an important political and social phenomenon, he began to strive to come to an understanding with me and make relations between us more bearable.[116]

Leo, the ambitious mayor who brought about the creation of Greater Cracow (see chapters 3 and 4), had been something of an academic wunderkind, earning his doctorate in economic law at the age of 23 at the Jagiellonian University, and winning tenure at 27 and full professorship at 30. He was still a professor at the time he was elected mayor in July 1904, choosing to remain on faculty in a state of unpaid leave. Most important, however, was his obvious transformation from conservative to democrat. Sensing the shift in political winds at the beginning of the twentieth century, Leo successfully steered his career in the direction of pragmatic populism and economic reform, staying in power until his death in 1918. In so doing, he was similar to Vienna's famous Karl Lueger or Budapest's István Bárczy, fellow mayors in the Habsburg Empire who sought urban development and reform on behalf of the poor and the petite bourgeoisie. Leo's commitment to economic rationalization, modernization, urban development, trade schools, and the creation of Greater Cracow made him popular with the average literate Cracovian—precisely the kind of person who would have read the popular press and complained about germs at the meat market or the servant market beneath the statue of Mickiewicz.

CONCLUSION

Like Vienna, its imperial capital, Cracow in 1900 tended to be rather "socially, economically, and politically out-of-date" and concerned with appearances.[117] "The Little Vienna on the Vistula" mimicked the capital in its obsession for uniforms, bureaucracy, and theater, while taking on a Viennese style of life, down to the Kaiser rolls, coffee, and eggs Viennese-style that most citizens had for breakfast.[118] As in other Habsburg cities of the day, Cracow's citizens were obsessed with status and respectability, from the ubiquitous honorifics among the educated or social elite and the presence of servants in petty bourgeois homes to the black bowler hats—as in Budapest—on the heads of manual laborers.[119] Religion and custom dictated the rhythm of everyday life; people largely knew their place, played their roles, and were readily recognizable according to social type, from the haughtiest aristocrat to the lowliest beggar. Historicism and patriotic commemoration of the past predominated in a city known for its obsession with funerals.[120] The fact that Cracow in 1900 had more servants, doormen, and widows than any other city in the empire betrayed the fact that it was not an especially forward-looking sort of place.

Many of the city's elite would have been happy to keep things as they were, but by the turn of the century the influx of new inhabitants and new ideas made such a reactionary position increasingly untenable. Changes in the arts, literature, and religion matched the demographic shifts that had been occurring now for almost twenty years. Cracow's population had been ballooning since the 1880s, as villagers from the Galician countryside flocked to the city seeking a better life. The life they found was almost always harsh, but by 1900 they and their masters increasingly recognized the novelty of their surroundings and the necessity for change. Little Cracow was becoming a big city, and with it came a growth in crime and disease but also in novel opportunities. During the first decade of the twentieth century, perspicacious municipal politicians began to implement solutions to the demands of modern urban life such as the installation of running water and electric streetcars, electrification, city sanitation, the expansion of paved roads and infrastructure, the construction of schools, and the incorporation of the suburbs. Ordinary citizens, many of whom were first-generation literate, increasingly began to call for such things themselves. Enterprising journalists recognized the growth of a metropolitan readership for whom these issues, along with sensationalist stories from home and abroad, would matter most, and thus they facilitated the process by which Cracow and its citizens became increasingly metropolitan.

CRACOVIAN TYPES, 1870s–1880s

Ignacy Krieger, Photographer

Two men from the Kelderash Roma camp in Cracow, c. 1870.   [MHK3481/K]

(left) Cracovian market woman, c. 1870–80. [MHK4468/K]

(left) Village artisan, c. 1870–80. [MHK4506/K]

(above) Beggar Woman/Ragpicker, c. 1870–80. [MHK4564/K]

(above) Boy from Bronowice Małe,
c. 1870–80. [MHK4600/K]

(left) Cracovian woman from Krzeszowice,
c. 1870–80. [MHK4714/K]

(above) Austrian Army Officer, c. 1880
(note sideburns in the style of Francis
Joseph). [MHK5382/K]

(right) Cracovian woman, c. 1880.
[MHK6131/K]

INHABITANTS OF CRACOW AND SUBURBAN VILLAGES, C. 1900

Natan Krieger, Photographer

(above) Couple in traditional dress holding hands.   [MHK2443/K]

(right) Woman with crossed arms (note large crucifix and skirt sewn of factory-made fabric).   [MHK2449/K]

Family in traditional dress, with son in modern dress.   [MHK2469/K]

(above, left) Schoolgirl wearing factory-made fabric and traditional vest. [MHK4881/K]

(above, right) Suburban community chief (Piotr Rosół of Nowa Wieś Narodowa?). [MHK4992/K]

(lower, right) Young woman in traditional dress. [MHK5015/K]

(left) Bourgeois children, early 20th century.
[MHK5739/K]

(below) Night watchman with dog, c. 1900.
[MHK6166/K]

Priest, c. 1900.

[MHK6274/K]

(left) Older Jewish man, c. 1890 [MHK4512/K], and *(right)* young Jewish man, c. 1900
(note modern hat and lack of earlocks). [MHK6615/K]

MODERN METROPOLITAN CRACOVIANS

Natan Krieger, Photographer

(*above, left*) Cracovian burgher, c. 1900. [MHK5991/K]

(*above, right*) Pilot, c. 1915. [MHK6339/K]

(*left*) Cracovian woman, c. 1910–1915. [MHK6399/K]

(*right*) Dapper Cracovian, c. 1900–1910
(indistinguishable from modern metropolitans
elsewhere). [MHK6996/K]

THE INTERURBAN MATRIX

Local News and International Sensations

in Cracow's Popular Press

—When is there a drought of Galician newspapers?
—Whenever "Neue Freie Presse," "Neues Wiener Journal"
  and "Berliner Tageblatt" are a day late.
—When does a catastrophe occur?
—Whenever the delay lasts for two days.
—*Liberum Veto*, April 20, 1903

In 1903, the Cracovian humor magazine *Liberum Veto* jokingly remarked that the Galician press maintained an April Fools' atmosphere throughout the year. "Monstrous" articles printed for April 1st gradually make their way, "from the English press to the French, from the French to the German, from the German to [Vienna's] *Neue Freie Presse*, and from thence on the northern train to Galicia; in the Cracovian and Lvovian press they appear more or less in June, July, or August, while some even appear in December, January, and March."[1] If the joke poked fun at Cracow's backwardness and dependence on its western neighbors for its sensationalist news, it simultaneously underscored the city's connectedness to the news and views of other European metropolises. Even if it was usually a few days behind, Cracow's Polish-language press, it went without saying, was simply part of a chain of appropriation that began, at least in this case, with April Fools' jokes in the English press and worked its way south and east. Thanks to the train, the telegraph, the telephone, and especially the modern newspaper, which benefited from all three inventions, Cracow, like other cities at the time, was part of an interurban matrix of words and images describing the modern world.

Cracow's popular press was deeply connected to similar papers abroad. Not only did it plunder stories from them; its very existence was the result of creative mimicry as enterprising local journalists sought to create local versions of successful papers from other European cities. Thoroughly enmeshed in press developments taking place across the globe at the time, Cracovian journalists such as Ludwik Szczepański (1872–1954) and Maryan Dąbrowski (1878–1958) revolutionized the city's media by applying the lessons of the "new journalism" to the particularities of their city.[2] This brand of journalism, as pioneered in the United States, Great Britain, and France, relied on the "familiar aspects of sensationalism—crime news, scandal and gossip, divorces and sex, and . . . the reporting of disasters and sports" while innovating the use of prominent headlines, "lavish use of pictures," and sympathy with the "underdog."[3] The result was a delightful admixture of old and new. Employing seemingly timeless elements of sensationalism and village gossip for modern purposes, the popular press bridged the chasm between the villager and the citizen, the barely literate and the urbane. Rotary presses, telephones, telegraphs, and automobiles helped relay the shocking stories and local city news that made these papers so attractive. Just as in other cities during this period, Cracow's popular press was an evolving medium, shifting to adapt to the needs of its citizens while in turn assisting in their transformation into modern metropolitans.[4]

In the era before the Great War, boulevard newspapers were one of the principal vectors for disseminating an increasingly globalized urban popular culture. Thanks to its focus on Cracow and other cities, the Cracovian popular press was a major factor in developing a modern, urban ethos among its readers while enabling them to see their commonalities with urbanites abroad. As Polish-speaking Cracovians began to see themselves as metropolitans, they found that archetypical models of Polishness from gentry or folk traditions often failed to apply. In the discourse of big-city life, Cracovian journalists consistently compared their city and its inhabitants to cities and citizens abroad. Picturing their city as an aspiring modern metropolis, they challenged and reinterpreted backward-looking, nationalist narratives of Cracow as a historic center of Polish culture.

THE BOULEVARD PRESS IN CRACOW

Cracow's first boulevard newspapers, *Kuryerek Krakowski, Nowiny dla wszystkich,* and *Ilustrowany Kuryer Codzienny,* represent Cracovian manifestations of an overall trend in the history of the press at this time, namely, a movement away from political papers catering to specific audiences toward urban newspapers catering to broad audiences.[5] Until the introduction of *Kuryerek Krakowski* in 1902, all four previously available Cracovian dailies could be classified, as they were at the time, as examples of the "political" or "serious" press. Each was linked to an audience defined according to political affiliation: the conservative *Czas* (Time), the liberal-democratic *Nowa Reforma* (New Reform), the nationalist, antisemitic *Głos Narodu* (Voice of the Nation), and the socialist *Naprzód* (Forward). *Czas* was founded in the revolutionary ferment of 1848, but the other three papers were all quite recent; *Naprzód* published its first daily editions only in 1901.[6] At the beginning of the century the four papers combined had about 8,000 subscriptions, half of which belonged to *Głos Narodu*.[7] *Nowa Reforma* achieved greater circulation throughout the decade by appealing to the city's most popular constituency, the liberal democrats, but it never took on the tenor of the popular illustrated press.

Publications from outside of the city were also available. In addition to reading *Czas* or *Nowa Reforma*, educated Cracovians had long read Viennese papers such as *Österreichische Zeitung, Die Presse, Neues Wiener Tageblatt,* and *Neue Freie Presse* in order to stay connected to affairs in the imperial capital and throughout the empire.[8] Cracovians could likewise subscribe to several of the Polish papers from the provincial capital, Lemberg. Illustrated weeklies and fashion journals from Vienna, Germany, and Russian Poland—including the venerable *Tygodnik Illustrowany* (Illustrated Weekly) from Warsaw—were available as well. Even so, there was definitely an untapped market for a Polish-language illustrated weekly and especially for a daily boulevard paper appealing to the tastes of Cracow's large *drobnomieszczaństwo,* or petite bourgeoisie.

Popular illustrated newspapers—frequently called boulevard papers or the "gutter press" (*prasa brukowa*) because they were sold on the street—had first appeared in the Habsburg Empire around the turn of the century. Budapest's first boulevard newspaper, *Esti Újság* (Evening News), appeared in 1896.[9] *Illustriertes Wiener Extrablatt,* a liberal/populist illustrated daily, had premiered in Vienna in 1872. One of the first major illustrated papers in Europe, it downplayed political news in favor of sensationalist and local news while remaining deferential to the emperor.[10] Until the turn of the century, it was not really a boulevard paper, however, relying more on subscriptions than street sales. The *Pražský Ilustrovaný Kurýr,* which was modeled on the *Extrablatt,* premiered in 1874 as an extra edition to a political newspaper and began independent publication in 1893.[11] In Cisleithania (the Austrian half of the empire), the passage of a law eliminating the periodical-press stamp, beginning on January 1, 1900, allowed for the proliferation of inexpensive illustrated dailies. *Illustrierte Kronenzeitung*, so named for its monthly sub-scription cost of one crown, premiered in Vienna the next day. *Kronenzeitung* quickly became the most popular paper in the imperial capital, with a circula-tion of 100,000 in 1906 and 200,000 just six years later.[12] *Wiek Nowy* (New Century), which was directly modeled on the successful Viennese paper, appeared in 1901 in Lemberg.[13] Cracow's first boulevard paper, *Kuryerek Kra-kowski*, went into print on August 9, 1902, in the hopes that a local alternative to *Wiek Nowy* would prove even more popular.

Like its Viennese and Lvovian models, *Kuryerek Krakowski* was clearly a new kind of newspaper. Like *Kronenzeitung*, its monthly subscription cost was one crown, while its daily cost was only two cents. Unlike the politi-cal press, which was printed in full-sheet format with six columns of small text in running columns (stories at the bottom of one column continued at the top of the next) and did not include illustrations, *Kuryerek Krakowski* appeared in a small format of eight half-sheet pages. Lively illustrations, often reprinted from publications abroad, graced each cover and smaller sketches appeared throughout. The paper drew deliberate distinctions between itself and the political press, claiming that the "great" papers, "so called because they print on big paper," love to preach and are full of glowing phrases but are "as quiet as a sleeping princess" when ordinary people need it most. "When local artisans are threatened," it wrote, "they are silent."[14] *Kuryerek Krakowski*'s editors, Jerzy Kluczowski and Feliks Mrawinczyc, were betting on the fact that speaking directly to issues that affected the petite bourgeoisie and working poor would attract a new audience of read-ers, previously overlooked by the political press.

Beginning December 1, 1902, the popular city councilor, feuilletonist, and humorist Kazimierz Bartoszewicz took over the editorship and shortly there-after changed the paper's name to *Kuryer Krakowski* (Cracovian Courier), the name of a short-lived newspaper he had edited more than a decade before. Despite a good mix of local news with sensations from home and abroad, the paper never achieved mass circulation, printing only 3,000 papers a day.[15] It is difficult to say whether Bartoszewicz would have succeeded in expanding the paper's readership; the appearance of Ludwik Szczepański's *Nowiny dla wszystkich* in May 1903, which sought the same market and had more funds in its coffers, assured that he would not have the chance.[16]

Despite the elimination of the stamp tax, several barriers to a truly free press remained, such as a rule forbidding street sales and the continued presence of censorship. In Cracow, at least, the authorities generally turned a blind eye to the boys and, eventually, girls on the streets hawking the news. The 1912 painting of Market Square at night (see the frontispiece) offers one example that this was the case. In the picture, a flower girl and a newsboy ply their trades in plain sight of a police officer standing guard. Evidence from the press itself makes it clear that street sales were routine in the city. Stories about boys who sold papers—including a story in *Kuryer Krakowski* that complained of a flock of boys selling *Kronenzeitung* in Cracow as an example of unfair German competition—were not uncommon, and advertisements for newsboys and, by 1912, newsgirls appeared regularly.[17] In fact, it was so unusual for the police to do anything about street sales that popular newspapers decried any interference in outrage whenever it occurred, at times even providing the identification number of the "new officer in town" who had harassed a colporteur.[18] Finally, the fact that printing runs were generally double or triple the number of subscriptions, testifies to the major significance of street sales for the popular press.

Censorship or confiscation, as it was known at the time, was the more serious obstacle to the growth of the boulevard press. According to the Austro-Hungarian Press Law of December 1862, publishers were required to submit a copy of their publications to the local prosecutor for screening 24 hours prior to distribution. Typically, once the prosecutor had determined the inappropriate text(s), the issue would appear with a blank spot where the offending material had been. The law stipulated that a copy of the paper be sent to the Ministry of State, the Ministry of Internal Affairs, local administrators, and approved libraries at the time the prosecutor received a copy, so in theory someone investigating the archival copy later on could read the offending material.[19] In practice, the original versions of confiscated issues are not always in the final collection. If they are, the reader can see that the editors occasionally baited the prosecutor whenever they were angry about a previous confiscation or knew that other parts of an article would not pass muster. In one instance, *IKC* likened the prosecutor's use of the red pencil to that of "a knife in the hands of an idiot, or fire in the hands of a child," and even threateningly reported a telephone call from Vienna that suggested the censor's days on the job were numbered.[20]

With daily publications, the 24-hour rule must have been particularly difficult to obey and enforce. Because the rule applied to the moment of distribution, rather than when the issue was printed, publishing controversial material was always something of a gamble for daily newspapers. If the prosecutor did not confiscate an issue quickly enough, many copies of the paper may have already been sold. (This did not eliminate a court date to determine if the prosecutor's confiscation was indeed merited, but at least the offending issue had gotten out beforehand, thus recouping some of the costs of printing with street sales.) Quite frequently on the day after a confiscation the paper would exult that several thousand copies had already been released in the city beforehand.[21] Still, the possibility of losing an entire run of the paper could be quite costly for the publishers. For publications such as the men's humor magazine *Bocian* (the Stork), which typically featured drawings of sensuous, buxom women in décolletage and was rife with double entendres, the likelihood of confiscation as "pornography" was too high to risk losing an entire printing. Instead the semi-monthly publication would print only one or two copies of an issue for the prosecutor and wait for his response before printing the newly amended issue.[22]

According to his detailed study of court records for confiscations in Cracow from 1900 through 1914, historian Andrzej Garlicki has determined that of the various topics most likely to result in confiscation and a case in court, "criticism of the government and authorities" and "pornography" were the most common, though there were many other categories, including blasphemy and antisemitism, that could result in confiscation.[23] The socialist newspaper, *Naprzód*, was subject to the most confiscations by far, with approximately 21 percent of the total. Boulevard papers like *Nowiny* and *IKC* came in (a distant) second place, however.[24] Confiscations were much more common in the early period—40 percent of all cases from 1900 to 1914 occurred before January 1, 1905—and tapered off during the middle of the decade, the potentially incendiary years of revolution in Russia notwithstanding. Cracow's censor, prosecutor Roman Daliński, despite being "a bureaucrat to the marrow of his bones, a typical old-Austrian civil servant who blindly held to the letter of the law" according to an *IKC* retrospective, was clearly less restrictive as the twentieth century progressed.[25] Garlicki concludes that the publishers learned how to test the limits without overstepping them, while the prosecutor and his staff relaxed in their interpretation over the years. Garlicki also notes that, by the second decade of the twentieth century, the number of publications that were exonerated in court also increased. Finally, the sheer number of publications available in the years before the war must have made government oversight increasingly difficult.[26] Censorship was clearly on the wane. While it remained a nuisance, censorship was not so oppressive as to limit in any significant way the kinds of sensational stories that were the lifeblood of the gutter press.

By the end of the decade, newly acquired rotary printing presses enabled the efficient publication of boulevard papers in great quantity. Truly mass circulation papers, *Nowiny dla wszystkich* and *Ilustrowany Kuryer Codzienny* outstripped their competition, precisely because they sought to write "for everyone." Circulation figures for *Nowiny* are disputed, with the highest estimate at 35,000 (for 1912) as compared to 9,000 for the same year in another study.[27] *Nowiny* claimed to print as many as 9,000 copies by the end of 1904 and announced holiday issues of 20,000 by 1908. No one disputes the huge success of *IKC*, which began in late 1910 with runs of 20,000, had doubled by 1912, and reached 67,000 during the height of the Balkan Wars in the years 1912–1913.[28] Forty to sixty thousand copies in a city of 150,000 was a huge share of the market, even if some of the papers went to subscribers outside the city. If one considers the likelihood that many issues were read by multiple readers, whether at cafés or in individual households, then it becomes apparent that by the second decade of the twentieth century, the popular illustrated daily press in Cracow was nearly ubiquitous.

Ludwik Szczepański—Cracovian Press Pioneer

Among the most innovative journalists and publishers of this period was Ludwik Szczepański, the founder and chief editor of the democratic popular daily, *Nowiny dla wszystkich*. Szczepański was perhaps an unlikely candidate to establish the city's first successful boulevard newspaper, given his patrician background and affection for decadent poetry.[29] Born in 1872 in Cracow, the son of Alfred Szczepański (1840–1909), a writer and journalist, and Helena Zieleniewska, the daughter of the first factory-owner in Cracow, Ludwik Szczepański spent his youth in Vienna, where his father had a position in the Länderbank and also worked as a newspaper correspondent. After two years studying law at the university in Vienna, Szczepański moved to Cracow to continue his studies. He quickly became involved in café life and published his first decadent poetry in 1894, earning fame for the line "through an ocean of black coffee I swim to the island of relief," and establishing a place for himself among the ranks of the nascent Młoda Polska (Young Poland) movement.[30]

In 1897, Szczepański made the bold move to establish an artistic-literary weekly journal, *Życie* (Life), with some of his friends and associates. The flagship of the Young Poland movement, *Życie* was an impressive publication that featured art, articles, and poetry by nearly all of the movement's "greats," including Stanisław Wyspiański, Stanisław Przybyszewski, and the Tetmajer brothers, Włodzimierz and Kazimierz, and represented a Polish take on the waves of modernism sweeping European metropolises at the time. The magazine was a bold, progressive voice among Polish publications, publishing the works of international and expatriate writers—most notably Przybyszewski, whom Szczepański succeeded in convincing to write in Polish. Women, too, played an important role. The editor of scholarly and social issues was the noted sociologist Zofia Golińska-

Daszyńska, and the progressive writer Gabriela Zapolska, who was most likely Szczepański's lover, wrote pieces for *Życie* as well, including a spirited attack of the antisemitic *Głos Narodu*.[31]

Szczepański's brash stewardship alienated some of *Życie*'s initial readers, and high publication costs made it difficult to keep it afloat. Szczepański's son, Jan Alfred, later wrote that a family letter showed the family no longer wanted to underwrite *Życie*, after having sunk 63,000 crowns into the endeavor.[32] After less than a year Szczepański passed the editorial helm to his colleague Artur Górski, who shortly turned it over to Przybyszewski. In his memoir, Przybyszewski recalls Szczepański as the instigator of "Young Cracow," affirming his pioneering role as an enthusiastic proponent of European modernism in the city, which, "though already a little stale, was entirely new for Cracow." He concludes his assessment of the young innovator remarking that, when Szczepański gave up control of the journal, "he must have come to profoundly loathe it, because he never returned." The journal went out of print in 1900, only three years after its inception.[33]

Szczepański's next move was to publish an illustrated weekly for a larger, more mainstream audience. Taking the Berlin publication *Die Woche* as his model, Szczepański launched *Ilustracya Polska* (Polish Illustration) on September 18, 1901.[34] The weekly targeted a patriotic Polish audience, desirous to see its nation progress. As its editor saw it, the publication was to be "for Poles, about Poles," richly illustrated with 20–40 illustrations per issue, unbiased, and "accessibly priced."[35] The journal featured theater reviews by Szczepański, as well as art and poetry by Szczepański's colleagues from the Young Poland movement. It also participated in disseminating a folksy "Polish style" of furniture and architecture, proclaiming the Zakopane style the national type, for example.[36] In addition to making its readers familiar with national culture, the magazine invited them to generate their own contributions, sponsoring contests for amateur photography and short stories. Yet the editor closely guarded entrance into the society of letters; as was the case in other publications of the time, examples of poor poetry or verse were occasionally published along with rejection letters.[37] Still, the weekly's nationalizing project was open to a wide Polish audience, even to those who may not have regularly read the magazine. A prominent article complained about the prohibitive prices of the People's Theater in Cracow, accusing the city council of shortsightedness and stinginess that kept people from enjoying national culture.[38] While *Ilustracya Polska*'s primary audience and focus was Galicia, it regularly reported on affairs in Prussian and Russian Poland and clearly sought to speak more broadly at times for the Polish nation. Occasional articles addressed local urban issues, such as a review of the Cracow fire department, but on the whole the publication was concerned with national cultural issues.

In 1903, Szczepański and his wife, Lucyna, decided to launch an illustrated daily. *Nowiny dla wszystkich*, published from May 16, 1903, until December 21, 1913, proved Szczepański's most successful publishing endeavor. Whereas *Ilustracya Polska*—which had folded by the end of 1904—was concerned with national issues and the dissemination of high culture, *Nowiny* was clearly a city paper, designed to appeal to a range of local readers, especially the large population of artisans, shopkeepers, petty office workers, and other (lower-) middle-class readers in Cracow and Podgórze. The paper, which characterized itself as "democratic, but unaffiliated with any party," was accessibly priced at 2 cents (4 hallers—about the cost of a cheap bread roll) an issue in town and 3 cents in the province, making it the least expensive paper in the city. During its eleven-year run *Nowiny* never exceeded 6 cents per issue, even when it quadrupled in size (from four to sixteen pages) after its 1911 merger with the ailing peasant party paper, *Dziennik Powszechny* (the Universal Daily). Monthly and quarterly subscription rates were also affordable, at one and three crowns, respectively. After 1905, the paper appeared daily at five in the afternoon and at eight in the morning on Mondays.

From the outset, Stanisław Brandowski, Maryan Dąbrowski, Jan Pietrzycki, Józef Rączkowski, and the popular lawyer Włodzimierz Lewicki joined Szczepański on the editorial staff. Dąbrowski, who had worked with Szczepański at *Ilustracya Polska*, was the editorial secretary and was probably involved in introducing coverage of sport and fitness into the paper, as this was one of his major agendas during the middle of the decade.[39] Rączkowski was the author of a series of witty feuilletons about everyday life in Cracow signed "j.r."[40] It is difficult to determine individual roles, however, because no editorial records remain, and anonymity generally prevailed on the pages of the paper. As for funding, it was widely rumored that Szczepański's cousin from Wieliczka and especially his uncle Ludwik Zieleniewski, a wealthy industrialist, subsidized the paper.[41]

Szczepański's "descent" from *Życie*, arguably the premier Polish-language literary and cultural magazine of its era, to the "gutter rag" *Nowiny dla wszystkich* did not escape notice. A few weeks after the appearance of *Nowiny*, the humor magazine *Liberum Veto* presented its readers with "a charade" consisting of sample covers of *Życie*, *Ilustracya Polska*, *Nowiny dla wszystkich*, and a booklet entitled *Hugo Szenk: Famous Murderer of Women*, promising a prize to the reader who could explain how they were related. The answer, of course, was that at least the first three were edited by Szczepański and the fourth would be the natural conclusion of his descent into the depths of gutter journalism.[42] The next issue of *Liberum Veto* contained a hilarious spoof of *Nowiny's* debut in the city, imagining its first colporteur as a gramophone with an "anglicized" Cracovian accent that managed to sell 10,000 copies of the paper within seven minutes. In this imaginary account, everything on Market Square, from the occupants of the electric trams to the bronze statue of Adam Mickiewicz, riveted its attention on the mechanical representative of the paper, whose presentation cast "a throng of thousands [into] a trance." Even "pickpockets are so engaged they forget for a moment the possibility of easy pickings, that may never in eternity happen again." The first to break free from the trance, *Liberum Veto* pointedly suggested, was Mr. Kazimierz Bartoszewicz, who had received a package of "2,998 unsold copies of *Kuryer Krakowski* from a printing of 3,000" just that morning.

> One could hear, as with tears in his eyes at the loss of "our dearly beloved" *Kuryerek*, with jealousy in his voice at the sight of the tremendous success of *Nowiny*, and with melancholy in his whole soul, he muttered: "Ah, so this is the island of relief?! —the port to which one sails through an ocean of black coffee? . . . Well, well, who could have predicted this five years ago?! These decadents are not as dumb as I had thought, after all!"[43]

Recalling Szczepański's most famous line of decadent poetry, *Liberum Veto's* Bartoszewicz took a humorous stab at the poet's descent into commercialized sensationalist journalism. Offering a final explanation, he surmised that perhaps it was Szczepański's recent marriage that compelled him to earn his daily bread pushing newspapers, citing a familiar saying: "He who marries, changes" (*Kto się ożeni, ten się odmieni*). With a circulation of ten thousand, the spoof implied, the mass illustrated press would certainly prove a more profitable enterprise than decadent poetry or highbrow journalism.

In its first years, *Nowiny* was clearly more populist and revolutionary than the conservative and liberal-democratic press in Cracow. Its coverage of socialist events was generally unbiased or even sympathetic, and at least initially its attitude toward the socialist daily, *Naprzód,* was ambivalent. This initial ambivalence is significant given *Nowiny's* obvious antipathy for the nationalist, antisemitic daily, *Głos Narodu*, with which it waged a rather fierce turf war for readers.[44] While *Nowiny* was generally not antisemitic, it never pressed this issue in attacking its potential rival. *Nowiny's* attacks on *Głos Narodu* were less ideological forays than tactical smears in order to attract the latter's readership. In this regard, it was very much a new sort of paper in Cracow, designed to attract the largest audience, not press a political stance. In 1905, *Nowiny* covered revolutionary events in Russia and Warsaw, unabashedly condemning the tsar while supporting "the people." Unlike the conservative *Czas*, which condemned "irrational" violence by Poles in the Kingdom of Poland, *Nowiny* made sure to put the initial blame on the "barbarism" of the Russian authorities when explaining revolutionary violence.[45] On May Day, 1905, the paper shut down in support of working people, an action it did not repeat after 1907, when to do so could have implied support for the Social Democratic party. By the end of the decade, the paper regularly mocked May Day celebrations in the city, claiming that "the more intelligent workers" had already figured out how pointless the "holiday of hatred" was.[46]

This significant shift in the newspaper's political position came about in 1907 because new Austrian laws enfranchised a large part of its readership by extending the vote to all adult males. After supporting universal suffrage for several years (an article in 1905 boldly declared: "The Polish people are knocking at the door" in reference to electoral expansion), the paper became much more concerned with local and Austrian politics in 1907.[47] *Nowiny* had long reported on local government, but now it became overtly political, encouraging its readers to vote for the Democratic Union ticket, while disparaging the socialists, and to a slightly lesser extent the conservatives, who until recently had run the city. Before 1907, *Nowiny*'s coverage of Ignacy Daszyński, Cracow's most important socialist politician, had been favorable. But once the Social Democratic leader challenged a ticket that included Szczepański's relative Edmund Zieleniewski, Daszyński and his newspaper *Naprzód* were subjected to ridicule.[48] Articles and illustrations from 1911 lambasted the socialists for failing to bring about the workers' paradise their slogans supposedly promised. One cartoon absurdly blamed the socialists for inflationary food costs, for example, because rolls and meat had cost less in 1906—before the Social Democrats had any clout in parliament—than in 1911 when there were 89 socialist representatives. Other illustrations depicted churches turned into marketplaces, with vodka being sold at the pulpit, children being assigned numbers by a socialist government instead of being baptized, and peasants receiving equal-sized but miniscule plots of state-owned land.[49]

Despite its basic allegiance to democratic principles, *Nowiny*'s political stance after 1907 could be a bit confusing. When in 1909, Szczepański sought to hire Stanisław Stojałowski as a political correspondent in Vienna, Stojałowski replied, "It's hard for me to write for you, sir, seeing as I don't know where you stand in this present chaos."[50] According to its competitors, *Nowiny*'s allegiances were simple to deduce—they merely followed the highest bidder. A gloating piece in *IKC* in 1913 claimed that "since the very beginning *Nowiny* has sought some political party, to which it can hitch its wagons, expecting of course, money from the deal."[51] In 1909, the paper briefly supported the National Democrats (who were a much better match with *Głos Narodu*) and was accused by the peasant party paper *Dziennik Powszechny* (the Universal Newspaper) of accepting a large sum of money for doing so.[52] Then in 1911, *Nowiny* absorbed the ailing *Dziennik Powszechny* and found itself trying to smooth the differences between the latter's peasant readership and its own democratically minded urban readers, suggesting that "their goals [were] the same" and that only methods had been different. "The working inhabitants of the cities and the villages can both push for democratic reform," the paper noted hopefully.[53]

But for the most part, *Nowiny* was not a political paper. It was drawn into politics by the changes that came about because of universal male suffrage and the need for financial support, but its political positions were not the reason for its appeal. The paper remained attractive because of its mix of local news and interurban sensation (described more fully below). It may have cast about for financial support by seeking political endorsement, but *Nowiny*'s very inconsistency on this front demonstrates that it was not a party paper like *Czas*, *Głos Narodu*, or *Naprzód*, which all hewed faithfully to their core party's interests. *Nowiny* backed the parties that the majority of its readers would find most attractive, the democrats and the overlapping coalitions that formed within this group over the years, the Democratic-Urban Coalition (Grupa Demokratyczno-Mieszczańska) and the Civil Servant Party (Stronnictwo Urzędnicze).[54] Until its last few months in print, *Nowiny* was fiercely loyal to the leader of the democrats, City President Juliusz Leo. As it turned out, however, President Leo outlasted the paper. The venerable mayor died in office just a few months before the end of the war in 1918; *Nowiny* had ceased to exist before the war began.

A major reason for *Nowiny*'s eventual collapse was the introduction and resounding success of *Ilustrowany Kuryer Codzienny* (*IKC*), a modern twelve-page illustrated daily edited by Maryan Dąbrowski, a former protégé of Szczepański at *Ilustracya Polska* and *Nowiny*. Dąbrowski had left *Nowiny* in 1906 and toured about Europe, observing the press in Rome, Paris, and Vienna. Seeking an opportunity to exercise more influence in Cracow's press upon his return, he joined a consortium that purchased *Głos Narodu* in 1908 and shortly became its managing editor. Yet when the new Polish Christian Social Party (Polskie Stronnictwo Chrześcijansko-Socjalne, PSChS) created by Dąbrowski and others affiliated with the paper failed to win much support in local or parliamentary elections and the paper failed to make a profit, Dąbrowski sought a clever escape. His decision to launch the mass circulation newspaper *Ilustrowany Kuryer Codzienny* in December 1910, with an initial press run of 20,000 copies, was seen as a betrayal by his former political associates at *Głos Narodu*, particularly because it was made financially feasible thanks to the editor's cooperation with some Jewish businessmen in real estate speculation. Dąbrowski even poached some of *Głos Narodu's* junior staff.[55]

Despite some early glitches with its much-ballyhooed rotary press, the fastest in Cracow, *IKC* quickly became a city favorite. A mere four days after its introduction, *IKC* bragged that it was already the most popular paper in the city.[56] For its first year, the paper was priced one cent less than *Nowiny* in town, at a cost of 5 cents in Cracow, 6 in the provinces. (After the paper had established itself for about a year, the price in town was raised to 6 cents.) In an effort to be the earliest paper available, *IKC* appeared at noon and was antedated, with the next day's date above the masthead.[57] Its business and stock reports were designed to appeal to the city's upper-crust businessmen, while special fashion sections targeted women readers. Showings at Cracow's favorite cinemas were featured along the side of the third page of each issue, and every cover had a dramatic half-page line drawing designed to draw in the reader. As if in reaction, *Nowiny* also began to publish regular business and fashion sections in its enlarged version of the paper, post-1911. An insert entitled "The Practical Housewife" appeared every Thursday. The threatened newspaper also published many more illustrations and photographs than before.

Yet these adaptations failed to make *Nowiny* sufficiently competitive. Despite having absorbed the peasant party paper in 1911, *Nowiny* quickly lost the support of its party leader, Jan Stapiński, who set aside so-called government press funds in Vienna in support of *IKC*. Press historian Czesław Lechicki remarks that if Szczepański had had better business sense, or at least as much financial support from his millionaire maternal grandparents as Dąbrowski got from Stapiński, *Nowiny* could have prevailed.[58] But this was not the case. With strong financial support, the city's largest press run, a well-organized and consistent layout, and plentiful illustrations, *IKC* outperformed its rival.[59] As *Nowiny* began to struggle, *IKC's* attacks on its erstwhile rival grew increasingly malicious. In one diatribe, *IKC* made fun of the paper's title, saying it "should be changed to 'Used' or 'Stolen News,' because all of the 'News' in the paper is like the jackets and trousers sold on the corner of Szpitalna St. by Mr. Gajer, which are neither new nor one's size," before accusing the paper of turning on President Leo because he was no longer willing to support their sinking ship.[60] According to *IKC*, *Nowiny's* efforts to "put a revolver to Leo's chest," only succeeded in getting about half the money the paper needed, and thus, "Ludwik could now perhaps spend the summer 'swimming through an ocean of black coffee' throughout Cracow, because black coffee is about how much he can afford."[61]

When a two-month Austria-wide printers' strike hobbled *Nowiny*'s already ailing finances during the winter of 1913/1914, Szczepański had to liquidate his beloved publication. On June 16, 1914, he sold *Nowiny* to Maryan Dąbrowski and joined the editorial board of *Ilustrowany Kuryer Codzienny* the next day.[62] Having forced Bartoszewicz's *Kuryer Krakowski* out of competition a decade before by producing a more innovative and better-funded popular newspaper, Szczepański now got a taste of his own medicine. His former protégé, Dąbrowski, "the Polish William Randolph Hearst," went on to become the head of the most powerful press conglomerate in interwar Poland.[63] Jan Alfred Szczepański later observed that his father must have felt that the saying "no man is a prophet in his own country" applied to him, as *IKC* won the battle for supremacy.[64] Both men had studied the foreign press and applied what they had learned to the particular conditions of early twentieth-century Cracow.

FEATURES OF THE POPULAR PRESS

"The News for Everyone"

As already noted, *Kuryerek Krakowski*, *Nowiny dla wszystkich*, and *Ilustrowany Kuryer Codzienny* resolutely claimed to be for everyone, avowing apolitical stances in an effort to garner as many readers as possible through subscriptions and quasi-legal street sales. *Kuryerek Krakowski* proclaimed no political program, only a desire to create a lively source of information "about things that interest every Pole . . . regardless of standing in society or religion," and that even the "most impoverished person" could afford to read.[65] The inaugural issue of *Nowiny* contained a similar message from the publisher about the purpose and intended audience of the paper, asserting, "We want a truly popular paper for every Pole . . . not just in the interest of a certain class."[66] In *Ilustrowany Kuryer Codzienny*'s premiere, Dąbrowski stressed the importance of having "papers of a popular-informative style" to supplement the political papers, "which, let's face it," he confided, "have a readership in the few thousands anyway." He cited examples from the West, including Paris and London, in justifying the appearance of his paper on the scene, pointing out that often the "serious papers" also publish a paper of popular-informative nature as well. Dąbrowski assured the complete political and class impartiality of the paper, asserting that it was the only independent daily paper in the country—a direct, though perhaps not unfounded, slight to *Nowiny*, which had failed to remain apolitical.[67]

The papers succeeded in meeting their target audiences. Advertisement and article content in each of the papers demonstrate wide readership, from the occasional déclassé noble trying to sell a manor in the countryside to young women seeking employment (or finding it) in advertisements that call for sales clerks in a confectionary.[68] Ads for service positions occasionally appeared in the popular press, but most advertisements tended to be about consumer goods and services for the artisans, bureaucrats, merchants, and shopkeepers of the city to buy and sell. Commercial advertisements in the May 23, 1907, issue of *Nowiny* included pitches for Hungarian wine, chocolate, bowling pins and balls, Ceylon tea, lily soap, sweets, hygienic rubber products, tailoring services, a Polish hotel, grave decoration, a notification of a change of business ownership, the Galician Zoological Company (which displayed "exotic animals" and sold "high quality pets"), watches for rent, and furniture.

The names of the merchants represented in advertisements often betray the mix of national backgrounds in business in the city, from clearly Polish names to Jewish, German, and Polish-German names (Polish first names and Polonized forms of German surnames). This merchant base is quite apparent in the articles in the daily newspapers that discuss, for example, numerous citywide meetings of shopkeepers, the occasional marriage of merchant families, or the winners of a recent beauty contest, all of whose fathers had Germanic last names and were listed as local businessmen. (In the beauty contest first, second, and third places were won by, respectively, Z. Gutmanówna, Marya Ferberówna, and Zofia Kellhoferówna. A note on page 2 mentioned that votes could be bought but assured that "it is this way the world over.")[69] Notices of meetings for the Chamber of Commerce and Industry abounded in *Nowiny* and *IKC*. Beginning in 1909, *Nowiny* introduced a section that targeted its principal readership entitled, simply enough, "Artisans and Shopkeepers." As mentioned above, *IKC* featured, from its first issue forward, a business section with stock reports out of Vienna. Not too long afterward, *Nowiny* issued a weekly section on economic issues in the city, "Economic Review," in an effort to compete for the same audience.

Working-class readers and petty artisans also read the popular illustrated press. *Nowiny* and *IKC* were the most popular dailies among joiners and furniture-makers, for example, according to a contemporary survey. In a study of young working-class men in 1912, Dr. Zofia Daszyńska-Golińska determined that almost all of her interlocutors were literate. Nearly all of the men read the newspapers, though sometimes irregularly and late. Most of the daily newspapers in Cracow were popular among artisans, she found, except for the conservative *Czas*.[70] Knowing that their readers were often working-class, the papers tended to be tolerant of strikes. In 1913, *IKC* offered an evenhanded report of a strike at the gasworks, scolding the mayor and the socialists (!) for inadequate support of the workers.[71]

Printed lists of promotional sweepstakes winners offer another glance at readership. The winner of an early contest in *Nowiny* was an upholsterer, a confirmation of the paper's success among petty artisans.[72] Many of the winners of a lottery in *Nowiny* from 1904 were pupils at area schools (or in one case, a schoolmaster); artisans and servants won prizes as well.[73] After its 1911 merger with *Dziennik Powszechny*, the failing peasant party paper, *Nowiny* appears to have had more readers outside Cracow than previously. Winners of "brain teasers" in 1912 came from all over western Galicia, including larger towns like Rzeszów, Tarnów, Wieliczka, Nowy Sącz, Zakopane, Żywiec, and little villages like Świątniki Górne, Skawina, and Podhajce. Only half of the winners were from Cracow and its surroundings.[74] This is no representative survey of the paper's readership, but it does give an indication of its expanded reach outside the city after 1911.

Youth read the illustrated press more than other newspapers. Illustrations and stories of local and international sensations naturally proved far more attractive to younger readers than the editorials of the political press. Serialized fictional stories that ran along the bottom of the newspaper—which could be a major motivation in securing subscriptions—likewise appealed to a broad audience that included the young. Boys took on the personae of famous fictional characters such as the American cowboy Nick Carter, the French "gentleman thief" Arsène Lupin, or the English detective Sherlock Holmes—all found in the popular press—in their games.[75] As the previously cited lottery results attest, school pupils participated in contests designed by the papers. Recognizing the value of attracting young readers, popular papers were also more willing to publish stories by or about youth. Magdalena Samozwaniec, the granddaughter of the famous painter Juliusz Kossak, recalled the publication of her humorous short story "Mama's Trip to the City" in *Nowiny* as "one of the most beautiful days in my life."[76]

The publishers and editors of the popular press deliberately sought women readers with special-interest stories, articles about women abroad (including woman suffrage movements), articles on housekeeping and child rearing, fashion articles, sensationalist dramas, fiction, and advertisements for all sorts of cosmetic products including "bust cream," corsets, and ready-to-wear dresses.[77] Occasionally a series or an article in the paper received floods of letters from women readers, as was the case when an editorial by a woman in July 1903 asserted that it was impossible to manage a family home on an average civil servant income. A few days after the initial letter ran the editors observed, "Our series has created a little revolution among the women of Cracow. Each day we have so many letters on the topic that to read them all and decide how to publish them would take a whole day of work."[78] One man who disagreed with *Nowiny*'s stance in favor of large city budget debts—a policy strongly opposed by the conservatives and the National Right party ("prawica narodowa") for which he was a candidate—threatened to revoke his subscription to *Nowiny*, only he feared his wife would probably not let him. "I like the *News* and my wife reads it from cover to cover," he admitted, "but perhaps she'll just have to pay for it herself."[79] One gets the idea that *Nowiny* was happy to report that even the wife of its political enemy read the paper from cover to cover. *IKC* was not above joking (about itself) that "only women read [the] *Daily Courier*." Almost exactly one year after the paper was founded, *IKC* began a series entitled "About Women, for Women" directly targeting this core readership.[80] Evidently the link between the popular press and female readers was commonly perceived.

It is difficult to assess the extent to which Jewish readers participated in reading the Cracovian popular press. Not until 1909 did the city have a Jewish daily, the Yiddish *Der Tag*, which, according to press historian Jerzy Myśliński, was largely assimilationist in nature.[81] In what was probably a veiled indication that it feared losing readers, *Nowiny* protested the introduction of *Der Tag*, saying that a Yiddish daily, even if it claimed to be apolitical, was unnecessary and would only foment antisemitism. "Some people argue that a Yiddish-language paper is the only way to speak to the Jewish masses," *Nowiny* wrote. "We believe that it will only keep them in the ghetto."[82] There is reason to believe that many Jews who were assimilated into the dominant Polish culture of the city indeed read the popular Polish-language press. When *IKC* ran a series about shopkeepers who were threatened by migrant fruit sellers, for example, it elicited "many replies from Jewish and Christian shopkeepers alike"—a clear indication that at least Jews of the target audience were reading the paper.[83] A personal advertisement in *IKC* for "a young Israelite woman, orthodox, who knows how to cook, sew and look after children" likewise implies that the advertiser expected to find a large enough sample of applicants among readers of the popular daily to fill the position.[84]

Yet, even if none of the papers was ever stridently antisemitic, *most* of them claimed a "Christian ethic" and were clearly nationalistic at times. (One exception was *Kuryerek Krakowski*, which, as cited earlier, deliberately made no distinctions regarding religious persuasion in its mission statement.) During election years, when Jewish votes were vital in supporting the democratic ticket, or during census taking, when it was advantageous for Polish Christians to have their Jewish neighbors claim Polish as their "everyday language," *Nowiny* courted Jewish support while decrying those Jews who failed to see its side.[85]

Articles about Jews were generally straightforward reports, occasionally manifesting slight Judeophobia or prejudice but never anything akin to the strident antisemitism of *Głos Narodu*. Juvenile delinquents with Jewish names, for example, were never seen as a Jewish problem but as part of a citywide problem with delinquency. In the only article I found that commented upon the Jewish identity of young troublemakers, the author merely observed that formerly "you never saw Jews [in jail]," but now, as the city has spread out, "Cracovian types" were showing up in Kazimierz, too.[86] Significantly, their criminality was due to the growth of the big city and not to their religious or ethnic background.

The popular illustrated press thus cut a wide swath through Polish-reading society in and around Cracow, missing only its conservative-elite and radical edges. *Kuryerek Krakowski, Nowiny dla wszystkich*, and *IKC* were widely popular, especially among the merchants, artisans, and journeymen of the city. The increased readership of women, children, and members of the working class demonstrates, in addition to the results of greater literacy, the economic imperative in creating a modern mass circulation publication. Expanding the readership by eliminating partisan appeals, by more explicitly inviting female readers, and by pitching to working-class readers meant greater sales and thus greater profits. The papers broadcast to the largest possible audience, picking fights only with groups who were presumed not to read the paper anyway. Always claiming to be non-partisan and for all classes, these papers provided the news for *almost* everyone.

More important, however, than the actual readership of these papers—which I have attempted to characterize by analyzing circulation figures, advertising and content, occasional lists of contest winners, and a contemporary survey— is the fact that *Kuryerek Krakowski, Nowiny*, and *IKC* consistently *presented themselves* as newspapers for everyone. Their self-presentation as the news for everyone, even when some groups such as conservatives, socialists, and certain Jews and other non-Poles may have had reason to feel excluded, is more important than their "actual" readership. In asserting that they published the news for everyone, the papers were mostly correct (they certainly sought a larger audience than their predecessors), but of course they were also giving respectability to their average readers in suggesting that all classes read boulevard papers, when their appeal leaned more toward middlebrow and lowbrow tastes. Artisans and shopkeepers were their primary audience, not aristocrats and professors.[87]

Immediate Truth

In an effort to appear modern and fresh, all of the papers also emphasized their immediacy or novelty. "Telegrafem i Telefonem" (By Telegraph and Telephone) was a daily section of the papers that reported news wired or phoned to the headquarters of the newspapers. The title of the section deliberately drew attention to the newspapers' use of modern technology to provide news quickly. *Nowiny* and *Ilustrowany Kuryer Codzienny* each fought to be the first paper on the streets in the afternoon, trying to outstrip the afternoon editions of *Nowa Reforma* or *Czas*, so that their readers could "get the day's news first."[88] And whenever there was a dramatic event in town such as a murder or a murder trial, the papers printed special editions so that readers could get "the latest developments." In its first report of the shocking death of Włodzimierz Lewicki, the popular lawyer who had contributed to the paper in its early days, *Nowiny* bragged that its illustration of the grisly scene had been drawn on location only "four hours after the incident"[89] (see Fig. 1). Readers were given an immediate view of the victim lying in his nightshirt on a bloody pillow where he had been found (or left) by his erstwhile lover and client, Janina Borowska. (In what became perhaps the biggest story in the popular press during this era, Borowska was later accused, tried, and acquitted of murdering Lewicki.)[90] The illustration gave readers the opportunity to discover the victim themselves, offering an intimate gaze on the dead man in his apartment mere hours after his demise.

This voyeuristic effect occurred each time the papers published a dramatic illustration of a sensationalist event. Drawings almost always depicted the moment of discovery. The illustration for "Death in a Barrel" acknowledged that the picture, "taken from the Viennese press, shows the moment when the unfortunate victim was discovered," but in most illustrations this truth was left unstated.[91] Viewers were present as the train conductor ran back to see the woman his train had struck; they were in the bathroom as the maid and a family member found a suicide victim in her bath; they saw the moment that a crazed young cadet opened the door to show his neighbors the family members

Fig. 1—"**How Was Dr. Lewicki Found?** (An exclusive drawing by *The News*' staff artist 4 hours after the incident)." *Nowiny,* June 6, 1909.

he had murdered with an ax.[92] Pictures that did not exactly show the moment of discovery still illustrated the artist's idea of the most dramatic moment of a given event, a fiction that gave the viewer an intimate, if somewhat falsified, perspective. "In the relentless pursuit of sensation," *Nowa Reforma* once complained, "[the popular press] illustrates such terrible scenes, . . . composing situations that the illustrator of course has never seen."[93] The sensationalist weekly *Nowości Illustrowane* employed a staff photographer to snap pictures of the effect of a crime or suicide, but such photographs were rare. One gets the idea that dramatic illustrations may have been thought to provide a truer picture anyway, as evidenced by the reporting of a "lovers' drama," one of the magazine's most common local stories, in the October 1, 1904, issue. The reader was treated to a photograph of a woman who committed suicide on a park bench in all its gray banality and authenticity, *plus* a drawing of her lover at the moment of discovery. Again, the viewer participated in the shocking discovery, seeing the ultimate moment of truth.

Implicit in the "moment of discovery" drawings was the blurring of subject and object (the reader), something that scholars of the popular press from other eras have noted.[94] The link between subject and reader was explicit, of course, in the daily chronicle section of the papers, where Cracovian artisans and shopkeepers, maids and juvenile delinquents, could regularly read about themselves or people much like themselves in the afternoon paper. The daily chronicles were the perfect venue for the overlapping of subject and object of the text. Names and often addresses of the persons described in this section were provided, thus connecting a story to real people or real buildings and places in town. Reports of merchant weddings or meetings for shopkeepers, already cited here, well illustrate this tendency.

The papers also excelled in depicting average citizens visually. A particularly enjoyable series of illustrations in *Kuryerek Krakowski*, entitled "Cracovian Scenes," showed a number of Jewish citizens in front of the Hotel Londyński, a trio of day laborers talking about their poor prospects for the winter, and a line of ordinary people waiting to buy lottery tickets (see Fig. 2).[95] The soldier, the schoolchild, the middle-class mother, the maid, the dandy in the bowler hat, the day laborer, the poor Jew, and the wealthy Jewish businessman rendered in these drawings represented archetypal Cracovians, and as such would have been instantly recognizable.

A common variation of this theme would make it clear that the subjects of a story in the news were *not quite like* the readers of the press, because they were less respectable—a reverse affirmation of the reader's identity and respectability.[96] Such was the story of Wojciech Frączkiewicz, a "curbside merchant," which was told in such a way as to resonate with respectable merchants in town, by suggesting that the street seller "apparently" wanted to be just like them:

> Wojciech Frączkiewicz apparently wanted to be a merchant above all, but, because he doesn't have a store, he sells on the street. He sells tombac [an alloy of copper and zinc] rings, which he sells to the naïve as gold. Just on the eighteenth of last month he was caught and arrested for this kind of trade and already yesterday he was called "under the telegraph" [i.e., to the police station] for the same crime. Apparently he still hasn't gotten over his mania.[97]

*Fig. 2—***Cracovian Types in the Lottery Line.** *Kuryer Krakowski*, February 12, 1903.

The humor in the entry about the curbside merchant arises from framing an issue of deceptive selling practices in terms of desire for respectability—as if Mr. Frączkiewicz did not sell counterfeit jewelry on the street to make a quick crown or to survive in desperate financial circumstances but because of a "mania" to be a merchant. Given these circumstances, the respectable reader was safely distanced from the petty criminal, his status above the phony merchant assured, and thanks to his reading of the paper, he would be less likely to be deceived by his wares.

The Blurry (Column) Lines between Fact and Fiction

If the distinction between reader and subject was sometimes obscured in each of these papers, so too was the line between fact and fiction. Generally, the reader could expect to find fiction—novels in installment form—in specific parts of the paper, so that news and fiction maintained different spaces. And yet, topically, there was regularly a strange synergy between the two, making the differences between them far less distinct than their spatial distance would imply.[98] All of the papers ran fictional pieces about crime; often the stories seemed oddly similar to an actual news story about a crime elsewhere on the page or on another page of the paper. Both *Nowiny* and *IKC* initiated their premiere issues with a "story of crime based on actual occurrences in Cracow" in the case of *Nowiny dla wszystkich* or in the case of *Ilustrowany Kuryer Codzienny* "an original romance set against the background of relations in Metropolitan Cracow." "Flower of Death" and "Bloody Key," respectively, treated their readers to stories of crime in their city, based on "actual" events reported in the press and located in decidedly familiar places. The choice of both papers to begin publication with this kind of story affirms the presumed appeal of mixing fact and fiction in a daily newspaper "for everyone."

Readers apparently wanted to read fiction that was still somehow "true" because it took place in familiar surroundings. As in the pictures of the moment of discovery, readers could feel as if they were present as the story unfolded before them, thanks to its familiarity or proximity. Here, obviously, proximity was geographical, as the characters of the stories walked the same streets that Cracovians frequented daily, and the readers could therefore easily reconstruct the scene in their minds. In the story "Limping," which ran in *Nowiny* in 1907, Mrs. Helena Montferrat, a Polish-speaking murderess (or murder suspect) with an exotic French surname, strolled down Sienna Street to attend the famous "Sztuka" art exhibit inside the central building in town, the Clothiers' Hall. All the while she was being followed by the intrepid Mr. Inspector Ślimak, whose unfortunate last name means "snail." He pursued her carefully through the exhibit as she paused to look at paintings currently on display by Stanisław Wyspiański and other famous artists.[99] The reader, too, could spy on the imaginary Mrs. Montferrat, easily imagining her environs because they were part of his or her everyday life in the city. He or she, like Ślimak, was *reading* the suspicious woman's behavior.

This uncanny overlapping of fiction and fact across sections of the paper was not always intentional, but the decision to include actual persons and streets in semi-fictional pieces made it likely. In fact, sometimes readers took the fictional segments too literally. One distraught reader wrote in to complain about the portrayal of his café in a fictional piece, assuring everyone that it was well lit and not dark and dank as the story put it![100] It remains unlikely that the majority of readers could not distinguish narratives that were mostly factual from those that were primarily fictional; spatial boundaries more or less defined fact and fiction in the paper. Yet this does not mean their deliberate blending ceased to function as a central component of the discourse. Readers seemed to favor facts that seemed fictional and fiction that was close to fact. "Spectacular reality," as Vanessa Schwartz has shown for the Parisian press, was a major source of these papers' appeal.[101] Readers sought a sensationalized, but "real," slice of modern urban life. They recognized themselves and their neighbors in the didactic dramas of everyday life.

In an era of increasing universal education, popular newspapers found ways to put science and statistics to the contradictory purposes of education and entertainment, fact and fiction. Readers of *Ilustrowany Kuryer Codzienny* in 1911 encountered illustrated tables at least once a week, where they could see how much coal or soap the great nations of the world used, how many dreadnoughts each state had, the percentages of the nationalities in the Austro-Hungarian army, how many Poles had emigrated to America in the past two years, and so on. *Nowiny* tended to use statistics even more creatively. The author of an article summarizing recent city statistics proclaimed, "Statistics are in general dry and boring, but can be very interesting for those who know how to read figures" and then went on deliberately to misread the figures for the month. He concluded, for example, that old bachelors cling to life more fiercely than married men, because so many more married men of the same age died. (Of course, there were numerically many more married men in that age group.) He made moralizing asides about the numbers of illegitimate births in the city ("many more than in other cities") and suggested that Cracow's low number of suicides (6) in a period when Vienna had 150, testified to the fact that Cracovians were simply too poor to afford poison or a revolver.[102] Another series of articles in 1907 *Nowiny* likewise used police statistics to define (or divine) the *morality* of the city.[103]

The marshalling of statistics for moral purposes was quite in keeping with a major imperative in the way stories were told in the news. Many news stories were described not in a way that simply imparted information, as in the recently developed Anglo-American tradition of the news, but in interpretative, moralistic tones.[104] The story accompanying the aforementioned illustration of the woman who committed suicide in her bath began, not with a description of who the victim was, where she lived, and when her unfortunate suicide occurred, but by postulating that "no time of year sees as many suicides as spring," and only after a full paragraph about the tragedies of youth in love, did it provide the particulars of the alluring illustration. The same pattern held in the story of a worker who met his untimely demise in a flour bin, which began with a lengthy exposition on the "terrible lot" of the machinist worker, or another report about some children who fell through ice and drowned, which rhapsodized for four paragraphs about the "tragedies of nature," before revealing the victims' names and when and where they had died.[105] Clearly the moral had precedence over the facts in such didactic dramas. Gunther Barth notes that American newspapers began to employ the "five W's" (who, what, when, where, and why) in the 1890s, thus escaping the "'straightjacket' of stylized news reporting" that had preceded it. In Cracow, and in continental Europe generally, the tendency to moralize first, however, was still intact.[106]

In Cracow at least, the moralizing tone in the popular press persisted in part because newspapers had not fully replaced or superseded the traditional role of rumor as a medium of communication. While metropolitan life could make verbal gossip difficult because of the sheer numbers of strangers inhabiting the city, the tropes and strategies of traditional gossip worked well in a society still growing accustomed to textual communication. The paper frequently followed up on rumors racing through the metropolis, confirming or disproving their veracity, and it was certainly not above rumor mongering itself. On one occasion, when a maidservant's newborn was rescued from the sewer after an attempted infanticide, *Nowiny* maliciously, if not libelously, noted that the child had "semitic features" and that the mother's Jewish master "had exhibited strange emotions throughout the whole affair."[107] Despite the feelings of isolation that may have accompanied immigrant life in the metropolis and its suburbs, the press was thus a reminder of gossip from home, even if the stories were now frequently examples of "big-city" (*wielkomiejskie*) crime (see chapter 5).

Ever since Georg Simmel's famous essay "The Metropolis and Mental Life," scholarship on the popular press and the modern city has stressed the enhanced visual aspect of the urban experience and the ways that the press orchestrated spectatorship in the city,[108] but the press's representation and facilitation of public conversation was also a central part of its appeal. The boulevard press appealed to the eyes *and* the ears; just as vivid front-page illustrations and brash headlines drew in readers, so did the cries of colporteurs who announced the biggest news of the day. Written in the language spoken where they were consumed—the street, the café, the parlor, the park—popular newspapers were part of conversations throughout the metropolis. The boulevard press picked up on snippets of dialogue throughout town and presented them to readers for further conversation with friends and associates. The daily chronicle section in *Nowiny* was called "Co słychać w mieście?" ("What's the word in town?" or literally, "What [do you] hear in town?"). The title implied that readers could tap into existing conversations all around them, eavesdropping on the most interesting ones. Whether in advocating for the masses against the exploitation of the rich and powerful or in seeking to express the mood of the day, Cracow's popular press claimed to be the *voice* of the people, and eventually "the voice of millions."[109] In the period before the Great War, few newspapers in Central Europe ever reached millions, but they were by far the most popular medium of communication in the great cities of the age. For their thousands of readers, from housewives to house servants, shopkeepers to shoppers, popular newspapers were the dominant, but not the only, voice in an ongoing conversation about the joys and dangers of everyday urban life.

Taken together, the moralizing stories and "factual fictions" of the popular illustrated press were a central part of its attractiveness.[110] But to focus on these aspects of the press alone would miss another major reason for their appeal, especially in a smaller metropolis like Cracow. As already seen, many of the sensations that peppered the pages of the press were clearly taken from newspapers abroad. The daily juxtaposing of sensationalist stories from abroad with close coverage of the city was the ultimate secret for these papers' success. There were ways to tell the two kinds of texts apart, both spatially and topically, but it was their resonance, finally, that helped readers develop a sense of being part of what they called "modern civilization." Even though stories from cities abroad were often more sensational and dramatic, increasingly they were similar enough to provide a story line for interpreting the dramas of big-city life at home.

THE INTERURBAN MATRIX— LOCAL DETAILS, FOREIGN SPECTACLES

Covering the streets on which they were sold, boulevard newspapers focused their gaze on the daily spectacles of the city. As Peter Fritzsche observes, as soon as the press in fin-de-siècle Berlin began reporting metropolitan issues, its readership swelled.[111] In numerous ways these papers helped their readers know how to behave in the urban environment. Examples of people defrauded in the big city could serve as cautionary tales, while articles about proper and improper behavior on the streets or in the trams were primers in urban relations. For example, when a reporter for *Nowiny* noticed two women having a long conversation in the doorway of the tram, thus keeping a crowd of people from entering, he printed a paraphrase of their entire conversation in all its banality and repetitiveness in the next day's paper.[112] Inexpensive announcements (classifieds) helped a variety of people find work, apartments, or marriage partners in an arena larger and more complicated than the village. The paper's daily delivery of staccato notes and news captured the fleeting inconstancy of the cityscape. Popular papers could be read in the way one read the city, by browsing their tantalizing headlines and arresting advertisements as one would browse the storefronts downtown for new wares, or scan streets and parks for interesting people and other snippets of urban spectacle.[113]

In feuilletons and daily chronicle sections with fetching titles like "What's the Word in Town?" and "What the Day Brings," *Kuryerek Krakowski*, *Nowiny*, and *IKC* reported the vagaries of Cracovian existence. Feuilletons under the regular title "From the Cracovian Streets" described characteristic moments of urban life, such as the experience of seeking a new apartment, a woman's frustration with social customs that required a man on her arm in public, or the seeming smirk of an electric streetcar aware of its control over the citizenry.[114] In the chronicles, arrest reports of pickpockets or prostitutes accompanied announcements of the newest plays at the People's Theater or the meeting times of a variety of voluntary associations. Chronicles usually appeared on the second or third page of the paper and contained a hodgepodge of snippets for the day, ranging in length from three lines to two paragraphs. The narrative style was generally informal and conversational. In the first issue of *Kuryerek Krakowski*, chronicle readers learned among other things that a boy fell from a second-story window on Gołębia Street, an actor was arrested for boisterous behavior then released, and a silver vest and a woman's watch were found downtown.[115] In earlier issues, especially, the language and content of the chronicles made the city seem more a provincial community than a big city. People featured in the chronicles were introduced by name, occupation, and often address. Subscribers could read about people like themselves, easily imagining the streets and shops in which their fellow citizens lived and worked. Cracow was thus rendered small and knowable, comprehensible in terms of human relationships, whether real or imagined.

Such attention to local detail did not mean that these papers were merely insular neighborhood chronicles. To the contrary, the popular illustrated press was an emphatically international, interurban medium, voraciously appropriating stories and images from abroad. Late-breaking international news arrived directly via telegraph and telephone while less time-specific sensations were usually translated from the foreign press (see Fig. 3). The first issue of *Kuryerek Krakowski* relayed the latest on the Dreyfus affair from *Débats*, a French paper, a story of "a terrible marital drama . . . in Tungermünde" that must have been originally reported in a German paper, a report about the Romanian minister of health's edict forbidding corsets at public schools, as well as an interview with a cannibal, originally conducted by an American journalist, that came to Cracovian readers via *L'Illustration*, a Parisian daily.[116] Often *IKC* and *Nowiny* carried variants of the same story from the international press, running the illustrations in different sizes or translations with slightly different points of emphasis. Other examples of pilfering the international press include stories by Marc or Mark Twain, the spelling of which often depended on the language of the newspaper from which the Cracovian papers took the story.

Sensations from abroad contributed to the image readers had of the world beyond Cracow and Galicia and were a major selling point for popular illustrated newspapers. Each issue featured a dramatic illustration on the front page, usually taken from the foreign press, designed specifically to lure potential readers. Recycled illustrations of a subway catastrophe in Paris, a woman and child plucked from the Danube in Vienna, an automobile running over a military section in Berlin, and the London poor on eviction day, among countless other examples, contributed to the image readers had of life in big cities abroad.[117] Of course, pictures were not the only purveyors of international sensations from "great cities" abroad: readers of the world news section of *Nowiny* from August 17, 1910, for example, saw reports on the transatlantic Crippen wife-murder affair (which had begun in London), a sexual murder in Vienna, the gruesome removal of a living boy's heart for "medicinal" purposes in "dark" Madrid, and a discussion from the German press about the twentieth anniversary of the state executioner of Breslau who, incidentally, had cut off 87 heads since starting the job in 1890. These stories appeared during the same week the Cracovian press was abuzz about a brazen political assassination, committed in broad daylight next to St. Mary's Church downtown.[118] Readers thus had disturbing evidence that they were part of the interurban matrix of gruesome crime.

New technologies like automobiles and airplanes were a staple of the popular press (see chapter 5). Just as common were illustrations and stories about what must have been a fin-de-siècle fascination for wild animals out of place and out of control. In June 1912, readers of *Nowiny* and *IKC* could have seen the following features: a lion on a piano; a lion in Cleveland that

Fig. 3—**The Interurban Matrix.** *IKC*, December 18, 1910. This illustration from the first issue of *IKC* aptly depicts the way the railway, telegraph lines, and the popular press connected modern metropolitans to interurban culture.

leapt off a stage, snatched a child from its mother's arms, and carried it around alive in its jaws; a lion in a circus biting into a man's chest; and a so-called drawing from nature of lions and tigers that sat on stools and leapt over each other as their brave trainer goaded them on with a whip. The penultimate example ran in both *Nowiny* and *IKC* and probably made it to Cracow via *Die Neue Zeitung*, an illustrated Viennese newspaper, where it had been published a few days before.[119] A front-page illustration of a soldier barreling through the countryside in his automobile with his pet lion beside him brought together the two attractions, a double whammy of technology and an exotic beast.[120]

Images like these, along with fiction and sensational reports from the international press, were replicated in newspapers across Europe and increasingly across the globe. However hyperbolic, superficial, or inaccurate some of the reports or images may have been, they were clearly part of a new interurban culture now available to many Cracovians, thanks to the popular press. Dance steps, fashions, detective stories, sensational crimes, and the like were increasingly international and, more specifically, interurban phenomena. In the first few months of 1914, as the tango seemed to catch on worldwide, *IKC* abounded with drawings of the sensual dance, including one picture of the German police studying two dancers so they would know whom to arrest, and one of the Pope watching another pair so he could make a decree on it—both taken from foreign papers.[121] In the summer of 1912, Cracovian readers were informed of the new custom of young men appearing in public without a hat, which had begun to catch on in Paris. "Seeing as Parisian trends always end up here anyway," the paper quipped, "it's most likely that we'll see bareheaded men on the A-B line, strolling about with snow in their hair or on a bald dome. We have a suggestion: let's just adopt the style now, while it's still warm! There's no need to wait the customary couple of months."[122] Of course, the images and stories that made up this new common culture did not ensure identical interpretations in each incarnation. What matters here, however, is the mere likelihood that Cracovians and citizens of other metropolises could have read many of the same stories, while performing similar urban rituals like riding the tram or sitting in a favorite café.[123]

Not surprisingly, popular newspapers often integrated foreign terms and ideas into the Cracovian context. Most of the time, local versions of international sensations proved to be rather pale imitations, but not always, as in an example of a Cracovian Jack the Ripper. Like Sherlock Holmes, who appeared in translation and in original fictional stories about mysterious crimes in Cracow, Jack the Ripper was an adaptable international trope, regularly appearing in articles from abroad and at home.[124] The original Jack the Ripper had been one of the primary reasons for the success of the "new journalism" in London in the 1880s—a lesson not lost on the publishers of the popular press thereafter.[125] Whenever a grisly sexual murder occurred in a large city, the term was trotted out, usually to head the article. *Nowiny* carried several stories on Rippers from New York City and Berlin, as well as a story about "Jack-the-Suffocator" from London.[126] The paper also reported Cracovian variants of the infamous criminal. At least twice, within a week of reporting a Jack-the-Ripper attack in Berlin, *Nowiny* followed up with a local version of the story. In one instance, "The bestiality of [Cracow's Ripper] exceeded even that of the Berlin Ripper," according to the report, which went on to describe a young woman found by the turnpike, "sliced into strips" and "poked like a sieve," but still breathing.[127] In the other instance, the "Cracovian Ripper" was nothing more than a petty thief, a young man who met an unknown young woman in the park, walked briefly with her, and then told her she would remember their meeting for a long time—a prophecy that came true when she got home and realized that he had "ripped off" her wallet! The girl claimed to have been frightened when he first approached her because she had read newspaper stories about a Ripper in Berlin.[128] When on other occasions, local sexual predators sliced the "lower regions" of their young victims, they were described as Rippers, too.[129] Readers, like the young woman who lost her wallet, recognized the trope from popular press stories translated from abroad. When Rippers appeared closer to home, Cracow seemed more like the other big cities they read about in their newspapers—dangerous but exciting.

Occasionally, Cracow was the site of sensations that launched it into the interurban matrix of the foreign press. Whenever articles about Cracow appeared abroad, the local press took note.[130] The trial of Janina Borowska, the married medical student accused of murdering her lover Włodzimierz Lewicki, in January 1910 is an ideal example. In a signed editorial after the trial in which he had been called as a witness, Ludwik Szczepański told his readers that the foreign press had covered the trial in detail. Several foreign papers concluded that it was a travesty because the judge so bullied the defendant. The censor cut much of Szczepański's impassioned statement to this effect but allowed the editor's citation of *Reichspost*, which argued much the same thing, to remain.[131] Here readers got a story filtered through the foreign press, even though it had taken place in their town! Several days later, they were reminded of their place in the sunlight of international sensation when notices in "What's the Word in Town?" reported that Borowska, who was declared not guilty, had received letters from all over, including America. Someone in Ukraine offered to take care of her child, and a manager of a convalescent home in Hungary offered her a two-month recovery at his resort.[132] Again, Cracovians could feel like worldly urbanites because, for good or ill, their city was part of the matrix of international sensations.

Comparisons to Great Cities Abroad—Cracow as Sibling City

One of the most common ways foreign cities appeared in the Cracovian press was as a point of comparison with Cracow. Journalists for the popular press were often aware of conditions in other European metropolises, whether from visits as correspondents or from their daily scouring of the foreign press. Not surprisingly, they regularly compared Cracovian peculiarities with those of other cities. An early article in *Kuryerek Krakowski* pointed out that just as Venice has its pigeons at St. Mark's and Vienna its Madelen, Cracow has a claim to fame or, rather, infamy: the brazen dog-catchers who trapped their quarry in broad daylight in front of pedestrians downtown.[133] A piece from 1913 placed Cracow among the ranks of European art centers, asserting that in each of the bigger cities there seemed to be a certain artistic specialty. "Vienna is known for its musicians, Munich for its painters, Warsaw for its actors, and Cracow for its writers," the journalist contended, perhaps a bit self-servingly.[134] In other instances, Cracow's main boulevard was likened to Parisian boulevards and its meadow park to the Prater in Vienna.[135] Journalists consistently compared Cracovian street criminals to their counterparts in London, Paris, Berlin, Vienna, Warsaw, and Lemberg, commenting on the particular characteristics of thugs in each city.[136] Statistics from other cities helped place Cracow in context, as in articles about working-class housing costs in a variety of European cities or the size of urban police forces, or a piece entitled "Cracow's Stomach," followed a week later by "London's Stomach," which detailed the amounts of food consumed per day in the respective cities.[137] A well-informed article about Cracow's lack of suburban development made numerous references to Vienna, Prague, Dresden, Warsaw, and even Bielsko-Biała, as examples of cities with developed suburbs and garden districts.[138]

Often articles complained that Cracow lacked the full luster of European civilization or was only a junior member of the family, as in a piece that likened Cracovians to children on the European scene because they had not yet mastered some basic skills of urban life, such as walking in crowds. The article observed that Cracovians did not know how to pass each other on the street, as their "older" European siblings did, further grousing that they did not know how to eat properly at restaurants or enjoy themselves in the city.[139]

Another piece discussed the city's night guards, who with their big beards and halberds seemed a laughable leftover from the Middle Ages. "Seeing as we're a European city," the article queried, "why don't we get a competent, well-paid, complete force of night guards?"[140] An article entitled "Cracow Gets Civilized" discussed the need to improve the city's public toilets, concluding: "The city must Europeanize itself [musi się europeizować] and cannot preserve the unhygienic and disgusting particularities it has had to this point."[141] Another article bemoaned unhygienic conditions in the shops and stores in the city, berating Cracow's tendency to cling to tradition instead of embracing modern, civilized techniques. After complaining that "even in a first-rate store," assistants wrap butter with filthy hands, people at the market still taste cream with their fingers, and patrons of the public library can be so "uncivilized" as to steal pages from the books, the author asserted that "[a] visitor from the civilized west must have a strange experience if for a moment he stops on Galician territory and gets to know ancient Cracow, [where] everything is still done according to the old accepted model."[142] The journalist's hope, of course, was that some of his thousands of readers would embrace more modern ways. "Today, the world over, even in old medieval cities upheld by tradition [i.e., Cracow], new orderly ways are being introduced," the author contended. "The gleam of culture and civilization does not disfigure old monuments; it does not injure the past." Reconfiguring the backward-looking, conservative, historicist vision of the city, the journalist called for the creation of a genuinely modern Cracow.

Comparisons with other cities at times could be nationalistic, but far more often they relied on civic pride, as when a journalist compared Cracow to its rival to the northeast, Warsaw. "We like to set up examples of the 'culture' of places like Berlin, London, [or] Paris," the writer began. "'Look how things are over there in the West!' 'And here?' we say in a loud voice. And then follows an appeal to our 'Western' hearts that we should be more like them."[143] The rest of the article was supposed to shame "European Cracow" by demonstrating that even in supposedly "wild," "Asiatic" Warsaw, the fire department and rescue services were much better developed. When another article complained that Cracow's cinema selection was on par with the entertainment industry in Bochnia and Wiśnicz, two medium-sized Galician towns, readers could be sure that Cracow was not living up to its self-proclaimed status as a center of culture.[144] Here culture was not determined in terms of historic monuments and statues—the measure of Cracow's greatness in the second half of the nineteenth century—but by its level of modern, urban civilization. In the popular press, the connections implicit in the interurban matrix often edged out the national narrative.

CONCLUSION—REFLECTIONS ON THE
INTERURBAN MATRIX

During the first decade of the twentieth century, the mass circulation popular press developed in Cracow, as innovative journalists such as Ludwik Szczepański recognized that conditions there were ripe for a new type of newspaper. Popular papers in other European cities served as models for the new publications in Cracow, which were now economically viable thanks to legal and demographic changes. The papers sought the broadest possible audience by downplaying politics, using illustrations and lively prose, and stressing novelty. Fictional pieces took place in actual places, and factual reports tended to be literary and moralistic. Science and statistics, the language of fact-based modernity, were playfully put to other uses. In these ways the papers were much like analogous papers abroad. Due to the metropolitan interconnectedness of editors and journalists like Szczepański and Dąbrowski, who read foreign languages and had been in other cities, the papers they contributed to were part of an interurban matrix of local and international sensations.

Thanks to the popular press, thousands of Cracovians were aware of the currents of urban life in their city and familiar with spectacles from big cities abroad. Whenever local journalists sought improvements in their city, they relied on their readers' sense that they belonged in the civilized (i.e., urban) culture of the West, while comparing their city to its larger European siblings. Even in an era of profound nationalism, the primary theme of these newspapers was the exploration and glorification of urban—not national—identities. The nineteenth-century definition of Cracow, as a center of national high culture and reliquary of monuments from the nation's glorious past, gave way to a new definition of the city in the press as one of many European metropolises, experiencing similar developments and dangers. In autumn 1914, when the archetypical cities of Paris and London had become official enemies, *IKC* still ran sympathetic articles about life in London during the war.[145] Even during the first months of wartime, readers had a glimpse of the familiar world where curiosities transcended national borders and the interurban matrix linked their city with others.

CHAPTER **3**

WE'LL MAKE
OURSELVES INTO EUROPE!

The "Greater Cracow" Survey Series, 1903–1904

Of course we would expect lights, paved roads, water lines,
police, and all the other things one should expect from the city.
—Jan Konik, Community Chief of Łobzów, 1903

On May 27, 1903, in just its tenth issue, *Nowiny dla wszystkich* launched a series of survey articles entitled "Wielki Kraków," designed to address, as the paper put it, "a matter of great import for our city: the incorporation of the suburbs into the community of Cracow."[1] The series lasted for more than two months and resumed again in early 1904. A flurry of coverage surrounding the outbreak of the Russo-Japanese War in the first week of February 1904 interrupted the series after only one installment, but it resumed—at the insistence of the editor, Szczepański—already by the middle of the month. During March, a meeting of delegates from many of the proposed districts with the deputy mayor, Leo, prompted a variety of news stories on the topic. The series officially ended on April 1, but articles on the topic continued for the rest of the month, concluding on April 29 with the publication of a map of the proposed "Greater Cracow" and a lengthy article justifying the plan. Attention to Greater Cracow tapered off in May 1904, while the paper covered two dramatic local murder stories, but *Nowiny* had already demonstrated its stake in reporting and endorsing Cracow's expansion. The newspaper had taken the lead in pushing the subject in 1903, at a time when the political press was essentially silent on the issue, and continuously kept the topic alive during the decade of wrangling over incorporation that followed. Staunchly committed to city Vice President (and later President) Juliusz Leo's vision of Greater Cracow, *Nowiny* kept the idea before its readers until it could report its realization in April 1910.

While its reports of city council meetings and, eventually, the sessions of the Galician Sejm (parliament) to determine the future of Greater Cracow were generally similar to coverage in the political press, *Nowiny's* initial series in the years 1903–1904 was radically different from anything on the topic in the other papers, to date or thereafter. "Greater Cracow: A Survey by the Editors of *Nowiny*" set out to get "the opinions of the most competent personages in this matter. . . . people who know Cracow and its suburbs, [and] who, as the result of many years of observation and experience, are capable of appreciating the benefits or costs" of incorporation.[2] The paper defined such people widely and creatively. Most were district mayors, whose communities faced the prospect of uniting with Cracow in the coming years. *Nowiny* spoke with the popular city councilman Kazimierz Bartoszewicz and the deputy mayor Juliusz Leo to get a Cracovian municipal perspective on expansion as well. Interviews with Bartoszewicz and Leo could be expected, particularly in light of the paper's favorable opinion of the plan. Yet the paper also interviewed the locally acknowledged "king of the smugglers" for his opinion on how Greater Cracow's new (and greatly expanded) tariff zone would affect his "business," and it featured a full-length opinion piece by a resident of one of the suburban districts that thumbed its nose at Cracow's urbane pretensions. The "lounge-chair journalists" of *Nowa Reforma* would never have interviewed a smuggler or printed the rants of suburbanites.[3] In giving voice to the village mayors and their citizens, *Nowiny* was also treading new ground. By featuring the opinions of suburbanites, the paper acknowledged the perspective of villagers who would eventually reside in "Metropolitan Cracow." *Nowiny* hoped to warm them to the cause of Greater Cracow and, just as important, to win their subscriptions.

Nowiny's series was at once a colonizing mission to the readers beyond the turnpike and an acknowledgment of the future place of these readers in the big city. From its first day in print, *Nowiny's* masthead read "Kraków-Podgórze"—a clear indication that its proposed audience would extend beyond the boundaries of Cracow proper. Publishing the "Wielki Kraków" series was one of the first ways the paper sought to attract readers outside Cracow, the thousands of residents who had regular contact with the big city but who officially still lived in separate communities. The paper's colonizing efforts, like so many territorial expansions of the day, carried with them notions of cultural superiority and a civilizing mission. Attention to the interests and concerns of suburban villagers did not mean that the paper necessarily agreed with them. Quite often the reporter assumed the voice of an intrepid explorer, who looked upon his subjects with bemusement and condescension. Braving the mud and puddles of suburban roads in order to meet with the community chiefs, the reporter sought to win suburbanites to the cause of "Greater Cracow" by offering them the benefits of urbanized civilization.[4] But the village mayors were hardly gullible or naïve. Thanks to their cunning and awareness of big cities abroad, they were often prepared to bargain for the most Cracow had to offer, and they parried the reporter's remarks with gusto and a bit of condescension of their own. Ultimately, the conversations with district mayors and Cracovian politicians alike revealed that both sides had a desire to become "civilized" or "European," though they may have understood the concept differently.

URBAN PLANNING AND INCORPORATION— CONTEXT AND BACKGROUND

During the nineteenth century, the unprecedented growth of big cities as a result of industrial capitalism presented novel challenges to state and (increasingly) municipal governments, who were at first completely overwhelmed by the effects of urbanization. "As was true of technology," Paul Hohenberg and Lynn Hollen Lees note, "the economics of capitalism were more effective in promoting urbanization than in coping with it."[5] Friedrich Engels famously observed the wretched conditions in Manchester in the 1840s as the old city failed to accommodate the influx of population. Human and animal waste befouled the ground and air, people were crammed in makeshift rooms within or attached to formerly bourgeois apartment buildings, and carcasses and green industrial effluvia clogged the River Irk. For Engels, it was obvious that capitalism and by extension capitalists themselves cared little about the "horror and indignation" caused by "the industrial epoch."[6] Some sort of intervention was needed.

The most famous example of state intervention comes from France during the Third Republic, where Napoleon III—who came to power in part by placating the sort of industrial workers Engels hoped to incite to revolution—and his Prefect of the Seine, the baron Eugene Haussmann, inaugurated a pattern of urban planning by fiat that took the latter's name. The intents of Haussmannization were twofold: to open the city to troops while preventing the barricades of prior revolutions and to open the city to the circulation of people and goods. Accordingly, narrow medieval streets were destroyed to make way for broad boulevards, plumbed below with water lines and sewers. The former inhabitants of those neighborhoods frequently found work in tearing them down, and then had to relocate to the *banlieue* on the edge of the city, because they could not afford homes on or near the boulevards they had helped to construct.

Plenty of cities sought to follow the Haussmann model, particularly in the capitals of southeastern Europe, whose newfound autonomy enabled grand state projects. Bucharest's mayor Emanoil Protopopescu, for example, was praised as the "Romanian Haussmann" for creating boulevards and squares that brought clean air into the city.[7] In Habsburg Central Europe, meanwhile, the model was, of course, Vienna where the famous Ringstrasse arose on the space formerly occupied by the city wall and its glacis. For many central European cities, the path to urban modernization followed the *Großstadt* model of Vienna, with the construction of ring roads and the incorporation of surrounding districts.[8] Also influential were German models of urban planning, which relied on local municipal self-government (*Selbstverwaltung*) to meet the challenges of modern urban development.[9]

As the cities of the Habsburg Empire received autonomy in the 1860s, their elected officials increasingly looked to Vienna and other cities in the empire and abroad for models of urban planning and incorporation. If in the beginning of the nineteenth century, Cracow's church cemeteries downtown had been covered up and a municipal cemetery constructed outside of town by imperial fiat, now local officials had much more say in urban planning. It comes as no surprise, then, that Cracow's first mayor after autonomy, Józef Dietl, inaugurated its phase of modern urban planning.

On January 1, 1892, Vienna became Gross-Wien, expanding in size from 55 to 178 square kilometers, thanks to the incorporation of nineteen of its suburban districts. Overnight the population of the metropolis increased from 801,176 to 1,355,979.[10] Concurrently, Cracovian politicians had begun to explore the possibility of creating Greater Cracow. Almost exactly two years after the formal creation of Greater Vienna, Cracovian city councilor Piotr Górski reintroduced an 1890 initiative to explore the possibility of incorporating the left-bank districts beyond the turnpike—Grzegórzki, Prądnik Biały, Prądnik Czerwony, Czarna Wieś, Nowa Wieś Narodowa, Krowodrza, Półwsie Zwierzynieckie, and the village of Zwierzyniec—into a newly constituted Greater Cracow (see Maps 1 and 2). Górski's idea was not entirely derivative; shortly after Cracow gained autonomy in 1866, several of these communities had submitted petitions to formally join or rejoin the city. Separated, however, by the ring of fortifications surrounding the city, none of their requests had gotten very far. In 1894, recent Viennese success notwithstanding, Górski's investigation determined that "for the time being," the benefits of expansion did not outweigh the costs.[11]

By 1897 disputes over the administration of the city cemetery, which lay beyond city boundaries in the territory of Prądnik Czerwony, brought the question of incorporation back to the fore. An 1898 letter to the branch of municipal government responsible for urban infrastructure called for investigation into the "data and materials" necessary to undertake incorporation of the left-bank districts.[12] The following year, the community of Czarna Wieś submitted a petition to the Cracovian city council requesting connection to municipal gas lines and (re)annexation. (Historically administered by the Cracovian city council since shortly after its founding by Casimir the Great in 1361, Czarna Wieś had been severed from the city by Austrian administrative decisions a century before.) Despite the thoroughness of the proposal, which included Czarna Wieś's municipal budget and transcriptions of a document from 1363 (in Latin and Polish) from King Casimir that placed the district under Cracovian administration, Cracovian officials were not prepared to act.[13] Even in a city obsessed with history, historical precedent was not compelling enough. The Cracovian city council proved reluctant to take on the expense of incorporating a single district, especially without an overarching plan for all the districts. Over the next two years, Cracovian city councilors requested, and got, detailed reports from municipal bureaucrats regarding the proposed costs of policing and lighting the new districts, along with positive feedback from most of the proposed districts.[14]

A global credit crisis that affected Galicia most severely from 1900 to 1903 likely undercut plans for expansion, and it seems that little was done until 1902 when Cracow's First Vice President Leo, who played a much more active role in the position than his predecessors, took up the issue of constructing a port in Cracow, while reinvigorating older plans for incorporating some of its suburban communities.[15] The political climate in Austria was auspicious for such an approach to incorporation. In an effort to combat the absolutely stultifying effects of national competition in the Austrian parliament, the new prime minister, Ernst von Koerber, had introduced a plan for the economic development and integration of the monarchy. The "Koerber Plan," which passed in 1901 as the Investment Bill, called for the development of more direct railway communication from Prague to Trieste, and from Lemberg to the Hungarian Plain beneath the Carpathians. It also included provisions for the regulation of major rivers and the construction of canals to facilitate trade and integrate the Habsburg economy.[16] Leo saw the Vienna–Cracow canal, which was to link the Vistula with the Danube, and eventually the Dniestr, as a vital mechanism in reconstituting Cracow as a city of industry and trade. The commission he headed decided to treat as one the issues of creating a port and expanding the city. Surveying the situation, Leo determined that it made no sense to expand the city in only one or two directions. The commission selected twelve "left-bank communities, along with four right-bank communities and the city of Podgórze to create so-called Greater Cracow."[17] The thankless task of determining taxes began in 1902/1903. According to Leo's biographer, Celina Bąk-Koczarska, much effort went into guaranteeing that no community would suffer financially because of incorporation. Of the 18 communities, 14 agreed and sent delegates for a conference in March 1904. Płaszów, Krowodrza, Grzegórzki, and the city of Podgórze declined on the grounds that they doubted Cracow could handle the weak economies of the incorporated communities.[18] During this period of early negotiation, the popular illustrated press was fundamental in popularizing plans for Greater Cracow, particularly in the suburban districts themselves.

FROM "COWS AND PIGS" TO "PAVING AND LIGHTING"

The first installment of the "Wielki Kraków" survey series provided a brief history of the concept, beginning its narrative with the 1894 initiative of city councilman Piotr Górski. According to the installment, negotiations were currently taking place between village and city officials. Meanwhile, Vice President Leo had proposed the ambitious plan of annexing Dębniki and the city of Podgórze, two communities situated on the other side of the Vistula. The paper suggested that the most difficult task ahead of the negotiators was reconciling the vast differences in taxation among the various districts. The installment set forth the goals of the series, including interviews with the "most competent" personalities on the topic, and closed by saying that the editors aimed to present a fuller picture of the future Greater Cracow.[19] The second installment asked if the structure of the present police, water, and gas systems could possibly suffice for Greater Cracow and what could be done and at what cost to improve them.[20]

Following the two introductory installments, *Nowiny* began by interviewing Kazimierz Hajdziński, the mayor of Czarna Wieś. The conversation set the tone for the interviews to follow, with the village mayor enumerating his requirements for incorporation in lively banter with the journalist. As in most of the interviews, both sides felt they had something to offer and something to gain. The community leaders implicitly offered their land, citizens, and resources, while the reporter offered the amenities of big-city life that would come with incorporation. "I am not an emissary of Mr. Leo," began one installment, "but because of the nature of things I must discuss with each of the surrounding chiefs the benefits that would come to his community if it were connected to Cracow."[21] Village mayors in favor of incorporation hoped for urban improvements such as running water, streetlights, paved roads, gas, and electricity, and sometimes the construction of schools—all on Cracow's bill. Yet they also expressed discomfort with urban regulations that seemed out of place in their predominately rural districts, including building codes and laws against keeping livestock. Notions of good governance were also a point of contestation. The specter of Cracow's presumed bankruptcy fed into impressions of inadequate administration, which as the village mayors saw it, did not bode well for the newly acquired districts. At times *Nowiny's* reporter sympathized with the community chiefs in their sense of mistreatment by big-city bureaucrats; at other times he offered a spirited defense of plans for annexation, while pointing out their greediness in making unrealistic demands.[22]

Mayor Hajdziński said that his district had voted to join Cracow, but reluctantly. Several years before, the community leaders of Czarna Wieś had approached the city about getting on the line for gas lighting, offering to pay for the service, but they were rudely ignored. Sympathizing with the mayor, the reporter wondered why the petition from Czarna Wieś had been placed "in the wastebasket." Asked what he required from the city, Hajdziński said "just little things," adding that because the other communities were "bargaining a bit with you all," he did not think incorporation would come about anytime soon. Hajdziński reminded his interviewer that it was not only Cracow that had claim to history, pointing out that Czarna Wieś also had "privileges from [King] Casimir the Great." He said his fellow citizens, many of whom made a living supplying Cracow with dairy products and vegetables, did not want to "drown" in Cracow. The rule in Cracow forbidding keeping livestock could not apply to them if they were to be connected to the city. "If you want to have us," the district chief summed up, "you'll have to take us with our cows and pigs."[23]

Later interviews with village mayors in favor of incorporation fit into the discursive pattern laid out in the Hajdziński interview, differing only in the style or level of clarity with which they were expressed. Mr. Maksymilian Szalwiński of Grzegórzki, "a well-known and much-admired citizen in our town" and personal friend of the editor Szczepański, was roundly praised in his interview for having a clearly stated set of stipulations from his community for Cracow. Szalwiński said he was very much in favor of incorporation "because of the good it can do for the community." He pointed out that Grzegórzki lacked the resources "to give the community what the newest culture demands . . . so it would be best to sacrifice personal ambition and the comforts of separatism so that the community could reach a European standard." In agreeing to join Greater Cracow, Szalwiński was admitting that while it may not have been personally gratifying for someone who stood to lose power and prestige from the deal, incorporation would be the only way to assure the community's access to the benefits of modernization, thus lifting it to "a European standard." Szalwiński clearly connected the creation of Greater Cracow with his community's modern, urban future.[24]

In consenting to join, however, Szalwiński had eight specific demands of Cracow, including: "2) that it assigns, at least for a short time, building relief and allows the keeping of cattle and non-horned animals; 3) that it tries to eliminate the demolition receipts [the rule that forbade building anything in the vicinity of the already obsolete Austrian military fortifications surrounding Cracow, separating it from the suburban districts]; . . .[and] 7) that the holdings of the district will be used above all for its own needs." In other words, Szalwiński wished to assure that the incorporation would bring about the promised economic and administrative rationalization in a way that was fair to the new districts. Like Mayor Hajdziński, he thought it unrealistic to expect his citizens to abandon their livestock or bring their homes up to city fire code standards at once.

Aware of the way incorporation took place in Vienna, Szalwiński concluded his interview by suggesting that community representation on the city council of Greater Cracow should follow the Viennese model, with two to three councilors elected from each new district to serve on the council.[25] Marshalling evidence from the capital of the empire to buttress his argument for continued political power after incorporation, Szalwiński demonstrated another aspect of the discourse of negotiated assent, namely, an appeal to other cities, and especially Habsburg cities, as models.

Jan Konik, community chief of Łobzów, fit entirely into the pattern of negotiated assent, though without the well-articulated program of Szalwiński. He said that his district lacked strong opinions either for or against incorporation. "Of course," he said, "we would expect lights, paved roads, water lines, police, and all the other things one should expect from the city." He was also firm about keeping livestock and assuring that the building codes that existed in Cracow would not pertain to Łobzów.[26] To this generalized list of demands, Wincenty Jelonek, the community chief of Ludwinów, added the stipulation that Cracow build a community school.[27] In the "Wielki Kraków" series at least, this basic list set the terms for joining Cracow. Even districts that had once opposed annexation eventually began bargaining for the items on the list. Dębniki, whose mayor Tomasz Mól had berated Cracow for its insensitivity in June 1903 (see below), asked—nine months later—for gas lighting, paved roads, the building of a school, and better transportation facilities. (Mól's change of heart came after Cracow proved the only source of assistance to his district following a terrible flood in July 1903.)[28] Whether through reading the results of other interviews in *Nowiny* or through mutual observation during negotiations with Cracovian municipal officials, most village chiefs began to voice the same stipulations for incorporation. In this way, the community leaders and their interviewers at *Nowiny* set the terms for a discourse of negotiated assent. Central to this discourse was the conception of the city becoming more "European" as urban improvements were added.

"WE'RE NOT SO DAFT AS TO FATTEN YOU WITH OUR BLOOD."

But in 1903 at least, not all of the small districts had come around to supporting annexation. The paper's second and third interviews in the "Wielki Kraków" series were with community chiefs who opposed incorporation into Greater Cracow: Adam Zbroja of Krowodrza and Piotr Rosół of Nowa Wieś Narodowa. If Mayors Hajdziński and Szalwiński set the terms for negotiated assent, Mayors Zbroja and Rosół would make the case for disaffected dissent. Their observations, too, would influence the statements of village mayors in later interviews, even if the village mayors supported incorporation. Significantly, none of these mayors contested the value of urban modernization in the guise of running water, street lamps, and the like. Rather, it was the way that Cracow treated them or their sense that Cracow could not really make good on such sweet promises that caused their dissatisfaction with the plan.

Mr. Zbroja's central argument was that Krowodrza could take care of itself and had no need to join with an already bankrupt Cracow.[29] Piotr Rosół proved an even tougher audience. The community chief of Nowa Wieś Narodowa "listened to [the reporter's] colorful fantasies of Greater Cracow with something close to pity" before replying that, despite the "golden heights" Cracow was promising, a look at its outlying districts told another story: "Go sir, to Wielopole, or even better, Rybaka, and look around. It's a shame how disorderly they are! No cobbled gutters, no lights, there's nothing there! And if that's how you take care of what is so close to you," he asked, "would you really take care of our community, so far away, separated by the railway and the army fortifications? Bah! You'd take our money; tax us—as much as you could. You like the smell of our district's wealth. And we have 100 crowns in landholdings and cash. But we're not so daft as to fatten you with our blood." Rosół continued, saying that his villagers were poor, getting by only on produce from their gardens. He argued that unification would cause his villagers to become "completely impoverished" because the building codes would make their homes illegal and their gardens would disappear when the land was regulated.

> We don't need any Cracovian charity. We're about to build ourselves a school, because to this point we've had a shared one with Łobzów; we're making a good sidewalk through the whole community and we're protracting a concrete canal. We'll make ourselves into Europe!

While Rosół seemed to agree that his community was poor and backward, and that getting running water and new schools were positive developments that would make it more "European," he took issue with Cracow's paternalism and doubted that the Cracovian Magistrate, the executive branch of the city's municipal government, would really look after his district anyway. As he put it, he and his fellow citizens had no desire "to fatten [Cracow] with [their] blood."

Rather than arguing these points, Nowiny's reporter simply asked if there were any benefits the community could expect from uniting with Cracow. Mr. Rosół thought a bit and then replied that if the demolition receipts could be officially abolished, Nowa Wieś Narodowa could develop some manufacturing industries. He recalled when, a year before, "some Schwabian or Moravian" came to him desiring to build a factory. He told the man that he was welcome to build on the land near the fortifications, but "tomorrow he could be commanded to tear it down and the Good Lord could only say He's sorry, but that's the way it is. And so he left, no doubt to make some brewery in his Vaterland." Here Rosół agreed with the Cracovian municipal authorities, who also found the ramparts a major obstacle for development. The old defense system was outdated and slated for destruction, but because the new fortifications were not yet underway, the city was unable to develop the lands on either side of it.[30] Rosół was still complaining about the fortifications when he was interrupted by a village woman who wondered if the community government would release her from paying taxes on her horses, because, according to witnesses, "one was blind and the other had pains in his side." "Not wishing to interfere in governance," the reporter quipped condescendingly, "I left the chancellery." He concluded his report with the observation that despite its "heaping wealth," Nowa Wieś Narodowa paid onerous taxes, while as a major transportation artery between Cracow and Łobzów it would shortly become the most busy and active suburb of Greater Cracow. Indulging in a homely metaphor of his own, the reporter concluded: "But Mr. Rosół does not wish to swallow the beer his community must drink down."[31]

Mayors Rosół and Zbroja had opposed unification largely on the grounds that Cracow could not be trusted to render assistance, an assumption based on the sense that the city was too financially strapped to take care of outlying districts, especially when it had trouble meeting its own needs. Both men preferred the gradual, minor improvements that they could expect by relying upon themselves rather than the prospect of relinquishing their autonomy to Cracow. In the end, one senses that the men were too proud to give in, despite the general inevitability of the plan. Another of *Nowiny*'s interviews revealed many of these themes, despite the interviewee being a community chief who at least originally favored annexation. Like Mayor Hajdziński of Czarna Wieś, Tomasz Mól of Dębniki disparaged Cracow's big-city attitude in ignoring the efforts of his community to join the movement on its own terms.

The central theme of Mr. Mól's conversation with *Nowiny* was Mól's sense that the Cracovian Magistrate had repeatedly ignored and spurned his community. In the colorful language of a simple man, Mól began his litany of complaints. First, Cracow had never officially invited Dębniki to join, even though his community submitted an application to be included a few years before.[32] Because of this, he and his fellow citizens had begun to wonder if it would be worth it anyway: "Two years passed and to this point we haven't gotten any response. And it's probably for the best.... We sent in our application in the heat of the moment; now we've had a number of reflections on this matter. The idea, though it glitters, it isn't gold—at least not for us." Mól asked why Cracow had not thought of large-scale expansion sooner. The reporter interjected, using the examples of Vienna and Berlin to demonstrate that Cracow was right on schedule in its plans: "If I may sir, not even ten years have passed since Berlin and Vienna had a similar thought. We, who are always about half a century behind, are in this matter actually following right in the footsteps of these two western capitals."

"But the mayor dismissed this with a wave of his hand," claiming that Cracow sought unification with the suburbs because its real estate "is so financially burdened that it couldn't possibly be burdened anymore." Mól asserted that Cracow was "bankrupt" and only wanted the "debt-free holdings beyond the fortifications" as a "foundation for more loans." "Cracow, a soiled aristocrat, wants to marry the crown of its suburbs, a wealthy plebian, in order to salvage his crest and the splendor of a capital city with her gold. And he fattens himself with our dowry, but does he offer us anything in return?"

Mól recalled another petition to the Cracovian Magistrate, an application for city gas. For two years Dębniki waited for a reply. "So long as we can't expect anything from you when we offer serious money, what's going to happen when we've melted into you and must ask for your graces for your various civilizing measures? There's a trial run for you of how you behave as a stepparent," Mól continued. "Or maybe you're behaving in this way in order to humble us, so that we'll feel so fortunate to be united with you?" "And then Mr. Mól looked at me with such pity," the reporter admitted, "that I felt in that moment like suffering and blushing for the one hundred thousand residents of Cracow."

Mr. Mól ended on a defiant note, however, asserting that once the port planned for the left bank of the river was built, Cracow would have to come crawling to Dębniki. "We'll get our own port and then, without Cracow, we'll grow so much that we'll need you . . . for horseradish!" The reporter suggested that Dębniki might still need Cracow's running water.[33] Mayor Mól, aware of the periodic problems with Cracow's water, often noted in *Czas*, said that they could do without the *crenothrix* bacteria. Fed up, *Nowiny's* reporter resorted to mudslinging, pointing out the common perception in Cracow that Dębniki's primarily working-class citizens were rough and rowdy: "Where you live they beat each other up!" Mr. Mól was undaunted by this insult:

> Fairy tales, most glorious sir! I would prefer to walk through the whole of Dębniki at night, than at day on your Zwierzyniecka Street, chock full of pubs, where there are always brawls that they later blame on Dębniki. Oh, the Cracovian newspapers like to smear us wherever and whenever they can.

"Hearing this," the reporter concluded wryly, "I thought it would be best to give leave to the district chancellery *cum dignate*. Where there is talk about smearing, your servant is never there!"—a delightfully ironic remark from a newspaperman.[34]

Despite the interview's descent into mudslinging, it remains a powerful example of the terms of debate surrounding the creation of Greater Cracow. Mól resented Cracovian arrogance in rebuffing his community's desire for the "civilizing measures" the big city seemed poised to offer. Protesting Cracow's dilatory attitude toward the needs of his district, he asked why the city had not begun addressing the issue of incorporation sooner. Significantly, the interviewer's response looked toward the models provided by European great cities, Vienna and Berlin, as justification that Cracow was "following right in the footsteps of these two western capitals." Finally, Mól's reference to Cracow as "a soiled aristocrat" fattening himself with the "dowry" of the "plebian" suburbs alluded not only to the medieval past but also to the perceived class difference between the typical citizens of each population. The reporter's jab that Dębniki's inhabitants were all working-class roughs only underscored this distinction.

Perhaps worn out from such heated discussions, *Nowiny*'s reporter took a break from interviewing village mayors for the next three installments in the series. The first installment after the interview with Mr. Mól was a matter-of-fact investigation of the toll system in place around Cracow and the measures that would have to be taken in order to more than triple its circumference with the creation of Greater Cracow. The article hypothesized that the reorganization of the toll system would be so complicated that Dr. Leo's dream for Greater Cracow could not be realized until 1910.[35] The next article in the series led off with the suggestion that a discussion of the toll road would not be complete without conversing with someone whom it would affect most: a smuggler.

The tone of the piece, as usual, was wonderful and witty. As a matter of journalistic discretion, readers were informed, the "universally acknowledged king of Cracovian smugglers" would remain unnamed, but he was described as looking "like a Russian peasant, with a great beard and a shaggy crop of hair." According to the report, the smuggler was honored to have his opinion considered on the topic of Greater Cracow and kindly greeted the journalist. The reporter began by asking about smuggling conditions in general and then launched into discussion of Greater Cracow. The smuggler attested that conditions for smuggling were increasingly difficult. With the new turnpike in place, movement of contraband would be even more difficult. The interviewer tried to cheer him by suggesting that it would be easier to get through fifty kilometers of road than fifteen, but the old fellow disagreed. He had his ten-year-old son describe a recent smuggling experience. The elder smuggler smiled with pride at his son's cleverness. He was certain things would be more difficult for him, however. "Not wishing to look at the pain of his fatherly soul," the reporter concluded, "I left his apartment through a little door like in a beehive, deliberating in my soul on the increasingly difficult occupational conditions of the rising generation."[36]

PATRIOTISM, EUROPE, AND MODERNITY DEMAND IT

In a radical shift of perspective, the paper went from interviewing an elusive, if relatively benign, criminal to "one of the most popular city councilors [and] one of the nicest and most popular men in Cracow," Kazimierz Bartoszewicz.[37] The introduction justified the paper's choice by fawningly suggesting, "whenever something is done in Cracow, people ask, what does Bartoszewicz think of it?" The city councilor pointed out that he was not on the committee responsible for the creation of Greater Cracow and so did "not know the budget calculations and figures" but could speak about it generally. Bartoszewicz felt that incorporation was overdue, commenting that there was no longer any need to maintain "anachronistic, silly, and senseless" "medieval" borders between cities. "That is why we see how in all cities of western culture, they are joining together with their suburbs as a unified whole." Councilor Bartoszewicz thought it difficult to foretell what sort of benefits the incorporation would bring to Cracow. He was confident that real estate prices for the former outlying districts would increase, which would be good for the owners but more expensive for the occupants. In general, he said, prices would go up, so that inexpensive food and living costs in communities presently outside of the city would soon cost as much as they did in the city. This, he predicted, would cause a change in the physiognomy of the people of Cracow.

Bartoszewicz also commented on how a "Greater Cracovian City Council" should be structured. Asked whether he thought the expansion of the electorate due to incorporation would greatly change the makeup of the city council, Bartoszewicz said that the radical element could successfully agitate in the new districts, increasing, "if not the actual size of their party, at least the number of votes it got. And such success would have a certain moral meaning. [The closer the votes are] the more the majority would have to deal with the minority." In the end, Bartoszewicz seemed to favor the plan, but not because he saw any immediate benefits. He favored it because it was a necessary step for "cities of western culture" and a step toward eventual rationalization of urban growth, but most of what he talked about here, in rather dispassionate terms, highlighted the political complications and price hikes that could result from it.

Juliusz Leo was interviewed in early 1904 but could not be so speculative about his pet project. Instead, he stressed its advantages while underpinning his argument with a pitch to national duty:

> I think that the entire matter should be looked at from a general national and cultural position. Cracow, after all, will remain a center of Poland, not only because of its national historical monuments, but also because of its intellectual and artistic life. In light of this, it behooves us to ask: Should Cracow, as such, get larger or not? If we answer affirmatively, then we should do our best to make Cracow into a great, European city, which undoubtedly calls for the construction of a water canal, because through it, Cracow will become as well a city of trade. Once again I repeat emphatically that one should look upon the issue of incorporating the 17 communities above all from the position of the nation in general.[38]

To this, *Nowiny*'s interviewer rejoined that some of the communities were "not exactly eager about the idea of incorporation." Leo replied that this came from misunderstanding what was "in their best interest," adding that such was the case with Podgórze. Leo explained that Podgórze feared paying more taxes because Cracow's taxes were higher, but he pointed out that current community taxes in Podgórze would no longer be needed once the city was part of Cracow's overall budget. Inhabitants would still have to pay for services, but it would not be a simple matter of adding Cracovian taxes to what they already pay. "And in the end," he argued, "the national position that I emphasized to you earlier, sir, demands certain sacrifices." When the reporter mentioned another grievance Podgórze had against Cracow, Leo replied that it was "too bad" that they felt that way but reminded his interlocutor that there was "a principle that the little one unites with the big one, and never the other way around." Leo concluded by stating that he would try to print extractions of current municipal studies and reports about Greater Cracow in the newspapers.[39] Vice President Leo, like City Councilor Bartoszewicz, justified incorporation in terms of European civilization and urban rationalization. Eager to win support, Leo also tied the creation of Greater Cracow into the late nineteenth-century trope of Cracow as the center of Polish history and culture. In a way both condescending and pragmatic, he offered the districts the benefits of big-city life while appealing to their sense of national duty to assuage any feelings of loss that would come with joining the big city.

Leo's technique proved quite successful. *Nowiny*'s next article on Greater Cracow, which informed readers that the city's report had been released and meetings with the community leaders had begun, pointed out that most communities seemed pleased with the report and stood to gain a good deal. "The incorporation will actually be most difficult for Cracow itself," the paper reported, "which will now have to take the main role of being the taxpayer for these communities."[40] A policy of a twenty-year freeze on tax increases for all of the new districts assured that the burdens of incorporation would not fall on the shoulders of the new communities. The double-barreled approach of essentially free urban improvements and appeals to patriotism helped smooth the way for incorporation to take place. *Nowiny*'s next interviews with community chiefs demonstrated that Vice President Leo's silver-tongued rhetoric of urban improvements and patriotism had been effective—at least initially.

THE COLONIZING MISSION OF THE SERIES,
AND A PROUD RETORT

Not long after his discussion with Vice President Leo, Szczepański sent out a reporter to interview more community leaders for their opinion on the latest negotiations with the deputy mayor. Taking advantage of the boost in sales that accompanied the outbreak of the Russo-Japanese War, Szczepański called in a reporter to resume the "Greater Cracow" series. Szczepański said that despite the interest in the war, the paper could not overlook "important local matters," pointing out that the negotiations were currently taking place. The journalist's first article on the topic drolly recounted his false enthusiasm upon receiving the assignment and made a big deal of his arduous journey to one of the outlying communities in a tram, a carriage so bumpy that he imagined he was getting "seasick, like on a Japanese warship," and then on foot through mud and slush—"[all] for the public good."[41] In this and his other reports, the reporter assumed the language and tone of a colonial emissary, begrudgingly leaving the comforts of the metropolis to fulfill his duty in the outskirts of civilization. Cynical and worldly-wise, the reporter mocked what he saw as the simple earnestness of his compatriots on the other side of the river and was uncertain whether the muddy fields he traversed would be of much worth to Cracow.

Wincenty Jelonek, the community chief of Ludwinów and the first mayor with whom the reporter met, was in favor of incorporation. Given his district's problem with mud, he was eager to get paved streets from Cracow, along with "lighting of some sort" and a school. Listening to Mr. Jelonek explain that the excise tax system would "be like in Vienna, after the incorporation of communities into a single whole," the reporter burst out, "Mr. Leo must have really sweet-talked you!" The village mayor agreed and relayed the deputy mayor's argument with enthusiasm:

> Naturally! He said that patriotism demands that we pull together and work alongside each other, because only in this way can we achieve what we truly deserve. He spoke for quite a while and rather beautifully. He is a professor, after all. . . .

> Think about it sir, as a result of the attachment of the communities, Cracow will gain about 50 thousand. Then it will be a powerful city, which will count even in Vienna.[42]

After hearing Vice President Leo's vision so eagerly repeated, *Nowiny's* worldly reporter left, not knowing "whether to laugh or cry." As he traveled through more muddy roads alongside snow-covered fields on his way to his next appointment, the reporter wondered what benefit would come to the city from uniting with these rustic districts: "What would Cracovian money do in this great mud, I thought, and the spirit of Dr. Leo whispered the answer in two words: 'Wielki Kraków.'" The report that followed this observation, however, only underscored the rural disorderliness of the place. The community of Zakrzówek and its citizens were hardly material for a grand vision of metropolitan glory.[43]

If *Nowiny's* reporter had his doubts about the plan, so too did some citizens of the provincial communities he had lampooned. A little more than a month after the interview with Ludwinów's mayor, *Nowiny* printed a three-column tirade by "Mr. Jacenty from Ludwinów" on Cracow's urbane pretensions and Jacenty's profound doubts that Cracow could ever live up to its heavenly promises toward the suburban communities. Apparently resenting the paper's portrayal of his community as muddy and rusticated, Jacenty jabbed at Cracow's glaring disorder, filthiness, and lack of civilization, especially as it appeared from his side of the river.[44]

"Not long ago a reporter from *Nowiny* came to visit us," Mr. Jacenty began his harangue. "His efforts were all for nothing, however, because neither the community chief nor the other people he spoke to adequately explained to him how we feel about the blandishments Cracow arrays before us." Pointing out that Cracow had never taken much interest in their communities until now, Mr. Jacenty declared that Ludwinów and Zakrzówek had good reason to be suspicious of the city's recent overtures:

> So where does this sudden kindness come from, that Cracow turns its merciful gaze upon us [and] suddenly desires to embrace us? From whence such generosity, that it invites our delegates over and promises us gifts? It promises to build us schools and sidewalks, [it] promises lighting, electric trams, water lines, its police force, and so on, and so on. In general, it promises to create a paradise for the people of Ludwinów and Zakrzówek, if we would just unite with it.

Mr. Jacenty recalled the common saying, "fools are taken with fine promises" (*ale obiecanka cacanka*) and warned, "those who lure us with such sweet words are prying into our interests and our savings." He cited an example of Cracow's duplicitous behavior in undercutting Podgórze's cattle market by founding its own—an issue that had received a good deal of coverage in *Nowiny*—to prove that Cracow was only pursuing its own interests.[45] There was good reason, then, to doubt that all the urban improvements he had enumerated would come to the outlying districts soon. Like the recalcitrant mayors interviewed in *Nowiny* several months before, Mr. Jacenty doubted that Cracow would make good on its rosy promises.

Unlike the mayors, however, he also took issue with the notion of Cracow as a national treasure. Assaulting the conception of the city as "the precious treasury of our traditions and national memorials," so recently upheld by Vice President Leo as a motivating factor, Mr. Jacenty pointed out that Cracow was hardly deserving of such high self-regard. From his perspective on the other side of the river, Cracow was a sad picture of decrepitude and poverty. "In cities that care about their appearance and the health of their citizens, the riverbank is always the prettiest part of town," he asserted. "There are parks where citizens can stroll in the fresh air, free from the dust of the city. There are wondrous edifices that give the city a distinctive appearance. And what do we have in Cracow?" he asked.

> Old, moldy boats, thrashed fishermen's huts that are falling apart, useless tubs and other bits of trash lie about on the banks of the Vistula, and in between that rubbish, [discarded boards] jut out like scarecrows. Not far from such tatters the banks are occupied by Cracow's street urchins [who] bask in the sun by day and go out like wolves on the hunt at night.

Moving from the disarray of driftwood, old boats, and garbage to the moral corruption of the petty criminals who lurked there, Mr. Jacenty felt compelled to add one more layer of filthiness to his description: "So that our picture can be abominable in its entirety, we look to the lower shores of the black canals, which appear like the open jaws of the Cracovian dragon, belching a foul odor into the Vistula [that afflicts] the inhabitants of the other side day and night." In this vision of the city, the idealized "silver ribbons of the Vistula" were perpetually violated by the foul effluvia of urban life, the visage of the riverbank marred by debris, and the moral health of the city jeopardized by predatory youth. Peering at Cracow from across the river, Mr. Jacenty saw only disappointment and decay.

Then, indulging in a travelogue of his own, Mr. Jacenty described a voyage into the heart of the city, which he contended was no less disgusting than its rotten exterior. In Jacenty's depiction the muddy fields of his native Ludwinów paled in comparison to Cracow's big-city muck. His first target upon crossing the bridge into the city was the repulsive public toilets that assaulted the senses with their overpowering stench. Next, he took on impoverished Kazimierz. Assailing "one of [its] three principal streets," Bożego Ciała (Corpus Christi), he leveled the same sort of complaint *Nowiny*'s reporters had made of the suburban roads and then continued to demonstrate that Cracow's streets presented a greater problem than just ruts and mud:

> [If] you haven't broken a leg on its uneven pavement or at least lost your galoshes in the mud, and if you have strong nerves that don't submit to sea-sickness then go, brother, to New Square [and] Bawół Square along Ciemna, Wązka, Jakóba, and Dajwór Streets, and you'll find not mud, but a stinking, heaping mass of excrement [and] putrefaction—you'll find it there and in abundance along the streets . . . [in short] you'll find the stables of Augeas, but no Hercules to clean them.

If the ride to Ludwinów had reminded *Nowiny*'s reporter of "a Japanese warship" on choppy seas and its abundant mud had cost him a pair of galoshes, the streets of Kazimierz were far worse, according to Mr. Jacenty, and required a much stronger stomach.[46] And if *Nowiny*'s elitist reporters had resorted to Latin phrases in summing up their arguments, here was an allusion to Greek mythology to illustrate the mythical extent of Cracow's filthiness. Reversing the roles, Mr. Jacenty's letter demonstrated that a sub-urbanite could also wield the discourse of cultural superiority—or at least match it, tit for tat.

Continuing, Mr. Jacenty asked rhetorically whether the citizens of Kazimierz were any less deserving of good governance than the rest of the city: "Do they not lift the same burdens as those who live on Market Square?" he queried. "Why have they been forgotten?" He hastened to point out, however, that theirs was not the only dirty district. Students had to dodge mud "even worse than what we have in Ludwinów" on their way to classes, and much of downtown was in need of "serious cleaning." He pointed out the awful state of disrepair that many of the city's historic churches found themselves in and bemoaned the lack of even a sidewalk leading up to the decrepit former castle complex of Polish kings, Wawel. In his tirade, Jacenty's humanistic benevolence toward the Jews of Kazimierz faded in the face of his distaste for the preponderance of German-speaking Jews (as attested by signs in German on either side of the national museum), which he saw as an affront to the Polishness of the city. He railed against Jewish control of the city, especially in the guise of "Bazes and his group."[47] Mr. Jacenty remarked that there were Jews in Ludwinów, but "they don't have us reigned in. They are our fellow citizens, but not our rulers." He concluded his diatribe with a call for Cracow to "take on Polish colors" and show that it has enough capital to meet its own needs, "and then maybe we'll believe that all it has promised us in Ludwinów—that is yet to be fulfilled even in Cracow—will come to pass."

Ultimately, Mr. Jacenty did not dispute Cracow's national significance so much as declare that it was failing to live up to its reputation. Like Vice President Leo, he appealed to nationalism in making his arguments. Unlike the future mayor, however, Mr. Jacenty saw no visions of greatness for the city. Approaching the city from its soft underbelly on the other side of the river and moving on through crowded Kazimierz, he saw only filthiness and failure. Mr. Jacenty's vision of Cracow was at once anti-cosmopolitan and anti-urban, even if it essentially called for a tidier riverbank and cleaner streets. As a major part of its rhetorical strategy, it cast aspersions on the city's ability to bring civilization to the countryside while questioning the value of big-city life in the first place.

Mr. Jacenty's negative letter and the concurrent efforts of officials from Podgórze to dissuade the districts on its side of the river from backing the plan must have had an effect on Mayor Wincenty Jelonek of Ludwinów. Ten days after the letter ran in the paper, *Nowiny* printed a list of rigid demands from the formerly compliant and eager mayor and some of his city councilors, Paweł Nowak, Jan Długoszyński, and Maurycy Abrahamer.[48] Among the stipulations was the demand that Cracow provide a strict timetable for "the building of a new school, paved gutters, gas lighting, water pipes (with the mention that for 20 years, the community [would] not pay the four percent fee for the water supply), and sewers"—as if in response to Mr. Jacenty's hunch that the big city would never make good on its promises. The four-person delegation demanded that Ludwinów be able to elect four representatives to the Cracovian city council and automatically hold some posts in the Greater Cracovian municipal government. The delegation called for a twenty-year grace period from taxes as well. *Nowiny's* editorial staff could not resist commentary: "Well, well, the gentlemen of Ludwinów seem to think that they are giving Cracow a great favor and honor in condescending to unite with it. . . . It's worth noting that the entire district of Ludwinów has 2,089 inhabitants, and a district holding of 5 crowns! But they're putting up a fight for it!" *Nowiny* concluded, "All of Ludwinów marches to the beat of the Jelonek family, which truly fears its loss of influence in the case of the incorporation of Ludwinów to Cracow and is therefore against the project."[49]

The paper reported a few more controversial meetings between the leaders of the Wieliczka powiat (the administrative unit that included Podgórze, Dębniki, Ludwinów, and Zakrzówek) and the repressive efforts of Mr. Nowak, the police chief of Ludwinów, to thwart meetings of citizens there in favor of the plan for Greater Cracow.[50] Nowak had been one of the drafters of the "excessive" demands put forth by Ludwinów. The paper concluded that such measures were "examples of what happens because of intrigues spun up to thwart a plan that is indubitably beneficial for many suburban communities," adding, "whether it is good for Cracow remains to be seen."[51]

Appropriately, the concluding article of the series addressed that question, striving to sway Cracovians themselves to the plan by stressing its inevitability and logicality. Asserting that average citizens did not know much of the plans, the paper justified its front-page map of Greater Cracow as an effort to familiarize its readers. The article stated that many city councilors might question the value of incorporating the surrounding communities, which "are impoverished and in very poor shape" but argued that it was certain the plans would have to proceed in some form. Greater Cracow was "an absolute necessity" for the growth of both Cracow and the suburban communities. "Czarna Wieś, Nowa Wieś, Krowodrza, Dębniki, Zakrzówek, Ludwinów, Półwsie Zwierzynieckie and Grzegórzki, which today are *simply extensions of Cracow*," the paper argued, should be officially amalgamated into a single administrative unit, and it made no sense to allow differing laws and administrations to govern them (emphasis original). As an illustration, the paper pointed out that brawls near the People's Theater on Długa or Krowoderska Streets might be broken up by a Cracovian policeman, only to have the perpetrators run "a few hundred steps to the turnpike . . . beyond the borders of Cracovian authority, where they can thumb their noses and start up the storm all over again." The article recalled Professor Rudolf Sikorski's assertion, printed in a previous article, that Cracow was the most densely populated city in the Austrian Empire and occupied the smallest territory. The city had no room to grow and lacked gardens and squares. "On a territory of 6.8 km^2 (including the [uninhabited] Meadow) 95,925 inhabitants are cramped together." In addition, the plan for Greater Cracow was important from the stance of re-channeling the Vistula and building a river port. "Because of this, Dębniki, Zakrzówek, and Ludwinów *must* be united with Cracow." Whatever the "financial difficulties" of the project, the paper determined, "the creation of Greater Cracow is *an unavoidable necessity* if our city is not to be cut off in its growth, if we don't want it to sink completely" (emphasis original). As such, the energy and efforts of Vice President Leo toward its realization were "in every way beneficial and merited."[52]

CONCLUSION

The "Wielki Kraków" series that ran from May to July 1903 and again from February to April 1904 demonstrated above all that Greater Cracow was a vision, a dream of civilization and greatness that both Cracovians and suburbanites felt they lacked. Its central motif was the drive toward "European" standards of living and an acknowledgment of Cracow's place among European cities. From the Cracovian perspective, the city would "sink completely" in relation to its European counterparts if it did not expand its boundaries and horizons. As the geographically smallest and most crowded Habsburg city, Cracow's chances for growth were doomed, unless it "follow[ed] in the footsteps of [Vienna and Berlin]" and incorporated its suburban communities like a genuine "great city." The chance to be part of something great, both for the city and, as Dr. Leo put it, for the nation, was not without appeal in the rural communities. Recall, for example, Mayor Jelonek's references to Vienna, parroting the deputy mayor's arguments, "as in Vienna," and "[then we'll] count even in Vienna," or Mayor Szalwiński's willingness "to sacrifice personal ambition . . . so that the community [could] reach a European standard." Even village mayors who were dubious about incorporation acknowledged the value of "[making themselves] into Europe." Rational modernization itself was not under attack so much as the way in which Cracow claimed it could bring it about.

In this conflict, the medieval past found itself confronting the modern future, and there was little doubt about which side would eventually win, even if at times the battle was hotly contested. Invoking his community's privileges from Casimir the Great, Mayor Hajdziński of Czarna Wieś proved reluctant to give up the customary medieval distinctions that separated his community from its larger neighbor. It was these same boundaries and the differing laws that accompanied them that Kazimierz Bartoszewicz found "anachronistic" and "silly" in his assertion that the city should modernize by incorporating its suburbs. Exemplified by the turnpike, which set a toll on goods coming into the city, antiquated customs that were increasingly out of step with the modern world were slated for extinction (or at least rationalization) with the creation of Greater Cracow. Indeed, in September 1903, during the hiatus of the Greater Cracow series, *Nowiny* had run an article about Cracow's night watchmen who seemed a laughable leftover "from the Middle Ages, with their big beards and battle axes," which called for their replacement with a modern police force.[53] And yet this was precisely the image one opponent of Greater Cracow chose to employ in creating a dark vision of the modernized future of Greater Cracow: "I'm telling you, sirs, if you unite with Cracow, your children will curse you for it. Today you have a nightguard with a halberd; later you'll have a man in a black shako," said the man, referring to the stiff cylindrical cap worn by Austrian policemen. "I won't tell you anymore, you can imagine the rest yourselves."[54]

Indeed, part of the reason for clinging to pre-modern sensibilities came from the differential of power expressed in the relationship between Cracow and the suburban communities. The attraction of the night watchman with his big beard and halberd was his familiarity and relative harmlessness—he was there to protect, not enforce. (An illustrated article several years later in *IKC* entitled "Extinct Cracovian Types," which showed an organ grinder, a night guard with halberd, a female fruit vendor with a huge hat brim, and a Jew with earlocks, declared that the night guard, despite his dangerous weapon, was a friend to the men returning late from the pubs.)[55] The "man in the black shako," meanwhile, represented a more insidious bureaucratization of force. People like Mr. Jacenty and some of the community mayors opposed the creation of Greater Cracow because it reinforced their sense of inferiority vis-à-vis their neighbors in the big city. Hastening to point out the flaws and filthiness of big-city life, Mr. Jacenty rejected the grand vision of Cracovian greatness, a vision that could only come about with a perceived loss of personal and local autonomy.

The loss of autonomy would come at a cost and could probably not be avoided, given Cracow's size and strength. With the exception of Podgórze, which was large and financially secure enough to oppose on its own terms, most of the communities seemed to sense the inevitability of the plan. Their task, then, was to negotiate their incorporation in the most favorable terms possible. The case of Wincenty Jelonek of Ludwinów, who originally seemed swayed by Vice President Leo's grand words and then made stiff demands of the city a month later, is instructive. If at first he called for a generalized list of improvements and reveled at the opportunity to make Cracow "count even in Vienna," after more reflection he chose hard-nosed bargaining instead. Leo's double-barreled approach of patriotism and pragmatism ultimately proved effective, but it was the pragmatic side that seems to have mattered most to the suburban mayors in the "Wielki Kraków" series. In the discourse of negotiated assent, patriotism proved less of a motivating factor than the urban amenities that could bring the suburban communities to "a European standard."[56]

MUNICIPAL, NATIONAL,

AND EUROPEAN ASPIRATIONS

The Creation of "Wielki Kraków," 1904–1915

Long live great, wonderful Cracow, metropolis of the Polish lands!
—Juliusz Leo, *Nowiny*, April 19, 1910

Like the suburban mayors, whose attitudes toward incorporation tended to be idealistic in their dreams of making it "into Europe" but staunchly pragmatic in the everyday demands they made, Juliusz Leo's motivations for striving so diligently to create Greater Cracow were also primarily pragmatic, though in public speeches he often stressed the national significance of such an endeavor. Recognizing the power of patriotism, Leo continued to note Cracow's place as the spiritual capital of Poland, while espousing plans that would radically reshape the historic capital of kings into a modern city of industry and trade. Yet with the exception of the debates in the provincial parliament, where nationalistic justifications could help sway patriotic delegates, the discussion surrounding the creation of Greater Cracow demonstrated that far more pressing than Cracow's nationalistic meanings was the city's economic and administrative situation. In the governmental publications justifying the expansion, just as in the "Wielki Kraków" series, national claims were virtually non-existent. Local and pan-European justifications held precedence.

THE DEMANDS OF PROGRESS

Within a few months after the completion of the 1904 negotiations with suburban mayors, Leo's ability to oversee the creation of Greater Cracow was enhanced even more. On June 30, 1904, President Józef Friedlein—

having lost much of his party's support and under long-standing pressure from the democratic minority—finally relented and submitted his resignation. Within a few days the city council elected Leo president, with 47 of 60 possible votes.[1] Leo made the creation of Greater Cracow his major program. In his inaugural speech, the young mayor alluded to Cracow's "splendid past" and the "great responsibility to the entire nation [its citizens had] to stand guard over the most sacred national treasures, [and] watch carefully, so that the most magnificent flame of Polish art and learning does not blow out."[2] Citing Cracow's monumental first city president during the period of autonomy, Józef Dietl, whose grand vision for the city had been more or less successfully fulfilled by subsequent mayors, Leo called upon his listeners to work for a better future: "'The great past has passed, and the present is sad, but the future is ours, if we work straightforwardly, sensibly, and enduringly for it.'"[3] In a move characteristic of those who sought to modernize the city, the president had skillfully shifted from Cracow's obsessive historicism and depressing present reality toward hope for a glorious future of capitalistic development. Leo, whose academic training was in economic law, then outlined his proposal to "institute harmony and order" in the city's finances, take out judicious loans for urban improvements, and commence "in the very near future, a number of great undertakings, which in my opinion," he said, "will determine Cracow's entire future economic growth." These were to protect the city from future floods (Cracow had experienced its worst flood in a century the summer before), build the port and canal, and "expand the territory of the city, in other words, the creation of so-called 'greater Cracow.'"[4]

As the plans for Greater Cracow accelerated, the rhetorical shift from historic, symbolic Cracow to big-city Cracow began to appear more frequently in the press. That autumn, *Nowiny* printed the acceptance speech of the new second vice president, Stanisław Domański. Though he seemed more connected to the historicist ideal of the city as a center of Polish memorials and culture, Domański understood well the importance of pointing toward Cracow's "obligation to move with the spirit of the times" in keeping with its Western heritage. He began by recalling Cracow's glorious past, remarking that the city was becoming more and more like it was in the times of Casimir the Great, the capital of art and learning for all of Poland. Yet, Domański noted, Cracow's historical participation in Western civilization meant that the city had "the obligation to move with the spirit of the times" and meet, "for the good of the people," the demands of "progress."[5]

In Domański's articulation of the discursively constructed vision of modern Cracow, the demands of progress impelled the city along the path of European civilization. Cracow was at once singular in its national significance, and commonplace in its imperative to modernize like the rest of "the West." Little wonder that this vision of the city held less allure for the second vice president (it meant that the city was behind, rather than at the fore of something), but he grasped, nonetheless, how important modernization, or "well-understood progress," was for Cracow's long-term benefit.

Meanwhile, a group of city employees under the leadership of the director of the Cracow Magistrate, Władysław Grodyński, and of Professor Rudolf Sikorski continued their research into incorporation. The result, a nearly 200-page document entitled *A Study of the Matter of Incorporating the Neighboring Communities into Cracow*, was published in early 1905. The study—based on research into the incorporation process in Vienna, Prague, Dresden, and other cities, as well as continued research into the costs and logistics of incorporation—offered a series of general and particular reasons justifying incorporation. The study was not ashamed of being derivative; the pattern of other cities that incorporated their suburbs provided an excellent model for Cracow's particularly compelling case. In general terms, the study assured its readers that "progress" demanded it, while in Cracow's specific case incorporation was imperative because the city had no room to grow and the suburban communities, unburdened by strict urban regulations and accompanying taxes for urban services, were developing at the city's expense.

The opening paragraphs of *A Study* are utterly saturated with the language of modernity, growth, progress, change, and development. In an era of "increasing education among all strata of society" and "increased understanding of the hygienic needs that this style of life requires," the study asserted, people would desire to follow the "trend of progress" in seeking "growth of the most perfect kind." Painting urban growth as a result of improved education and the desire to have better jobs and more comfortable homes, parks, and gardens, the introductory paragraphs suggested that cities would continue to grow until their former territories became completely insufficient. As the number of homes increased within the city borders, the authors contended, "narrow, medieval streets" would not accommodate "modern traffic" and the city would have to expand beyond its borders. In this situation, the surrounding communities would begin to grow violently, and so much so, their growth would come at the expense of the big city, undercutting its economic growth.[6]

The study then turned to the examples of Vienna, Prague, Innsbrück, Dresden, Poznań, and closer to home, Rzeszów, to demonstrate that other cities had in similar circumstances succeeded in incorporating surrounding communities.[7] The study stressed that among the most important reasons for incorporation in each of these cases was the inconsistency of tariffs and the resulting economic disadvantage to the big city vis-à-vis the suburbs, and in the following pages it explored this matter in more detail as the pattern played out in Vienna, Prague, and Rzeszów.

According to the study, Cracow's suburban communities benefited from municipal amenities in Cracow, including hospitals, public transportation, cultural institutions, and educational facilities, without paying for them directly.[8] Because living conditions in the increasingly urbanized communities outside of the city were cheaper, not only poor people but also bureaucrats and artisans and even industrialists and professors chose to live there and commute to the city to work.[9] Thus, despite Cracow's rapid population increase from immigration in the years 1880–1910, growth in the suburban districts was even greater. During the period 1890–1900, for example, the populations of Dębniki and Ludwinów grew at a rate ten times greater than Cracow itself (see chapter 1). Furthermore, even if the outdated fortifications and the river that separated the city from the suburban communities kept it from growing, they were poor defenses against outbreaks of disease likely to develop because of poor hygienic standards in outlying villages. The problem of sanitation control, as well as adequate policing and tax administration, could only be resolved through incorporation.

The study then enumerated four major reasons for incorporation: the Danube–Vistula canal, the planned destruction of the next ring of fortifications, Cracow's exceedingly high population density, and the cost of improving the infrastructure of the suburban districts, which would likely come from Cracovian capital, with no assurance of direct return on the investment. The first three merit further discussion.

The creation of a vast canal system connecting the Vistula with the Danube on the west and eventually the Dniestr on the east was a major dream for Leo. Part of Prime Minister Koerber's economic plan, the canal system had been approved in parliament in 1901 with a planned completion date of 1912.[10] In his memoirs, Ignacy Daszyński noted that the Poles and Czechs in the Austrian parliament had won backing for the Danube–Morava–Odra–Vistula canal by supporting the construction of a series of railways between Trieste and the capital. But the general ambivalence of the Polish nobility toward industrialization thereafter amounted to a situation in which the railways in the south got built, thanks to the taxes paid by these nobles, while Galicia ended up with nothing.[11] (Alexander Gerschenkron later asserted that the canal's failure was more due to the subtle and secretive lack of support from one of his eventual teachers, the finance minister Eugen von Boehm-Bawerk—a contention that has been downplayed in later scholarship, not least because Koerber knew that Boehm-Bawerk and the agrarians remained ambivalent.[12]) The realization of the canal would have been a tremendous economic asset for Cracow by making it a central intersecting point for trade routes from the Baltic and the Black Sea into Vienna and the rest of Central Europe. Aware that businesses connected directly with trade concentrate as close to ports as possible, Cracovian leaders and Leo, in particular, were keen not to let a right-bank port be built without officially incorporating that area into Cracow. Vienna had found itself in a similar position vis-à-vis the construction of a port on an opposing bank that did not belong to the city and so in 1904 set about incorporating the districts of Florisdorf, Leopoldau, Kagau, Hirschstalden, Stadlau, and several others.[13] A number of the articles in the "Greater Cracow" series had mentioned the plans for the port; negotiations with Podgórze and the other communities on the right bank of the Vistula could not avoid the topic. Leo made the canal and port a major part of his political efforts in Vienna when he became a leading member of the Polish Circle (Koło Polskie) in the Austrian parliament in 1910, but the plan had already started to falter in the years before the Great War, due to competing aims in the various crown lands and the sense in the Ministry of Finance that canalization would prove vastly more expensive than initially thought.[14] Still, as late as 1916, a formal map of Greater Cracow included the port in the right-bank community of Płaszów (east of Podgórze), and as late as June 1917 the municipal government in Vienna organized an international conference to discuss the plan. During the period of negotiations, of course, everyone expected that the canal would be built.

The second immediate reason for incorporation was the decision of the Austro-Hungarian military authorities to demolish the fortifications from the Vistula to Prądnik Czerwony, in order to construct new fortifications further outside the city, encompassing the Kościuszko Mound.[15] From the Cracovian perspective, it was crucial that Cracow obtain rights to the newly available lands and regulate the growth that would otherwise occur there pell-mell were the various districts to build on their own. In an analogous situation, Prague had lost out to its suburban communities. If the municipality of Cracow gained rights to the land, the study pointed out, affordable working-class housing could be built on a larger scale.[16] Besides, existing city services including the cemetery, waterworks, and municipal slaughterhouse already existed beyond the fortifications.

A third crucial reason for rapid incorporation was Cracow's amazingly small size and "exceedingly high population density." In 1900 only Prague, with an official size of 14 km^2 and a population of 201,589, could vie with Cracow for the densest population in the Austrian monarchy. Prague's population density was slightly higher, but only if one included Cracow's 1 km^2 City Meadow as livable space. Without the uninhabited meadow, Cracow had the densest population, with 15,851 people per square kilometer.[17] Over the decade, as Prague incorporated more surrounding communities, its situation bettered, leaving Cracow as the most densely populated Habsburg city. The study relished pointing out that conditions in Cracow were markedly worse than those in Vienna before its incorporation in 1891.[18]

Altogether, the study stressed the costs of the current situation to Cracow's potential for growth. Only well into the second section did it enumerate the benefits that the suburban communities could expect from unification. These were, as in the "Wielki Kraków" series, improved "public safety, roads, streets, curbs and sidewalks, water lines, market facilities, community health, care for the poor, and schools."[19] The remainder of the study was a detailed presentation of budgets and potential costs of incorporation. Nowhere did the study refer to Cracow's role as the "Polish Athens."

FROM NEGOTIATION TO INCORPORATION, 1905–1910

President Leo's plans in office addressed both aspects of Cracow's character, its national and historic significance as well as its development into a modern metropolis. In 1905, the city gained rights to the Wawel Castle complex from the Austrian military and began its restoration. The Florian Gate, the Old Theater, and St. Mary's Church were renovated during Leo's tenure, as well. In 1910, while the city celebrated the 500th anniversary of the Battle of Grunwald, President Leo opposed altering the Barbakan, a medieval fortress tower, in order to install a panorama of the famous battle inside; his opposition was based on the grounds that the alterations would jeopardize the historical integrity of the site.[20]

In 1905, the year that restorations began on Wawel, Stanisław Tomkowicz declared in *Czas* that "for intellectuals" interest in old buildings was "a natural reaction to the uproar and distractions [of the modern world], a longing for the silence, peace, and harmony that the view of edifices from centuries that did not know trains, telegraphs, newspapers, factories, capitalism, strikes, and bombs can provide."[21] While Tomkowicz positioned the old as an antidote to the new, Leo eagerly embraced both aspects of Cracow's character, boldly marshaling elite support for Cracow's ancient splendor to bring about some of the very changes that elites like Tomkowicz may have feared. Even if he sought to avoid the bombs and strikes of revolutionary Warsaw, "trains, telegraphs, newspapers, factories, [and] capitalism" were certainly part of Leo's plans for the city.

Leo believed that Cracow needed to be "[a center] of manufacturing, industry, and trade," as opposed to its previous role as "[an assemblage] of the intelligentsia."[22] In addition to his ambitious plans for the canal and port, including a number of projects designed to re-channel the Vistula and its tributaries completed between 1905 and 1907, he sought funds for the construction of eight vocational schools in order to create an educated artisanate to work in manufacturing. Leo also sponsored a number of programs to aid the city's poor, including the expansion of the city slaughterhouse and the eventual importation of inexpensive meat from Argentina, city coal delivery, rent relief programs, and the hiring of nurses and dentists for city schools. When in 1905 the military relinquished the lands around the fortifications, Leo began negotiations with military and railway officials and the ministers of the treasury for the purchase of the land. In late 1906, after more than a year of negotiations, Leo succeeded in obtaining a portion of the fortification lands for city use.[23] His plans for the terrain included factories and affordable working-class housing. By 1911 the ambitious mayor had succeeded in gaining a majority share of the tram company for the city, thus enabling the rational development of tram lines throughout Greater Cracow while channeling the company's lucrative income into city coffers (see next chapter). Further efforts to improve business and transportation in the city included the freight railway station and the "Third Bridge" over the Vistula, both completed in 1913.[24]

Not only did Leo disagree with conservatives like Tomkowicz about the dangers of modernizing the city, he openly aroused their ire by abandoning their party. In 1907 Leo and a few key conservatives had switched from the Conservative Party to the Democatic Union, sensing a shift in power that would come about with the implementation of universal male suffrage that year. Aligning himself with the liberal-democratic *Nowa Reforma* (and to a lesser extent, *Nowiny*) rather than *Czas*, Leo signaled the end of conservative dominance in Cracow—the historic preeminence of the Stańczyk faction, whose ideas had held sway in the city for four decades.[25] In city council debates over Greater Cracow that autumn, only two city councilmen out of the 40 who voted opposed the plan, Adolf Gross of the Party of Independent Jews and Karol Łepkowski, a conservative representative.

Articles in *Nowiny* from this period were quite optimistic; a report following the September 19 city council vote approving the plan went so far as to proclaim Greater Cracow an established "fact."[26] The conservatives did not go down without a fight, however. Once the resolution passed to the Sejm, the Cracovian conservatives launched an all-out attack on Leo and his plans for Greater Cracow.

Councilman Łepkowski had argued that the city was not prepared for the financial demands of incorporation, an accusation that the conservatives would harp on for nearly a year. The proposal was debated in the Sejm in late 1907 and then again in late 1908. Throughout the winter of 1907/1908, *Czas* launched frequent attacks on Leo's administration, asserting that it was deep in debt, poorly run, and hardly ready to meet the demands of incorporating the new communities.[27] Meanwhile, in a rare signed piece by Ludwik Szczepański, *Nowiny* defended the administration's budgets to its readers, underscoring the importance of judicious loans to assure "the constant, favorable, further . . . growth of the city."[28] A few days later the paper reported an important speech by President Leo to the magistrate that laid out his plans for Cracow's economic and political development, while setting forth the democratic platform in Cracow and Galicia.[29] During the following months, attacks by *Czas* continued. In early April, *Nowiny* printed a mock "Ten Commandments of the Conservatives" in response to the repeated efforts of the conservatives to torpedo Leo's plans.[30] In *Nowiny*'s sarcastic critique, the conservatives were pictured as clannish and snooty intellectuals who opposed growth and "progress" in favor of "stagnation and dead economics." As in other stories about Greater Cracow, the depiction of the conservative intelligentsia as "the guard of the traditions of Cracow" conjured up an image of the medieval past in opposition to the modern future. Like Cracow's anachronistic night watchmen who, despite centuries of tradition, were being replaced by a modern police force, the conservatives were merely defending their outdated ways while protesting their replacement by Leo's democrats.

The conservatives' most significant attack on Leo's plans for Greater Cracow was a study by Jagiellonian University professor Włodzimierz Czerkawski in September 1908, which attempted to show that the city could not handle the financial and organizational burdens of incorporation. Czerkawski's brochure created doubts in the Sejm about whether incorporation was possible, and Leo and his supporters had to work vigorously to prove that the plan would still work. President Leo and his long-term colleagues in the creation of Greater Cracow, Magistrate Director Grodyński and Professor Sikorski, wrote a response.[31] An article in *Nowiny* entitled "The 'Deficit' in Lesser and Greater Cracow" took issue with *Czas*'s assertion (based on the Czerkawski document) that Greater Cracow would have a deficit of 664,988 crowns. *Nowiny*'s article reported that the persons on the committee for the creation of Greater Cracow had countered the accusation point for point, demonstrating its errors, incompleteness, ill will, and willful misinterpretation. "The deficit for the first year will only be 135,857 crowns so Prof. Czerkawski missed it by 527,131 crowns, or 389 percent!" the paper remarked. "The budget is so well thought out, in fact, that shortly it will bring profits to the city, without raising taxes as drastically as Czerkawski accuses."[32]

Meanwhile representatives in the Sejm continued to debate the details of the proposal. While the representatives concurred with the previous Sejm in agreeing to the creation of Greater Cracow in principle, they sought to assure that the city indemnify the districts of Cracow and Wieliczka for the loss in tax revenue they would incur once incorporation went into effect.[33] The marshal of the Wieliczka district, Karol Czecz, whose jurisdiction included the right-bank communities that were slated for incorporation into Greater Cracow (Dębniki, Ludwinów, Zakrzówek, and Płaszów), took up the conservative cause in the Sejm as a strong opponent. Arguing that the creation of Greater Cracow would cause great financial loss to his district, he put forth a plan for the creation of a "Greater Podgórze" as a counterweight to Greater Cracow. In response, *Nowiny* called the marshal by his full aristocratic, and German-sounding name, Karol de Lindenwald Czecz—even though previous articles had only called him "Mr. Czecz"—and printed his proposal with parenthetical insertions of exclamation points and question marks at points of disagreement.[34] When his proposal for Greater Podgórze failed to garner any support in the Sejm, Czecz sought to lengthen the period of tax relief in the communities from twenty to thirty years. This, too, was defeated.[35]

Patriotic bombast probably eased the passage of the plan in the Sejm. In her biography of Juliusz Leo, Bąk-Koczarska notes that Cracow was a symbol of Polishness that spoke to representatives of all classes: "Therefore all of the representatives, when speaking on behalf of their clubs [parties], brought up Cracow's significance and historic role, expressing their approval that they had the opportunity to assist in the creation of new conditions for the growth of the former capital of Poland."[36] Unlike the community chiefs, who ultimately preferred pragmatic results to patriotic sentiment, the Polish representatives in the Sejm seemed to have reveled in patriotic justifications. After lengthy negotiation over details, the representatives chose to couch their support in terms of Cracow's national significance as a center of Polish culture.

But the national significance of the city was only a minor part of the formal analysis that representatives Jakób Bojko and Antoni Górski presented to the Sejm on October 26, 1908. In their "Report of the Community Commission of the Country Department on the Subject of Incorporating the Neighboring Districts and Manorial Districts to the City of Cracow," the representatives noted that the matter required careful study and that their fellow representatives should not accept incorporation because "the national interest and meaning of the city of Cracow as the capital of Poland require[d] it." Nor, they noted, should the matter be approached exclusively from the perspective of "financial effects and the increased burden on the population" (the Czerkawski argument). "The truth," they argued, "as usual, lies somewhere in between: Cracow had and may still have times of great glory, even if its edifices are not large, nor its industry well-developed." Even if Cracovians and others worshiped its old buildings, "the spirit of the times demand[ed]" that Cracow do all that it could to meet the "various imperatives of a growing big city anywhere." Particularly in a "poor country like ours," Cracow's industrial growth was to be welcomed. For these reasons the Community Commission recommended that the necessary tax increases, even if they would prove burdensome to the poor, the working class, and the suburban citizens, were not excessive and were ultimately worthwhile.[37] The remainder of the document stressed the practical aspects of incorporation. As in Deputy Mayor Domański's 1904 speech, the report acknowledged the necessity of moving with "the spirit of the times" to help the city and its "poor" province keep up with urban growth elsewhere. The national and spiritual meanings of the city were not insignificant, but they ultimately mattered less.

On November 3, 1908, just two days before the closure of the session, a plan that called for the incorporation of Zwierzyniec, Półwsie Zwierzynieckie, Dębniki, Zakrzówek, Czarna Wieś, Nowa Wieś, Łobzów, Krowodrza, Prądnik Biały, Prądnik Czerwony, Olsza, and Grzegórzki was approved. Ludwinów and Dąbie would not be included. Celebrations in Cracow were not long in coming. That week, at an ovation for President Leo in front of the Franciscan Church, a *Nowości Illustrowane* photographer used too much magnesium for the flash and caused a terrible explosion that broke some lower panes of one of Stanisław Wyspiański's famous stained glass windows. Worse, some of the falling pieces struck President Leo on the head, cutting him badly, "slicing an artery and causing a great flow of blood."[38]

Shortly after passage in the Sejm, the Galician viceroy and fellow Jagiellonian University professor Michał Bobrzyński assured Leo he would see that the plan made its way to the emperor as quickly as possible. Francis Joseph's sanction came a year later, on November 13, 1909. In consultation with Czecz, Leo set the date of April 1, 1910, as the day that incorporation should go into effect.[39] Greater Cracow would gain ten new districts, created from the 12 communities slated to join that day, increasing its size more than fourfold, from nearly seven square kilometers to nearly 30 km².

On April 10, 1910, Cracow took over the legal and financial accounts of the incorporated districts. A week later the city celebrated the occasion.[40] Guests at the ceremonial breakfast were seated according to an elaborate seating chart that classified them in one of four groups: "A. Named platform guests; B. Representatives, religious leaders, government leaders, and invited guests; C. City councilors, village and community mayors, members of the Magistrate, and editors; and D. Delegates of the suburban communities, and municipal civil servants" (the largest group).[41] The breakfast menu, with cuisine from all over Europe and presented in an appropriately multilingual format, can be read as a tacit acknowledgment of Cracow's place in European civilization. French dishes predominated, but the menu was delightfully ecumenical:

Bulion w filiżankach (Bouillon in cups)

Tourne-Dos de Boeuf aux Truffes

Jarzyny à L'Impérial (Vegetables à L'Impérial)

Kapłony Styryjskie (Styrian Capons)

Kompoty – Sałaty (Compotes – Salads)

Pêches Soufflées

Owoce (Fruits)

Kawa czarna – Likiery (Black Coffee – Liqueurs)

Madiera dry

Chateau Margeaux

Hochkeimer

Pommery & Greno

None of the alcoholic beverages appears to have been locally produced, though the soup at the ceremonial dinner that afternoon, "Polish broth with vegetables," gave the meal a local flavor.[42] The meals only proved what everyone already knew and what the creation of Greater Cracow hopefully affirmed: modern Cracow and its citizens were part of European civilization.

In his speech, President Leo began by stressing Cracow's future as a great city but quickly reverted to the late nineteenth-century trope of its historic greatness. Asserting that in this "Polish acropolis" the "spirits of kings will direct us along our new paths, [as will] the spirit of our greatest poet, whose remains [lie in Wawel's crypts]," Leo claimed that Cracow had not ceased to be "the Athens and Rome and capital of Poland." And just as great things had occurred there in the past, he intoned, so "now we must create . . . a city that will be an example to others, whose gates we may one day open with pride, when they fulfill the dreams for which we have sacrificed. In that hope," Leo concluded, "I say: Long live great, wonderful Cracow, metropolis of the Polish lands!"[43] All of the other speakers, including the mayor of Lemberg, Stanisław Ciuchciński, acknowledged Cracow's symbolic place as a "sacred city" for the Polish people.[44] The festivities and speeches of the day, mirroring the mayor who largely brought it all about, proclaimed Cracow's historical and national greatness while marshaling in its future as a big city.

WINNING PODGÓRZE

Although the events of April 1910 were cause for celebration, President Leo's combination of Polish patriotism and urban improvement had still not won for Greater Cracow the jewel on the far side of the river: Podgórze. Unlike the other suburban communities, Podgórze was a town in its own right, with 22,057 inhabitants (in 1910) on a territory nearly as large as pre-1910 Cracow. The two cities had an established rivalry, particularly in the realm of economic development. With Podgórze's own municipal services already in place, including electric lighting, there was not much Cracow could offer it by way of urban amenities—at least according to Podgórze's elected officials. As early as 1905 Podgórze city councilor Władysław Liban said, "We have no benefits from uniting with Cracow. After all, we have everything here ourselves. We have paved roads, lighting, and our water from Krzemionki is markedly better than in Cracow."[45] His statement reflected a clear understanding of the terms of negotiated assent that were articulated in the "Wielki Kraków" series in *Nowiny* a few years before. Convinced of its inapplicability in their case, Liban and his fellow municipal authorities resisted every overture Cracow made in the following years. Above all, leaders and residents of Podgórze were convinced that incorporation would only hurt them financially.

Yet with the creation of Greater Cracow an established fact, Leo could argue for the inclusion of Podgórze from an increasing position of strength. In September 1910, at the beginning of a new term as city president, Leo pressed for "the incorporation of Podgórze in the near future."[46] A series of articles in *Nowiny* that month discussed the debate between Cracow and Podgórze.[47] In the final article, *Nowiny* appealed to a shared sense of urban identity in its effort to persuade Podgórze to join Greater Cracow. The article conceded that the incorporation of "a city of 25,000 should not be done sloppily" but said that the need for relative haste was apparent. Pointing to the Galician economy, the article showed that most of the province's natural resources, including oil, coal, stone, iron, timber, and people, were produced for export instead of being used locally in cities and centers of industry. "Growth of cities here would stop at least half of our emigrants from departing and keep them in the country, where they would find work and make a living," the article declared. "Everyone who cares about the good of our cities and our country should push for this goal." The article stated that "overvalued member[s] of the privileged classes" and "foreigners" could not be counted on to push for urban vitalization. The piece concluded with a call for "inhabitants of cities [to] stand on their own two feet as pioneers of [Galicia's] economic rebirth. In order to meet this goal we must unite our strength, and we shouldn't put it off any longer than absolutely necessary!"[48]

In light of the current political climate, in which the Agrarian party, the socialists, and the Ukrainian parties were gaining ground in the Austrian parliament, *Nowiny's* pitch to a shared sense of urban identity was a shrewd move, but not unexpected. Indeed, the strongest political affiliation in Cracow and Podgórze at the time was the Stronnictwo Mieszczańskie, a party of urban middle-class democrats. It is hard to tell to what extent *Nowiny's* effort to underscore a common sense of urban identity proved persuasive among its many readers in Podgórze, but a 1913 article in *Nowiny* related that the Mieszczańskie party in Podgórze was in favor of incorporation, while according to a poll from a few weeks before, artisans and industrialists were withholding support until a few demands were met.[49] When it came to persuading inhabitants of Podgórze of the necessity of incorporation, the paper recognized that national appeals would not be as convincing as appeals to middle-class, urban identities.

Meanwhile, Ludwinów and Dąbie, communities to the west and northeast of Podgórze, respectively, had submitted applications for inclusion in Greater Cracow.[50] They were officially incorporated on April 1, 1911. Negotiations were under way to incorporate Płaszów, the large community to the east of Podgórze, where the port was to be built. Karol Czecz held some 550 acres of manorial land in Płaszów that he had been unwilling to sell in 1907. When President Leo renewed his initial offer in 1910, however, Czecz accepted. The emperor's sanction came on November 29, 1911, and went into effect on February 1, 1912.[51] Podgórze was effectively surrounded on three sides by Greater Cracow (see Map 2).

Despite Leo's strategic move, Podgórze's authorities continued to hold out, making new demands with each new offer from Cracow. Articles in *Nowiny* and *IKC* during the years 1911–1913 kept the issue of Podgórze's incorporation alive until an agreement between the two cities was officially signed on June 7, 1913.[52] In early January 1912, President Leo relied on his old tactics, claiming that "Europeanization" demanded unification and "so too [did] Podgórze's residents," who expected big-city accoutrements that Podgórze

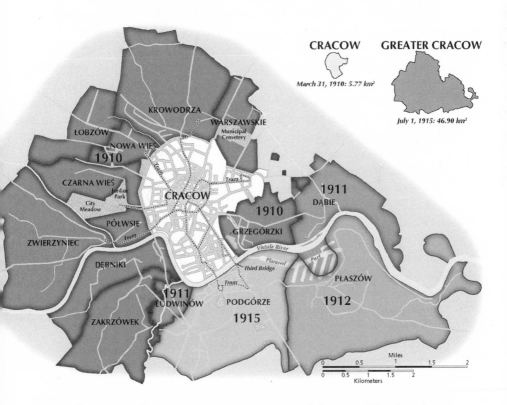

Map 2—The Creation of Greater Cracow, 1910–1915. Note the location of the planned port, which was never built, east of Podgórze in Płaszów.

would be incapable of providing without involvement with Cracow.[53] For at least some members of the Podgórze city council, this argument seems to have had some clout by this point. In April 1913, at a meeting in which the council finally agreed to incorporation, city councilor Emil Bobrowski claimed that even though he was "not much of a friend with Dr. Leo, [he had] to attest that the idea of unifying the two cities . . . was good from the perspective of the nation, the economy, and society." In language strikingly reminiscent of then Vice President Leo from almost a decade before (see chapter 3), Bobrowski stated that a number of examples of English and German cities demonstrated "that little communities like Podgórze cannot meet all of the needs of a great-city populace (tramways, running water, sewers) and for this purpose smaller cities unite with big ones."[54]

Immediate reactions to Podgórze's acquiescence after years of difficult negotiations tended to be somewhat triumphalist and mean-spirited in *IKC* and *Nowiny*, before the papers moved on to the business of the future.[55] Particularly delightful was a drawing in *Nowiny*—mockingly rendered in a "symbolist-futurist style" that was symbolic but certainly not futur-ist—depicting Cracow and Podgórze shaking hands across the river.[56] In it, Cracow, represented by an aged king in partial armor and cape, offers a gloved hand to a skinny, barefoot, balding, and bespectacled Podgórze in the attire of an Austrian officer. Cracow's historic scepter leans against his shoulder, while Podgórze holds a scepter, too—topped with a hand in a symbol of rude defiance (see Fig. 4).

Podgórze's defiance had paid off. Not only would the city have a guar-anteed position in the Greater Cracovian city presidency, it had also won a number of concessions, some of which would benefit its former govern-ment. Lengthy negotiations in Lemberg determined that Cracow would pay the Wieliczka district 44,000 crowns a year for 25 years in compensation for the loss of Podgórze. President Leo had little choice; it was seen as a very expensive arrangement for the city already deeply in debt, but the conserva-tives would not back down. Not until February 26, 1914, did the proposal go before the Sejm, where, as with the previous discussion surrounding Cracow's expansion, a patriotic mood prevailed.[57]

The emperor's sanction came on August 22, 1914, but because of the outbreak of the war, it was not announced until May 28, 1915.[58] Incorpora-tion was delayed until the summer of 1915—well after the siege of Cracow had ended. After leaving the city during the siege, President Leo made a "calculated" return in late 1914, when, as Ludwik Szczepański (now writing for *IKC*) sarcastically put it, "the city still appears to be in danger, but the worst of it has passed."[59] In early July celebrations began. On the first of the

Fig. 4—"The Union of Podgórze with Cracow. A futurist-symbolist picture." *Nowiny*, April 22, 1913.

month, President Leo met with Podgórze city officials, introducing himself as "the new president and a longtime citizen of Podgórze." He praised Mayor Franciszek Maryewski for his invaluable service and said he looked forward to working with him in the presidency of Greater Cracow.[60] On July 4, while refugees from the siege continued to return to the two cities, Cracow and Podgórze celebrated their union. The "Third Bridge" was decorated with fir branches and banners in Polish and Cracovian colors as dignitaries from each city, in black coats and top hats, met each other for speeches and mutual celebration. A cordon of gallantly dressed firemen surrounded the speakers for crowd control. On either side of the bridge hung a large sign with the word "Welcome!" (*Witajcie!*).[61]

Yet for many of the inhabitants of Podgórze, July 4, 1915, was not a day of rejoicing but one of sadness. According to an investigative piece published in *IKC* two days later, few ordinary citizens of Podgórze attended the commemorative events that day, rendering the cordon of firemen on the Podgórze side rather superfluous. Despite a week of earnest advertising, the article pointed out that there were fewer than a hundred citizens of Podgórze waiting behind the firemen to walk over to the Cracovian side. The reporter noted the general disinterest of the small gathering there and overheard an invalid saying, "Oh, here they've written in big letters 'Welcome!' From that side it's all well and good, but here they should have written, 'Say Good-bye!'" The gathering erupted in laughter. Later in the report, the journalist found himself in a bar with some artisans from Podgórze who were clearly depressed about the whole occasion until an optimist among them pointed out that Cracow had a shortage of workers like them and they should find it more easy to get work on the other side of the river now that they were all part of the same city.[62]

In a high mass at 10:30 that morning, President Leo addressed the gathering, underscoring the national significance of the occasion. He also affirmed the city's loyalty to Emperor Francis Joseph, wishing him long life. As in the celebrations of April 1910, President Leo was not alone in hearkening to the nation. Dr. Władysław Jahl, the representative of the provincial government, remarked that the "long-awaited" event was of "uncommon significance for the whole country (i.e., Galicia), [and] for all of Poland." "Behold the powerful spiritual capital of Poland, a metropolis with a thousand years of culture, the treasure trove of our art and learning, this national Mecca, to which our descendants will come for encouragement and hope forevermore."[63] Dr. Jahl, like the other dignitaries involved, configured the incorporation of Podgórze in national terms. Even if the creation of Greater Cracow was explicitly about remaking the city as a modern center of industry and trade, in such celebratory discourse Cracow was still configured as "the Polish Athens," or "the Polish Mecca."

CONTESTING THE MEANINGS OF GREATER CRACOW

Yet the myth of Greater Cracow as the Polish Athens or Mecca was by no means universally accepted. For worldly artists and intellectuals, such expressions of patriotic greatness could seem a bit overblown. Taduesz Boy-Żeleński later recalled that the expression "Wielki Kraków" was "a self-negating term, a combination of words that could only bring a smile." (*Wielki*, of course, means both "large/big" and "great/wonderful.")[64] According to Boy-Żeleński, Leo felt himself to be a big-city mayor, under the gaze of all of Poland, so he set out to make Cracow into a Polish great city.[65] Boy-Żeleński concluded that the city's obsession with the past was so overpowering that few people could really comprehend Greater Cracow on its own terms: "Cracow had become specialized in sorrowful ceremonies, not joyous ones; [it was] trained to look to the past, not to the future. In the face of this, Greater Cracow was a concept that was just too abstract."[66]

Boy-Żeleński was not the only one to question Cracow's place as a great city. On April 16, 1910, just two days before President Leo's first speech celebrating the creation of Greater Cracow, *Nowiny* led off with an article entitled "Finally, a Voice of Criticism," which debated Cracow's position as a center of culture. The article begrudgingly admitted that the city may be "the Polish Athens," at the fore of Polish culture, art, and music, "but Cracow, even this Greater Cracow," it asserted, "is still a small, provincial town." Based on a recent publication by Professor Klemens Bąkowski, the article attested that artistic opinions in Cracow were limited to a small clique of two to three thousand people who made up the same faces at the theater and art galleries. It blasted the city for its lack of a civic orchestra and its inadequate art criticism in the press. Citing Bąkowski, the article harangued Cracow's contemporary art scene for being derivative and misguided.[67]

In 1913 Adolf Nowaczyński, a Podgórze-born satirist and prominent figure in Cracow's bohemian artistic community, premiered "New Athens: A Satire of Greater Cracow" in the city's rival to the northeast, Warsaw. The play acerbically ridiculed Greater Cracow's pretensions and hypocrisy, deflating its claims of exclusivity while reminding viewers of the humble origins and worldviews of its inhabitants. "Your Greater Cracow," wrote Nowaczyński, "[y]our little city, dear citizens, is essentially a mainstay of humanism, but it is also a capital of hypocrisy, a cradle of cheap lunacy, and a hatching ground of snobs."[68] A brief review of the play in *IKC* was not very enthusiastic.[69] Like Boy-Żeleński and Bąkowski, Nowaczyński called into question Greater Cracow's symbolic meaning as a "great city" and the "Polish Athens."

Ultimately, the creation of Greater Cracow was much more about modernization and urban rationalization than national glory. Nationalistic speeches aside, citizens and politicians knew that the incorporation of the suburban districts would do little to augment Cracow's role as a center of national historic culture. Just a few days after Podgórze's incorporation into Greater Cracow, *IKC* stated that city officials now had a great task ahead of them: "to straighten up, manage, [and] in a word, create a technical-management organization [befitting] a unified and modern western city."[70] The tasks ahead, just as in 1910 after the first round of incorporations, included

> investing in the roads and canals, assuring that lighting is of an equal standard throughout Greater Cracow, expanding the network of city plumbing, erecting schools in outlying districts, creating new parks for the public and the youth, expanding Jordan Park at the expense of the city racetrack, improving the Sanitation Department, rationally supporting building development in the

city, a radical obviation of housing costs through building new developments like the one at Salwator, and cooperating with working-class neighborhoods in creating factories.

Even in wartime, *IKC* understood that the chief purpose of Greater Cracow was to modernize the city. Appropriately, a report in the chronicle that day noted that the city was working on improvements, including the installation of a new tramline.

Numerous articles from the autumn and winter of 1910 attest to this same imperative to rationalize and modernize after the first round of incorporations into Greater Cracow.[71] New sidewalks and lighting were clear demonstrations of the reality of incorporation in the newly acquired communities. Already by December 1910, main streets in the new suburban communities all had gas lighting, and the side streets had provisional lighting until more permanent poles could be put in place.[72] Both the magistrate and the suburban communities understood the illumination of the new districts in symbolic terms. As in the *Nowiny* interviews of 1904, the effort to illuminate the benighted districts beyond the turnpike was a direct example of the spread of civilization and with it, Greater Cracow's control over the new areas.

Despite the assumption that most residents would desire the streetlights and sidewalks that signified their new place in a modern European city, nearly all of the suburban communities experienced episodes of lantern smashing shortly after incorporation. *Nowiny* reported in early January 1911 that the lighting "just recently provided for public use in the communities incorporated into Cracow has undergone barbaric treatment by the local people. Lanterns and lights, which were installed at great cost, are systematically smashed . . . stolen, or in the best case, put out." The article reported cases in eight of the eleven new districts, one case even being perpetuated by Christmas carolers![73]

Wolfgang Schivelbusch has written about lantern smashing in European history, arguing persuasively that streetlights were nearly always a symbol of authority and control. As such, their destruction was a source of particular delight, because it represented a direct affront to authority: "Every attack on a street lantern was a small act of rebellion against the order it embodied," he writes, "and was punished as such."[74] It was no accident, then, that *Nowiny* referred to the perpetrators of lantern smashing in the new communities of Greater Cracow as "barbaric": in smashing the new lights they were directly rejecting the symbolic and actual changes street lamps represented in their communities. They were rejecting "civilization."

If the city's intellectuals like Boy-Żeleński, Bąkowski, and Nowaczyński had chosen to attack Greater Cracow's rhetorical significance as a great Polish city, the discontented denizens of the suburban districts, in smashing the new street lamps, were attacking the symbols of Cracovian intrusion and, to some extent, the notion of European civilization itself. And in many ways their acts of protest were more to the point for, at least locally, the creation of Greater Cracow was much more an issue of adaptation to modern, urban development than a continuation of the city's historic role as the "Polish Athens." As Boy-Żeleński recognized, Cracow's predisposition for commemorations of the past made it hard to understand Greater Cracow on its own terms as a forward-looking phenomenon. One presumes that in recognizing this fact, President Leo invariably coupled his plans for Cracow's dramatic modernization with the nationalist and historicist image of the city in order to ease its acceptance. This is not to say that Leo himself was not a Polish patriot, he was—just as he was a committed Austrian and a proud Cracovian. Most important, however, was his decision, voiced as early as 1904, that the creation of Greater Cracow should be considered from the perspective of the nation, despite the fact that it had very little to do with Cracow's identity as the "Polish Athens" and everything to do with economic and administrative administration. Among the lantern smashers, however, there seems to have been no confusion about what they chose to destroy. In breaking the lanterns, they were challenging the essential meaning of Greater Cracow as emblematic of the city's modernization.[75]

Of course, not all suburbanites opposed the modernization of their districts. There were certainly plenty who felt that Cracow was not doing enough to bring civilization and control to their communities. After a year or two both *Nowiny* and *IKC*, in an effort to appeal to the new citizens of Greater Cracow, responded to complaints that changes were not occurring quickly enough there—an affirmation that both readers and journalists tacitly understood urban modernization as a major part of the creation of Greater Cracow.[76] "When Czarna Wieś was a community with a chief at its head," one citizen wrote in to complain, "one had to endure disorderliness due to dust and mud, but now, when it has been attached to the city and bears the name Greater Cracow, changes ought to come about."[77] The citizen called for the magistrate to exercise authority in enforcing rules against walking cattle in the streets and dumping trash in forbidden areas, and to police the community. Clearly desiring the order and control that city authority should provide, this citizen upbraided the magistrate for failing to live up to its responsibilities in the new communities.

Despite complaints like these, there was no doubt that the creation of Greater Cracow was the source of dramatic changes in the realm of urban infrastructure. During the years 1910–1915, Cracow witnessed the modernization of its telephone and lighting systems, the expansion of tramlines, the dramatic expansion of sewer and water lines, the building of new businesses and buildings, and the creation of additional streets and roads throughout the enlarged territory—all under Leo's initiative. An article from 1913 entitled "New Cracow" exulted that someone returning to Cracow after being gone for just a short while would notice a host of changes, including many of the items listed above.[78] President Leo's vision for the city had created tremendous change in just a matter of years. Franciszek Klein stated in 1926 that Cracow's growth and progress, which had been interrupted by the war, came to an end with the death of Leo in 1918. And the very same Klemens Bąkowski who had criticized Cracow's parochial artistic community spared no words of praise for the late Juliusz Leo, attesting "his services for the city were colossal."[79] Bąk-Koczarska writes that although Leo was unable to see many of his initiatives to fruition, "already by 1915 Cracow was a completely different city than it had been a decade before."[80]

CONCLUSION

In reconfiguring their city as Greater Cracow, not only were Cracovians becoming more European, they were also becoming less obsessed with the city's Polish past. In public speeches, political elites like Juliusz Leo asserted that Greater Cracow had to be considered from the perspective of the nation. In deploying this powerful symbol Leo managed to garner a good deal of support for the project in the Galician Sejm and among political elites in Cracow. Within the city, however, the practical concerns of urbanization proved far more significant than nationalist and historicist symbolism. Proponents and enemies of Greater Cracow alike recognized that its creation was a plan for "European" modernization and urban development. The nineteenth-century trope of Cracow as the Polish Athens made increasingly less sense as the city became a modern metropolis. The imperative to create new canals and tramlines, for example, did very little to enhance the city's reputation as a center of historical monuments and artistic culture. Popular newspapers fully supported the change—*IKC*, for example, berated the magistrate for being too conservative regarding questions of esthetics in preserving certain "historic" parts of the city that got in the way of its modernization—and one can presume that many of their readers did as well.[81] Overall, the city had chosen to follow its European neighbors in embracing the vicissitudes of modernization.

PLANES, TRAMS, AND AUTOMOBILES

The Dangers and Allure of Modern Technology

Those inside the tram complain that it goes far too slowly,
while those who look at it from the street lament that it tears
by out of control.

—*Nowiny dla wszystkich*, October 8, 1903

Modernization and urban improvements were not always top priority in Cracow. In 1888 Cracow's autonomous municipal government, faced with the fiscal decision of building a grand new theater or installing running water, opted for the theater.[1] Thirteen years later, on February 14, 1901, Cracow's city waterworks finally began operation. Almost exactly a month after that, the city's first electric trams began service. At the dawn of a new century the appearance of electric trams and running water signaled a significant shift in the city's character, a change contemporaries readily noted. The humor magazine *Djabeł* published a poem entitled "Nowy Wiek w Krakowie" (A New Century in Cracow) that playfully pointed out the novelty of electric trams and running water in town, while the admittedly pessimistic feuilletonist for *Nowa Reforma* noted that, had they actually been in service on January 1, 1901, perhaps the first day of a new century would have been less humdrum.[2] If in the second half of the nineteenth century, Cracow was dominated by a conservative historicism that hearkened to the city's glorious past while stressing its importance as a center of Polish culture, the first decade of the twentieth century marked a period of urbanization and modernization that necessitated looking to the outside world for models. While

Cracovians generally viewed running water as a welcome improvement, the political press and the humor magazines politicized and lampooned its failures. In the case of the electric tram, which was loud, fast, and powered by a seemingly dangerous energy source, fears of new technology came to the fore. By 1901 Cracow was ready for urban improvements, but not without some acclimatization.

This pattern was generally the same for automobiles and airplanes, which also made their initial appearances in the city during the first decade and a half of the twentieth century. Electric trams and automobiles arrived at the beginning of the decade, while the first airplane took off from the city racetrack in 1910. In an environment largely accustomed to animal-powered transportation, the appearance of these new machines was greeted with surprise, wonder, and even shock. Memoirist Eleonora Gajzlerowa recalled her sense as a child that the electric streetcars rumbled down the tracks "like a 'drunk' [and] I always had the impression they would leap off the track."[3] Numerous articles and illustrations in the press depicted the new machines as instruments of death for the new century, sympathizing with the horses and people endangered by their erratic coursing through the city and countryside. Despite connotations of danger and death associated with new transportation technologies (something the popular press was apt to exploit), the overarching message regarding the machines in the press was one of familiarization and acceptance. The tram quickly assimilated into the rhythms of urban life. Citizens expected it to work effectively and complained when it did not. Newspapers may have exploited accidents for dramatic effect, but above all, they indicated the public's expectation that the machines work as designed, safely and efficiently.

Automobiles and airplanes remained exotic novelties during this period, never shedding their implication of danger and death, but they were also lauded as symbols of the profound achievements of the age and, as such, remained noteworthy even when they did not crash. Whether domesticated, as in the case of the tram, or exoticized, as in the case of the automobile and airplane, the new technologies represented modernity on the ground and in the air. Coverage of them in the popular press further contributed to the existence of modern, urban sensibilities among newspaper readers.

ELECTRIC TRAMS IN THE CITY

On the evening of March 16, 1901, Stanisław Wyspiański's *Wesele*, a masterpiece of twentieth-century Polish drama, premiered in the Municipal Theater in Cracow, the very venue built at the expense of the installation of running water more than a decade before. In March 2001, the centenary of the playwright's most famous work was upheld in his hometown with great pomp and ceremony. Newspaper articles discussed the continuing significance of the play, which was celebrated in the museum dedicated to its legacy and was restaged for a fortnight.[4] Another hundredth anniversary was commemorated that month in Cracow, though with less publicity. On March 16, 2001, Cracovians had the opportunity to witness the coursing of an antiquated streetcar along their tramlines. Careful readers of entertainment and weekend guides might have noticed an announcement for an exhibit at the Museum of City Engineering about the hundredth anniversary of electric trams in the city. The exhibit made much of the fact that on the very day Wyspiański's drama premiered in 1901, Cracovians could have taken their first ride on an electric tram to get to the performance. Although it remains a mere coincidence that such an important work of modernist drama premiered on the same day as the modern electric streetcar, it bears pointing out that the latter introduction has also had a tremendous impact on the city, even if its inaugural date is less well-known.[5] Cracovian middle-school children, who for genera-tions have struggled with difficult passages in Wyspiański's drama, almost certainly got to their lessons on an electric streetcar. Though they may have thought nothing of their ride on the tram to school, at the time the play and the trolley were introduced, the electric tram was surely the greater sensation among school-aged youth and the populace at large. Memoirist Stanisław Broniewski confirms this supposition, remarking that far fewer people attended the premiere of Wyspiański's play that night than had stood along the tracks gaping at the new electric trams.[6]

The morning papers for Saturday, March 16, 1901, wrote much more about the impending inauguration of electric trams than about the evening's premiere, which could be assessed only afterward. By the evening editions, *Czas* and *Nowa Reforma* had already reported on the pageantry of the morn-ing's events in glowing terms. At nine o'clock that morning, the ceremony began in front of the city magistrate building with provincial, military, and municipal authorities present, including the city president Friedlein and First Vice President Leo. A large crowd of curious onlookers had gathered around waiting for a glimpse of the new trams. About half an hour later, an electric tram with a renovated horse-drawn tram in tow pulled up in front of the edifice, its bells ringing and its frame festooned with flowers, the city crest, and flags in both national colors and the city colors of blue and white. A second decorated electric trolley pulled up just moments later. The director of the Cracovian Tramways Company, Leopold Mussil, stepped out of the first tram and invited the dignitaries aboard. Along with a few representatives of the press, they boarded the trams and rode to the train station, Market Square, and Cracow Park, and then to the power station on Gazowa Street, where they observed two electric generators capable not only of powering the trams but, as readers of *Czas* were informed, of lighting Cracow and its surrounding districts as well. At 11:30, the city authorities breakfasted in the adjacent tram station with the board of the Tramways Company, a Belgian joint stock company that had won the contract to build the city's electric tram network. (The editor of *Nowa Reforma* saw fit to point out that, while much of the equipment at the station had been installed by Czech and German workers and thus had German instructions, these would shortly be replaced as Polish-speaking workers were trained for the job.)[7]

In some ways, the inauguration of electric trams in Cracow was as much about pageantry and entertainment as was the play that night. Not only had the ceremonial ride and breakfast been a staged performance of civic pride and the embracing of new technology, the trams themselves were also first seen as entertainment, something of a novelty, like a ride at the fair or a night at the theater. *Nowa Reforma* made the comparison explicit. In the Monday-morning edition, the paper chronicled the varying forms of recreation sought by Cracovians that weekend, mentioning outings to the countryside, walks in the Ring-Park, and Wyspiański's play. "Downtown," the paper pointed out, "there were many people, crowds in fact, who found another entertainment. They simply couldn't ride the new electric rail enough. Without any need, well, just for fun and to kill time, the crowds jammed themselves in the wagons of the tram like sardines in a bucket for several hours 'using' the electrics." Crowds at the tram stops had to compete for tickets; clearly this premiere was sold out. Much to the presumed delight of Mr. Mussil, the chronicler noted, the public "rode and rode them until late into the night."[8] *Czas* likewise reported, "Among the public there were many people who rode not out of need, but for the pleasure of experiencing a ride on an electric tram; especially the school-aged youth used this novelty."[9]

Reading the "serious press" one would have thought that the first weekend of electric streetcar service in Cracow was an overwhelming success. Yet there was a dissenting voice in the press that weekend. To put it mildly, *Głos Narodu* was less enthusiastic about the new technology on Cracow's streets. The nationalist antisemitic newspaper dedicated two articles—almost two columns of front-page text—in the Monday-morning paper to the trams. A bitingly sarcastic piece painted the public's reception in darker tones than those depicted in the blithe reports of *Nowa Reforma* and *Czas*. "Cracow's little people greatly enjoyed their trams yesterday," the article began. "The stations were besieged, and there were actual fights for a space in the horseless vehicles." Nothing could sour the disposition of the crowds, the article continued, until they found out the price of the universal fare for a ride:

> A particularly pleasant surprise awaited those who, setting out for a ride on the "electrics," brought along enough money to cover the former fare, [only] to find out that, for example, from Market Square to Rajska Street would now cost them 16 halers a person.[10] We were ourselves witnesses of how one woman, surprised in this manner, spared no words in praise for the affable Belgians.

And that was not the only problem of the day. One of the trams broke down, and in several of the wagons "the electrical current melted some wires or caoutchouc [rubber], resulting in metaphysical odors." "Besides that," the article concluded wryly, "the first day of travel passed happily without any more serious incident."[11]

Głos Narodu, like *Nowa Reforma* and *Czas*, made it clear that it was the common folk—the "public" or the "crowd," as all three of them put it—who were most using the trams as entertainment. The decision to mention the "little people" in *Głos Narodu*'s report (*ludek*, diminutive of *lud*, or people) made this connection more explicit. This distinction is significant. While the elite rode the trams as a matter of public display during the inauguration, the "serious" press viewed the public's use of the trams during that first day more as a matter of frivolous entertainment.

Głos Narodu's emphasis on the tram company's flaws for the day, instead of its tremendous financial success, arose from its nationalist politics as well as its dislike of its competitor papers and the audiences for which they wrote. *Głos Narodu* cast its rival papers as apologists for a foreign tram company, which was clearly in cahoots with the Jewish city council members and the local bourgeoisie in taking advantage of the average Pole. Thus, the other article about the trams in the Monday paper reported that the "little breakfast arranged by the tram company management" was poorly attended. "Of the 60 city councilors, only seven prepared their mouths for the Belgian fare," and the grand total in attendance including journalists "and the Belgians came to about 20 people." "And it's a pity," the paper intoned, for had more people come, "they would have seen [all the] German or foreign workers at the central station, they would have read the exclusively German placards and instructions." *Głos Narodu* went on to complain that the breakfast language was German and that Mr. Mussil replied to the city's servile toasts "in the Belgian tongue [*sic*]." The remainder of the article took issue with *Czas*'s glowing assessment of the company's ability to supply the city and its surroundings with electric power and its claim that the company was making a healthy profit from its new business. A follow-up article the next day continued a rather boring sparring match with *Czas* on the numbers of tickets sold and money made.[12]

What is most important here—internecine battles between clearly opposed political papers aside—was the real tension over having a foreign tram company in Cracow. In this the city was like many of the lesser metropolises of the world at the time. Elsewhere in Europe and South America, for example, already established tram companies from abroad frequently won contracts to supply smaller cities with electric streetcars.[13] In Cracow as early as 1882, British, Austrian, and Belgian companies had competed for bids on building and operating horse-drawn tramlines in the city.[14] And as in other cities where the tram company was owned and operated by foreigners, this fact often figured into complaints that citizens had about their new forms of transportation. Electric trams, pictured negatively, were thus *doubly* foreign: out of place in a world accustomed to animal-powered transportation *and* operated by foreigners. In the Cracovian press this dynamic was readily apparent. Comments about trams in the newspapers regularly fit into two often related categories: complaints about them as a dangerous new technology or complaints about the Tramways Company management, which failed to run the streetcars as well as it should. As Cracovians became accustomed to the noisy trams careening down their narrow streets, the complaints in the popular press turned from cursing the frightening new technology to lamenting the tram company's inefficient operation of it.

From "Too Sudden and Violent" to "Too Slow and Heavy"

Before electric trams were introduced in the city some Cracovians, especially the elite, worried that the new technology might not fit the particular kind of urban life to which they were accustomed. After all, did electric trams really belong in a city studded with statues and monuments, rhetorically positioned as the locus of Poland's glorious national past? The trams would give Cracow the look and feel of a big city; some Cracovians were not sure they wanted or even needed the noise and confusion the trams would create. A characteristic article in *Czas* in September 1900 indicated fear that the noisy electric tram would interfere with national displays on Market Square.[15] *Bocian* and *Djabeł*, the city's humor magazines, delighted in pointing out the apparent incongruence of an electric tram, a symbol of modernity, clanging its way around the city's medieval landmarks, squeezing itself down Cracow's narrow historic streets (see Fig. 5).

*Fig. 5—**Trams on the Main Square.** Note the contrast between the famous St. Mary's Church and the modern transportation (including, by this period, automobile taxis) in the foreground. From a photograph from the 1920s, originally published in Polaczek-Kornecki, *Zarys Monografji Komunikacji Wewnętrznej Miasta Krakowa*, 1930.*

Both magazines printed bogus contracts between the city and the Tramways Company. The first of *Bocian*'s clauses required the destruction of Cracow's famous medieval Clothiers' Hall, so the electric tram could get from one side of Market Square to the other without having to skirt the large building. Both magazines suggested that the tram would interfere with the ordinary life of citizens on the streets where it ran. "On streets touched by the tram," *Bocian* joked, "moving furniture to and from apartments and provision of coal, ice, and so forth is prohibited." Another clause suggested that "fiacres, droshkies, and one-horse carriages" would not be allowed on those same streets "for the purpose of eliminating unhealthy competition." The mock statutes did not avoid the issue of the Tramways Company's apparent dominance of city politics either. The second clause in *Bocian* stated that Mr. Mussil would become "*co ipso* the president of the city," and the next clause gave Leon Rothwein, the city councilor responsible for relations with the tram company, the greatest honor a Cracovian could ever hope for: "§53. The councilors will give Rothwein, for defending the interests of the community, a constant pension of 20,000 crowns and give him the right to cast his figure in bronze (or in another bronze-colored material) and place it in the spot where the figure of Mickiewicz stands."[16] Embedded in the absurdity of the jokes there was a real sense that the electric tram represented a new order, a novel and perhaps menacing vision of the metropolis, that challenged Cracow's meaning in Polish national mythology. If in the old world, the joke implied, we made statues of our greatest national and cultural figures, now a bland bureaucrat, a harbinger of the new world, would occupy the position of the great bard. Meanwhile, the Clothiers' Hall, the very center of town for centuries, could be razed for the modern principle of efficiency, if taken to the extreme.

Nearly a month before the electric trams officially began service, a reader of *Czas* contributed a thoughtful, if somewhat mistaken, opinion on their introduction in Cracow. In a full column of text printed in the chronicle section, he remarked that technology should simplify life, becoming in a short time so useful as to seem necessary. He asserted that the electric trams would be an aesthetic improvement for Cracow, giving it a great-city feel, at least making it a "big small city" (*wielkie małe miasto*). Yet the contributor worried that the electric streetcars would not prove particularly useful in Cracow because of the way they were supposed to run.

> Well then, how will it be with traffic itself? —How will we use this new form of progress? Everyone replies: no differently from before. Traffic will be quicker; we'll all get to our destinations more quickly. Yes, but who will this

help if the tram moves too quickly to leap out of it, and a person has to turn around and walk back to the spot to which he needed to go? . . . Will this be practical? Will the tram still help the person who desires comfort and seeks speed, so absolutely necessary today?

Probably not, he concluded. "The tram will be too sudden and violent for those seeking comfort and too slow and heavy for the clients."[17] The concerned reader clearly had difficultly fathoming the new configurations of space and time that would accompany the introduction of the electric tram in the city. Still thinking of the city as a walking city, or at least a city in which one could stop one's droshky or carriage precisely where one wished to, the concerned reader could not comprehend how the trams would truly prove beneficial if they overshot his mark by a block or two.

But it was not overshooting one's mark that concerned average Cracovians most when the electric streetcars made their first appearance. If queried whether the new trams would be "too slow and heavy" or "too sudden and violent," there was no doubt that most people feared the latter option. Just two weeks after the trolleys were introduced, *Nowa Reforma* complained that the "electric tram drives along the streets of Cracow at the speed of a passenger train; it is a wonder no fatal accidents have occurred." A month later when an electric tram struck a horse-drawn wagon, killing the horse, the report in *Nowa Reforma* clearly indicated the public's sense that the trams were indeed too fast and violent. Eyewitnesses to the accident stated that although the horse was "at a gallop," it was not fast enough to avoid "the lightning-fast electric wagon."[18] Actually a horse *could* outrun the electric trams of the day, which operated at average speeds of little more than six to eight miles an hour.[19] Yet neither horses nor people reacted well to the electric competition on their streets. To the passersby, the tram seemed too fast to outmaneuver; the hapless horse stood little chance.

This attitude came in part from preconceptions about the new technology as something that was inherently life threatening. *Djabeł* and *Bocian* both had clauses in their introductory "contracts" about recourses for the unlucky people who would certainly be struck by the swift new machines. *Djabeł's* jokes got at the issue of reparation: "those killed by the tram," the magazine quipped, "may bring the issue before the Magistrate and demand that Mssrs. Mussil and Rothwein be present at their funeral as representatives of the Company." Another clause intimated that Mr. Rothwein, who was also a lawyer in town, would be ideally suited to represent "[all] those seriously or lightly injured by the electric trams"—an obvious conflict of interest. *Bocian* put it more forcefully, suggesting that victims of the technology would simply be viewed as unfortunate obstacles: "Persons run over by the trams, without regard to whether they remain in this life or move on to eternity, shall be held responsible in court, where they shall pay the Company in compensation for the alarm and the pause in the schedule [caused by their accident.]"[20] Within a year of the introduction of electric streetcars *Djabeł* could joke in a brief definition of Cracow that "its inhabitants can be expected to live as long as they avoid being run over by a tram." In its "Devil's Dictionary" (Słownik Djabelski) from October 1902, an electric tram was defined simply as "a type of traveling guillotine." (Coincidentally, according to Roshanna Sylvester, the nickname "Belgian guillotine" appeared in Odessa, as well, where journalists also dubbed the streetcar "a tool for the modern death penalty.")[21] Jokes about the electric streetcar as a modern mechanism of death clearly betrayed deeper fears of its power source, speed, and seemingly blade-edged metal wheels.

During the first few years that the electric trams were in service, Cracovians plainly had trouble adapting to the new technology. Though it may be difficult for a person one hundred years later to imagine the danger of a streetcar traveling along a *fixed track* at less than ten miles an hour, the electric tram in motion appears to have befuddled and frightened people on the streets of Cracow in the first years of the twentieth century. Reading the reports of accidents from these years, one is struck with how often "incautious" citizens were struck by the trams. Too often, reports in the press describe how the victim—who often survived, one may presume, thanks to the streetcar's moderate speed—simply misjudged the velocity of the oncoming vehicle, thinking it could be evaded. In March 1903, shortly after a new set of tramlines was inaugurated, two near accidents in as many days involved teenage girls who misjudged the speed of the tram.[22] Only a month later Herman Żabner was struck while urging his son across the street in front of an electric tram at full speed. The man, who was dragged for 30 meters before the tram came to a complete stop, suffered numerous lacerations, broken bones, and "a cracked skull" but was not killed (see Fig. 6).[23] A report in *Kuryerek Krakowski* from September 1902 noted that Rachela Rubinson, "a 79-year-old Jewess," was the victim of an accident with an electric tram. Fortunately, the old woman was not run over, only knocked on her back.[24]

The tram was no respecter of persons (a railway worker lost his lower leg in an accident with an electric streetcar in 1905), yet accidents with the elderly, women, and children attracted the most attention because they exemplified the dangers of the new technology.[25] A fatal accident involving a six-year-old boy who was sliced stem to stern elicited a moralizing line from *Nowiny dla wszystkich* about the need to regulate the speed of the trolleys and watch over children on the streets, but unlike in other cities, the newspapers in Cracow never reported a campaign to eliminate child deaths due to the streetcar.[26] Even so, according to at least one early report, all Cracovians were reduced to the status of children in the way they behaved toward the electric trams:

> Our new lines were just put into use and already we have a second unhappy accident to report. And what's most original is this, Cracovians act entirely like little children; they're used to the old tramlines, and "approach them as part of everyday life," but just let the tram company erect a few new poles and dozens of pedestrians surround them and stare for hours. Better yet, let a tram appear on a new line and—oh boy! Half of Cracow runs in the way, as if they had nothing better to do.

By reducing Cracovians to children, the article drew attention to the relative immaturity they exhibited in the face of new technology. Like "little children," the piece implied condescendingly, they simply did not recognize the danger of the novelty before them. Cracovians were already street savvy with the older tramlines, but their inexperience and wonder regarding the new lines made them vulnerable. The new lines had not yet entered the realm of "everyday life." For now, until citizens grew up by becoming accustomed to the new technology, accidents with the "incautious" would unfortunately occur. Thus the 22-year-old servant girl whose death was the reason for the above moralizing was described as both "unfortunate" and "incautious."[27] Like a little child she was blameless in the face of something she did not understand; yet it was her carelessness that had endangered her most.

The front-page illustration of the servant girl laying helplessly on the ground as the streetcar hits her in the back reinforced the sense that she was a consummate victim, careless yet blameless (see Fig. 7). Like the depiction of Mr. Żabner's ill-timed dash in front of the tram, it shows the moment of impact, just as the tram strikes its unfortunate victim. This visual angle was characteristic for the popular press, allowing the viewer the voyeuristic horror—and pleasure—of witnessing the accident firsthand from the most dramatic point of view. Not only do the pictures allow an unobstructed view of the accident, they also encourage a sort of empathy with the victims—and the drivers. In both cases the faces of the victim and driver are rendered simplistically, with exaggerated space around the dots of the eyes, indicating surprise. Simplified faces also enable viewer participation: by reducing the faces to the most basic features, the characters are effectively made into symbols, everyman and everywoman.[28] The viewer shares their shock.

Fig. 6—**Mr.** Żabner's **Ill-timed Dash.** *Kuryer Krakowski*, April 2, 1903.

But there are some significant differences in the two pictures, which at first glance seem quite similar. What separates the depictions most is the measure of agency exhibited by the victims. While the man runs foolishly, yet heroically, after his son, the servant girl lies, inexplicably, in a tragic pose that seems to suggest she was supine before the tram ever hit her. He is active; she is merely acted upon. The gender stereotypes do not stop there. In the illustration of Mr. Żabner's accident, the passengers seem unaware of the tragedy unfolding in front of them; in the case of the servant girl, two male passengers observe the spectacle from either side of the machine, gripping the handrails as they peer around the front windshield. Whether this distinction was intentional, the placement of the men at the privileged spots astride the driver reveals some-

Fig. 7—"**Under the Wheels of the Tram.**" *Kuryerek Krakowski,* November 2, 1902. Note the victim's tragic pose, the simplified look of surprise on the driver's face, and the male passengers who observe from the handrails.

thing of the way one's relationship to the electric tram was represented as a gendered and age-specific experience. In these illustrations, men—not women or children—rode on the front steps, where the view was best, while women and children (or childishly incautious people) were the typical victims.

Another illustration (from a Munich newspaper and reprinted in *Nowiny*) of "a grate for incautious people" reinforces the gendered types of the female victim and the male witness.[29] In this picture, which illustrated a new safety feature rather than a particular accident, a hapless female cyclist lies in the safety net while three men observe her from the tram above and a police officer watches from the street. Just as in the picture of the servant girl's imminent death, technologically savvy men watched from their position on the steps while a woman lay helplessly prostrate in front of the roaring machine. Men, these drawings implied, had mastered the speed of the electric tram, while carelessly incautious women and children still had reason to fear.

The deadly combination of "carelessness" and speed figured into accident reports until 1903 but seems to have held little clout in the popular press thereafter. People could still be careless, of course, but the tram's speed was no longer to blame. The previous examples, which called attention to the childlike feminine nature of most accident victims, already point to the shift in mentality that was occurring as people grew accustomed to the trolleys on their streets. The trams may have been fast, but the articles signaled that it was only incautious people who had reason to fear. As the speed of the tram faded in significance, accident reports became much more matter-of-fact. On September 10, 1905, readers learned simply that there were two accidents, neither of them mortal, but one quite severe. In this and later reports there was none of the characteristic commentary readers expected in sensationalist articles, precisely because the accidents were no longer seen as so sensational.[30] Typically, the paper reported that an accident had occurred and attempted to ascertain who was at fault. If before, the tram "[drove] along at the speed of a passenger train" or was "lightning fast," by late 1903 *Nowiny* could simply point out that the tram's speed was relative: "Those inside the tram complain that it goes far too slowly; while those who look at it from the street lament that it tears by out of control."[31] To the person on the street in 1903, the tram may have still been lightning fast, but from the perspective of a passenger, this explanation was less convincing. Indeed, as more and more people used the trams, the popular illustrated press increasingly took their point of view. Figuratively and often literally, the paper's perspective was now from *inside the trolley, not from the street.* Often read from inside the tram, it is no surprise that the popular press generally took the passenger's point of view.[32]

Accordingly, within a few years the popular press described the electric streetcar as decidedly too slow. In 1909 *Nowiny* declared that the tram "was traveling at its usual turtle speed" when it broke down, lamenting that one may as well get out and walk rather than endure "Cracow's damn [slow] trams."[33] Three years later, *IKC* used the same phrase in describing an incident with the trolley, which was traveling at its "usual turtle speed," when a footstep broke out from under a passenger.[34] A "fortune teller" writing for *Nowiny*'s Christmas Eve issue of 1911 predicted that "despite the invention of the aeroplane, the systems of transportation [for 1912] will remain the same: trains, trams, droshkies, automobiles, bicycles and everything [else] that can help a person get around. *Only the Cracovian tram will not be regarded as a system of transportation, but rather as a pedagogical device, designed to teach people patience.*"[35] A few months after reporting the original "turtle-slow" tram, *Nowiny* made it clear that speed was not the issue in the case of two accidents with electric trams. "Cracow's famed tram, traveling at 'painfully' slow speeds, still has its accidents," the piece began. The first accident was more serious, breaking the lights and windows of the tram and seriously injuring the horses of a cart driven by Mr. Szostak, "*who didn't notice the tram coming* on Basztowa [Street]."[36] Another accident report illustrates the shift convincingly. Readers learned that a tram struck a wagon driven by a "villager" on the corner of Grodzka Street and Dominican Square. "The blame falls entirely on the villager, who haplessly steered a young and easily frightened horse," the report concluded.[37] And, as if coming full circle, another report in 1911 of an accident between a horse-drawn cart and a streetcar indicated that the motorist (streetcar driver) had been brave in his handling of the situation, when without warning, a spooked horse "leapt *lightning fast* in front of the tram."[38] By then the trolley had become something constant and predictable; it was the *horse's* erratic "lightning" speed that caused the accident.

Even if "easily spooked" equines still had trouble adjusting to their electric competition on the streets, it appears that by the middle of the decade Cracovians were thoroughly acculturated to the electric tram. Mentalities shifted as more and more people rode the streetcar. The tram company sold 2.7 million tickets in 1901, coming to an annual average of 31 rides per citizen. By 1905 these figures had nearly doubled (5.3 million, 52 rides per citizen), and by 1910, 7.5 million tickets were sold (or 72 rides per citizen of pre-Greater Cracow).[39] Wolfgang Schivelbusch has demonstrated that Europeans' reactions to the steam locomotive followed a similar, though lengthier, trajectory. If before steam travel had seemed "an annihilation of space and time," something unnatural and thus intrinsically dangerous, by the middle of the nineteenth century the "subliminal fear" of "the accident" subsided as people grew accustomed to the speed and uncanny smoothness of travel by rail. As he puts it, "the railroad had become part of everyday life . . . the new geography created by the railroad (and first experienced as a shock) had become second nature."[40] People were initially terrified, though fascinated, with the new technology, becoming accustomed to it within a quarter of a century. This seems to have happened in Cracow with the introduction of the electric tram in the span of half a decade at most. New geographies, mental and literal, had been created in the city by the daily coursing of the electric streetcar.

Schivelbusch argues that when accidents occurred the "repressed" initial fears came to the surface. Citing Ernst Bloch on the nature of the technological accident, he discusses how the sublimated fear of the "demonic nature of first railroads" erupts when an accident occurs. "Only the accident still reminds us of it sometimes," Bloch affirms, "with the crash of collision, the roar of explosion, the cries of maimed people—a production that knows no civilized schedule."[41] One cannot doubt that Cracovians involved in tram accidents continued to experience this shock, yet their trauma no longer made news in accident reports in Cracow's popular illustrated press. Like an everyday automobile accident today, it was worth reporting but had simply become too banal to garner dramatic coverage. Once the rapid period of acculturation had passed, reports of accidents were matter-of-fact, even in the most sensationalist newspapers in the city.

"Zawsze One"—Persistent Commentary

The primary reason that newspapers no longer milked accidents for their sensationalist effect was due to the shift in perspective—from the pedestrian's to the passenger's. Although accident reports could attract interest for a while, it was more likely that complaints about the tram's lack of efficiency, rather than its danger to pedestrians, would resonate with readers/riders. As accidents were sublimated into the quotidian pulses of the city, it no longer made sense to dwell on them in a moralistic sense. Far more important was the general efficiency of the new technology, its ability to meet its task of cheap and effective transportation.

Articles in the popular press could assist in the process of acculturation. One went so far as to describe how to board or leap off a moving tram—even though this was illegal—because so many men seemed to attempt it anyway. "Everyone knows that the railway laws severely forbid boarding and de-boarding a tram when it is in motion," the paper explained. "Yet many fellows pay no attention to these rules. For these men, we provide the following observations." Readers were then told how to leap in the direction of the tram, using one's right hand to push off. Here, the newspaper seemed to acknowledge that men ("fellows") could even do something seemingly incautious, because of their ability to understand the technology.[42] A number of articles anthropomorphized the increasingly familiar machines. Trams were said to "smile" or "flap along."[43] One delightful feuilleton described a tram's last "gasps and lurches," before becoming completely "paralyzed." Bystanders and passengers personified the "wounded" machine, playfully calling out for the emergency rescue service, as they would have done for an accident victim. Indeed, one may suppose it was their witty observation that prompted the tone the feuilletonist employed in describing the breakdown. Fully enjoying the metaphor, he wrote that "the conductor tried to play doctor" but was unable to "revive . . . the mortally paralyzed" victim.[44] Such anthropomorphism helped make sense of machines in a world still accustomed to animal power.[45]

Of course, riding the tram regularly did even more to make it seem familiar and, ultimately, indispensable. Not surprisingly, the most common articles in the popular press about electric streetcars were complaints about poor service. During its brief independent existence, *Kuryerek Krakowski* hitched its fortunes to the clattering trolleys on Cracow's streets, betting that frequent criticism of the new technology would resonate with its readers. For the first several months, the popular newspaper commented on the trams under various headings, but shortly after Kazimierz Bartoszewicz assumed editorial control, readers saw the first of what would become one of the most common subheadings in the chronicle section.[46] An article entitled "[It's] Always Them" (*Zawsze One*) expressed disgust that a local lawyer on his way to the offices of the paper was compelled to pay twice for the same ride, because a conductor on the second line refused to honor the lawyer's previously purchased and validated ticket. In the same article there was also a complaint that trams were speeding along narrow city streets, despite poor weather conditions.[47] The article and its title implied that conductors and motorists were always the source of trouble, a nuisance to honest passengers like the lawyer in this story, and were prone to drive their dangerous machines recklessly. The next complaint about trams in the paper, which lamented how dirty and smoky tram stops had become, used a different title, but thereafter, whenever the editors wished to comment on trams or their conductors, they entitled their reports, "[It's] Always Them."[48] Within a few weeks the headline had become the paper's most common title. Hardly a week went by without at least two or three "Always Them" reports about the electric trams, their drivers, or the Tramway Company's management. In early April 1903, for example, there was a five-day stretch with an "Always Them" story in each issue; another report bombastically suggested that problems with the trams and their management were so recurrent that the chronicler could "fill several columns of text a day" with commentary.[49] Eventually, the "zawsze one" commentary became so ubiquitous that it entered popular discourse: One month after *Kuryerek Krakowski* ceased to exist as an independent daily, a contributor to *Nowiny* used the phrase. The contributor, a doctor at the emergency rescue service, spurted "Zawsze one!" when he received a telephone call that a tram had struck an old woman: "Aha, a tram! It's always them! I'm on my way!" (*Aha, tramwaj! Zawsze one! Zaraz jadę!*)[50] Functioning as metonym for the tram or its management, the expression signaled dissatisfaction with the way the trams functioned in the city.

Kuryerek Krakowski exploited tram accidents in the paper, printing front-page illustrations and full-length articles for several dramatic cases. Yet even during the frightening period of acculturation to electric trams in the city, the majority of the newspaper's complaints about the tram were about its management, not its dangerous speed. In *Nowiny* and *IKC* the prevalence of reports about the ineffective management of the streetcars continued to rise, while comments about their dangerous speed disappeared altogether. Of the 90 reports on trams in the popular press (*KK*, *Nowiny*, and *IKC*), for which I have significant notes or a copy of the article itself, more than half (52) could be described as comments or complaints about the management or functioning of the tram in the city. Only 6 articles could be said to imply the dangerous speed of the tram, none appearing later than 1903. Significantly, reports of near accidents also disappeared around that time, due to an apparent lack of interest in reporting anything other than a confirmed collision.[51] Complaints in the popular press about the electric tram betrayed frustration over the efficiency of the new technology and ultimately the management of the company. Not surprisingly, failure to run the trolleys on schedule consistently drew fire from the popular press, almost always with an aside about how the Tramways Company management was "not meeting the needs of the public."[52]

In the summer of 1907, *Nowiny* went so far as to pronounce a "tramways plague" in the city, decrying the company's monopoly and blatant "lack of respect" for the citizens of Cracow. Asserting that the Cracovian Tramways Company had taken advantage of a poor contract made years before, the paper complained in language that would resonate with its major audience of artisans and shopkeepers that the firm was not run "as a business" (*po kupiecku*) but as "organized robbery, [designed] to yank away as many coins as it can." The article protested that "1.) Tickets are horrendously overpriced, and 2.) The way in which the trams run is extremely flawed and causes the public thousands of inconveniences." Passengers had to wait at times for half an hour for the Market Square–Cracow Park Line, "which isn't pleasant in the rain." And even though the city "grows by the year," the article continued, "the German management" sees no need to add new lines or trams. "In a word," the diatribe concluded, "[the management] does everything it can to show the city nothing—that it cares nothing for the city."[53] This sort of commentary, of course, went a long way in winning supporters among the paper's target audience of Polish-speaking, petty bourgeois urbanites. For anyone who had been caught in the rain waiting for a late tram or who felt that tickets were overpriced, the argument was sure to strike a chord. There was no need to report a grisly accident to win readers; complaints like this were compelling—and convincing—enough.

Nationalist impulses affected the way newspapers interpreted the foreign management of the tram company until it was ultimately taken over by the city, which bought a majority of shares in 1910.[54] Yet complaints were by no means simply nationalistic. In the previous example, the "German management" of the company certainly did not help its case, but the principal reasons for frustration were corporate greed and poor service, not who was in charge. Indeed, the city magistrate often bore the brunt of the paper's wrath when trams failed to function as citizens thought they should—even while the company remained under foreign control. When a city ordinance caused trams to cease operation too soon to take people home from the theater, the paper complained.[55] When muddy streets made travel by tram a dirty, unpleasant affair, the newspapers were vociferous advocates for inconvenienced passengers.[56] By the middle of the decade, the majority of readers were seasoned urbanites who expected their trams to operate efficiently. Popular newspapers resolutely took their readers' point of view, whether this meant critiquing the company or the municipal government.

AUTOMOBILES AND AIRPLANES

"Death in the Twentieth Century"

The overwhelming emphasis on urban demands for efficient municipal transportation does not mean that the discourse of danger and death associated with new technology disappeared from the popular press. To the contrary, it shifted to commentary on the automobile and the airplane, exotic new technologies that were yet to become vehicles of mass transport. Unlike the electric tram, which readers used regularly, the automobile and airplane remained unfamiliar novelties, fast and dangerous. And while the popular press did much to domesticate the new machines, making its readers familiar with them by running numerous articles about their wondrous capabilities, automobile and plane accidents still elicited dramatic sensationalist reports and images throughout this period. The moralizing that accompanied early tram accidents was there in full force, as well. Both machines were regularly linked to danger and death, as the electric tram had been in its first years. Thus another reason that tram accidents no longer commanded much attention in the illustrated mass press was that car and plane accidents, thanks to their exotic unfamiliarity, were far more thrilling.

In June 1903, the humor magazine *Liberum Veto* ran an illustration entitled "Death in the Twentieth Century," representing "How the vacationers staying between Poitiers and Paris imagine death after the recent automobile race" (see Fig. 8).[57] The picture, drawn by a regular contributor to the magazine, shows a skeleton in driving goggles and cap at the wheel of a stylized automobile running over people and farm animals, leaving a trail of carnage in its wake. Except for the flocks of scavenging birds flying in for a feast, all of Nature seems to protest the car's intrusion: even the trees along the road appear to wail, humanlike, in shock at the massacre before them. With skulls for headlights, a skeleton driver, and a black cat running for its life in front, the car proclaims itself as the modern incarnation of superstitious death. However macabre it may be, the cartoon is hilarious, from the skeleton's stony grin to the details of flailing fingers, feet, and feathers under the wheels and the pig's posterior in the background. Even the artist's signature looks like roadkill! One sees the knowing condescension of the artist, who gently mocks the vacationers' hyperbolic sentiments. And yet the humorous exaggeration, as in *Djabel*'s dark joke about the tram as a traveling guillotine, conveys a broader fear of the subject it lampoons. From the perspective of people (and animals) caught in its path, the speedy automobile was indeed an instrument of death for the new century.

However original—and witty—*Liberum Veto*'s artist may have been in his depiction of "Death in the Twentieth Century," plenty of other artists across the globe had similar ideas, lending credence to the idea that not just the purported vacationers between Poitiers and Paris associated fast new machines with death. The image of a skeleton driving the fast new machines of the age was a worldwide phenomenon, from Cracow to Paris to Latin America. According to Anton Rosenthal's study of fin-de-siècle Montevideo, "[t]he front page of one Sunday paper [in 1907] featured a ... cartoon entitled 'Macabre Things'" that likewise depicted the Grim Reaper at the controls of a new machine: "[a] trolley driven by a smiling skeleton with large black birds hovering overhead carrying scythes. Alongside and behind the trolley people are lying in the street or caught under the car, screaming, while in front a dog and several people flee. The caption reads, 'Progress is something that appears much like barbarism.'"[58] And Rosenthal has found several other depictions of mechanized Grim Reapers in the Latin American press from this era, including a similar illustration by the Mexican satirist Guadelupe Posada.[59] Thanks to the interurban matrix of words and images from the international press, these ideas were apt to disseminate quickly.

In the summer and autumn of 1911, four illustrations of skeletons and aircraft appeared in the Cracovian popular illustrated press. The first of these, a triptych in *IKC* entitled "Flying Death," featured a skeleton reaching out to grab an airplane soaring through the air. The picture accompanied a report of a French pilot's death and was probably recycled from the French press.[60] A little more than a month later, *Nowiny's* staff artist, TĘCZA, added his interpretation to the genre. "The Flight of Death" shows a skeleton gripping the steering wheel of a plane equipped with menacing scythe blades for propellers (see Fig. 9). Readers of the accompanying article learned that the drawing was influenced by the idea of "a French artist [who] has modernized the image of death."[61] Later images in this vein had moralizing titles such as "For Fame and Fortune" and "Fatal Effects": comments on the bold but foolish victims of the new technology. The second of these pictures shows a plane full of passengers plummeting into a lake, while the Grim Reaper arises from the surface to take his spoils.[62] In all of these illustrations, the new machines were tantamount to an icon of death: the newest tools in the Grim Reaper's scythe shed. The drawings suggest that modern vehicles of transport, for all their allure, merely amounted to a swifter route to death.

"The Automobile and Culture"

In these iconic illustrations, Death could strike the operators of the new technology or its innocent bystanders. The victims in the drawing of the automobile were animals and people on the road; while in the case of aircraft the victims were the pilots and passengers who chose to risk their lives by leaving the earth in such fragile machines.

In automobile accident reports—as in the illustration "Death in the Twentieth Century"—the newspapers generally identified with the victims on the road, not the drivers or passengers. This identification came largely thanks to the way people associated automobiles with the people who could afford them, the aristocracy and wealthy bourgeoisie who, significantly, were not presumed to be the average readers of the popular press. Readers of *Nowiny* in October 1907 learned of an accident on the road from Czyżyny to Cracow in which an automobile belonging to "Mr. Count" ran into a wagon, breaking it apart and seriously injuring several occupants.

Fig. 8—"**Death in the Twentieth Century.**" *Liberum Veto*, June 20, 1903. Note how all living creatures, including the trees, bemoan the coming of the car—except, of course, for the scavenging birds!

The paper and its readers likely had little sympathy for the unnamed nobleman whose car, which was "totally responsible for the accident," was spun around upon impact and simply drove off the other way. Thanks to a combined sense of class-consciousness and fear of the new technology, readers would have more readily identified with one of the victims, Chaim Blumenfrucht, than the unnamed count, regardless of the victims' presumed ethnicities.[63] Earlier that year, a report in "What's the Word in Town?" noted that the late Count Andrzej Potocki, the former viceroy of Galicia assassinated by a Ukrainian nationalist, had been memorialized in the "Galician Automobile Club," of which he had been a member.[64] Clearly this was not the sort of club to which average readers could expect to belong. When, in 1909, wealthy shopkeeper and city councilor Wiktor Suski struck and killed a worker on the streets of Cracow while driving his car, *Nowiny* viciously blamed him for the accident. The paper made much

Fig. 9—"**The Flight of Death.**" *Nowiny*, July 28, 1911.

of the class difference between the driver and the victim, a day laborer who left behind a wife and two young children. It called for stricter laws regarding automobile speed in the city and blasted Mr. Suski, who did not have a driver's license, for "acting like a chauffeur" by driving himself, instead of leaving the responsibility to a trained driver.[65]

In the report of Mr. Suski's accident, as in other articles, the newspaper betrayed another commonly held conception regarding automobiles, namely, that they should be driven by a chauffeur. Cars were still viewed as a means of transportation driven by someone for someone else or as a means of entertainment. Even in 1916, "the art of driving . . . without a chauffeur" was still a new skill, requiring a special handbook.[66] The mental model of the horse and carriage, typically driven by someone other than its privileged passengers, persisted, even in the design of a sleek car featured at the Monte Carlo Auto Show named the "Torpedo," which featured an aerodynamic back and a full roof, "such that the chauffeur is also covered."[67] In a charming feuilleton relating the conversation of a family of four who dreamed of winning the lottery, it made perfect sense for the wife to remind her husband that their imagined automobile would require a chauffeur as well.[68] Unsurprisingly, the newspapers seemed to find it easier to relate to chauffeurs, who were just working-class men doing their job, than they generally did to most automobile owners. A few days after Mr. Suski's tragic accident, when another car struck a five-year-old boy, the paper remarked that it was thanks to the chauffeur's competent handling of the situation that the boy was not killed. In another instance, the chauffeur who maneuvered the flaming car of a visiting Moravian baron onto Cracow's City Meadow and then leapt out was praised for his professionalism in getting the car away from people and buildings.[69] When Princess Lubomirska's automobile frightened the horse pulling the carriage of two Cracovians so badly that it upset the carriage and caused the death of one of the men, *IKC* pointed out that, contrary to popular opinion, the chauffeur of the car had not been driving too fast; rather, "the horse itself was very easily spooked, having had trouble earlier near Market Square."[70] The next day the paper printed a front-page illustration of the accident, milking the story for its full effect, but it refused to blame the chauffeur for the fatality.

If the stereotypical victim of the streetcar had been a child or a woman, the stereotypical victim of the automobile was a "villager" or a peasant. In focusing on villagers the papers underscored the class difference between technologically savvy urbanites and their backward brethren in the countryside. Numerous accident reports involved cars that upset horse carts or struck villagers on the roads that led into the city.[71] Like the tram a few years before, cars seemed regularly to shock and maim people who had trouble comprehending them. "[Our] country will have to get used to sport-automobiles," *Nowości Illustrowane* mused after an accident on a rural road in 1904, "and unfortunately, that acclimation will leave bloody tracks."[72] A compelling cover illustration from 1912 depicted a gaily attired couple, he in a top hat and she with a bouquet of flowers, sitting in the back of their chauffeured automobile, smiling obliviously as a barefoot peasant child was about to be crushed between their rear wheel and fender. Readers of the related article discovered that the setting of the drawing was a country road leading into Lemberg.[73]

The peasant boy in this illustration looked especially vulnerable; not all those threatened by automobiles on country roads were as passive and helpless as the barefoot child, however. Several articles discussed peasants or street urchins who vandalized automobiles, including a case in which some "local peasants" exulted that they had "busted the 'stinkmobile'" (smrodochód, a play on samochód, the Polish term for "automobile") that coursed between Cracow and Myślenice.[74] An accident report in IKC from July 1911 made a special effort to explain that, contrary to rumor, local villagers did not steal from victims or loot the car.[75] Evidently, urbanites perceived that there was enmity between villagers and automobiles.

That same summer, amid numerous reports about automobile accidents on the roads into Cracow, IKC ran an article entitled "The Automobile and Culture," which expressed the conflict of cultures that was occurring as automobiles and villagers increasingly came into contact. The author complained about how badly he was treated in his automobile on the road to Zakopane by the highlanders (górale), who deliberately obstructed his path, dug holes in the road, and refused to move their sheep. He used words like "civilization" and "culture" to describe what the locals lacked in understanding modern technology, and he recommended having priests explain to their parishioners that it was a sin to interfere with an automobile, because they could cause its driver to die or become crippled if they deliberately got in his way.[76]

The article got many replies from "sportsmen" and "the spheres of the people" alike. A summary of the responses printed a few days later stated that there could be "no talk of restraining [car use]," because "automobile traffic will continue to increase day by day." The affected parties, therefore, would have to learn to get along. Automobilists would have to exercise caution and, "above all, tact" in their dealings with villagers, while "the people" needed to develop a better understanding of the technology, which could come about only with an increase of "awareness and culture." The paper recommended that villagers learn to accept automobiles as "'a necessary evil', while thinking of ways to reduce that evil to a minimum." There was much to do to familiarize peasants with the modern machines, the article intoned, more than the pamphlets occasionally dropped by automobilists about how to handle a horse frightened by a car. Perhaps the automobilists could offer "old folks and children" a ride, it continued, "just to help them become familiar with the 'devilish travel' firsthand" or talk with locals about the machines "over a beer" in their pubs in the evenings.[77] Familiarity, the article implied, would do a great deal to resolve the urban/rural divide regarding automobiles. Yet even if the paper's summary showed greater sensitivity toward villagers than the original opinion piece (no patronizing priests here!), it essentially agreed that the villagers' lack of civilization and culture impeded their acceptance of the automobile.

A year after the debate surrounding the automobile and culture, *IKC* launched a tremendous publicity campaign: an automobile journey throughout Galicia. The car was supposed to reach two hundred cities and villages and travel more than five thousand kilometers—"a Galician automotive record"— while promoting the paper and reporting the news of the provinces.[78] The proselytizing goals of the journey were clearly twofold. On one level, at least, the newspaper was practicing what it had preached a year before by bringing the automobile, and with it "awareness and culture," to the countryside. The second goal, which was related to and even more important than the first, was to align the paper with the automobile, as a symbol of modernity and the future. As a promotional tool, *IKC* was confident that the automobile journey would reinforce the paper's status as a symbol of progress.[79] The paper obviously delighted to report meeting a villager outside of Lipnik who embraced the automobile's occupants as his advocates in the larger world. The man was impressed to learn that the car and its riders were from Cracow, but when he found out that they were in the *IKC* automobile, his face lit up and he exclaimed, "Our little Courier!" and invited them to dinner. "So long as you are driving around asking people what they think, I'd really like you to endorse voting reform," he chipped in. "We really need it out here."[80]

Although villagers were the stereotypical enemies of automobiles, the villager outside of Lipnik proved an enthusiastic supporter of the *IKC* automobile because he connected it with progress and a future of increasing empowerment. Obviously, cars could stand for the glorious future, as in illustrations from abroad that showed the wonders of great-city transportation, including a picture of a man stopping his auto on a city street to make a telephone call or a multi-tiered drawing of subways, trams, automobiles, elevated trains, and airplanes in one of the world's megalopolises. "We contemporaries . . . don't have any idea of how much and in what direction great-city travel will grow in the near future," gushed the commentary to the second picture. "Just twenty years ago only humble horse-drawn trams enlivened the streets of big cities; today, showy electric trams and automobiles cruise along the streets while underground trains roar and resound below in the black, mysterious distance."[81]

Yet for all the rhapsodizing about the wonders of great-city transportation, other reports in *IKC* from this period were not so optimistic. An article entitled "A Terrible Statistic," which detailed the horrific number of pedestrians struck by automobiles, electric trams, and horse-drawn vehicles in Paris, said that in the course of two months, some 441 people had been run over, coming to an average of 12 victims a day. Of these, more than half had fallen under the wheels of automobiles.[82] *IKC*'s automobile tour of Galicia demonstrated its sense that cars were a good way to advertise the paper's commitment to progress and modernity. But the paper, like the public that bought it, could not abandon entirely the discourse of danger associated with the new technology.

"Kings of the Air"

Airplanes, too, were multivalent symbols of modernity. They were astonishing proof of the new century's superlative achievements, but they were also seen as instruments of death. In addition to the examples of skeletons and aircraft, there were numerous articles and images related to pilots who lost their lives in airplane crashes. The death of Patricia Quimby, an early female aviator whose successes had appeared previously in the Cracovian popular press, attracted special attention.[83] Not only did the press exploit the danger that planes caused their pilots and passengers, it also pointed out the threat they posed for innocents who happened to get in their way.[84] On several occasions, consumers of the popular press saw illustrations from other European newspapers of airplanes crashing into bystanders. One popular image depicted a plane plummeting into the upstairs window of a house where two women were drinking tea! Another dramatic illustration with commentary showed an airplane striking a female cyclist in the back. Thankfully, the rotor was stopped in the illustration, so viewers were not treated to an image of splattering blood and flesh.[85] A particularly gruesome case, reminiscent of the villagers who opposed the "stinkmobiles" on their roads, involved an old farmer and his wife who stubbornly refused to leave their field, despite efforts to move them from the potential path of an airplane. When the plane began to have difficulty it flew low over their field, hitting the pair, who were too slow to run away, slicing off the woman's head and "cutting the man so badly that he died on the spot." According to the report, the pilot burst into tears. The airplane was lightly damaged.[86]

In these accidents, the victims had been unintentional casualties of unruly machines, but readers of the popular illustrated press were fully aware of the airplane's potential as a weapon of war. As early as 1911, *Nowiny* and *IKC* ran cover illustrations of airplanes used for military purposes in the Italian-Turkish War.[87] Less than a year later, consumers of the popular press could read about practice flights of military aircraft on Cracow's City

Meadow, under the direction of Lieutenant Stanisław Miller, "a Cracovian well known for his participation in the Berlin-Vienna flight competition." The paper warned the public to follow the commands of soldiers directing them away from dangerous spots where the planes needed to land. (Readers who remembered the story of the old farmer couple killed by a landing plane—printed in Nowiny just ten days before—must have had added incentive to obey the officers' commands!)[88] As a fortress city for the Austrian army, Cracow was frequently the site of aerial exercises. While many of these were seen largely as entertainment and spectacle before the war began, the sight of Austrian and Russian planes overhead during the first months of the war must have been unsettling for Cracovians.[89] After all, what safety could their fabled fortifications provide in the face of an aerial attack? As it turned out, the Russian planes were only spying on Austrian military formations, but the possibility of aerial attack remained. A propagandistic image from the beginning of the war of a German airplane dropping an ultimatum for surrender while soaring over the Eiffel Tower suggested that even Paris was susceptible to an attack from the air.[90]

In 1908, well before the actual use of aircraft for military purposes, Nowiny published an installment novel by its editor Ludwik Szczepański about an aeronautical invention that precipitated a pan-European conflict. "King of the Air," which was published in the same year as H. G. Wells's "War in the Air," was set in the near future date of 1911 and told the story of an "aeromobile" created by Jan Silnicki, a Polish engineer from Poznań.[91] Despite Silnicki's peaceful intentions for his invention, the existing geopolitical situation meant that his aeromobile quickly became the cause of instability and war because it was viewed as a weapon of disproportionate power for any country able to manufacture it. In the conclusion of Szczepański's story, which proved less apocalyptic and more realistically prophetic than Wells's grand morality tale, British knowledge of the Germans' possession of Silnicki's plans led to a preemptive naval attack, resulting in German defeat, an economic downspin, and an eventual continental war "that reshaped the map of Central Europe."[92]

The story begins with the idealistic Silnicki flying Wolność (Freedom), his appropriately named aeromobile, triumphantly over Berlin. Pressed as to whether his invention would ever serve military purposes, the good Polish engineer avers that it would only serve cultural not military aims, rhapsodizing about how in the air "borders wouldn't matter, military secrets wouldn't be secret anymore," and one would just "be a free citizen of the world."[93] But the German army is far too interested in the invention, and quickly the young man is compelled to discuss his invention with Kaiser

Wilhelm himself. In delightful moments for Polish readers, Silnicki stands up to the emperor, asserting that he is not a loyal subject of the empire and that he will not sell out, Prussian might notwithstanding. Meanwhile, an "energetic, 'clean-shaven'" American offers to buy the machine and the rights to its future production.[94] Before any deal can materialize, however, Silnicki is arrested as he leaves the opera with his fiancée, Anna. Anna and Silnicki's loyal sidekick Kruszek escape to Paris in the aeromobile just as the German authorities move in to confiscate it. Silnicki's arrest and the pair's brave escape create an international sensation; newspapers brim with stories about the landing in Paris and the two pilots become world celebrities. But when the Germans refuse to release Silnicki, Kruszek and Anna decide to take to the air again to press for his freedom.

They fly over Berlin and drop an ultimatum, threatening to bomb a dreadnought docked at Kiel if Silnicki is not immediately released. Their request unmet, they proceed to sink an unmanned vessel in the harbor but are struck by shrapnel fired from below. Astonishingly, they drift on partial power from northern Germany in a long southeasterly path, conveniently passing over Cracow at dawn and crashing in the author's—and much of Cracow's—beloved Tatra Mountains near Zakopane. (Faithful readers knew that Szczepański had just returned from holiday in Zakopane.) They survive, assisted by a highlander, and meet up with the recently released Silnicki for a London wedding and a trip to America, where Silnicki and his American investor found "The Worlds Aviatic Company" [sic]. The epilogue informed readers that Szczepański's next crowd-pleaser, "The Siege of Cracow," would describe the pan-European conflict caused by Silnicki's machine. As if to reassure women readers, the epilogue also noted that the account would be "softened by a love story that takes place during the joint attack of the Prussians and Russians" on the city.[95]

However patronizing and ridiculous parts of Szczepański's story may seem today, "King of the Air" wonderfully depicts the competing senses of fear and wonder regarding the infant field of aviation. While it is clear that the aeromobile would prove the cause of war, the potential violence of the airplane in the story is kept to a minimum, left mainly to an epilogue of dark predictions that nonetheless allowed the possibility of a resurrected Poland. Unlike Wells's story, which anticipates the horrors of the Second World War in its graphic depiction of aerial bombardment of cities, Szczepański's story describes only the destruction of an unmanned dreadnought and the downing of a Zeppelin over Berlin. There was much to render aviation attractive. Some of Szczepański's descriptions of flying are absolutely delightful and imaginative, especially when Kruszek and Anna enjoy French bread, pâté, and wine while drifting their way across Germany, or when they escape Berlin, seeing it for the first time from the air, flattened into its numerous parts: "[like] a monstrous spider, extending its iron-rail tentacles in all directions, mottled by red factories belching black wreaths of smoke."[96] Discussions of aviation history in the story dovetailed with articles that continued to appear in the paper about the new technology, including several reports on the Wright brothers' most recent successes.[97]

The novella masterfully captured the world of international sensations that its author knew so well, commenting on the hastily compiled, erroneous reports in German newspapers hungry for information about the whereabouts of the aeromobile, or the "interview"—the English word was used—and Kodak snapshots Anna and Kruszek were subjected to upon arrival in Paris.[98] The airplane itself, of course, was a sensation *par excellence*, and Szczepański's choice to write about it was a deliberate effort to capitalize on public fascination with the new technology. Like *IKC*'s eventual auto tour of Galicia, "King of the Air" was a calculated attempt to underscore *Nowiny*'s close relationship to novelty, modernity, and the future.

Numerous articles and images made the most of the airplane's novelty. Races that pitted automobiles against airplanes were recurrent stories from abroad. Readers also had the opportunity to read about the first childbirth in an airplane, which raised the important question of how to determine place of birth.[99] Cracovian journalists thrilled to print that the proposed Paris–Peking flight in 1912 would touch down in Cracow en route, but by then Cracovians had already witnessed an airplane in their city.[100] In 1910 *Nowiny* made a big deal of the first airplane built in Cracow, dragging the story on for several days before finally revealing the pair of Czechs who were constructing the plane in a Cracovian auto garage.[101] And a Blériot-type plane, flown by a man named Otto Hieronymus in numerous Habsburg cities including Cracow, Prague, and Lemberg, was a big story for much of April and May of that year, until the engineer's successful Cracovian flight (after several weather-related and mechanical failures) on May 22, 1910.[102] Stanisław Broniewski recalled that the Blériot plane flew up some twenty or so meters into the air and then awkwardly landed, "like a drunken duck. Observers uniformly pronounced: 'Such a toy as this, sir, has no future. . . . Zepplins, good sir, now those are something worthwhile, but such a jumping flying machine is only good for children.'"[103] Szczepański's novel "King of the Air" went on sale in book form that spring, amid several articles about Polish and Galician involvement in aviation, creating a groundswell of popular interest in airplanes. For all their inherent danger, airplanes had tremendous appeal.

CONCLUSION

Ultimately, technological danger and death did not matter most in the popular press, however titillating the topic may have been. In the case of the electric tram, the discourse allowed for sensationalist pictures and attracted readers, but the less flashy and much more ubiquitous complaints about management meant more in the end. The majority of reports about the trams indicated a willingness to live with the potentially dangerous technology, because its benefits far outweighed its costs. After 1903 popular newspapers did not sensationalize trolley accidents because the accidents were no longer so shocking. As the technologies became necessities, complaints in the popular press called for their rational, effective use. Nationalist impulses affected the way the Belgian company was treated in the press, but the city attracted negative attention as well when it failed to live up to the demands of the average urbanite—who was also the average reader of the popular press. When one considers that the papers complained about the tram in the same ways they lambasted the failures of city water or sanitation, it becomes clear that the functionality of the machines, not the nationality of those who owned them, mattered most.

The discourse of danger and death continued in articles and illustrations about automobiles and airplanes, but even then, the popular press proved a willing supporter of the new technologies. Unlike with the electric tram, which many ordinary readers rode daily, the association of danger and death generally remained with the exotic automobile and airplane. After all, readers could not be expected to share passengers' perspectives because only the privileged could afford to ride in the new machines. Significantly, the moralizing that accompanied accident reports often emphasized the social distance between owners and victims. As with the tram, the standard victim of the automobile was naïve, yet stubbornly foolish, regarding the new technology. Only "an increase of awareness and culture," the papers suggested, could save villagers from more run-ins with automobiles.

But an increase in "culture" was precisely what the papers offered their readers, safely distancing them from the simpletons who refused to adapt to the modern world. Cracow's mass circulation illustrated press supported the new technologies in ways that ordinary political newspapers did not. *IKC* emphasized its use of automobiles to deliver its newspapers and organized an automobile tour of Galicia to rally support for the paper. Articles on aviation, including Szczepański's innovative installment novel in 1908, abounded in the popular press. Thus even with these two implements of "foreign" technology, which average readers could only view from a distance (if at all), the discourse of danger and death was not what mattered most. The attractions of the machines assured that they would receive ample coverage, whether they crashed or not. Depictions of automobiles and airplanes helped educate readers about the new technologies, breeding familiarity and "culture."

Both *Nowiny* and *IKC* delighted in proving the city's connection to the newest technologies of the age. Thanks to the interurban matrix, readers were aware of the latest developments from abroad, while local coverage of automobile accidents and airplane flights from the City Meadow reinforced the city's relationship to the new technologies. Cracow got its first electric trams the same year as London and saw its first manned flight during the same spring as Prague and Lemberg. This is not blithely to equate cities: London already had an underground rail system by 1901 and plenty of "lesser" cities had electric trams long before Cracow, while some larger cities such as Warsaw, for example, got electric trams later (1907). The point remains that Cracow participated more or less simultaneously in this general period of rapid technological development and disperson. Popular illustrated newspapers stimulated and in turn reflected the nodes of popular discussion regarding the new machines of the twentieth century, contributing to modern sensibilities among their readers. Cracovian readers, like readers abroad, viewed the machines with a mixture of fear and rapt fascination. If Wyspiański's difficult drama represented a new modernist voice in Polish theater, the introduction of the electric streetcar (and later automobiles and airplanes) in the city represented dramatic proof of Cracow's modernity on the streets and in the air. Though not immediately well understood, both kinds of innovations were well received. And the popular illustrated press was a major vehicle in assuring their generally favorable reception.

CHAPTER 6

"BIG-CITY MUCK"

Images of the "Great City" in the "Gutter Press"

Serious, esteemed Cracow, of high morality according to
police statistics provided by us yesterday, hides within
itself . . . so much filth, that one could without hesitation
call it a great city.

—*Nowiny*, January 8, 1908

Despite the popular press's endorsement of Cracow's development into
Greater Cracow and its promotion of new technology such as electric
streetcars and automobiles, there was one perspective on modern urban
life that consistently drew negative attention in the pages of *Nowiny* and
IKC. The association of the "great city" with filth and crime—a concept that
had a storied history in nineteenth-century European thought—was readily exploited in the Cracovian popular illustrated press. Numerous stories,
headlines, and comments in the papers demonstrate that for writers and
readers the expression carried a number of negative connotations. Chief
among these was the notion that the big city was a place of corruption and
filth, capable of poisoning and ruining its inhabitants. As in discussions of
the typical victims of technology, comments on great-city filthiness also
tended to focus on the city's presumably weakest denizens: women, children, and the poor. But it was not enough to locate those who were most
susceptible, for great-city filthiness was not limited to feminine or youthful
bodies—even if that was where it could be most cogently observed. Thanks
to increased understanding of the mechanisms of infection and the concurrent obsession with hygiene, bourgeois writers and readers sought to
control and isolate the sources of literal and moral contagion in the city

before they spread to the rest of the body politic. The mass circulation press helped both define the limits of this discourse and also negotiate the range of responses and solutions to it.

While Cracow's popular press betrayed fears of "great-city filth" (*wielkomiejski brud*) and crime, articles about the actual state of sanitation and crime in Cracow consistently called for the city magistrate and the police to control the problems effectively—and complained bitterly when they did not. Just as articles with urbane complaints about inefficient trams in the city accompanied and ultimately supplanted the sensationalist discourse of danger and death, specific calls for improved city sanitation and effective policing ran alongside and ultimately outnumbered more sensationalistic articles about "great-city filth." Articles that focused on local problems with sanitation and policing indicate that, despite fears of great-city filthiness and crime, Cracovians endorsed modern, big-city solutions to their problems, rather than simply bemoaning the dangers of the modern world. While the great city abroad stood for depravity and filthiness, it was also a model for the solutions to these problems. As Cracow became a big city, its police and magistrate were expected to meet their tasks of protecting the populace by controlling urban filth.

ELITE ATTITUDES TOWARD THE "GREAT CITY"

In the nineteenth century, the term "great city" (*Großstadt, wielkie miasto*) generally meant a city of more than 100,000 inhabitants—a category that, due to the unprecedented urbanization of the period, mushroomed from 23 European cities at the beginning of the century to 143 by its end.[1] Cracow's population in 1900 of 91,323 put the city quite close to this group. Even without the creation of Greater Cracow in 1910, the city would have surpassed the 100,000 mark by that time. As the formerly provincial Cracow became a "great city," its citizens looked to other great cities of the age for models of big-city life, following a pattern of metropolitan emulation already common in Europe. In 1854, the conservative Bavarian journalist Wilhelm Heinrich Riehl had observed, "In the eighteenth century, every German residential city was expected to be a Versailles; now each one is supposed to become like Paris and London. Even the smallest city now desires at the very least to *impersonate* a big city, just as every citizen wants to play the part of an aristocratic gentleman."[2] By the last third of the nineteenth century, central and southeast European cities from Cracow to Cetinje sought to emulate London and especially Paris in their patterns of urbanization.[3] In nineteenth-century Bucharest, the locals joked that the distance between their city and

Paris was "about three centuries."[4] Yet rapid modernization in the last third of the century changed that. The city deliberately emulated Paris, which after all was the capital of the quintessential Latin-speaking nation. Early in the twentieth century, a visiting Englishwoman saw Bucharest as "the Paris of the East," approvingly noting its wide boulevards "after the French style," restaurants "run on French lines," women wearing "the latest Paris fashions," and food "directly from Paris."[5] Cracow's Western models, meanwhile, included Vienna, Paris, London, and Berlin. On the one hand, Cracovians sought to bring themselves to a "European" standard by replicating the urban attitudes and amenities of great cities abroad. Yet on the other hand, one of the most common representations of the "great city" in Cracow's press was the conception of it as the locus of disease and immorality.

The notion of the "great city" as a "seedplot" of crime and vice was prevalent in early nineteenth-century London and Paris. Middle-class commentators in London generally assumed, for example, that youth on the streets would be corrupted by the wickedness that surrounded them.[6] During the era in which Pasteur discovered the role of micro-organisms in causing disease, the language of great-city filthiness increasingly relied upon metaphors of contagion and infection. In 1843 Robert Vaughan, an Englishman who praised the great city as a center of association where intelligence was bound to increase, nonetheless admitted that there was also greater "hazard for infection" in big cities. "Nowhere else," he wrote, "does man acquire such expertness in iniquity, and nowhere else has evil so large a space over which to diffuse its pestilential influence."[7] Much more critical than the liberal Vaughan was his conservative contemporary, Riehl, who roundly upbraided large cities for obliterating national sentiment, reducing social differences to naked categories of rich and poor, and corrupting their inhabitants. Riehl claimed that Europe was "becoming sick as a result of the monstrosity of its big cities."[8] As European and especially central European cities grew exponentially in the last third of the nineteenth century, writers and artists increasingly reacted to the urbanization of their societies by calling upon the discourse of great-city filthiness and disease.

The attitudes of nineteenth- and early twentieth-century Polish writers toward big cities ranged from antipathy to ambivalence, often mirroring, whether intentionally or not, the general European critique of modern urban existence. Jerzy Jedlicki argues that despite the fact that anti-urbanism is seen as a mainstay of Polish and Slavic thought generally, Polish attitudes toward the great city were nearly identical to those penned in western Europe. In critiquing modern urbanism, Polish intellectuals were merely part of the same European tradition.[9] Wojciech Gutkowski writes that Young Poland

artists and writers tended to represent the city in "'archtypical' architec-
tonic motifs, above all [in] the universal, eternal opposition: the holy city
(Jerusalem)—the city of the damned (Babylon)."[10] Generally, Polish writers
preferred the charms of the countryside to the grime of the big city, though
this was beginning to change by the end of the century. Historically the
Polish elite was limited to the landed gentry who, though they may have had
apartments in the city, were socially conditioned to pine for the tranquility
of their country manor houses. In the middle of the nineteenth century, the
Polish émigré Stefan Witwicki wrote from Paris that Polishness (*polskość*)
was to be found in the "village home" (*wiejski dom*) and not in the city.[11]
Until the nineteenth century, urban dwellers in many Polish-speaking areas
were predominately Jewish (or to a lesser extent German, Armenian, or
Greek).[12] The Polish gentry eschewed trade, and as such, the Polish idiom
remained idyllic rather than urbane in its perspective.

Adam Mickiewicz's masterpiece *Pan Tadeusz* (1834), for example, glorifies
the fields and boreal woods of his Lithuanian fatherland. In his melancholy
epilogue (published posthumously), Mickiewicz (1798–1855) contrasts the
noisy streets of Paris, where he lived in exile, to the countryside of his youth:
"the lands of childhood," where flowers, meadows, linden trees, "and every
little rivulet and stone [were] known."[13] From his city apartment he clings to
the moment when "evening greys," and he can

> sit with a few friends and lock the door,
> And by the fireside shut out Europe's roar,
> Escape in thought to happier time and tide,
> And muse and dream of [his] own countryside.[14]

While Mickiewicz's nostalgic idyll of childhood may not have been explicitly
anti-urban, it certainly favored the countryside over the distractions and cold
impersonality of the big city. Only at night, when the city's noises could be
"shut out" and forgotten in the company of friends around a crackling fire,
could the poet find happiness in his recollection of rural Poland.

Mickiewicz's desire to "shut out Europe's roar" in favor of a rural ideal
sits in marked contrast to the attitude of those Cracovians and suburbanites
who saw in the creation of Greater Cracow the desired "Europeanization"
of their city a little more than half a century later.[15] This attitudinal shift
came in part from the marked urbanization of Polish society in the late
nineteenth century and in part from the failed revolutions of that century
and the more conciliatory, practical ideologies that arose from those expe-
riences. Polish positivism, which was adapted from the ideas of Auguste

Comte and espoused the maxim of "small-scale work," called for the modernization of Polish society through improved farming, growth of industry, and development of cities.[16] The democrats in Cracow actively endorsed Galicia's modernization and urbanization, challenging the conservatism of the Stańczyk faction (conciliatory toward the Austrian authorities but not necessarily in favor of modernization), eventually defeating it during the first decade of the twentieth century. Juliusz Leo's switch from the conservatives to the democrats was among the most important signals of this change. Significantly, the stronghold of the liberal democrats was in the cities and larger towns of Galicia, especially Cracow.

It is intriguing that Cracovian fiction of the day, from Wyspiański's *Wesele* (1901) to Konstanty Krumłowski's *Królowa Przedmieścia* (Queen of the Suburb, 1898) to Gruszecki's *Cygarniczka* (1906) all reached to the suburban villages. The protagonist of *Wesele*, like the loquacious intellectual on whom he was based (and the playwright himself), married a peasant girl from the village of Bronowice, northwest of the city. *Królowa Przedmieścia* is about a suburban woman, while *Cygarniczka* tells the story of a fisherman's daughter from Półwsie Zwierzynieckie who, rather than becoming a servant like her girlfriends, goes to work in the tobacco factory. *Cygarniczka* seems most willing to accept modern urban life, but of course it is also an exposé of the difficult, if occasionally empowering, experience of factory labor. Wyspiański and his contemporaries, Włodzimierz Tetmajer and Lucjan Rydel, all of whom married peasant women from Bronowice, seemed concerned more with bridging the gap between city and countryside for national and personal reasons than with embracing a modern urban existence. Cracovian literature and its literary figures at the beginning of the twentieth century seem to have remained somewhat ambivalent about modern urban life.

IMAGES OF THE "GREAT CITY" IN THE CRACOVIAN POPULAR PRESS

Discomfort with the big city was not limited to artists and writers. In fact, reading newspaper articles in which reference to the "great city" appears, one gets the sense that, because of a tendency to associate big cities with crime and squalor, many Cracovians did not wish to think of their city as a "wielkie miasto," akin to Warsaw, Vienna, Berlin, or more remotely, Paris and London. The fact that most of the news they read in their paper regarding those cities was generally sensationalist must have helped in forming this perception. Readers of the popular press regularly saw pictures of urban depravity, poverty, violence, or spectacle reprinted from the pages of the foreign press, from Parisian hooligans with studded wristbands and knives to a two-part picture of a ruined English gentleman and his faithful hound scrounging for scraps in the gutter.[17] Of course, articles about big cities abroad did not always paint the metropolis in such garish tones and there was much that rendered the great city attractive, if not seductive. But the imperative to focus on its immorality persisted.

"Night Life in Big Cities"—Decadent Delights

Big cities at night were at once morally suspect and alluring, a challenge to notions of propriety and a source of guilty pleasure. "An Evening in Paris," published in 1908, began with the delights of *flânerie* on the Parisian boulevards, where "waves of strollers" walking past the Café de la Paix between five and seven o'clock provided an ever-changing spectacle of humanity. Later the lights of the city sparkled like "diamonds" and the multiple entertainments of the theater represented a continuation of the joys of big-city spectatorship.[18] An article in this vein from 1912 claimed, "Like the Athenians of antiquity, the Parisians know how to live." After a long workday, the reporter asserted, they take to the streets and boulevards "in waves, like ants, filling the cafés, concert halls [and] theaters," bringing with them an attitude as clear and "bubbly as [their] champagne." Yet there was certainly a sense that, effervescence aside, the joys of the big city were at their core decadent and depraved. The article concluded:

> Silent and dark during the day, the "establissement de nuit" famous the world over, suddenly glistens under millions of colorful lights, jaunty music thunders out with bacchanalian tumult, matched outside by the roar of thousands of automobiles driving in a crazy rush all over the humongous city. The monstrous, red sails of the "Moulin Rouge" turn slowly over the frenzied crowd and you could say that here—audaciously, openly, insolently—Satan celebrates his triumph.[19]

A report in *IKC* a year later, "Night Life in Big Cities: How Does Paris Amuse Itself?" confirmed the depravity of Parisian nightlife, commenting on the "craze of lascivious orgies and . . . licentiousness" that befell "the capital on the Seine" at night. In the cabarets, "Parisians and foreigners applaud the sensual dances of half-naked virgins, reveling in the disgrace of corruption and demoralization." After this moralizing, melodramatic introduction the correspondent then described his own experience in "Heaven," a Parisian nightclub, where naked young women danced at the gates of heaven, and St. Peter, rather than holding keys, held a pair of scissors. As part of the act an eighteen-year-old young man was told that to get into heaven he must undergo an operation that would make him suitable. The lights go out and the crowd hears a snip, as the boy becomes a eunuch.[20] The nightclub's sacrilegious reconfiguration of heaven as a place full of seductresses and emasculated boys, like the report from a year before that described Satan's triumph over the city, clearly underscored the big city's brazen assault on Christian morality.

"Night Life in Big Cities" sparked a number of similar stories in the following months, including reports from New York, London, Vienna, Berlin, and an unnamed city in Australia—where nightlife was actually so dead that a visiting Ignacy Paderewski could not get a bite to eat after his concert.[21] In December 1913, a feuilleton from a correspondent in Berlin depicted the phoniness and vulgarity of big-city life, as illustrated by a jewelry store on Friedrichstrasse, whose electric lights gave a false impression of the luster of its wares and a cabaret where so-called "*artists*" blatantly revealed their most "*secret places to satisfy the big-city masses.*"[22] The reporter concluded that the "foreign newcomer feels encompassed by fear and aversion" when faced with the "primeval roar of animalism" witnessed in big-city Berlin. Of course, he willingly attended the cabaret there, and he could only assume that the majority of his readers would react to his report with a similar mixture of delight and disgust. Like the report from Paris a few months before that condemned the degeneracy of Parisian nightlife while at the same time gleefully reporting its salacious details, this report contained the impulse to condemn *and* enjoy the great city at night.

Reports of the city at night were part of a long tradition of urban journalism that had its beginnings in the first gaslit metropolis, London, in the middle of the nineteenth century. Thanks to "intrepid" nocturnal explorers (including Charles Dickens), who ventured into the chiaroscuro of gaslight and shadow of nighttime London, bourgeois readers comfortably ensconced at home could envision the otherworldly aspect their city took on after dusk.[23] Gaslight brought unprecedented levels of visibility to the city but, unlike electric light later, retained something of the mystery of primeval night because of its flickering flame.[24] In these reports the city at night was not the same as the city by day. In the glare of the gas, the metropolis seemed strange, foreign, and bizarre. Stories about the city at night generally ended at dawn, when the city began to take on its more familiar, reassuring characteristics. Having taken their readers through the netherworld of the city at night, the reporters brought them safely back to the quotidian shores of the metropolis by day.[25]

Despite the fact that the bacchanalian scenes *IKC*'s correspondents described in Paris, Berlin, and other large cities were usually bathed in the glow of electric lights, the narrative structure of their reports also clearly conveys the sense that the city was much stranger—and more animalistic and vulgar—at night than during the day. "By the light of day all manner of wonders occur [in Paris] that are hard to believe. Oh, but what must happen in this center of laxity when the 'darkness of night falls[!]'" one piece proclaimed.[26] Just as in the archetypal stories of the city at night from London many decades before, these reports posited the nocturnal city as a place of mystery and danger. And like those stories at least one Cracovian example, "Night Life in Big Cities," also ended with the reassertion of the quotidian. After the wild show at "Heaven," the reporter and his artist friends went out at dawn and saw strong men loading fruit stands along the river. They bought a cheap breakfast and watched as city life rolled on around them.[27] In ending his narrative with the mundane details of daytime Paris, the correspondent reinforced his claim that the city was more debauched and depraved at night, while at the same time demonstrating that the great city defied simple categorizations. It contained both the irrational hedonism of revelers by night and the rational behavior of workers by day. Yet the city never ceased being a source of spectacle for middle-class flâneurs like the correspondent and his friends. Even in the certainty of daytime, there was still something to sit and watch.

Like the articles from London half a century before, this article gave its readers the disturbing details they desired to see without personally exposing them to any danger. In using this narrative structure, the authors of stories like this one were probably not deliberately following precedent; rather, both sets of writers implicitly recognized the desire of middle-class metropolitan readers to experience the city vicariously by focusing on its moral danger. Of course, a significant difference between the tales of London by gaslight and *IKC*'s series on great cities at night was the relationship of the audience to the city under question. In the former case, the average reader was also a citizen of the city described, whereas in the latter instance, the readers could not be expected to identify directly with the daytime city firsthand.[28] The quays of the Seine were as unfamiliar to them as the windmill flag of the Moulin Rouge. In this respect, big cities abroad were even less a source of danger than a source of delight. Twice removed from the city under discussion, Cracovian readers could safely enjoy (and deplore) the immorality of nightlife abroad.

Given the metropolitan culture of the time, big cities were always spectacular, sensationalized spaces, whether by day or at night. The focus on the city at night, however, served to reinforce the big city's degeneracy. In the uncertainty of night, when the natural and the artificial promiscuously crossed paths, the moral dimensions of big cities seemed most clear. The popular press of this period pictured great cities at night as centers of riotous iniquity, seductive and depraved.

Great-City Crime

If the great city at night was morally dangerous, news of atrocious crimes from abroad demonstrated that great cities were also physically danger-ous. Reports of bizarre murders from London, Berlin, and Budapest, for example, were shocking proof of great-city depravity and crime.[29] In these articles, serial murderers were incriminated because the remains of their victims were found in the city. In the case of Albert Crossmann, a habitual wife-killer from London whose story was related in *Nowiny* in April 1904, the stench of a corpse from his home finally gave him away. According to *IKC* articles, a murderer from Berlin, a 30-year-old cook, had scattered his boy lover's body parts, wrapped in green paper, throughout the city, while Jan Rumpf, a criminally insane murderer in Budapest, had ridden around town in a tram with a packet containing parts of his young victim's body, leaving a bloodstain on the seat of the tram. In these reports, strange men unable to control their degenerate lusts had preyed upon the weak—women and children—in the dark corners of the great city. Emboldened by the ano-nymity of the big-city crowd, two of the men had even wandered throughout the city with the body parts of their victims. Appalled (and enthralled) by such criminal acts, the translator of the Crossmann story could not refrain from a moralizing comment of his own: "And such things take place at the beginning of the twentieth century in the great capital of this civilized coun-try."[30] Despite the British reputation for civilization and advancement, the remark implied, in Britain's sprawling capital city, reprehensible criminals could perpetrate their heinous crimes virtually undetected. All three stories underscored the sense that the relative anonymity of the big city was the ideal environment for horrific crimes.[31]

Of course, spectacular crime that was "homegrown" got even more press space in *Nowiny* and *IKC*. As with other boulevard papers, both publications had a feeding frenzy whenever a shocking murder or court case occurred in town. In these instances, Cracow's "great city" status could be a derogatory marker, indicating its depravity and immorality. For example, in 1904 two young men who attempted to murder an entire family, including a ten-month-old infant, were described as "rather ordinary types in great cities, under-educated and misled." *Nowiny*'s introduction of the two criminals indicated that they had "taken in theories from here and there" and, having joined the socialists, "lost their faith in God." "Misunderstanding the true principles of socialism," they lost their sense of "respect for others' property" and then, having committed a few crimes, they decided to try a murder-robbery, to see if they could do something really big.[32] The story of a poor family from Dębniki who lost their apartment and, after living on the streets of Cracow, one by one ended up in jail was portrayed as "a sad illustration of big-city poverty [*wielkomiejska nędza*]."[33] The chronicle report of a husband who murdered his wife in the Greater Cracovian suburb of Łobzów in 1911 likewise alluded to great-city poverty and its connection to crime: "And once again, a tragedy of the sort that abounds in great-city chronicles," the article began. "A cramped, oppressive apartment, large family, extreme poverty [and] alcohol [was the backdrop for] yesterday's horrible incident."[34] In these instances, Cracow was like the big cities whose newspapers the editors daily scoured, a place where people behaved differently, compelled by frightening, larger forces and ideas they did not understand. At least temporarily, Cracow's conditions matched those of the other "great cities" readers and editors alike daily observed in the press.

Ordinary Cracovians seemed to associate large cities with terrible crime, generally doubting that Cracow had enough crime to be considered a "great city." They were not above blaming fellow Poles from the big city of Warsaw for crimes in their neighborhoods, however. This is apparent in the intriguingly titled piece "Bandit in Skirts," which told the story of a woman who left her servant girl at home to look after the house only to find it completely ransacked upon her return, with all of her valuables missing. The girl's explanation to her mistress included a "'very tall' young man" who forced her to tell him where the valuables were. When the neighbors heard about the crime, word quickly spread that "only Warsaw bandits could have done this."[35] Of course, the irony, given the title's clue, is the fact that the maid herself wreaked so much destruction. Beyond the potential issues of class hatred, gender typing or, at the least, simple personal animosity remains the intriguing fact that the neighbors could not—or did not want to—think of their fellow citizens in this way. Fellow Poles, Warsaw bandits, could have perpetrated the crime, but its enormity precluded the notion that anyone from Cracow could have been responsible. The neighbors' incredulity suggests that such behavior was conceivable in a big place like Warsaw, but not in their own neighborhood—a sentiment betrayed in other crime reports, as well.

Indeed, whether by word of mouth or by reading the sensationalist press, or more likely because of a combination of both, the explanation of Warsaw bandits became a stock response. For example, several articles under the title "Banditry in Warsaw" in May 1906 may have helped in forming this impression.[36] Several years later, *Nowiny* reported a mysterious robbery in which a 68-year-old jeweler was attacked inside his closed shop by an assailant who entered the store from an interior hallway, just after the jeweler opened the door. Despite the criminal's apparent knowledge of the locale, the paper nonetheless included testimony that indirectly linked an outsider to the crime. The article also mentioned how rumors had begun to fly throughout the city that a bandit "from beyond the cordon" (i.e., from Russian Poland) must have committed the crime.[37] It was easier to believe that Varsovian bandits were to blame than fellow Cracovians. Such observations underscore Cracovians' reluctance to acknowledge that they, too, lived in a big city where such crimes were possible.

"Great-City Muck"

Bourgeois observers throughout Europe were preoccupied with the filthiness and squalor of the modern city, particularly in its connection to youthful and feminine bodies. Precisely as modern sewage systems were putting filth out of sight by directing it into subterranean channels, filthiness—symbolic and real—became a public obsession. Big cities experiencing rapid urbanization were dirty, grimy places, especially in the ramshackle slums of the poor. Bourgeois observers projected this filthiness onto the bodies of the working poor, tautologically equating the apparent deviance of their behavior with the apparent squalor in which they lived.[38] They feared that the immorality of the poor would spread, like the cholera outbreaks they were just learning to control, to other populations of the city. Not surprisingly, hygiene movements captured the attention of reformers and politicians alike. Perhaps most cogently, this preoccupation with filthiness and contagion was used to justify the regulation of prostitution, as prostitutes and other working-class women were subjected to inspection in London and other large cities.[39]

As in other European cities, commentary on urban filthiness and squalor in Cracow was not limited to muck on the streets; the dark, dirty places where criminals and the poor lived proved excellent fodder for Cracow's "gutter press" as well. In its first year, *Nowiny* featured a series called "Secrets of Cracow" about the darker, stranger side of the city, including installments on "Brother Albert's Homeless Shelter," "Dog Catchers," "Cracow's Holes and Dens," and, in the Christmas issue, "Vagabonds"—printed a few pages after another fine article for holiday reading about venereal disease among youth![40] "Cracow's Holes and Dens" deliberately invoked London and Paris to introduce the hangouts of the city's misfits, remarking, "Cracow is not really

London or Paris, but terrible poverty here in this little Cracow gives rise, as in great centers of population, to holes and dens." This statement, hyperbolic and humbling at the same time, suggests that while Cracow could not compare to the archetypical great cities of London and Paris in size, its poverty was bad enough to give it some "great city" characteristics.[41] In 1907 the paper featured a series of feuilletons about the squalor and poverty in which its poorest citizens lived, entitled "How They Live"—a title strangely reminiscent of Jacob Riis's famous exploration of New York City tenements from sixteen years before, "How the Other Half Lives."[42] The efforts of the police to control the moral health of the city by periodically arresting registered prostitutes who failed to keep their medical check-up appointments were regularly reported in "What's the Word in Town?" Segments about "police round-ups" and "sanitary round-ups" (obławy sanitarne) detailed how many women of "low conduct" were sent to the hospital after the previous night's raid.[43]

The rhetoric of contagion was not limited to controlling venereal disease alone. One article jokingly characterized Cracow's problem with theft in terms of an epidemic caused by a bacterium known as bacillus debaucherius.[44] And when a spate of murders occurred in and around Cracow in May 1903, Sowa (the Owl), a feuilletonist for Nowiny, wondered if perhaps the idea of murder had, like a disease, become contagious. His suggestion in the same article that the sexual abuse of two teenage girls by their teacher Zygmunt Gesser may have been partially enabled by schoolchildren's access to the [mildly] pornographic magazine Bocian made clear the connection in his mind between moral filthiness, contagion, and criminality.[45]

Infanticide by servant girls, regularly reported in the popular press, presented a clear example of big-city corruption. The reports were so common that the newspapers developed their own shorthand, generally describing each sad story with several pat phrases. In these stories the women, faced with the temptations of the metropolis, "through their carelessness" and "in a moment of weakness," "fell from virtue." When "the fruit of their carelessness" was born, fearing that the child would "only be a burden," the women decided "to rid themselves of the child."[46] In one such story a 31-year-old maid tried to bury her child in a coal bucket, right after it was born. Shortly after, her master saw the blood in the lavatory and sought her out. He heard the whimpering of the infant from the coal bucket and took the mother and child to a gynecologist. Nowiny concluded its report with the following moralizing statement:

> Marytkówna is a typical example of what can happen from the carelessness of a girl who finds herself in a great city. She easily grows accustomed to the moral corruption that lies in wait for her at every turn, then she falls, and

after her fall, she plummets lower and lower, descending all the way to the path of crime. Marytkówna, only thanks to happenstance, did not become a child murderer.[47]

According to this narrative, vulnerable servant girls faced with the corruption of the great city were apt to lose their virtue and then, a few slippery steps later, could even become child murderers. Marytkówna's more advanced age (31) presented a slight problem for the standard narrative about young girls who make a momentary mistake and fall from virtue. Nonetheless, the newspaper reported, "Despite her mature age, Marytkówna did not resist depravity and fell, becoming the victim of her own carelessness and the infamy of her seducer."[48]

The set of associations for juvenile delinquents and great-city filthiness was even more developed. An arrest report in *Nowiny*'s daily chronicle from July 14, 1904, laid out much of the discourse of juvenile delinquency that appeared in a limited range of permutations in articles over the next decade:

> [Piotr Krzysiak, 13, and Stefan Zieliński, 18] both represent typical young tramps, morally neglected [*zaniedbani moralnie*], not able to read or write even their last names, soiled, ragged, dirty, disheveled, who—just as they've begun, will end up in crime. There is no saving this type; they are lost from society forever (because we lack reform homes and forced labor for homeless children) and they will continue to sink lower on their declining path of vice and crime until they reach its very bottom.[49]

According to the discourse, Krzysiak and Zieliński, whose ragged appearance and presumed lack of parental care was supposed to explain their crimes, were "lost from society forever." Without forced labor and reform homes, they would undoubtedly continue along the "declining path of vice and crime" until they ended up in hard prison or worse. Thanks to the "unbelievably flawed prison system in Austria," as another piece on juvenile delinquents put it, "these immature offenders [would] become professional thieves, [wandering] from one jail to the next."[50] While the article about Krzysiak and Zieliński clearly distanced its respectable readers from the poor boys on the street (consider the long list of repellent adjectives—soiled, ragged, dirty, disheveled—that described the very antithesis of a respectable child), it concluded on a more compassionate note: "And yet it is worth noticing," the report summed up, "that for the most part these kinds of children perish as a result of having an uncared-for upbringing, a lack of protection, and what is most important . . . from hunger."[51] Only in reform homes in the countryside—"in the open air, far from city life, far from bad company"—could juvenile delinquents be saved.[52] Just as in the discourse of servant girls who became child murderers, the great city served as the prime instigator of a descent into wickedness.

As with tram accidents, "careless" villagers, women, children, and the poor were presumed to be most susceptible to the corruptions of the great city. This did not mean that Cracow's privileged citizens were immune, however. Just as tuberculosis could spread from beyond the poorest districts of Dębniki and Ludwinów to the homes of the intelligentsia in Piasek or downtown, so too could great-city filthiness spread to other segments of the population. Even bourgeois women and children were apt to lose their virtue, often by abusing the freedoms afforded by city life. One article in the popular press discussed the "degenerate romanticism" among bourgeois youth of the city, who met downtown or on the City Meadow for clandestine trysts.[53] "Miss 'Modern,'" a feuilleton that compared two young women conversing on the street—a "modern" girl and her traditional, respectable friend—made clear that the modern urban woman was "depraved" and would "eventually expire all for naught." The article began with Stanisław Wyspiański's derisive definition of a "modern" young woman: she cares little about her appearance, and even less about her family's care; she spends most of the day outside the home, "drinking absinthe, black coffee, and smoking, talking a lot about art in simplistic banalities that sound nice all the same, and for show she 'studies,' meaning she 'goes to the university' or 'out for art' and she paints." The feuilletonist suggested that, in her desire to play the role, Miss Modern would ultimately do "what no young woman who is not 'modern' would do," just to differentiate herself from others. "Coffeehouse poets write her verses; cabaret artists paint her"; and the reader was left to assume both kinds of men would readily compromise her virtue.[54] Seduced by the temptations of the metropolis, the article implied, even educated young women from good homes were apt to "fall" from virtue.

Other articles condemned urban life as being bad for children's mental and moral health. In one of these, a doctor argued the merits of taking children on a summer holiday, far from the distractions of the city, "without the little balls, theaters, circuses, and concerts, in a word, all the pleasures that, experienced too early, exert such a detrimental influence on the normal development of a child's mind and taint a young, sensitive soul."[55] Like numerous other articles that associated the big city with moral and physical filth, this article argued that bourgeois children were not immune from the corruptions of the big city.[56] "Normal" development could only occur, the doctor argued, in the countryside. This was not so different from the desire to quarantine street boys from the corruptions of the city in the "fresh air" of rural workhouses. If working-class youth went to the countryside to work, it only made sense that respectable children should go there to play. In both cases, it was presumably for their benefit.

According to newspaper narratives, "great-city filthiness" was a major explanation for why the weak would depart from the path of normal behavior. In the discourse of deviance, as soon as uncared-for youth and uncareful servant girls had stepped onto the slippery slope of moral ruin, they were prone to slide into further crime and long-term imprisonment. While individual cases of deviance rarely fit the discourse exactly, the papers persisted in applying it to many reports as a ready-made interpretative framework. In the creation of a meta-discourse about urban deviance, one might say that Cracow's popular press indulged in a "moral panic." According to Stanley Cohen's original definition, a moral panic occurs when "a group of persons [is] defined as a threat to societal values and interests [and] presented in a stylized and stereotypical fashion by the mass media."[57] Yet rather than demonizing deviants, Cracow's popular press tended to create an inclusive discourse of urban deviance. Despite fears of moral danger, deviants such as juvenile delinquents were rarely depicted as devils. Article after article called for the redemption of "our servants," "our children," and "our women" through paternalistic intervention—before it grew too late.

Early in 1908, *Nowiny* printed a series of articles about the morality of the city based upon police statistics from the previous year. In the first of these articles the writer concluded that Cracow was a rather moral place, considering the fact that it had only a few curious crimes such as "youthful howling" and failure to close pubs on time.[58] The very next day, however, the paper ran an article about a male "fortuneteller's" scandalous seduction of a gullible fifteen-year-old nursemaid. Under a large headline, "Cracow's Secrets," appeared the following introduction: "Serious, esteemed Cracow, of high morality according to police statistics provided by us yesterday, hides within itself . . . *so much filth, that one could without hesitation call it a great city.*" After a little more commentary, there began the narrative of a "handsome young man" who, finding the nursemaid alone in an acquaintance's apartment, tried to read more than just her palms, specifically mentioning his effort to palm-read her breasts. The article concluded with the girl telling her mistress the whole shameful experience during an outing to the countryside. The mistress then passed the story to a male friend, who "as they inform us, conveyed it to the police."[59] In its retelling, the newspaper declared in disgust that Cracow had enough "dirt" to be called a "great city," all of its morality notwithstanding.

Despite its "dirty" topic, however, the author told the story with a certain irreverence and distance that perhaps undermines his claim of initial shock. The reader could voyeuristically imagine the seduction, feeling both pleasure and outrage at the same time. Indeed, it seems odd that the groping of a maid would be newsworthy in the first place, given the ubiquitous association of servant girls with sexuality (see chapter 1). Still, the fact that the author equated immorality with the "great city" is significant, because of his assumption about the persuasiveness of such a statement. In order for the equation to work, the author had to expect his audience to concur that "filth" and "great cities" went hand in hand.

The next day another article on Cracow's morality appeared. Reassessing the level of morality in Cracow, the article admitted that the city had a real problem with theft, but could not go so far as to concede Cracow's "great city" status. It suggested that "the temperament of the city does not seem in any way akin to the temperament of the inhabitants of great cities," exclaiming that one need only compare daily newspaper chronicles in Warsaw or Vienna to Cracow's news to see the difference: "Good Lord! Let us read the chronicles of Warsaw or Vienna and then the chronicle of Cracow! Among us there were during the whole year only 56 public acts of violence. If we were to judge from this point whether Cracow is a great city or not, we would have to admit that, no, it is not."[60]

In answering this question the author was addressing both a small debate about Cracow's morality within the pages of the city's most popular illustrated daily and a larger issue concerning reactions to crime and urban growth. It is difficult to tell how serious the author was in claiming that, because there were only 56 public acts of violence in the previous year, Cracow was not a great city like Warsaw or Vienna. The author's concluding observation—that the "most painful statistic" is the number of citizens, most of them women, who are taken into the police station and then to a "discrete part of the hospital" for venereal diseases—confirms his distaste for the violation of female bodies that presumably takes place more often in big cities. "Were it not for this," he mused, "Cracow could vie for a prize in a virtue contest," an assertion he followed with the sarcastic remark, "Indeed" (*A jakże*).[61] The tongue-in-cheek ambivalence of the author of this piece betrays more genuine concern: Given its level of crime, was Cracow becoming a "great city"? Was crime really as bad as in Warsaw or Vienna? In his article, the author tapped into this question and answered it in the negative, though the evidence was hardly reassuring. Like the neighbors who could not believe that a humble servant girl had ransacked her mistress's home with an ax, the writer of this piece was reluctant to admit that he lived in a big city—at least not yet.

Commentary about Cracow's morality and the sexual danger of big cities was not limited to the internal discussion that erupted in the pages of *Nowiny* in January 1908. These topics resurfaced in other articles in *Nowiny* and then a few years later in the newly formed *Ilustrowany Kuryer Codzienny*, demonstrating their persistent discursive power. An article entitled "From the Drama of a Great City" ("Z dramatu wielkiego miasta") in *IKC* in December 1910—the same year that Cracow became "Greater Cracow"—confirmed the fear of dirt and danger in the metropolis, especially for the poor and powerless. In the same week that the recently introduced *IKC* attempted to expand its readership by promoting a contest to guess Greater Cracow's new population figures, the paper printed the following cautionary tale.[62] Illustrated by a line drawing of a girl lying dead in front of apartment buildings, the article began with the observation: "Colorful and rapid great-city life, alluring and enticing at first glance, contains within itself nevertheless so much squalor (*brud*) and poverty, so many silent and yet shocking dramas, that without a doubt great cities deserve to be called 'the modern Babylon.'"

The article then assumed the gaze of the "dame" riding by or the "banker off to make a quick profit at the market," who glancing through the glass windows of their carriages, see the parting crowd of poor people as a "single mass, instead of individuals created with just as much right to live in happiness." "And yet," the article asserted, "in that colorless, gray crowd exist thousands of beautiful and unfortunate people . . . for whom a little bit of money constitutes a great fortune. . . ." Only then, after three paragraphs of introduction, came the ostensible report: according to a recent chronicle notice, a flower girl in Berlin, Anna König, had died of hunger and cold.[63]

IKC's commentary on the relationship between the powerful and weak in the metropolis, manifest in the overt comparison between the gray masses and the privileged archetypes of banker (capitalist) or great lady (aristocrat), was pitched to strike a chord with working-class and petty bourgeois readers whose own experience of urban life was difficult and frequently humiliating. And as in many other articles of its type in the popular press, the imperative to moralize seems to have been just as important as the news itself. In the case of this article, apparently the staff of *IKC* had been scanning the Berlin press for news. Lifting a notice from the chronicle (*Kronik*) section about a dead flower girl, a minor piece of news in the larger scheme of things, they determined to make it an illustrated morality tale about the drama of "great city" life for their paper.[64]

By leaving the "great city" in the title unnamed, the editor could indirectly address the expansion of Cracow into Greater Cracow in a different light. Readers perusing the headlines and pictures of this issue would have had every reason to assume that the great city under discussion was their own, such was the simultaneous effort to promote the creation of Greater Cracow in the paper at the time. This rendering of "great-city" life did not mean that the editors were against the expansion of the city, rather, it reflects the ability of the newspaper to convey multiple meanings. During a week in which articles and promotional contests encouraged excitement about the city's continued expansion, this morality tale addressed concurrent fears about becoming a "great city."

Once again a violation of female bodies, a sexual threat to the city's most "helpless" denizens symbolized the squalor of the great city. In the case of this piece, the author took the liberty to assume that the poor girl had to resist repeatedly "the temptations that must have accompanied her job," only to have fallen from starvation in the end. As in the case of the "tiny nursemaid" whose diminutive status the author chose to emphasize or even invent, the young woman in this article was made to represent one of the city's most vulnerable inhabitants. In this discourse great cities implied squalor and filth, a condition most apparent among its presumably weakest members. Rapid urbanization was a threat to the body politic, an assault on public morality and traditional notions of decency.

Half a year after the publication of "From the Drama of a Great City," *IKC* ran a front-page exposé of Cracovian prostitution, and child prostitution in particular, under the telling title "Great-City Muck."[65] Again, the press inscribed great-city filthiness upon the bodies of women and vulnerable girls, though this time the "great city" in question was clearly Cracow itself. The article began by challenging Cracow's small-town sense of piety and wholesomeness in the face of its recent growth, reminding its citizens of the consequences of big-city development:

> Considering our complete love for our hometown, considering the complete piety reserved for its valuable historical monuments, . . . we cannot forget that Cracow, by strength of fact, is becoming as the years go by a truly *great city,* and it follows that great-city corruption—perhaps in a tempo faster than it should—strides alongside its actual growth.

Explicitly reifying the link between great-city growth and moral corruption, the article's opening statement asserted that reverence for historical monuments was no longer the only way for Cracovians to conceive of their city. They had to recognize that Cracow was becoming a big city with its attendant problems and dangers.

"It behooves us to bring up an unpleasant topic," the article continued, "which the newspapers (in our opinion wrongly) have considered only in short notices in the police reports." Thanks to a misplaced sense of prudishness, the article insisted, Cracovians had tried to conceal discussion about prostitution while it simply grew worse. Claiming that one merely had "to walk along Market Square or in the Ring-Park in the evening [to witness] the full hideousness of the trade of 'human flesh'" in audacious openness, the paper called for civil and charitable efforts to combat prostitution. Pointing out that there were "hundreds of humanitarian organizations" in Cracow but no organization for fallen women, *IKC* demanded such an institution. As in nearly every other article that decried the city's filth or backwardness, the paper affirmed that western European cities had done much more to deal with the problem: "Abroad the problem is long since practically solved." There, "according to a long-since-confirmed sociological theory," subsidized institutions have succeeded in their mission of returning "the fallen woman to society. Here meanwhile there is only dead silence in this field."

The remainder of the article told the sordid story of 13-year-old Mania Szumcowa, a pretty black-haired girl who was "sold by contract" for fifty crowns to her amorous 72-year-old neighbor, Feliks Borkowski, a street vendor, some two years before and then compelled by her mother into child prostitution after Borkowski raped her on a summer trip. After the pair returned, Szumcowa's mother demanded her daughter back, but Borkowski would not relent, based on their "contract." Mrs. Szumcowa took the matter to the police and Borkowski was arrested, thus returning the girl to her family. Forced by her mother and other relatives to continue in what she herself called, "this sinful Sodom," Mania began to write plaintive letters to old Borkowski begging him to take her back, preferring his love to the horror of prostitution for her family. Borkowski had admitted in court to raping the girl but was released. Now, the article informed, the police were taking up the matter again and had passed it to the criminal court. The results of the preliminary investigation "qualify as a slap in the face of the public morality," *IKC* opined. "They bring to light such abominable immensity," the author of the article gushed with melodramatic fervor, "that the hand begins to shake and the pen falls from it." The article concluded that young Szumcowa was "now a completely corrupted woman, cynical, and lost," despite its earlier injunction that fallen women could be returned to society. In a final jab, it remarked, "Such is a fine picture from a day in the life of 'god-fearing' Cracow."

IKC's moralizing exposé of Cracovian child prostitution—like its famous London prototype of nearly three decades before, W. T. Stead's "Maiden Tribute to Modern Babylon"—was a polysemous text.[66] It was at once a reproach of the appalling corruption of big-city life and a reveling in sensational material that was bound to attract curious readers. Like the "Maiden Tribute," "Great-City Muck" began with an accusatory claim that phony prudishness kept citizens from facing the actual conditions of big-city life, knowing well that an article of this sort would only attract readers. (Before running his expose, Stead had coyly observed that squeamish and prudish readers, "who prefer to live in a fool's paradise of imaginary innocence and purity, . . . *will do well not to read the Pall Mall Gazette of Monday and the following days*.")[67] And like the "Maiden Tribute," it exaggerated the role of childhood prostitution over other forms of prostitution for the sake of emotional argument. The introductory passages of "Great-City Muck," with their commentary on pimps and whores downtown and the need for a reform home, did not directly relate to the horrible story of Mania Szumcowa who was forced into private prostitution by her mother, but they were paired together nonetheless because the girl's story was a good way to attract sympathy for women who were otherwise employed in a legal, if despicable, profession.[68]

Like much of the commentary on prostitutes in other European cities, this article also conflated big cities and the filth of prostitution. An article appearing some two years later in *IKC*, for example, confirmed this association. "From the Monstrosity of a Great City" told the story of a poor girl trapped and nearly bullied into prostitution in Warsaw, where "of late, nothing grows and gets so powerful as prostitution."[69] The titles of both articles took it for granted that big cities and prostitution went hand in hand. What made "Great-City Muck" unique, however, was its claim that "by strength of fact" Cracow was "becoming . . . a truly great city" itself.

In confirming Cracow's status as a "great city" with an article about prostitution, the paper was affirming that Cracow was more similar to big cities abroad than Cracovians may have wanted to admit. Reifying the association of big cities with filthiness, this article implied that all protestations to the contrary, little "god-fearing Cracow" was increasingly on par with the dens of iniquity abroad. If opinion pieces from several years before in *Nowiny* had claimed that Cracow's chronicle reports could not possibly compare with those of big cities abroad, this article insisted that Cracovians recognize that "by strength of fact" their city was not so unusual, after all. In this regard, "Great-City Muck" was not really so different from the numerous articles that compared Cracow with other cities in order to incite change. Cracovians had merely to recognize their problem and, following the lead of big cities abroad, begin to address it.

As such, the rhetorical use of the "great city" abroad was paradoxical. While journalists and citizens almost universally used the trope negatively, the actual cities abroad that fit that category remained models for how to address big-city problems. Large European cities stood for civilization *and* corruption, the promising future *and* the immorality of decadence. As demonstrated in previous chapters, the interurban matrix enabled comparisons between cities on a scale previously impossible. As citizens read about the dangers and delights of big cities abroad, they began to identify with the metropolis, even if at times they may have feared "great-city filth."

Big-city corruption may have been unattractive, but urbanites did not really seek its alternative in retreating to the purported safety of the countryside. In a withering attack on "Galician Cleanliness" in 1909, a journalist for *Nowiny* argued that despite the fact that Heinrich Heine's mean-spirited verse, "An der Weichsel, wo da hausen/ Edle Polen, die sich lausen" (On the Vistula, where the noble Poles reside/ they pluck the lice from their hides [lit. they delouse themselves]), stung bitterly, the remark still rang true when referring to the people of the countryside and small towns, noting that there were still some inhabitants of Galicia who were washed from head to toe only twice, at birth and before burial.[70] Mickiewicz's idyllic "lands of childhood" were no longer so desirable. It is true that summer homes came into vogue during this period, and trips to the mountain resort town of Zakopane were extremely popular—at least among those who could afford them, including the editor of *Nowiny*, Ludwik Szczepański. Urban elites sought ways to experience the charms of the countryside, most notably by building suburban neighborhoods after the "garden city" model, or constructing homes and other edifices in the vernacular style.[71] But few wished to leave the city permanently. Few urbanites would be willing to give up their streetcars, streetlights, functioning sewers, and running water for the underdeveloped conditions of the countryside.

Indeed, according to the most urbane, even the newly incorporated communities of Greater Cracow failed to meet the standards of civilization that modern metropolitans might expect. An article written just a few months after the first round of incorporation into Greater Cracow in 1910 observed that the former city limits literally marked the edge of civilization. In Krowodrza, where the city tramline and streetlights suddenly ended and there were deep canals of dirty water instead of functioning gutters, one truly appreciated the value of civilization:

> Here and there is a little bridge [over the canals]; here and there there's not. There's no bridge precisely where it's dark and one would expect it. . . . To the inhabitants of Krowodrza, who walk barefoot, this is no problem, but if it happens that someone in shoes accidentally ends up in those parts, he

will then know how to appreciate the meaning of civilization. Indeed, just beyond the turnpike, nature begins. Not some parody of nature, but strong, powerful nature.[72]

In this context "nature" was hardly romanticized or sentimental but, rather, a symbol for backwardness and dirtiness. Like the articles associated with the creation of Greater Cracow, where the mud of rural life made the suburban districts so unattractive, this piece could not imagine a civilized existence outside of the city.

So what was worse, great-city muck or the mud of underdevelopment?[73] One solution, offered by the press of the time, would be to suggest that Cracovians would complain no matter the situation in which they found themselves.[74] Following this line of argument, the two conditions were equally bad. Yet, as already seen, streetcars, street lamps, and running water were clearly preferable to whatever preceded them—at least once people got used to the new technologies and the city succeeded in getting them to function properly. Even if they were disgusted by the physical and moral filth of the "great city," urbanites clearly preferred its benefits to the backwardness of the countryside. Accepting the Enlightenment tradition of belief in progress, they ultimately believed that problems of filthiness, whether urban or rural, could be ameliorated by modern science and good government. And Galician big cities such as Cracow and Lemberg were better equipped than rural areas to deal with these problems. The question, then, was not which kind of filth was worse but, rather, how could filthiness be overcome? Articles about hygiene and crime in Cracow make it clear that citizens had not given up on big cities in despair. Rather, they complained about filth in the hopes that something would be done about it.

HYGIENE AND CITY SANITATION

The plentiful articles in Cracow's popular illustrated daily press about hygiene and city sanitation during the first decade and a half of the twentieth century generally fell into three categories: (1) educational or special interest articles about hygiene, including discussions of disease in the city and how to avoid it; (2) complaints from readers or reporters about filthy shops and restaurants in town; and (3) most commonly, articles about mud and filth on the streets and the city's failure to deal with the problem. Collectively, the articles sought to improve cleanliness in the city, often by shaming citizens, businesses, and most importantly, the city magistrate into compliance.

Articles of the first category demonstrate the era's obsession with hygiene, ranging in seriousness from gently humorous discussions of the hygienic disadvantages of mustaches or kissing to detailed descriptions of how to prepare meat safely or how to avoid spreading cholera.[75] Several of these articles carefully explained germ theory, offering sophisticated but clear explanations of bacterial infection. Many of them were pitched directly to women, appearing in sections of *Nowiny*'s "Practical Housewife" (Praktyczna gospodyni) or *IKC*'s "For Women, from Women" (Dla kobiet, od kobiet). An early article in *Kuryer Krakowski* entitled "Hygiene, Formerly and Today" took care to point out that "the 'good' old days had their 'bad' side as well" and proceeded to enumerate the ways that everyone today was much better off than their ancestors in terms of cleanliness and health. Yet in affirming "daily bathing is as indispensable to us as bread and meat" and "today, even the busiest person finds time for a walk," the article was not so much describing reality as prescribing hoped-for behavior.[76] The articles presented principles of cleanliness and disease prevention with the assumption that readers would be grateful for the potentially life-saving advice. It comes as little surprise, then, that the organizers of the *Universal Hygiene Exhibition in Cracow* in 1911, which was designed to accompany the eleventh annual gathering of Polish physicians in Cracow, expected "a very large audience" for its "nine humongous pavilions" on the subject of hygiene. By providing free transportation to the event, planners hoped to get as many citizens as possible to participate, especially housewives from the suburbs and provincial towns.[77] Articles and exhibitions like these sought to spread the gospel of cleanliness to the ignorant while affirming the faith of the believers. In their missionary zeal, they relied on the power of peer pressure to encourage conformity to new standards that were clearly beneficial for all.

Whenever citizens or businesses failed to comply with the new hygienic standards, however, the newspapers stood ready to call them out. Articles of this type included complaints about shopkeepers handling meat and money with the same unwashed hands, laments from concerned citizens about filthy ice in cafes or open salt and pepper shakers at restaurants, and sightings of rats at restaurants, including a humorous tale of a rat that caused pandemonium at an outdoor concert when a concertgoer realized it was not a cat brushing against her skirts.[78] In March 1907, *Nowiny* published a sardonic feuilleton entitled "Enticements" (Wabiki), which featured the ironical argument of a "lifetime resident of Cracow" that the best way to attract foreign tourists to the city was not to flaunt its national treasures, which were in disrepair and would not be well understood, but instead to take photographs of a disgusting butcher's shop and other such "beauties" to make an album to send all over Europe. "Enticements" like these, he claimed, would "bring in tourists in droves."

> Hoho! We should show foreigners our butcher's shop behind the Dominican [Church]! Have you ever been there, sir! Of course you have. Is there a city in the world that has such a butcher's shop? So much filth [*brud*], what a stench, what disorder, what uncleanliness even on the chopping blocks! Sir, that is an enticement. You can see historic and artistic monuments abroad, but something like this, nowhere else.[79]

The feuilleton went on to describe the slovenly cooks downtown, the manure-covered square in Kleparz, and pointedly the dilapidated courtyard of the city magistrate building itself, "a veritable museum of 'provincial housekeeping' in a big city." Throwing Cracow's pride in its historic buildings on its head, this article implied that until the city got its act together, it would never draw Western tourists—or at least not for the right reasons.

Another article of this sort suffices to illustrate the major tendencies of the "complaint" category. "By chance I had to walk through Holy Spirit Square very early yesterday morning," wrote a reporter for *Kuryerek Krakowski* in late November 1902, "and I saw a picture so 'nice' and 'appetizing,' that for the rest of the day I was unable to bring even a tiny piece of meat to my lips." According to the reporter, the scene he witnessed—the unloading of raw "cheap" meat at the market from bloody, muddy, dung-covered peasant carts—was enough "to offend even the most primitive notion of cleanliness, formed in the mind of a wild person." The sight was "a photograph that the Sanitation Commission and the commissioners of the market [really] should retouch, if our city has even the slightest pretensions to be more European than the 'little capitals' of the caciques on the islands of Haiti, Fiji, or somewhere in Honolulu!" In a final moralizing statement, the editors added that it was "an embarrassment for the city authorities to allow the poisoning of poor folk" at the cost of their own hard-earned grosze.[80]

Encapsulated in this brief report were many of the themes associated with hygienic concerns in Cracow's popular press for the next decade and a half. One of these was the familiar reference to "Europe" as the standard of civilization and "Asiatic conditions" as the opposite—here pictured in a new twist as the "wild" islands of the New World. The term "Asiatic conditions" was always used as a negative marker in the popular press, connoting backwardness, venality, or filthiness. An article in *Nowiny* that accused wealthy Jewish businessman Gustaw Gershon Bazes of getting illegal tax relief carried the title "Asiatic conditions" as did a spirited complaint from local businessmen that storage areas at the train station were muddy, filthy, covered with garbage, and never cleaned.[81] Fundamentally, the term implied a civilizational difference between the two continents, symbolically construed. Using this rhetorical device, writers positioned Cracow precariously somewhere between European civilization and Asiatic barbarism. Cracovians felt themselves to be fully European, yet each example of "Asiatic filthiness" was "an embarrassment" that suggested their city still lacked a great deal of civilization and refinement if it truly hoped to be a European metropolis. Exploiting a perceived inferiority complex, arguments like this one questioned Cracow's level of civilization.

A second feature of the report was the sense of revulsion mixed with fascination felt by bourgeois observers and, presumably, the majority of newspaper readers as they witnessed the muck of big-city life. Often enough, the filth they observed was in public spaces, where it could seemingly contaminate widely. Yet in this story, the reporter offered an exposé of a practice that sullied the city, even if it did not threaten his health directly. Despite the editors' pandering plea for the poor people who regularly bought the contaminated meat, the reporter made it clear that he had not gone there to shop for himself. According to his introduction, he had merely been compelled to pass through at an inopportune time. While he and his fellow newspapermen were capable of sympathizing with the poor folk compelled to buy such dirty meat, their sympathy only went so far. In exposing the city's filthiness, they made clear the metonymic relationship between filthy practices and filthy people. Moreover, the peasants who delivered the meat were clearly beneath them, exhibiting as they did in the reporter's account, an inhuman disregard for the most perfunctory notions of hygiene. Even a "wild" person, with "the most primitive conception of cleanliness" he accused, knew better than to transport raw victuals in a shit-covered cart. As with the villagers who obstructed automobiles on roads into the city, these peasants could only become part of urban civilization with "an increase of awareness and culture."

Finally, and perhaps most significantly, despite their disgust for what was taking place in Cracow the editors and reporter illustrate a belief that the problem was ultimately soluble. Like much of the muckraking reporting of the day, the focus on filth, while titillating in itself, was not there only for shock value. Appeals to "city authorities," "the Sanitary Commission," and "the commissioners of the market" were not idle laments; they suggest a basic optimism that with effort, education, and effectively enforced rules, the situation could be bettered. This belief in the possibility of eventual improvement is a crucial feature of nearly all reports about hygiene and city sanitation during the period of this study. Reporters and citizens did not expect instantaneous improvements—experience had taught them not to hope for too much—but, given the rapid changes in urban infrastructure they had witnessed in just a few short years, they had every reason to believe that sensible improvements were possible and worth demanding from civil authorities.

"Please Deign to Consider this Matter, Most Glorious Magistrate of Cracow"

Dripping with irony and in the outdated language of medieval patronage, boulevard newspapers addressed the executive branch of municipal government, the Cracovian Magistrate, in the hopes that it would better deal with the problems of filth and crime in the city.[82] "The Magistrate—excuse me—our resplendent Magistrate has had mercy on the plight of poor inhabitants," began an article about the use of three new street-cleaning machines in *Kuryerek Krakowski* in the spring of 1903. "But you can't really see the effects of their work," the paper sniped. "And besides they only clean the streets under the influence of city councilors."[83] A few months later *Nowiny* printed the laments of several citizens about crime and filth in town in which a reader begged the paper for help from the magistrate,

> which has forgotten that Zacisze Street is in Cracow and nearly the center of town. The street is full of mud, puddles, and potholes, in which today, when rain rather regularly visits us, one could easily drown; from the basements comes the odor of rotten potatoes; in general hygienic conditions are not to be envied. No surprise then, as the author attests, in home nr. 6 several persons have scarlet fever.

Nowiny concluded the report with the falsely obsequious injunction: "Please deign to consider this matter, most glorious Magistrate of Cracow."[84]

The magistrate eventually did consider the matter of sanitation, passing new regulations for garbage removal and street cleaning in 1906. During the debate over the new regulations that year a reporter for *Nowiny* "interviewed" "Jacenty," a municipal street cleaner, for his thoughts on the proposed changes. The city wished to bring in new street-cleaning tools and make more stringent rules about the removal of garbage. To set up the problems of the present system, the interviewer first described old Jacenty's lazy and ineffective technique, which was to sweep mud on the streets into piles or push it onto the grass instead of removing it. "After a few days, Jacenty appears again and looks for those piles, which by now have disappeared," the reporter commented laconically, "because the wind has obligingly blown them in the form of dust into neighboring windows or the lungs of the children who play in the Ring-Park." Another of Jacenty's purported techniques was to dump "trash, paper, and orange peels" into the nearest drain, because it would eventually end up in "the Vistula, and then [drift on] to Gdańsk," Jacenty explained, "'for the Germans.'" Of course, if it clogged the drain and flooded the streets instead, it would just help the neighborhood have the desire to clean its cellars, Jacenty pointed out, even if it did stink a bit. Asked what he thought of the proposed regulations, Jacenty suggested that little would come of them. The interviewer agreed, noting that they were just on paper, and it would remain to be seen if the magistrate could make good on its reforms.[85]

The municipal government officially instituted a number of sanitation regulations in November 1906, but as predicted, they were difficult to implement. Despite the use of sprinklers and eventually a new chemical solution called "Siployt" to clean the streets, they remained dirty, especially due to difficulties with garbage removal.[86] Citizens were unsatisfied because the new rules required higher taxes but did not seem to bring about the desired results, and the removal of garbage continued "in a manner that [was] very unhygienic"—if at all.[87] For much of the month of January 1907, house guards, knowing that the city had now taken the responsibility of removing garbage, no longer took out their buildings' garbage, and without clear instructions about when the city carts would come around, a great deal of trash had accumulated on the streets.

Given these circumstances, in late January *Nowiny* conducted another interview, this time with Chief Jan Nowotny, the administrator responsible for city sanitation. Mr. Nowotny explained that the magistrate's new rules, passed in November and implemented on January 1, had simply come about too quickly for the city to meet the new demands. As of February 1, he explained, Cracow would be divided into twelve zones that would have designated dumpster wagons. By May 1, the city would provide uniform bins with lids for each building that would be emptied regularly. This system, he assured, would be "most ideal and most practical."[88]

But problems with trash accumulation and dirty streets persisted. In 1910, when Halley's comet was scheduled to pass over Europe in a few days, one reader joked that the comet's long tail, which was presumed to actually penetrate the atmosphere, might do a better job of cleaning the city's streets than its municipal authorities had done of late.[89] Doormen frequently failed to observe rules regarding sidewalk cleaning in front of apartment buildings, and excessively muddy streets continued to bedevil pedestrians. *Nowiny*'s report on a meeting of the magistrate to deal with these problems in 1912 was titled emphatically, "Finally"—a clear indication of citizens' frustration with the failures of city sanitation. According to the article, the meeting was well attended by members of the city cleaning commission and others. The attendees determined "to empower a company to hire an appropriate number of workers and carters, in the purpose of immediately removing the accumulated mud. Simultaneously the Magistrate determined to send a notice to the police headquarters to observe house guards, who often ignore the rules regarding cleaning sidewalks in front of apartment buildings."[90] Another piece, published several months later, complained that "no city in the West" had such a problem with dust as did Cracow. "Could the city Sanitation Department please wake up?" cried *Nowiny*. "Could the doormen who are responsible for this please bring themselves to clean the sidewalks appropriately?"[91] Later that summer *IKC* relayed the dismay of a reader about how ineffectively the city was fighting the germs that caused tuberculosis. On his walk he observed a sign about the danger of bacilli, which one could take as a good measure by the authorities, but he then noticed how perfunctorily the street cleaners were doing their job, stirring up as many bacilli as they were getting rid of by using dry brushes and doing a sloppy job.[92] Just as "old Jacenty" and *Nowiny*'s reporter had originally surmised, it was indeed hard to implement sanitary regulations in Cracow effectively.

Yet, for all their complaining, the papers occasionally acknowledged that citizens themselves were also responsible for the muck on their streets and that real progress had been made. In September 1909 *Nowiny* tried to address the problem of city sanitation fairly. "Cracovians habitually love to criticize the order of the city and complain that despite a city sanitation department and despite the costs the community expends for sanitation, the city is still a mess," began a note in the chronicle. "It is our characteristic trait that we always criticize everything, [but perhaps for the wrong reasons]." The notice then explained the admittedly thorough process of city sanitation. Because traffic on some city streets had gotten so thick that only minor cleaning could take place during the day, some readers may have made the false assumption that the magistrate was doing little to keep them clean. Readers learned that the city employed 120 sanitation workers by day and 15 at night, when the heavy, and more cost-efficient, street-cleaning machinery could operate. Twice a week after the market days, all the paved and asphalt roads of the city were thoroughly washed "in the full meaning of the word" and dried with rubber push brooms.

"Despite [these efforts], some say, our streets are [still] not clean," the article continued. "And that is partially true, though in general we must attest that our city has greatly improved in recent times. If our streets still don't meet all expectations, then it is we, the public, who are most to blame." The public's custom of throwing coal and building materials on the streets as well as the frequent use of narrow wheels on freight wagons, outlawed by magistrates in other cities but not yet in Cracow, tended to negate the cleaning efforts of the city, leaving rutted and cracked areas on the streets that were impossible to clean. "We conclude that our Magistrate will also provide an appropriate judgment on this matter," the paper added hopefully. Finally, the report addressed the cleanliness of the Ring-Park. Claiming that walking paths were hosed down at the wrong times of day, it called for reform. In a familiar rhetorical strategy, the author referred to foreign cities as examples, pointing out that walking paths in France, Belgium, and Vienna, such as the path to Semmering, were paved with pitch. The article concluded with one more indirect request for the magistrate: "perhaps the Magistrate could at least try out one such path [here]."[93] Devoid of the bombastic language of other articles on this topic, *Nowiny*'s two-column article on city sanitation from September 1909 rationally addressed the progress and shortcomings of the magistrate and Cracovian citizens alike in matters of city sanitation, quietly admitting that conditions were improving.

In articles like these, popular boulevard papers represented their readers' concerns about urban hygiene, while pressuring the magistrate to redouble its efforts. Often pointing to specific cities abroad as examples to emulate, the papers called for the urban conditions they felt entitled to as citizens of a European big city. Cracovians and the papers they read admittedly loved to blame the municipal government for their problems, but ultimately they recognized that their city was a reflection of themselves. If they did not wish to disgust foreigners or themselves with "enticements" like the butcher's shop behind the Dominican Church, they would all have to make an effort to keep the city clean. Informative articles about hygiene, specific complaints about public health problems, and pointed demands of municipal officials were all efforts to bring this about.

CONCLUSION

In Cracow's mass circulation press from 1900 to 1915, there was a preoccupation with the grime and squalor of the city, particularly in the years leading to the creation of Greater Cracow in 1910. Of course, the "gutter press" succeeded in part precisely because it drew attention to the filthiness of urban life. Even though "great-city muck" seems to have been a uniformly negative trope, it was also titillating entertainment and, when viewed in its larger context, should not be taken as proof of antipathy for modern, urban life. To the contrary, one could almost say that filth and crime were one of the major attractions of the "word city" of the popular press.[94] Repugnant when experienced personally but entertaining when experienced vicariously in the press, big-city filth was one of the chief "enticements" of the popular press.

Even so, the trope of great-city filthiness could stand for a host of concerns about crime, health, and morality in the metropolis. By elaborating on symbols that readers readily apprehended, the press contributed to popular discourse about city growth. This discourse employed some of the same notions of filthiness and criminality articulated by bourgeois observers in other European capitals. While the writers of these stories may have been part of Cracow's cosmopolitan intelligentsia, their average readers were not. Shopkeepers, clerks, housewives, and maids all had reason to participate in this dialogue as well. The experience of increasing rental costs, dirty streets, and escalating crime reports must have assisted in creating this impression. As in mid-nineteenth-century London or Paris, or turn-of-the-century Berlin, the filthiness of the city was both imagined and real. The newspapers regularly reported the efforts of the municipal government to cleanse the city, which its citizens knew to be dirty. Reports on murders and suicides appeared in the paper frequently. In addition, thanks to sensationalist coverage of crime in other great cities, Cracovians who read the popular press had little reason to expect their city to get any safer as it continued to grow. The repertory of symbolic language about big-city criminality and filthiness seemed increasingly applicable in their town, too.

Unlike London, Paris, Berlin, or even Warsaw, Cracow had few factories and therefore lacked a large working class that saw itself as such. Instead, as these articles demonstrate, servant girls, rather than factory girls, represented the dangers of urban contamination. The paternalistic sense of noblesse oblige and Christian morality that were still strong in the city must have contributed to the sense of violation experienced when maids committed crimes or were victims themselves. The examples given here constitute part of Cracow's particular response to city growth and crime, a response that combines some of the universals found in other urban contexts with the particulars of Cracow's experience as a smaller, less-industrialized city.

Here, perhaps even more than in larger metropolises, discourse surrounding the "great city" became tied up with public morality. As the city grew larger, its perceived morality was increasingly jeopardized, a condition symbolized by filthiness and sexual danger. Cracovians who read the illustrated press knew that their city was becoming a "great city," both literally, with the creation of Greater Cracow in 1910, and symbolically, through the apparent increase of criminality and squalor. However positive the visions of the future city politicians might present, the use of the term "great city" in the articles considered here betrays the fact that many Cracovians were ambivalent about the changes taking place around them.

Yet as this chapter has shown, while the popular illustrated press may have reveled in exposing "great-city muck," it did not abandon the modern big city and its forms. Just because "great-city filthiness" and the fall from virtue were part of a master narrative that was subject to endless iteration does not really mean that people fully believed it. One gets the sense that a master narrative can be rattled off to assuage one's guilt about not dealing with the problem or to simplify it into its sharpest contours. After all, the children on the street who, according to the discourse, belonged in the workhouse or mandatory schooling also helped sell the very newspapers that reported their exploits. Not only young impressionable maids tried to kill their babies, and it seems unlikely that the women who did commit infanticide did so because of a single, momentary fall from virtue. Even the great city itself, much maligned for its filthiness, was not such a bad thing. Without any apparent sense of irony, the doctor who advised respectable parents to take their children to the countryside for the summer because of its salubrious effect spent the last third of his article detailing how to avoid illness due to typhus, dysentery, scarlet fever, malaria, rheumatism, stinging insects, poor drinking water, and open-pit toilets there.[95] Despite everyone's protestations to the contrary, maybe modern urban life was not that bad after all.

Numerous articles about hygiene and city sanitation demonstrate that even if citizens believed the *moral health* of the city was in jeopardy as it grew, they felt its *physical health* could be improved through effective hygiene and city sanitation. And in these articles Cracow's filthiness was more frequently depicted as the result of its backwardness, not its urbanization. Articles about sanitary matters demonstrated a basic optimism that it was worthwhile to complain about filthy streets. Even if results were not always immediate, the papers recognized that the magistrate's efforts were succeeding in cleaning the city. Streets were still dirty, crime could still flourish, and women and children were still in jeopardy, but with effort, the autonomously governed great city of Cracow could find its own solutions to these problems, quite often by looking to the example of great cites abroad.

CHAPTER

BECOMING METROPOLITAN

It's getting to the point that someone who goes to the cafés once
or twice a week seems strange, because most of us go *daily.*
—*IKC,* March 2, 1913

Ludwik Szczepański, the founder and chief editor of *Nowiny,* and Juliusz
Leo, the mayor and creator of Greater Cracow, were ambitious, forward-
looking men in a city that had tended to focus on its past. Szczepański
founded the avant-garde literary journal *Życie,* the city's first illustrated
weekly and, most importantly, its first successful illustrated daily newspaper. His editorials aggressively supported Cracow's urban development
and his installment novels, "King of the Air," "Upheaval," and "In the Year
1950," all pointed resolutely to the future. Leo, meanwhile, another "man
of the future" according to a contemporary profile, recognized the necessity of Cracow's economic and administrative modernization.[1] As the city's
deputy mayor and then as its chief executive, Leo oversaw the complicated
negotiations required to incorporate its surrounding communities into a
single administrative unit. He worked to shift the city's makeup and character away from its former status as an "assemblage of the intelligentsia"
to a diversified modern metropolis by constructing working-class housing, building vocational schools, and albeit unsuccessfully, pushing for
the creation of a canal system that could have made Cracow a vital port
city. Like Szczepański, Leo faced considerable opposition from the city's
conservatives, particularly after he abandoned their party shortly before
the implementation of universal male suffrage in 1907. But also like
Szczepański, he found substantial support for his ideas.

This study is not a biography of two of fin-de-siécle Cracow's "great
men." Rather, its main characters are the city of Cracow, the popular press,
and the thousands of citizens who, during the first decade and a half of the

twentieth century, were in the process of becoming metropolitan. In large part, Szczepański and Leo owed their success to the fact that their ideas were not out of step with those of ordinary Cracovians. The lasting presence of the illustrated boulevard press was a referendum on Ludwik Szczepański's hunch that Cracow had a ready market for an urban newspaper that offered entertaining coverage of local affairs, mixed with sensations from abroad. And Juliusz Leo's recurring political success, meanwhile, affirms that voters in his city borough and the majority of his fellow city councilors shared his vision for the city. While it is difficult to get at the attitudes of ordinary citizens, by carefully reading contemporary fiction, memoirs, and especially the popular press, one can determine that they were largely supportive of the city's modernization.

Ultimately, the popular press and its readers supported the spread of what they commonly called modern European civilization. In the popular imagination, Cracow was rhetorically positioned along an axis of civilization with "Europe" or "the West" at one pole and "Asiatic" backwardness at the other. Cracovians were confident that they belonged in the West but in the realm of urban infrastructure at least often feared that they were not yet fully there. Much like the communities slated to join Greater Cracow, they hoped to go from being "a suburb of Europe" to being fully fledged members.[2] The installation of running water and electric trams, the development of a shipping canal, the creation of Greater Cracow, and the ability to deal with urban filth and crime were all seen as examples of the desired "Europeanization" of the city. For many Cracovians, then, "Europe" represented modernity and progress. Although some intellectuals and nationalists may have scorned the West, among the general public this attitude of desired emulation seems to have been widespread.[3] Even community mayors who initially opposed incorporation into Greater Cracow wished to "make themselves into Europe."

This does not mean that support for Cracow's transformation into a modern metropolis was unequivocal, however. As already seen, fears of "big-city corruption" persisted in "God-fearing Cracow." Narratives of modernization and urbanization in the popular press portrayed villagers, women, and children as particularly vulnerable to the challenges of modernity and urban life. They were most susceptible to the dangers of tram and automobile traffic and most susceptible to the moral corruptions of the city. Stereotypes generally described their susceptibility in terms of a descent. Faced with the challenges of modern urban life, villagers, women, and children were most likely to "fall," whether in front of the roaring machine or from the path of virtue.

Yet far from being mere victims, villagers, women, and children were often the most eager to become metropolitan. Villagers, including the thousands of young women who flocked to the city to work as housemaids, made the conscious decision to move there and gradually became metropolitan as they grew accustomed to the rhythms of modern urban life. It was not easy for a villager to navigate the big city, and as the rural mayor Jan Słomka ruefully recalled and the papers readily confirmed, there were always plenty of city slickers ready to take advantage of hayseeds blundering about the metropolis. Employing a sylvan simile that wonderfully underscored his rural perspective, Słomka recalled feeling "lost in the forest of streets" when he first visited Cracow. Yet, "[later] I began to realize that it was not hard to find my way, especially since I could read the names at the corners."[4]

Literacy helped in domesticating the city, but it was not always enough. In 1903 a peasant came into the offices of *Kuryer Krakowski* with his two daughters and a son—none of them older than twelve—and asked, "Don't you know me? I have subscribed to your paper for two years." He then confessed that, upon coming into "your city" he had purchased a copy of *Czas*, "because that seemed the thing to do in the big city," but he was very frustrated that the prestigious paper had failed to announce a children's concert that would have been just right for his family. Instead, faced with the choice between the potentially scandalous *Miss Maid* (Panna Służąca) and Wyspiański's ponderous play *Deliverance* (Wyzwolenie), they had chosen the latter, and bored and perplexed, the children had slept through most of it.[5] The worldly wise editor Kazimierz Bartoszewicz was doubtless delighted to run this story—he gave it two full columns of text—for a number of reasons. The rustic earnestness of a peasant who presumed the staff of the paper would recognize his name was charming, as was his effort to get the most out of the city. Conveniently, the political press had failed him, while in running his story and maintaining his subscription *Kuryer Krakowski* could demonstrate its value for all those who were still determined to behave like urbanites in the metropolis.

For the suburbanites who frequented Cracow, big-city employment and especially big-city entertainments helped to cultivate metropolitan identities. Early in Artur Gruszecki's *Cygarniczka*, Stasia, the suburban protagonist from Półwsie Zwierzynieckie, attends an artisans' dance in Jordan Park. Stasia and her friend, along with their dates, take a paddleboat around a pond, tour the menagerie (because the cinema was too crowded), and of course, dance. The locals call out for "Our [dance]! Our [dance]!" and sing along to the Krakowiak:

I'm a little Cracovian, in Cracow I was born,
While I was still in school, I was already seducing the ladies.
(*Krakowiaczek ci ja, w Krakowiem się rodził,*
Jeszczem do szkół chodził, jużem panny zwodził.)[6]

When Stasia's date asks if she can dance the waltz, she replies with the ultimate affirmation of kinship in modern urban civilization: "What, d'ya think
I'm a hick?" (*Czy ja ze wsi?*)[7] Somewhat chilled by the night air because
she was too proud to cover her modest dress with her "dirty, old jacket,"
Gruszecki's Stasia sought to affirm her modern metropolitan identity by
enjoying its entertainments, even if she was not well-off.[8] Stasia's attention
to fashion, like her knowledge of local and Viennese dances, was evidence of
her effort to join modern, metropolitan culture.

If the adaptation to modern urban life was bracing for villagers and suburbanites, the changes for women in this period were potentially even more
radical. Bound by the tight strictures of bourgeois morality, young women
began by around 1910 to break free. Girls "from good families," who otherwise would have been utterly ignorant of sex until the shock of their wedding
night, got a much better idea by watching the movie stars of the day, such
as Asta Nielsen, kiss their leading men on the silver screen.[9] And the literal
strictures, corsets, began to disappear by this period, too. A few women even
donned the notorious trousers known as "*jupe* culottes" that took European
cities by storm in 1911.[10] More and more women were attending university,
entering the workforce, and appearing in public unaccompanied. An article
in *Nowiny* from 1909 on the "Newest Women's Questions" discussed an
upcoming conference in London that would address questions of women's
employment and marriage for love rather than money or station.[11] Most
newspaper articles pictured the new woman as an aberration, including a
cover image from *IKC* entitled "World Flipped Upside Down: A Picture
from the Near Future" that depicted a woman in a rocking chair, leaning
rakishly back, brazenly smoking and reading *La Mode*. Two men behind her
on the street in top hats and skirts were being chased by an angry mob, not
unlike the crowds that were harassing women in culottes that spring. In an
inset, a profusely sweating father was on his hands and knees with two of
his children on his back and two more making noise nearby. He too was in a
skirt (see Fig. 10).[12] While the artist had trouble truly inverting the gendered
world (if he had, the woman would have been reading a political journal
or perusing a magazine full of scantily clad men and the father would have
been doing housework rather than merely playing with his progeny), his
humorous illustration still functioned only as an exaggeration of the world

of altered gender relations he expected in the near future. "Miss Modern" may have offended masculine notions of superiority and feminine notions of respectability, but she was not going away.

The modern woman's attention to a French fashion magazine reflected another way in which Cracovians, women and men, were also becoming modern: by adopting Western dress. The priceless collection of photographs from the Ignacy Krieger studio, which includes some nine hundred photographs of Cracovians and regional villagers taken by Krieger and his son Natan from the late 1870s until the end of the Great War, offers clear evidence of the dramatic changes in fashion and self-representation in the city by the second decade of the twentieth century. If in the photographs from the 1880s, which form the bulk of the collection, people were readily identifiable whether as peasants, day laborers, tinkers, gypsies, Christians, Jews, rabbis, Orthodox or Catholic clergy, gentry, or aristocrats, by 1910, the distinctions

Fig. 10—"**World Flipped Upside Down.** A picture from the near future." *IKC*, March 29, 1911.

are no longer so clear. There are some "modern women," in corsetless skirts and blouses sewn of factory-made printed fabric, whose religious origins are not immediately legible, and modern men whose military uniforms or business suits likewise obscure their origins. They appear to be more or less interchangeable with moderns elsewhere.[13]

Images in the press drew attention to this shift in fashion, as well. The top half of a two-panel sketch entitled "Yesterday and Today" showed a goateed man in a top hat who was unable to hand a woman a bouquet because her hoop skirt was so large. In the lower panel a clean-shaven dandy in a gaudy striped suit and derby could not give a woman in a slender dress a diamond necklace because her hat was too big.[14] If the joke suggested that women's fashions remained impractical, it still made clear the dramatic change in fashion in a single generation. The diamond necklace, meanwhile, drew attention to the materialism of modern urban life.

Youth were also becoming modern metropolitans. The young, as usual, were on the vanguard of accepting new technologies, entertainments, and sport. They reveled in the popular literature published in installment form in the boulevard press. They learned to ride the trams and navigate the city streets, frequently becoming the most avid aficionados of the new machines. Several memoirists who were children at the turn of the century wrote about the introduction of the electric tram as a major event in their lives. One boy from a family of the intelligentsia marveled at the machines that coursed along his street and told his parents he wanted to be a streetcar driver when he grew up; another noted that boys of his generation memorized statistics on trams and locomotives much as boys in the 1960s became experts on fighter jets and rockets.[15] Privileged youth rode bicycles and roller skates before much of the greater population did. When the Kossak girls rode their bicycles around the City Meadow, traditionalists upbraided them for their "shocking" behavior, while others called out, "Miss, your panties are showing" or "give me a kiss."[16]

The growth of sport is a clear example of modern, interurban culture that truly expanded during the first decade and a half of the century in Cracow. If, in 1903, Józef Czech's "Cracovian Calendar" listed only Falcon (Sokół) exercise clubs and horseback riding clubs, by 1912, there were three major soccer clubs, cycling clubs, lawn-tennis clubs, as well as ice-skating and roller-skating rinks.[17] By 1910, many Cracovians followed the successes of their favorite local sporting clubs, Cracovia, Wisła, and Makkabi (a Jewish squad), in matches with clubs from other cities all over central Europe, and occasionally from as far away as England and Scotland.[18] (Significantly, as is often the case with sport, talent trumped ethnic exclusivity, allowing for the presence of Jewish players such as the goalkeeper Józef Lustgarten on the Cracovia squad. Further, *Nowiny*'s regular reporting on Makkabi in the same column as other local squads demonstrated a common sense of local urban identity, at least in terms of sport.) Cracovian journalists thought that the English and the Czechs were the best players and were pleased when a local squad, Wisła, joined their league, the International Alliance of Football Amateurs.[19] Reporters delighted in noting the popularity of the game, which drew more than a thousand spectators to a Cracovia match in 1913. This was especially impressive, one of them claimed, because the squads did not really advertise and yet managed to attract so many fans.[20] Newspaper coverage of the matches proliferated so much that the famed "Zielony Balonik" cabaret, which typically skewered local artists and politicians, portrayed a player for Cracovia and a journalist in one of its sketches in 1911.[21] Sport connected Cracovian men and boys to modern metropolitan culture while cementing their sense of local loyalties, as they rooted for "their boys" in games at home and throughout Europe.

Thanks to the interurban matrix, Cracovians were aware of an increasingly global urban culture to which they clearly belonged. They could dance the same dance steps, watch the same films, see airplanes and automobiles or read local and international stories about them, wear the same fashions, read the same fiction, and view the same sensational images—from a lion in an automobile to a woman leaping into the Danube.

The mere fact that Cracovians could read about such interurban phenomena as fashion, sport, or dance, however, was not enough to make them metropolitan. After all, a villager from a tiny place like Świątniki Górne who subscribed to *Nowiny* or *IKC* could also see the same images and read the same stories. It was the fundamental commonality of experience that enabled readers in and around Cracow to identify with the interurban culture of the age. Wearing Western dress, riding the trams, attending the theater and cinema, and patronizing the cafés did much to reinforce one's sense of urban selfhood. A chronicle report in *IKC* in 1913 titled "Coffeehouse Life in Cracow" affirmed that the city's café culture was vibrant, as in Vienna, while the old custom of home visits was fading fast. "It's getting to the point that someone who goes to the cafés once or twice a week seems strange, because most of us go *daily*," the chronicler noted, before sketching an image of a typical urban family enjoying a Sunday afternoon in the coffeehouse: the boy in his school uniform and the girl in a short dress, the father smoking and discussing the war in the Balkans while the mother gossiped with her friends.[22] During this period, Cracovians had access to their own parks, electric streetcars, cafés, art galleries, movie houses, shops, restaurants, and skating rinks.[23] In the

Fig. 11—"**Football in Cracow.**" *IKC*, April 21, 1911.

evenings or on the weekends they could stroll downtown or attend a concert or a play at one of several theaters, including the inexpensive People's Theater. The popular boulevard press was indispensable in providing the information —from theater showings and reviews to advertisements for desirable goods— that enabled citizens to enjoy the city.

Of course not all of Cracow's similarities to big cities abroad were connected to the pleasures of metropolitan life. During this period, Cracow had its own array of sensational crimes, including the rape and murder of several young girls.[24] Articles from abroad on the same topic would have resonated with Cracovians' own experience of such trauma. Although Cracow was no Berlin or New York City, it did have its slums and tenements, whose denizens also contributed to the metropolitan culture of the city. A story in *Nowiny* from 1910 that described the "bloody results of jealousy in lower-class apartment buildings" among "persons of loose morals" included the discovery of two lovers "in the closest of relations," a stabbing, and the appearance of several people in front of the apartment building, some in droshkies even, based on the rumor that a double murder had taken place there that night.[25] Stories of prostitution, infanticide, and suicide were common story lines in the Cracovian popular press. A dark review of suicide statistics in 1907, for example, morbidly enumerated the ways Cracovians had taken their own lives in the previous year. In addition to the 40 deaths by poison or firearms, "4 sought death in the waves of the Vistula, 3 by jumping from heights to the pavement, [and] 1 desperate person slit his throat and another soaked his clothes in oil and found death in the flames."[26] For the week August 31–September 6, 1911, there was an article about suicide in every issue of *Nowiny*.

One of those suicide victims from 1907—Hugo Launsky, a 25-year-old office worker—came from a respectable family that had nonetheless failed to succeed in the city. The father, an alcoholic, had died a few years before, leaving the family in financial difficulty. The eldest son quit university studies to work for a bank in Vienna. The youngest daughter, an "unusually beautiful" woman (as they always are in such stories), had been engaged to be married but took her own life when a doctor diagnosed her with a terminal illness. Hugo, the remaining middle son, and the mother suffered greatly and soon could afford only a kitchenette apartment. Hugo also quit university and went to work for a bank. When he chose to take his mother's life and then his own (this was not the first time this had happened in recent memory in Cracow: two years before a student on Długa Street had killed his mother and then himself), the pair was so financially strapped that they had rented hallway space in their tiny apartment to a working-class boarder, an employee of the Liban and Ehrenpreis Factory. Their lodger, Stanisław Krysta, heard the shots and discovered the awful scene. Polite to the end, "Hugo left letters for people, and for the police, and for his fellow workers."[27] If the "bloody family tragedy" of Hugo Launsky demonstrated the pressures of modern urban life, it also showed the way that metropolitans shared a common lot. Krysta, a factory worker, and the Launskys, a declining family of the intelligentsia, lived, thanks to their mutual poverty and the obscene cost of rents in Cracow, in the same cramped space.

Metropolitans recognized that the challenges of modern urban life were demonstrably different from those faced by their forebears. "People of the past," intoned an editorial condemning the artificiality and meaninglessness of modern urban life, "perhaps they were slower and more constrained, but at least they were real."[28] By the second decade of the twentieth century, a common advertisement in the popular press promoted a product designed to deal with "exhausted nerves." Plenty of Cracow's thousands of bureaucrats, men like Hugo Launsky and his coworkers, would have taken note of the ad, which showed a clerk at an office job hunched forward in his chair, with his handkerchief on his forehead, eyes closed, and his hand on his lower back. His wastepaper basket lay upset in the foreground. The other ad for this product showed the same man's mustachioed face, before and after taking the product that helped him feel better.[29] Already in 1904, in his article promoting the necessity of summer homes for children and "wearied mental workers" (see chapter 6), Dr. Wł. Chodecki acknowledged that in the old days, "summer homes, so fashionable now, were unheard of, and people may have been healthier or lived longer. Perhaps that's true, but formerly they lived differently than today, not so frenzied, not expending their nerves so quickly, and people did not age mentally and physically as quickly as they do now."[30] Demographic statistics would almost certainly disprove Dr. Chodecki's contention that life in the old days may have been healthier, but for a generation of urbanites who still had connections to the tempo of rural life, it was clear that metropolitan existence was demanding in new ways.

Recognizing this, Cracovians were also becoming metropolitan in deciding who they were *not*, most notably, by emphasizing the distinctions between themselves and their co-nationals in the countryside. A reporter for *Nowiny* in 1906 felt the need to stress to his readers that the inhabitants of the suburban communities, who while "not peasants, but not city-dwellers, either," were worth getting to know nonetheless. "Do you know, my Cracovian brothers, your closest suburban neighbors? Do you know Grzegórzki, Dąbie, Nowa Wieś? Łobzów etc. etc.," the article began. "Admit it brother, you don't know them, and you think it's not worth it either."[31] Why would city dwellers bother to go to the suburbs, he asked rhetorically: "Because what's to see there? Bad roads, potholes and puddles, dust or mud, a few pubs here and there; there's no Hawełka's or Wentzel's nor cafés with billiards; it's not a village, but it's not a little city either. The trams don't go there; to get there on foot, [one can expect only] fatigue and messed up shoes; to go by droshky you pay a lot to get shaken up. Why bother?"[32] To the reporter, whose article came off as condescending and not very heartfelt (even though it was ostensibly trying to encourage Cracovians to get to know the suburban communities), the differences between city dwellers and the folks who lived in the suburbs were clear. Their fellowship in the Polish nation mattered little in effacing these fundamental differences of lifestyle.[33]

And yet of course, the very people and villages the reporter was mocking were slated to become part of Greater Cracow. With time and "an increase of [civilization and] culture," they too could become metropolitan. Thanks to their greater connections to the city (running water, schools, electric lights, electric trams, and of course the popular illustrated press), they would have the opportunity to cultivate this identity. For the thousands of new Cracovian urbanites in the first decade and a half of the twentieth century who either moved to the city or lived in its incorporated suburbs, the popular press was a crucial guide to their new metropolitan lives. During this period Old Cracow became Greater Cracow, provincial Cracow was becoming a "great city," and the city's inhabitants were becoming metropolitan. These parallel developments were the central story line of the popular press.

In Cracow's popular illustrated daily newspapers, the principal source of identification, the "first-person plural" that led to the creation of an "imagined community," was not national but metropolitan.[34] Thanks to the interurban matrix, readers of the popular press had daily examples of urban sensations from abroad, and thanks to their papers' close coverage of the details of the city, they began to identify with modern, urban life. Even in an era of intense nationalism, the popular press and its average readers were more concerned on a daily basis with urban issues than national ones. The mass circulation press promoted modern secularized culture, a culture that increasingly connected the citizens of big cities, irrespective of national and religious boundaries. An article in *IKC* about the spread of *"jupe* culottes," the newest fashion craze from Paris, opined that the era of significant national differences was fading as a new global culture arose: "Gone forever are the times when national barriers *really* keep nations apart. All sorts of inventions become the property of the whole, whether their cradle is Kansas City . . . or . . . in our even more kind-hearted bare Galicia and hungry Ludomeria [*Golicya i Głodomierya*]."[35] Film stars, sports stars, famous criminals, heroes of aviation, and ordinary people caught up in the "spectacular reality" of modern urban life peopled this universe and were the subject of conversations from Kansas City to Cracow.

Urban and interurban culture may have been superficial and fleeting, but it was no less attractive for its immediacy and superficiality. Indeed, in an era of dramatic changes in urban infrastructure and individual lifestyles, metropolitan culture best matched the thrilling, if frequently unsettling, impermanence of modern urban existence. Its entertainment factor numbed the harsh realities and inequalities of life in the city, offering an opportunity to relish the triumphs and misfortunes of others. Its sense of shared spectatorship, too, offered the sensation of belonging to a community of people with similar perspectives and problems. Ultimately, recognizing and affirming one's urban selfhood was an empowering experience. For migrants, women, and children (the groups that urban men presumed to be most vulnerable to the dangers of great-city life), becoming metropolitan offered novel opportunities while challenging the constraints of traditional culture. For city planners and municipal leaders, metropolitan improvement promised popular support and the opportunity to "catch up."

In the realm of municipal government, becoming metropolitan was, as contemporaries well understood, entirely "symptomatic" of the advance of industrial capitalism across the globe. The demographic revolution and the spread of the global marketplace, respectively, pushed and pulled villagers from the impoverished Galician countryside to nearby oilfields, to Lemberg and Cracow, to German farms, mines, and factories, and to the expanding cities of the New World.[36] As Cracow, a central place city with regional pull, proved incapable of managing the flow of migrants to the city and the suburban communities, it increasingly made sense to do what numerous other European cities were doing by creating an overarching city plan that included incorporation. Tariff zones would be altered or eliminated to aid the flow of capital and goods throughout the city; tramways and roads would spread beyond the old turnpike to aid the flow of population throughout the metropolis; sewers and running water would spread health and hygiene; and the canalization of the Vistula and construction of a port, it was hoped, would fully connect Cracow to the fruits of global trade. If its location in the corner of the three partitions had previously limited Cracow's link to its "natural" hinterland, now, President Leo and others hoped, its connection to the river network would place it at the nexus of Danubian, Baltic, and Black Sea trade.

In the years 1900–1915, Cracow and its citizens took part in the interrelated set of structural, institutional, economic, sociological, and cultural changes associated with becoming metropolitan. By the second decade of the twentieth century, Cracow was no longer the sleepy lair for widows and maidservants it had been in 1900. With its greatly expanded territory and population, thriving boulevard press, new "normal gauge" tram lines (now under city control), trade schools, cleaned-up markets, a new bridge across the Vistula, riparian canalization, and plans for a new port, Cracow had become a "great city." Its inhabitants, Poles and Jews alike, joined sporting clubs, attended the cinema, and expressed interest in automobiles and airplanes. There were assuredly plenty of traditional people still in the city, people whose rank and religion were readily legible in their attire and demeanor, people whose rural background (and worldview) remained etched in their weather-beaten faces and thick work-worn fingers, but there was also no denying the presence of modern metropolitans there, too. Cracow and its inhabitants had donned "European attire," and though ill-fitting and a little shabby in spots, it was beginning to suit them.

Epilogue

The city is poisoning us. The city is killing us. No one reads
poetry anymore, they only read newspapers—such is the
drama of the city of Cracow.
—Jalu Kurek, 1926[1]

So what became of Cracow's nascent metropolitan culture during and after
the Great War? The war was a break, but perhaps not in the way we have
become accustomed to thinking. Typically, historians and contemporaries
alike have viewed the war as the ushering in of "the modern."[2] In Cracow,
at least, what the war ushered in was national independence and a surge of
nationalism and national feeling. But modern metropolitan life, of the sort
promoted by the popular press, was *interrupted* by the exigencies of war and
the creation of a new national state. Cracow was evacuated and besieged
early in the war and, like other Central European cities, endured a period of
municipal and especially imperial failure by the end, in which basic needs
could not be met and society began to break down. In April 1918, the city
was the site of a pogrom that, when considered alongside other pogroms
in Poland that year, irrevocably soured many Jews' attitude toward Polish
acculturation.[3] After the war, it took a while for modern urban life to resume.
Stories in *IKC* in 1918 and early 1919 obsessed over the national situation as
Poles set about creating a new state. Sports scores and local news were still
there, but the balance of coverage in the press had shifted to war, politics,
and the creation of the new state. It would take a few years for the balance of
popular culture and political culture to reverse itself. Modern metropolitan
life had to be resumed, but once it was, the process of becoming metropolitan was largely complete. Cracovians, for good and for ill, were now part of
modern European civilization.

When in 1924 Alfred Döblin, the renowned novelist from Berlin, jour-
neyed to Poland, he found a society wracked with the tensions of creating a
national state out of a territory inhabited by several different national group-

ings, including the Jewish community of his forebears. In repeated instances, he noted the irony of Polish nationalism in trying to create a state in its image after having been excluded itself for so long by other powerful states.[4] In Warsaw, Lwów, and Cracow he also found modern European civilization, a civilization that he found both familiar and unsettling.[5]

Cracow, "the cleanest, most beautiful city [he visited] in Poland," was for Döblin nonetheless a city of suffering both medieval and modern.[6] Drawn to St. Mary's Church, which he visited daily, he reveled in the profundity of the broken body of Christ and the horror of the world. Stepping outside the church, he saw an airplane fly overhead.[7] "Businessmen, lawyers, art lovers, and students" walked hurriedly by.[8] He marveled at the contradiction between old and new in this "ancient city," but unlike Ménie Muriel Dowie, who saw progress in Cracow as "hopelessly out of tune," for Döblin the contradiction was reconfigured as something poignant, the backdrop for a wistful embrace:

> In the evening, I often steal into this slender decorated building [the Clothiers' Hall], as airy as lace, the home to dense darkness. The tremendous wealth of the arc lamps is spread out across the large square. The ancient fragile structure appears clearly in the whiteness, like a ship on the vast ocean. Confusing, poignant—this proximity of two worlds: electric light, modern promenades, automobiles, and that, the Cloth Gazebo, and also that, the slender church of St. Mary. How they crowd each other, encounter each other, kiss each other over their shoulders.

"Is it a dead world and a new world?" he asked himself. "I don't know which is dead. The old one isn't dead. I feel intimately and violently attracted to it."[9] For Döblin the divide between old and new was not the same as the fissure between living and dead, and each aspect of the city had its own measure of vigor *and* corruption. Given the choice, however, he came to favor the "practical science of theology" embraced by the old world over the crass superficialities of modern urban life.[10]

Still, Döblin saw much of modern urban Cracow during his visit. A doctor by profession, he sat in on a surgical lecture at the university. Some students slept or chatted, others paid rapt attention. He noted the women, whose bright blouses and "pert bobbed hair" made a nice contrast with the young men's brown and black clothing and long slicked-back hair.[11] In the evening on the streets, he spotted more beautiful women, with their "full figures" and "piquant, sexy faces," laughing and strolling. People "sated themselves" with coffee and sweets, swaying in "coziness and delight." The "executed man" in St. Mary's Church still "[hung] in their midst," he noted, but they preferred not to think about it. "Life," he concluded, "wants to be heavy and sated."[12]

For Döblin, modern urban life, the European civilization that he shared with the people on Cracow's streets, was ultimately about this feeling of satiation, a sensation that blunted the pangs of suffering in the world. As in Warsaw, where he took in jaunty nightclubs, penny operas, and concerts, and in Lwów, where he saw a bourgeois couple in pince-nez and diamonds contentedly eat their roast beef under the glow of electric light bulbs, blissfully unconcerned with the compression of coal, dynamos, wiring, and human effort that made the illumination of their mundane act possible,[13] here too in Cracow, Döblin cast an ambivalent eye on the utter placidity of modern urban life.

While touring Kazimierz, he learned of the presumed rape and murder of a female university student who went missing and whose body was later found floating in the Vistula. Her parents were initially convinced she had been abducted by white slavers; others thought it was a suicide. Later in his narrative, Döblin reported that the autopsy indicated "heavy injuries, rape, death only a day ago. She was kidnapped, abused, murdered, her body thrown into the water." Her violent death, along with the disappearance of the sixteen-year-old daughter of a physician, who was later "found on the road, raped, moronic, insane," only confirmed Döblin's sense of the ineluctable universality of human suffering.[14] Yet according to the report in *IKC*, "despite rumors to the contrary, the autopsy of the student did not reveal rape or a violent death." She had in fact committed suicide—possibly, the paper speculated, because of philosophical and lifestyle differences between the "freethinking" young woman and her traditional Jewish parents.[15] Meanwhile no report of the missing doctor's daughter appeared in any issue of the newspaper that week.

In this instance at least, "great-city filthiness" no longer seems to have elicited the same level of shock among Cracovians as it had some two decades before. Just as stories of accidents with the electric streetcar, which had become matter of fact once the population had grown accustomed to their presence, so too had the tragic story of a young girl's death ceased to be reason for the outworn tropes. In an age when young women sat with young men at university lectures, observed flayed bodies beneath them, and went out on walks on their own, it was no longer so shocking when one of them, sadly, chose to take her life. Faced with such a tragedy, metropolitans desired not a morality tale, but the facts. They were accustomed to the terrors of modern urban life (and to death, after years of war) and, if Döblin was right, generally preferred to be sated by the pleasures of their cafés, concert halls, shopping arcades, dance clubs, and cinemas, rather than be constantly reminded of those terrors. Unconfirmed and unreported, the story of a bourgeois girl's abduction and rape—just the sort of story that would have sparked a frenzy of press interest some twenty years before—had somehow missed the editor's desk.

Notes

INTRODUCTION

1. *Nowiny dla wszystkich* (hereafter *Nowiny*), 7 October 1904, 5.

2. Francis W. Halsey, ed., *Seeing Europe with Famous Authors*, vol. 4, pt. 2, *Germany, Austria-Hungary, Switzerland* (1914; reprint, NY, 2004), 34–39. Emphasis added. Ménie Muriel Dowie (1867–1945) first published *A Girl in Trousers* in 1891. Subsequent editions shortened the title to *A Girl in the Karpathians*, and by 1892, the author's last name had been changed to reflect her 1891 marriage to Henry Norman. See also Ménie Muriel Norman, *A Girl in the Karpathians*, 5th ed. (London, 1892), 290–95, which renders the phrase about Cracow as a "gay capital . . . full of . . . *esprit*" rather than "wit."

3. The Polish-Lithuanian Commonwealth was partitioned by Russia, Prussia, and Austria in 1772, 1793, and 1795 and ceased to exist as an independent state in 1795.

4. Hanna Kozińska-Witt, *Krakau in Warschaus langem Schatten. Konkurrenzkämpfe in der polnischen Städtelandschaft, 1900–1939* (Stuttgart, 2008); Patrice Dabrowski, *Commemorations and the Shaping of Modern Poland* (Bloomington, IN, 2004); Jacek Purchla, *Krakau unter Österreichischer Herrschaft, 1846–1918. Faktoren seiner Entwicklung* (Vienna, 1993) and *Jak powstał nowoczesny Kraków* (Cracow, 1990). Purchla convincingly shows how Cracow's aristocratic elite shaped its modernization. See also Lawrence Orton, "The Formation of Modern Cracow, 1866–1914," *Austrian History Yearbook* 19–20 (1983–1984): 105–17; and Jan Małecki, "W dobie autonomii galicyjskiej (1866–1918)," in *Dzieje Krakowa*, vol. 3, *Kraków w latach 1796–1918*, ed. Janina Bieniarzówna and Jan Małecki (Cracow, 1979), 225–394.

5. Józef Dużyk, "Polskie Ateny," in *Kraków Stary i Nowy. Dzieje kultury*, ed. Janina Bieniarzówna (Cracow, 1968), 303–44; Kazimierz Wyka, "Kraków stolicą Młodej Polski," in *Kraków i Małopolska przez dzieje*, ed. Celina Bobińska (Kraków, 1970), 339–52; Czesław Miłosz, "Young Poland," in *The History of Polish Literature* (1969; Berkeley and Los Angeles, 1983), 322–79; Artur Hutnikiewicz, *Młoda Polska* (Warszawa: PWN, 1994). See also Piotr Krakowski, "Cracow Artistic Milieu around 1900," in *Art around 1900 in Central Europe: Art Centres and Provinces*, ed. Piotr Krakowski and Jacek Purchla (Cracow, 1999), 71–79; Harold Segel, "Cracow: Little Green Balloons," in *Turn-of-the-Century Cabaret* (NY, 1987); and David Crowley, "Castles, Cabarets, and Cartoons: Claims on Polishness in Krakow around 1905," in *The City in Central Europe*, ed. Malcolm Gee, Tim Kirk, and Jill Steward (Brookfield, VT, 1999), 101–17.

6. Jan Bystroń, "Pięćdziesięciolecie samorządu Krakowa, 1866–1917," in *Kalendarz krakowski Józefa Czecha na roku 1917* (Kraków, 1916), 66.

7. Stanisław Broniewski, *Igraszki z czasem, czyli minione lata na cenzurowanym* (Cracow, 1970), 101.

8. Mieczysław Smolarski, *Miasto starych dzwonów* (Cracow, 1960), 187. See also Władysław Krygowski, *W moim Krakowie nad wczorajszą Wisłą* (Cracow, 1980), 9–10.

9. *Ilustrowany Kuryer Codzienny*, 12 March 1913.

10. Perhaps the earliest-known version of the myth attributes the idea to bait the dragon to Krak, a proto-ruler of the city. Jan Adamczewski, *In Cracow* (Warsaw, 1973), 16.

11. The Austrian Commune Law of 1866 granted communal autonomy to villages, towns, and cities in an effort by the Habsburg authorities to counter the centralizing aspects of the 1861 February Patent. See Keely Stauter-Halsted, *The Nation in the Village: The Genesis of Peasant National Identity in Austrian Poland, 1848–1914* (Ithaca, NY, 2001), 79–81; and Jeremy King, *Budweisers into Czechs and Germans: A Local History of Bohemian Politics, 1848–1948* (Princeton, NJ, 2002), 49. I thank Pieter Judson for calling this to my attention.

12. Lawrence Orton, "The Stańczyk Portfolio and the Politics of Galician Loyalism," *Polish Review* 27, nos. 1/2 (1982): 55–64.

13. Dabrowski, *Commemorations*.

14. Robert L. Przygrodzki, "Tsar Vasilii Shuiskii, the Staszic Palace, and Nineteenth-Century Russian Politics in Warsaw," in *Polish Encounters, Russian Identity*, ed. Bozena Shallcross and David L. Ransel (Bloomington, IN, 2005), 144–59.

15. Brian Porter, *When Nationalism Began to Hate* (NY, 2000).

16. Jacek Purchla, *Matecznik polski. Pozaekonomiczne czynniki rozwoju Krakowa w okresie autonomii galicyjskiej* (Kraków, 1992).

17. Eugen Weber, *Peasants into Frenchmen: The Modernization of Rural France, 1870–1914* (Stanford, CA, 1976); Stauter-Halsted, *The Nation in the Village*.

18. For more on the term "self-identification" and justifications for using it, please see Rogers Brubaker, *Ethnicity without Groups* (Cambridge, MA, 2004), 28–63, esp. 41–42.

19. Dennison Rusinow, "Ethnic Politics in the Habsburg Monarchy and Successor States: Three Answers to the National Question," in *Nationalism and Empire: The Habsburg Empire and the Soviet Union*, ed. Richard L. Rudolph and David F. Good (NY, 1992), 246–47.

20. Pieter Judson, *Guardians of the Nation: Activists on the Language Frontiers of Imperial Austria* (Cambridge, MA, 2006).

21. For a contemporary example of this phenomenon in the highly nationalized space of Cluj, please see Rogers Brubaker, Margit Fieschmidt, Jon Fox, and Liana Grancea, eds., *Nationalist Politics and Everyday Ethnicity in a Transylvanian Town* (Princeton, NJ, 2006).

22. Markian Prokopovych, *Habsburg Lemberg: Architecture, Public Space, and Politics in the Galician Capital, 1772–1914* (West Lafayette, IN, 2009). Daniel Unowsky, *The Pomp and Politics of Patriotism: Imperial Celebrations in Habsburg Austria, 1848–1916* (West Lafayette, IN, 2005).

23. Eric Hobsbawm, *Nations and Nationalism since 1780* (Cambridge, UK, 1991), 11.

24. Harald Binder, "Urban Landscape and Printed Press in Habsberg Lemberg: The Kotsko Memorial of 1912," *East Central Europe* 33, pts. 1–2 (2006): 53–70.

25. *Nowiny,* 16 July 1910, 1, and 17 July 1910, 5.

26. Dabrowski, *Commemorations,* 159–83.

27. Robert Musil, *The Man without Qualities,* trans. Eithne Wilkens and Ernst Kaiser (London, 1979), 1:34, cited in Charles S. Maier, "City, Empire, and Imperial Aftermath: Contending Contexts for the Urban Vision," in *Shaping the Great City: Modern Architecture in Central Europe, 1890–1937,* ed. Eve Blau and Monika Platzer (Munich and NY, 1999), 25.

28. Benedict Anderson, *Imagined Communities: Reflections on the Origins and Spread of Nationalism* (NY, 1991).

29. Georg Simmel, "The Metropolis and Mental Life," in *The Sociology of George Simmel,* ed. Kurt H. Wolf (NY, 1950), 409–24.

30. Gunther Barth, *City People: The Rise of Modern City Culture in Nineteenth-Century America* (NY, 1980), 24, see also 1–6.

31. Gábor Gyáni, *Identity and the Urban Experience: Fin-de-Siècle Budapest,* trans. Thomas J. DeKornfield (Boulder, CO, 2004). See also my review of this work on H-Urban, H-Net Reviews, February 2009.

32. According to figures from the *Library Atlas of the World,* vol. 2 (Chicago and NY, 1913), 1910 populations for Berlin, Vienna, Budapest, Warsaw, and Prague were as follows: 2,071,000, 2,031,000, 880,000, 771,000, 640,000. Cited in Paul Robert Magocsi, *Historical Atlas of Central Europe,* revised and expanded ed. (Toronto: University of Toronto Press, 2002), 96. For the book that launched the expression "the age of great cities," please see Robert Vaughan, *The Age of Great Cities, or, Modern Society Viewed in Its Relation to Intelligence, Morals, and Religion* (1843; reprint, Shannon: Irish University Press, 1972).

33. As cited in Grodziska, "Gdzie to miasto zaczarowane," 115.

34. Józef Piłsudski, the socialist/nationalist revolutionary from Russian Poland and future president/dictator of Poland from his coup d'état in 1926 until his death in 1935, famously organized the Polish Legions in Cracow in August 1914 with the hope that they might assist in fighting for Polish independence during the coming war.

35. King, *Budweisers into Czechs and Germans* and "The Nationalization of East Central Europe," in *Staging the Past,* ed. Maria Bucur and Nancy Wingfield (West Lafayette, IN, 2001), 112–52.

36. The power of the teleological nationalist narrative is most evident in a brief article by Cracow's greatest living historian, Jan Małecki, who, given the task of describing the city's autonomous government from 1866 to 1918 at a conference sponsored by Jacek Purchla, chose to begin his story two centuries before, when Cracow was the capital of the Polish-Lithuanian Commonwealth, and end his account when the independent government of Poland was established in the 1920s, and the city was fully Polish again. See Małecki, "The Cracow Municipal Government in the 19th and 20th Centuries," in *Mayors and City Halls: Local Government and the Cultural*

Space of the Late Habsburg Monarchy, ed. Jacek Purchla (Cracow, 1998), 35–43.

37. I acknowledge that in substituting one myth for another, I could be accused of merely replacing one teleological vision with another. After all, "progress," "development," "modern," and "future" are all loaded terms that imply their own notions of directional movement toward a particular goal, modernity. In titling my work "Becoming Metropolitan," I choose to stress process rather than arrival. The *telos* is implied but remains unfulfilled—at least before the war. As in any sensitive study of the formation and articulation of national identity, this text seeks to explore the discourses of identification without reifying their claims.

38. For an important discussion of modernity, please see Marshall Berman, *All That Is Solid Melts into Air: The Experience of Modernity* (NY, 1982); Perry Anderson's critique of Berman, "Modernity and Revolution," *New Left Review* 144 (1984), 96–113, esp. 100–103; and Peter Osborne's critique of both, "Modernity Is a Qualitative, Not a Chronological Category," *New Left Review* 192 (1992), 65–84.

39. Lynda Nead, *Victorian Babylon: People, Streets, and Images in Nineteenth-Century London* (New Haven, CT: Yale University Press, 2000), 5.

40. *Cracow: Dialogue of Traditions,* ed. Zbigniew Baran, English version edited by William Brand (Cracow, 1991). Note the title.

41. Simon Hadler, "Der urbane Raum Krakaus als Medium des städtischen Images?" (De)Konstruktionen Galiziens. Kommunikation—Transformation—kultur elles Gedächtnis, Universität Wien, Vienna, 28 November 2008.

42. Olgierd Jędrzejczyk, *Niech Kraków zawsze Kraków znaczy* (Cracow, 1981), 83–85.

43. I thank Bill Johnston for this suggested translation of "*pomnikomania.*" Żeleński adopted the pen-name "Boy" in most of his work and is most frequently referred to as Boy-Żeleński, a pattern I follow as well.

44. Maria Bucur and Nancy Wingfield, eds., *Staging the Past: The Politics of Commemoration in Habsburg Central Europe, 1848 to the Present* (West Lafayette, IN, 2001); Brian Porter, *When Nationalism Began to Hate: Imagining Politics in Nineteenth-Century Poland* (NY, 2000).

45. The most famous work of Central European urban history is Carl Schorske's *Fin-de-Siècle Vienna: Politics and Culture* (NY, 1980). See also John Lukacs, *Budapest 1900: A Historical Portrait of a City and Its Culture* (NY, 1988); Peter Demetz, *Prague in Black and Gold: Scenes from the Life of a European City* (NY, 1997); and Gary B. Cohen, "Society and Culture in Prague, Vienna, and Budapest in the Late Nineteenth Century," *East European Quarterly* 20, no. 4 (January 1987): 467–92. *The Once and Future Budapest* by Robert Nemes (Dekalb, IL, 2005) illustrates the way that the multiethnic cities of Buda and Pest became a national capital. *The Garden and the Workshop: Essays on the Cultural History of Vienna and Budapest* (Princeton, NJ, 1998) by the late Péter Hanák is a collection of essays, clearly inspired by Schorske's work, on the cultural history of Budapest and Vienna. Gábor Gyáni's fascinating studies of the social and material culture of Budapest constitute the most thoroughgoing portrait of urban identification in this region. See Gyáni, *Women as Domestic Servants: The Case of Budapest, 1890–1940*

(NY, 1989); Gyáni, *Parlor and Kitchen: Housing and Domestic Culture in Budapest, 1870-1940* (Budapest, 2002); and Gyáni, *Identity and the Urban Experience*. See also *The City in Central Europe*, ed. Gee, Kirk, and Steward; and *Shaping the Great City: Modern Architecture in Central Europe, 1890-1937*, ed. Eve Blau and Monika Platzer (Munich and NY, 1999). *Mayors and City Halls: Local Government and the Cultural Space of the Late Habsburg Monarchy*, ed. Jacek Purchla (Cracow, 1998) is a very useful collection of articles about urban government in Habsburg Central Europe at the turn of the century. A recent special issue of *East Central Europe* 33, pts. 1-2 (2006) focuses on the urban history of East Central Europe. See also Prokopovych, *Habsburg Lemberg*.

    46. Peter Fritzsche, *Reading Berlin, 1900* (Cambridge, MA, 1996).

    47. Nathaniel D. Wood, "Becoming a 'Great City': Metropolitan Imaginations and Apprehensions in Cracow's Popular Press, 1900-1914," *Austrian History Yearbook* 33 (2002): 105-29. Much of this article focuses on the perception of criminality and filthiness associated with the "great city." I develop these ideas in chap. 6.

    48. Vanessa Schwartz, *Spectacular Realities: Early Mass Culture in* Fin-de-Siècle *Paris* (Berkeley and Los Angeles, 1998).

    49. Jürgen Habermas, *The Structural Transformation of the Public Sphere*, trans. Thomas Burger with the assistance of Frederick Lawrence (original German edition, 1962; Cambridge, MA, 1994) 170, 159-75.

    50. Habermas, *Structural Transformation*, 171.

    51. Jean Chalaby, *The Invention of Journalism* (NY, 1998), 153, 181. For an important discussion of Habermas, Benedict Anderson, and Chalaby, please see Michael Schudson, "News, Public, Nation," *American Historical Review* 107, no. 2 (April 2002): 481-96.

    52. Sylvester, *Tales of Old Odessa: Crime and Civility in a City of Thieves* (DeKalb, 2005).

    53. Fritzsche, *Reading Berlin*, 209.

    54. Schwartz, *Spectacular Realities*, 6.

CHAPTER 1

    1. Kazimierz Marjan Morawski, *Kraków przed trzydziestu laty* (Warsaw, 1932), 7.

    2. Ignacy Daszyński, *Pamiętniki* (Cracow, 1925), 96-97.

    3. A "central place city," as the title implies, draws in surrounding population, frequently because it is an administrative capital. See Paul Hohenberg and Lynn Hollen Lees, *The Making of Urban Europe, 1000-1994* (Cambridge, MA, 1995).

    4. Rudolf Sikorski, "Kraków w roku 1900, oraz jego podział administracyjny w ciągu XIX stulecia," in *Kalendarz krakowski Józefa Czecha na roku 1903* (Cracow, 1904), 88.

    5. Eleonora Gajzlerowa z Cerchów, *Tamten Kraków, tamta Krynica* (Cracow, 1995), 21.

    6. Mieczysław Hamburgier, "Śmiertelność z gruźlicy i zapalenia płuc w Krakowie

od 1900 r. do 1913 r.," *Gruźlica* 1–2, issues 3, 4, and 5 (1925/1926), 143. Bieniarzówna and Małecki, eds., *Dzieje Krakowa,* 3:315.

7. Krygowski, *W moim Krakowie nad wczorajszą Wisłą,* 12.

8. *Nowiny,* 15 November 1903, 5.

9. *Nowiny,* 19 January 1911, 2.

10. *Nowiny,* 20 May 1910, 3; 22 September 1910, 1–2; 3 December 1910, 1.

11. Nearly all of these destinations are mentioned in Magdalena Samozwaniec's *Maria i Magdalena* (Cracow, 1970). By the second decade of the twentieth century, the popular newspaper *IKC* had an office in Marseilles, to cater to the Riviera crowd of expatriates and Cracovians on holiday.

12. Magocsi, *Historical Atlas of Central Europe,* 28; Mieczysław Orłowicz and Roman Kordys, *Illustrierter Führer durch Galizien mit einem Anhang. Ost-Schlesien von Dr. Johan Kotas und Prof. Josef Londzin* (Vienna and Leipzig, 1914), 52. Incidentally, one cannot get to Vienna or L'viv any faster by train today.

13. The *Illustrierter Führer durch Galizien* (1914), for example, had 41 pages of text about Cracow and only 19 devoted to Lemberg. See also Karl Baedeker, *Österreich-Ungarn. Handbuch fur reisende* (Leipzig, 1903).

14. From notes in the archival copy of Baedeker's *Österreich-Ungarn* (1903) in the collections of the University of Kansas, Spencer Research Library.

15. For more on the Palace of Art, please see Urszula Bęczkowska, *Pałac Sztuki. Siedziba Towarzystwa Przyjaciół Sztuk Pięknych w Krakowie* (Cracow, 2002).

16. Jan Bystroń, "Rozwój demograficzny dzielnic Krakowa (Tworzenie się Centrum wielkomiejskiego w Krakowie)," *Ekonimista* 15, nos. 1–2 (1915): 112–60.

17. Both aforementioned memoirists mention Fischer's. See Krygowski, *W moim Krakowie,* 79–81; and Gajzlerowa, *Tamten Kraków, tamta Krynica,* 34–35.

18. The famous Zielony Balonik (Green Balloon) cabaret located at Jama Michalika did not begin until 1905, but the sweetshop itself had been open since 1892.

19. Sikorski, "Kraków w roku 1900," 83. The number of buildings in the neighborhood had increased by 270 percent since 1867, growing most rapidly in the last decade.

20. Archiwum Państwowe w Krakowie (APK), DPKr 439–442 (rejestry prostytutek).

21. Jacek Purchla, *Matecznik polski* (Cracow, 1992), 75–76.

22. The Archduke Rudolf Barracks were in the neighborhood of Kleparz. Fortifications and military installations were scattered throughout the city, particularly in the suburban communities.

23. Author's calculations, based on data in *Statystyka Miasta Krakowa za lata 1903, 1904, i 1905* (Cracow, 1908), 116, 88.

24. Bystroń, "Rozwój demograficzny dzielnic Krakowa," 160.

25. Artur Gruszecki, *Cygarniczka* (Warsaw, 1906).

26. *Nowiny* reported that several working-class Cracovians picked fights with the American Indian actors in the troupe, as they walked around downtown, or got into other fights at the show while trying to sneak in for free. In the paper's final

verdict, despite hauling in some 250,000 crowns, the show was a disappointment. Further violence occurred as frustrated Cracovians who felt the horseback riding, whooping, and "childish episodes of battles" did not live up to the advertising clamored for refunds. See *Nowiny*, 3 August 1906, 4–5; 5 August 1906, 4; 6 August 1906, 2; and 7 August 1906, 5.

27. Jacek Purchla, "Krakowskie mosty i ich znaczenie dla rozwoju miasta," in his *Kraków. Prowincja czy metropolia?* (Cracow, 1996), 111.

28. Andrzej Żbikowski, *Żydzi krakowscy i ich gmina w latach 1869–1919* (Warsaw, 1994), 13.

29. Sean Martin, *Jewish Life in Cracow, 1918–1939* (Portland, OR, 2004), 32.

30. Jan Małecki, "Cracow Jews in the Nineteenth Century: Leaving the Ghetto," *Acta Poloniae Historica* 76 (1997): 87–88.

31. Gajzlerowa, *Tamten Kraków, tamta Krynica*, 31; *Nowiny* 5 April 1904, 3–4. See also Żbikowski, *Żydzi krakowscy*, 272–79.

32. Małecki, "Cracow Jews in the Nineteenth Century," 93. See also *Krakowianie. Wybitni żydzi krakowscy XIV–XX wieku*, ed. Agnieszka Kutylak (Cracow, 2006), 92–95.

33. Małecki, "Cracow Jews in the Nineteenth Century," 91.

34. Martin, *Jewish Life in Cracow*, 37.

35. As cited in ibid., 39.

36. Żbikowski, *Żydzi krakowscy*, 269–95.

37. Tadeusz Boy-Żeleński, *Znaszli ten kraj?. . . (Cyganeria krakowska) oraz inne wspomnienia o Krakowie*, ed. Tomasz Wiess (Wrocław, 1983), 5.

38. Purchla, "*Krakowskie mosty*," 109.

39. Jarosław Żółciak, "Rozwój przestenny Podgórza," in *Kraków. Nowe studia nad rozwojem miasta*, ed. Jerzy Wyrozumski (Cracow, 2007), 530–86.

40. *Nowiny*, 17 January 1908, 1, compares Cracovian and Viennese prices. See also *Nowiny*, 27 October 1907, 2, which compares Cracovian rents to those in Paris, Vienna, Berlin, Lemberg, and London. Jan Małecki confirms the fact that Parisian rental costs were nearly half of Cracow's. See Bieniarzówna and Małecki, eds., *Dzieje Krakowa*, 3:357.

41. *Nowiny*, 30 April 1909, 1.

42. Bystroń, "Pięćdziesięciolecie samorządu Krakowa," 12.

43. Ferdynand Goetel, *Patrząc wstecz* (London, 1966), 7; Witold Zechenter, *Upływa szybko życie* (Cracow: Wydawnictwo Literackie, 1975).

44. Bieniarzówna and Małecki, eds., *Dzieje Krakowa* 3:315.

45. Bernadeta Wilk, *W 'Małym Wiedniu nad Wisłą'* (Cracow, 2008), 51; Baedeker, Österreich-Ungarn (1903), 333.

46. Bystroń, "Pięćdziesięciolecie samorządu Krakowa," 78; Wilk, *W 'Małym Wiedniu,'* 44–45; Robert Wierzbicki, *Wodociągi Krakowa do roku 1939* (Cracow, 1999).

47. Jacek Purchla, "Local Government and the Civilizational Space of Cracow in the 19th Century," in *Mayors and City Halls*, ed. Jacek Purchla (Cracow, 1998), 265–66.

48. Bieniarzówna and Małecki, eds., *Dzieje Krakowa*, 3:355.

49. *Słowo Polskie*, 11 February 1908, 1.

50. For a thoroughgoing study of this process in Budapest, please see Robert Nemes, *The Once and Future Budapest*.

51. Only Szlachtowski came from a Polish gentry family (from Lemberg). Zyblikiewicz was the son of a Ruthenian furrier from Sambór/Sambir. Leo's German-speaking grandfather came from Moravia in the early nineteenth century to work in the salt mines of Wieliczka. The other three mayors came from established Cracovian families of German origin.

52. Friedlein, who headed the city from 1893 to 1904, was known for his personable attitude and was often seen walking the city streets, conversing with citizens. Sadly, Friedlein's habit of conversing with strangers cost him a fine watch, according to *Nowiny*, which reported that a man with a Czech accent swiped it from the former mayor after asking him the time. The septuagenarian gave chase but failed to catch the thief. *Nowiny*, 5 August 1904, 5.

53. Goetel, *Patrząc wstecz*, 10–11.

54. Sikorski, "Kraków w roku 1900," 89–90.

55. Kazimierz Władysław Kumaniecki, *Tymczasowe wyniki spisu ludności w Krakowie z 31grudnia 1910 roku* (Cracow: City of Cracow, 1912), 33–34. Including the military, the percentage of Polish speakers drops to 90.84% while that of German speakers increases to 7.6%. For more on the census forms themselves and an analysis of the 1880 data, please see Lidia Zyblikiewicz, "Education and Social Structure according to the Cracow Census of 1880," in *L'enseignement des Élites en Europe Centrale (19e-20e siècles)*, ed. Victor Krady and Mariusz Kulczykowski (Cracow, 1999), 111–20.

56. Kumaniecki, *Tymczasowe wyniki spisu ludności*, 33–34.

57. *Nowiny*, 4 January 1911, 1–3.

58. *Nowiny*, 6 January 1909, 3.

59. *Nowiny*, 15 October 1908, 1.

60. Krzysztof Zamorski, "Rozwój demograficzny Krakowa w ciągu wieków," in *Kraków. Nowe studia nad rozwojem miasta*, ed. Jerzy Wyrozumski (Cracow, 2007), 872. See also Zamorski, "Kraków-przestrzeń społeczna," in *Kraków. Dziedziectwo wieków*, ed. Jan Małecki (Cracow, 2006), 74–101, esp. 94–96.

61. *Statystyka Miasta Krakowa za lata 1903, 1904, 1905*, 89. Sikorski, "Kraków w roku 1900," 87.

62. Żbikowski, *Żydzi krakowscy*, 41.

63. Jan Tambor, *Trwanie życia ludzkiego w Krakowie w okresie od r. 1881-1925* (Warsaw, 1930), 31. All told, during the period of Tambor's study there were seven Cracovians—four Jewish men and three Christian women—who lived 110 years or more.

64. Ibid., 31, 23.

65. *Statystyka Miasta Krakowa za lata 1903, 1904, 1905*, 89.

66. Zamorski, "Kraków-przestrzeń społeczna," 95; *Statystyka Miasta Krakowa za lata 1903, 1904, 1905*, 16–17.

67. Tambor, *Trwanie życia ludzkiego w Krakowie*, 8.

68. Kumaniecki, *Tymczasowe wyniki spisu ludności*, 31; Sikorski, "Kraków w roku 1900," 87.

69. Janina Bienarzówna and Jan M. Małecki, *Dzieje Krakowa*, vol. 3, *Kraków w latach 1796-1918* (Cracow: Wydawnictwo Literackie, 1979), 318. Males also had higher mortality rates and were more likely to emigrate from Cracow as young men.

70. *Kraków. Rozszerzenie granic, 1909-1915*, published by Karol Rolle, President of the City of Cracow (Cracow, 1931).

71. Bystroń, "Rozwój demograficzny dzielnic Krakowa," 160.

72. *Nowiny*, 19 September 1909, 1, and 24 September 1909, 1.

73. Samozwaniec, *Maria i Magdalena*, 47-48. Please see also Keely Stauter-Halsted, "Moral Panic and the Prostitute in Partitioned Poland: Middle Class Respectability in Defense of the Modern Nation," *Slavic Review* 68 (Fall 2009): 557-81.

74. Peter Hall, *Cities in Civilization* (NY, 1998), 174. The term likely came from Arthur Schnitzler, whose plays frequently featured a variant of an early love, a needlewoman. See Reingard Witzmann, "The Two Faces of Vienna," in *Vienna, 1890-1920*, ed. Robert Waissenberger (NY, 1984), 76.

75. *Kuryerek Krakowski* (hereafter *KK*), 5 March 1903, 4-5.

76. *Nowiny*, 7 April 1908, 2. After the old man kissed her, she said she would hit him over the head with a frying pan. The feuilleton concluded: "Her mistress took her back. Poor Marysia."

77. *Statystyka Miasta Krakowa za lata 1903, 1904, 1905*, 14.

78. Ibid., 91.

79. *Nowiny*, 4 June 1904, 1, 6; 20 March 1907, 1-3; 22 March 1907, 3; 23 March 1907, 1; 9 June 1907, 2-3.

80. Ménie Muriel Norman, *A Girl in the Karpathians*, 95-96.

81. *KK*, 16 January 1903, 4.

82. *Kalendarz krakowski Józefa Czecha na roku 1903*, 58-62.

83. Prince Lubomirski also funded an analogous home for girls. See Jacek Purchla, *Matecznik polski*, 75-76, and the illustrations numbered 55-61 following p. 80. The original photographs are housed in the Museum of the History of the City of Cracow.

84. The term *Antek/Antki* was in use in Warsaw and Lemberg, as well. Dictionaries of Varsovian and Polish slang show that the term was in use already in the middle of the nineteenth century. "Antek," a short story by Bolesław Prus about a village lad who ultimately leaves for the city may have popularized it even more. I thank Bob Rothstein for his reference to slang dictionaries. Cracovians also called the boys "Andrusy."

85. Marian Turski, "Czasy gimnazjalne," in *Kopiec wspomnień*, ed. Jan Gintel (Cracow, 1964), 86-88.

86. *Nowiny*, 13 April 1905, 5; 17 April 1905, 1-2; 18 April 1905, 3; 7 February 1906, 1-5.

87. Gajzlerowa, *Tamten Kraków, tamta Krynica*, 29.

88. *Nowiny*, 17 January 1908, 1.

89. *Nowiny,* 22 September 1907, 2.

90. Wilk, *W 'Małym Wiedniu,'* 38–39.

91. Broniewski, *Igraszki z czasem,* 52. *Dziad* has since come to mean beggar, but as a second definition.

92. Morawski, *Kraków przed trzydziestu laty,* 28.

93. Gajzlerowa, *Tamten Kraków, tamta Krynica,* 24–27.

94. For more on the founder of Brother Albert's shelter, please see Tadeusz Chrzanowski, "Adam Chmielowski—Saint Brother Albert or between Art and Saintliness," in *Cracow: Dialogue of Traditions,* ed. Zbigniew Baran, trans. William Brand (Cracow, 1991), 95–106.

95. "Ustawa nadająca statu miejski królewskiemu stołecznemu miastu Krakowowi," printed in *Kalendarz krakowski Józefa Czecha na roku 1901* (Cracow, 1901), 1.

96. Józef Buszko, "Kraków w dobie autonomii galicyjskiej (1866–1914)," in *Szkice z dziejów Krakowa od czasów najdawniejszych do pierwszej wojny światowej,* ed. Janina Bieniarzówna (Cracow, 1968), 371.

97. For more on Cracow's intelligentsia, please see Irena Homola, *"Kwiat Społeczeństwa . . ." Struktura społeczna i zarys położenia inteligencji krakowskiej w latach 1860–1914* (Cracow, 1984).

98. Jacek Woźniakowski, "Old City, Modern Art," in *Cracow. Dialogue of Traditions,* ed. Zbigniew Baran, trans. William Brand (Cracow: Znak, 1991), 82.

99. Zofia Muczkowska, "Pod Krukiem," in *Kopiec wspomnień,* ed. Jan Gintel (Cracow, 1959), 44. See also Gábor Gyáni, *Identity and the Urban Experience,* 64–65.

100. *Nowiny,* 3 June 1909, 1–2.

101. Tadeusz Boy-Żeleński, "Wielki Kraków," in *Boy o Krakowie,* ed. Henryk Markiewicz (Cracow, 1967), 121.

102. Bystroń, "Pięćdziesięciolecie samorządu Krakowa," 67–68.

103. Stefan Zweig, *World of Yesterday* (1943; reprint, Lincoln, NE, 1964), 88.

104. APK DPKr 436–437.

105. *Kalendarz krakowski Józefa Czecha na roku 1908* (Cracow, 1907), 169–71.

106. *Nowiny,* 29 January 1904, 4; 7 August 1906, 4–5; 9 August 1910, 3.

107. Sikorski, "Kraków w roku 1900," 90–93.

108. Goetel, *Patrząc wstecz,* 11.

109. Boy-Żeleński, "Wielki Kraków," in *Boy o Krakowie,* 121–22.

110. See also Piotr Krakowski, "Cracow Artistic Milieu around 1900," in *Art around 1900 in Central Europe,* ed. Piotr Krakowski and Jacek Purchla (Cracow, 1999), 71–79.

111. Ludwik Waryński, as cited in Karolina Grodziska, "Gdzie to miasto zaczarowane," 107.

112. Wilk, *W 'Małym Wiedniu,'* 111.

113. Orton, "The Stańczyk Portfolio and the Politics of Galician Loyalism," 55–64.

114. Maciej Janowski, *Inteligencja wobec wyzwań nowoczesności. Dylematy ideowe demokracji liberalnej w Galicji w latach 1889–1914* (Warsaw, 1996). See also Stanisław Pijaj, *Między polskim patriotyzmem a habsburgskim*

lojalizmem. Polacy wobec przemian ustrójowych (Cracow, 2003).

115. Ignacy Daszyński, *Pamiętniki* (Cracow, 1915), 188–89. According to the 1866 statute, the municipal government in Cracow was composed of 60 city councilors, elected to six-year terms with elections every three years for half of the body.

116. Ibid., 189.

117. Jacques Le Rider, *Modernity and Crises of Identity: Culture and Society in Fin-de-Siècle Vienna*, trans. Rosemary Morris (NY, 1993), 11. See also Hall, *Cities in Civilization*, 177–78. Undoubtedly, Vienna was a major seat of modernist art, music, and literature, and innovations in psychology, but in terms of its material culture and urbanization, it was behind Anglo-American cities, as John L. Stoddard, in his eponymous lectures from the period pointed out: *John L. Stoddard's Lectures*, vol. 6, *Berlin, Vienna, St. Petersburg, Moscow* (Boston, 1903), 138.

118. Irena Homola-Skąpska, "Mały Wiedeń nad Wisłą," *Zeszyty Naukowe Uniwersytetu Jagiellońskiego: Prace Historyczne* 121 (1997): 409–26.

119. An illustration of a workers' strike from 1905 shows that the majority of participants wore bowler hats. See *Nowości Ilustrowane*, 11 February 1905. For the sartorial customs of Budapest's skilled workers, see Lukacs, *Budapest 1900*, 76.

120. The best, though certainly not the only, discussion of Cracow's funerary obsession is Boy-Żeleński's. See "Wielki Kraków," in *Boy o Krakowie*, 121–28.

CHAPTER 2

1. *Liberum Veto*, 20 April 1903, 21. Even though *Liberum Veto* was joking, mistakes like this actually occurred (and still do today). In 1913, *Nowiny* reported an instance of other Galician newspapers mistakenly repeating an April Fools' Day spoof from a Warsaw paper, as if it were true. *Nowiny*, 4 April 1913, 4–5. The lag, obviously, was only one or two days.

2. Wiesław Władyka, *Krew na pierwszej stronie. Sensacyjne dzienniki Drugiej Rzeczypospolitej* (Warszawa, 1982), 5, 11–18; Marion T. Marzoff, "American New Journalism Takes Root in Europe," *Journalism Quarterly* 61 (1984): 529–36, 691.

3. Frank Luther Mott, as cited in W. Joseph Campbell, *Yellow Journalism: Puncturing the Myths, Defining the Legacies* (Westport, CT, 2001), 7.

4. Gunther Barth, *City People*; Fritzsche, *Reading Berlin*; Schwartz, *Spectacular Realities*; and Sylvester, *Tales of Old Odessa*.

5. This is the central, celebratory argument of Robert Park's "The Natural History of the Newspaper," *American Journal of Sociology* 29 (November 1923): 273–89. For more about the politics of the Polish-language press in Galicia during this period, please see Harald Binder, "Das polnische Pressewesen," in *Die Habsburgermonarchie 1848–1918*, vol. 8/2, *Politische Öffentlichkeit und Zivilgesellschaft*, 2. Teilband, *Die Presse als Faktor der politischen Mobilisierung* (Vienna: Austrian Academy of Sciences, 2006), 2039–90.

6. Czesław Lechicki, "Kartka z dziejów prasy krakowskiej XX wieku," *Małopolskie Studia Historyczne* 8, nos. 1/2 (28/29) (1965): 119–33. *Nowa Reforma* was

published from 1882 to 1926; *Naprzód* began as a semi-monthly in 1891 and switched to a weekly (1895–1900) and then daily format by 1901; *Głos Narodu* ran from 1893 to 1939. See Mirosław Frančić, *Kraków. Kalendarz dziejów od prawieków do wybuchu I wojny światowej* (Cracow, 1998), 179–80. Inexplicably, Frančić does not include *Nowiny* in his list of "Cracovian newspapers and periodicals of the second half of the nineteenth century and the early twentieth century." There were a few Jewish weekly or semi-monthly publications, but the first Yiddish-language daily did not appear until 1909.

7. Jerzy Myśliński, "Prasa polska w Galicji w dobie autonomicznej (1867–1918)," in *Historia prasy polskiej w latach 1864–1918*, ed. Zenon Kmiecik et al. (Warszawa, 1976), 125–27.

8. Homola-Skąpska, "'Mały Wiedeń' nad Wisłą," 409–26.

9. Lukacs, *Budapest 1900*, 152–53.

10. Daniel M. Vyleta, *Crime, News, and Jews: Vienna, 1895–1914* (NY, 2007), 75.

11. I thank Jakub Machek for this information.

12. Vyleta, *Crime, News, and Jews*, 74.

13. Władyka, *Krew na pierwszej stronie*, 18.

14. *KK*, 25 November 1902, 2–3.

15. Lechicki, "Kartka," 125. The more respectable *Nowa Reforma*, with better-established networks, was printing three times as many papers at the time.

16. *Kuryer Krakowski* may have coexisted for some time alongside its competitor, but because no copies remain from after 23 May 1903, it is impossible to know when it folded. Based on ads in *Nowiny*, it appears that the *KK* title persisted as a Monday addition to the paper as late as April 1904, but by then Bartoszewicz's paper had clearly been co-opted.

17. *KK*, 7 April 1903, 5. For other examples of stories of boys who sold the papers, please see *KK*, 15 March 1903, 4; *Nowiny*, 7 February 1906, 1–2, and 5 July 1908, 1–2. An ad for a newsboy can be found in *Nowiny*, 15 September 1910, 4.

18. See *Nowiny*, 31 August 1910, 2–3. "Perhaps the police administration could encourage this officer to spend his time looking for drunken rabblerousers rather than pestering the colporteur who is only trying to make a living," *Nowniy* suggested. See also *Nowiny*, 4 December 1912, 3, or the Lvovian paper, *Wiek Nowy*, 20 February 1904, 17.

19. Piotr Borowiec, *Jesteśmy głosem milionów. Dzieje krakowskiego wydawnictwa i koncernu prasowego Ilustrowany Kurier Codzienny (1910–1939)* (Cracow, 2005), 34.

20. See *IKC*, 22 March 1912, 4.

21. See, for example, *Nowiny*, 3 April 1906, 4, or 13 December 1912, 4.

22. Andrzej Garlicki, "Rodzaje konfiskat prasowych w Krakowie w latach 1900–1914," *Przegląd Historyczny* 54, no. 3 (1963): 460.

23. Ibid., 457–72.

24. During the period 1904–1907, *Nowiny* had the second most (8 as compared to *Naprzód*'s 61), and in the period from 1908 to 1912, *IKC*, which first appeared in December 1910, also occupied the second position, with 26 confiscations, while *Naprzód* recorded 57.

25. *IKC,* 20 November 1920, 20, as cited in Borowiec, *Jesteśmy głosem milionów,* 35.

26. Garlicki, "Rodzaje konfiskat prasowych w Krakowie," 471.

27. Lechicki asserts that *Nowiny* had subscriptions of 12,000 by 1912 and published 35,000 copies a day. *Nowiny* claimed the figure of 35,000 on June 2, 1912. Jerzy Myśliński puts circulation figures much lower, based on quarterly police records. Arguing that editors would have no reason to lie to the police about their circulation figures (because they were assured complete discretion and the records were kept from public knowledge), he presents circulations for *Nowiny* that average around 5,000 and peak at 9,000 in 1912. Some quarters were as low as 2,600. Jerzy Myśliński, "Nakłady prasy społeczno-politycznej w Galicji w latach 1881–1913," *Rocznik historii czasopiśmiennictwa polskiego* 4, no. 1 (1965): 115–33; Jerzy Myśliński, *Studia nad prasą polską społeczno-polityczną w zachodniej Galicji, 1905–1914* (Warsaw, 1970), 117.

28. Władyka, *Krew na pierwszej stronie,* 42.

29. At least in Russia, most of the editors of the boulevard press tended to be of peasant or lower-middle-class origin, successful in business, but not too far from "the people." See Louise McReynolds, *The News under Russia's Old Regime: The Development of a Mass-Circulation Press* (Princeton, NJ, 1991); and Daniel R. Brower, "The Penny Press and Its Readers," in *Cultures in Flux: Lower-Class Values, Practices, and Resistance in Late Imperial Russia,* ed. Stephen P. Frank and Mark D. Steinberg (Princeton, NJ, 1984), 151–52.

30. Lechicki, "Kartka," 119–20. For more on the Szczepański family, see Krystyna Zbijewska, "Saga rodu Szczepańskich" (Saga of the Szczepański Family) in *Kraków—magazyn kulturalny* (Cracow—A Cultural Magazine), no. 4 (1991): 45–46. The writer, editor, and alpinist Jan Alfred Szczepański's poignant memoir of his father, Ludwik Szczepański, can be found in *Godziny zwierzeń,* ed. Stefan Henel (Warsaw, 1983), 274–84. Sadly, most Polish encyclopedia references to Ludwik Szczepański note his early contributions to the Young Poland movement while downplaying or even ignoring his central role as an innovative journalist. Lechicki's article goes a long way toward rectifying this oversight, but even entries appearing after its publication still focus on Szczepański as a lesser poet and author instead of on his contributions as an editor and publisher of the popular press.

31. Lechicki, "Kartka," 121–23. For more on Szczepański's relationship with Zapolska see Krystyna Zbijewska, "Z dziejów słynnego romansu. Nieznane listy Gabrieli Zapolskiej," *Przekrój,* 8 September 1991, 8–9.

32. Szczepański, *Godziny zwierzeń,* 281.

33. Stanisław Przybyszewski, *Moi współcześni* (1926; reprint, Warsaw, 1959): 329–30.

34. *Ilustracya Polska,* 18 September 1901, 1–5.

35. Ibid., 23. The journal cost 30 halers per issue, a quarterly subscription cost 3 crowns, 90 halers. The price of a cheap bread roll at the time was 2–4 halers.

36. *Ilustracya Polska,* 18 April 1902, 364–66. "Styl polski" (the "Polish Style").

This article features photographs of and commentary about Stanisław Witkiewicz's large home, which was built in the Zakopane style. For more on the Zakopane style, please see Edward Manoulien, "Invented Traditions: Primitivist Narrative and Design in the Polish Fin de Siècle," *Slavic Review* 59 (Summer 2000): 391–405.

37. *Ilustracya Polska*, 11 October 1902, 80. "Korespondencya redakcyi" (Editor's Correspondence).

38. *Ilustracya Polska*, 11 October 1902, 78. "Teatr Ludowy w Krakowie" (the People's Theater in Cracow).

39. Borowiec, *Jesteśmy głosem milionów*, 52–56.

40. For a string of j.r's witty feuilletons, please see *Nowiny*, 20 March 1907, 2–3; 21 March 1907, 3; 30 March 1907, 6; 14 April 1907, 2–3; 19 April 1907, 1; 26 April 1907, 1–2; 15 June 1907, 1–3; 1 September 1907, 1–2; 8 September 1907, 3.

41. See Lechicki, "Kartka," 125; and Myśliński, *Studia nad prasą polską*, 96–97.

42. *Liberum Veto*, 1 July 1903, 20. The mock prize, incidentally, was a copy of "Flower of Death," the "sensationalist crime story on the backdrop of conditions in Cracow" by Walery Tomicki, then running in *Nowiny*.

43. *Liberum Veto*, 10 July 1903, 10–13.

44. *Nowiny*, 30 July 1903 and 14 August 1903.

45. *Czas*, 2 May 1905; *Nowiny*, 4 May 1905.

46. The issue published on 1 May 1909 called the International Day of Labor "a holiday of hatred." In 1911, *Nowiny* claimed that the "holiday" passed in Cracow "entirely without incident," while asserting that intelligent workers in Cracow, Prague, and Vienna had long since realized how pointless such marches really were. See *Nowiny*, 3 May 1911, 3.

47. *Nowiny*, 26 November 1905, 1.

48. For a positive article about Daszyński, please see *Nowiny*, 27 February 1904, 3. For some of the negative coverage in 1907, see 12 May 1907, 1; 24 May 1907, 1; 28 May 1907, 2; 14 June 1907, 1. Daszyński sued Szczepański for a drawing that depicted him accepting 400,000 marks from German Marxists and Jews. See *Nowiny*, 12 May 1907, 1; 21 August 1907, 2; and 1 September 1907, 1.

49. *Nowiny*, 8 June 1911; "Free additions" to *Nowiny*, 28 and 29 May 1907.

50. Myśliński, *Studia nad prasą polską*, 98.

51. *IKC*, 8 June 1913, 5.

52. Ibid., 99.

53. *Nowiny*, 1 January 1911, 1.

54. Both of these party names are difficult to translate into English. *Mieszczański* means both bourgeois and urban, while *urzędniczy* can be translated as bureaucratic, official, or civil servant. The *Grupa Demokratyczno-Mieszczańska* was founded in 1908 and evolved into a "circle" and then a "party" by 1911. Cracow city president Juliusz Leo was its leader both in Cracow and in the parliament in Vienna. *Stronnictwo Urzędnicze* was relevant in the 1911 elections.

55. Borowiec, *Jesteśmy głosem milionów*, 51–59; Myśliński, *Studia nad prasą polską*, 103.

56. *IKC,* 21 December 1910, 2–3.

57. Borowiec, *Jesteśmy głosem milionów,* 75, 67.

58. Lechicki, "Kartka," 126–27; Myśliński, "Prasa polska w Galicji," 127.

59. In fact by this period, Borowiec reports, *IKC*'s principal competitor was actually the liberal-democratic paper, *Nowa Reforma.* Borowiec, *Jesteśmy głosem milionów,* 71.

60. *IKC,* 8 June 1913, 5. Of course *IKC* just as rapaciously scoured the foreign press for the articles and images it eagerly reprinted.

61. *IKC,* 8 June 1913, 18, and 12 June 1913, 5.

62. Lechicki, "Kartka," 127. During the first months of the Great War, Szczepański wrote a number of fascinating editorials for *IKC* about the conflict and the ways Cracovians experienced it. As the war progressed, Szczepański's writings became increasingly subversive. Like his father before, who had been imprisoned by the Russians for his involvement in the 1863 uprising, Szczepański lost his freedom to the authorities of a partitioning power, spending nearly a year in an Austrian prison camp outside Linz. Jan Alfred Szczepański, *Godziny zwierzeń,* 278–79.

63. For more on the *IKC* press empire and *IKC* in the 1920s and 1930s, please see Władyka, *Krew na pierwszej stronie,* 42–60; Borowiec, *Jesteśmy głosem milionów;* and Adam Bańdo's *Nie tylko krew na pierwszej stronie. Problematyka kulturalna na łamach "Ilustrowanego Kuriera Codziennego" w latach 1918–1939* (Cracow: Wydawnictwo Naukowe Akademii Pedagogicznej, 2006), which stresses the cultural and political role of the paper, arguing that it was not just sensationalist.

64. Jan Alfred Szczepański, *Godziny zwierzeń,* 281–82.

65. *KK,* 9 August 1902, 1.

66. *Nowiny,* 16 May 1903, 2.

67. *IKC,* 18 December 1910, 2.

68. "Small announcements" in the 23 May 1907 issue of *Nowiny,* for example, included "20,000 crowns sought for a first mortgage"; "Two journeymen harness-makers and two apprentices needed"; and "An intelligent young woman who has finished the VI class, with a mastery of German, is needed as an expedient to a confectionary factory." For sale in the same issue were, among other things, "A manor, 11 km from Bochnia" and an "Automobile using 6hp for 4 persons, very cheap."

69. For example, the 17 June 1905 issue of *Nowiny* included the following items in its daily chronicle: "Sunday rest for merchants; Seat of the Chamber of Commerce; [The] Marriage of Miss Marya Hułko, daughter of Wilhelm and Marcela of Stibów with Mr. Zygmunt Ślimakowski, a merchant, will occur . . . ." The report of the beauty contest was printed in *Nowiny,* 25 July 1911, 1, 2, and 4. The –ówna ending on the winners' surnames simply designates their status as unmarried women.

70. Zofia Daszyńska-Golińska, "Robotnicy młodociani w rzemiośle i rękodziełach w Krakowie," *Czasopisma Prawnicza-Ekonomiczna* 14 (1913), 41.

71. *IKC,* 22 January 1913, 5–6, and 24 January 1913, 5.

72. *Nowiny,* 20 May 1903.

73. *Nowiny,* 12 January 1904, 4; 13 January 1904, 3; 14 January 1904, 6. For some winners, no occupation was listed.

74. *Nowiny,* 11 December 1912, 2.

75. The first issue of *IKC* (18 December 1910) mentioned all three! See also Aleksander Słapa, "Chłopięca pasja książek," in *Kopiec wspomnień,* ed. Zygmunt Gitel (Cracow, 1964), 178–202, esp. 182–89 for his youthful fascination with Sherlock Holmes and Jack the Ripper.

76. Samozwaniec, *Maria i Magdalena,* 41. Samozwaniec does not specify how old she was when the story was accepted, but it seems from the context that she was not yet a teenager.

77. *Nowiny,* 21 May 1911, 4.

78. *Nowiny,* 11 July 1903, 3. For more replies, see *Nowiny dla wszystkich* for the first two weeks of July 1903.

79. *Nowiny,* 29 March 1908, 1.

80. *IKC,* 4 September 1912, 4. The article, about the hotel of the future, addressed the reader and then addressed instead the female reader, playfully acknowledging, "only women read our *Daily Courier.*" For the inaugural "For Women, about Women" column, see *IKC,* 10 December 1911, 11.

81. Circulation of *Der Tag* ranged from 1,500 to 5,000. Myśliński, "Prasa polska w Galicji," 138.

82. *Nowiny,* 27 November 1909, 2.

83. *IKC,* 9 July 1911, 4.

84. *IKC,* 9 January 1914, 7.

85. For examples of the census issue, please see *Nowiny,* 4 January 1911, 1–3, and 18 January 1911, 3.

86. *Nowiny,* 5 January 1910, 2.

87. Karol Estreicher, the son of a Jagiellonian professor and grandson of the famous bibliographer and director of the Jagiellonian University library Stanisław Estreicher, recalled in his memoir that in 1912 his father's primary paper was *Czas,* but he also bought *Nowa Reforma* and *Naprzód* to follow local stories. See Estreicher, *Nie od razu Kraków zbudowano* (Warsaw, 1956), 18.

88. *Nowiny,* 18 February 1908, 1.

89. *Nowiny,* 6 June 1909, 1.

90. For more on the Borowska trials, please see "Procesy Janiny Borowskiej," in *Pitaval krakowski,* by Stanisław Salmonowicz, Janusz Szwaja, and Stanisław Waltoś (Cracow, 1974), 310–67.

91. *Nowiny,* 11 September 1904, 1, 3.

92. *Nowości Illustrowane,* 1 September 1904, 1, 4; *Nowiny,* 4 June 1912, 12; *Nowości Illustrowane,* 22 October 1904, 1.

93. *Nowa Reforma,* 19 December 1910, 2.

94. See for example, Lennard Davis, *Factual Fictions: The Origins of the English Novel,* 69.

95. *KK,* 3 and 4 December 1902, 1; *KK,* 12 February 1903, 1.

96. Please see Roshanna Sylvester, *Tales of Old Odessa,* for more on the

relationship between the popular press and definitions of respectability.

97. *Nowiny,* 22 January 1908, 2.

98. For more on this phenomenon, please see Deborah Wynne, *The Sensation Novel and the Victorian Family Magazine* (London, 2001); and Vanessa Schwartz, *Spectacular Realities,* 32–33.

99. *Nowiny,* 1 January 1907, 2, and 2 January 1907, 2.

100. *Nowiny,* 26 September 1903, 4. The editors sarcastically replied, "We will take this information into account and wish from all our souls for Mr. Wójcik that the sun will as often and as long as possible continue to shine in his café."

101. Schwartz, *Spectacular Realities,* see esp. chap. 1.

102. *Nowiny,* 28 September 1903, 3.

103. *Nowiny,* 9 January 1908, 2, and 10 January 1908, 2. See chap. 5 for more commentary on these articles.

104. Jean Chalaby has argued that journalism, with its discourse of objectivity and neutrality, is a relatively recent, primarily Anglo-American invention. Contrary to the venerable tradition in press history that places the roots of modern journalism in seventeenth-century nouvelles and broadsheets, Chalaby argues that the discursive structure that defines modern journalism arose only in the nineteenth century, spreading from the United States and, to a lesser extent, Great Britain, to other parts of the world. Chalaby, *The Invention of Journalism.*

105. *Nowości Illustrowane,* 15 September 1904, 1, 5, and 14 November 1904, 1, 4.

106. Barth, *City People,* 68.

107. *Nowiny,* 2 January 1906, 2.

108. Georg Simmel's notion of the primarily visual aspect of urban life is well-known. See his 1903 essay "The Metropolis and Mental Life." For more on the ways that the press orchestrated spectatorship, see also Fritzsche, *Reading Berlin*; Schwartz, *Spectacular Realities*; and Sylvester, *Tales of Old Odessa.*

109. Borowiec, *Jesteśmy głosem milionów.*

110. Davis, *Factual Fictions.*

111. Fritzsche, *Reading Berlin,* 18.

112. *Nowiny,* 31 August 1907, 3.

113. For an illuminating commentary on "browsing," see Fritzsche, "The City as Spectacle," chap. 4 in *Reading Berlin,* 127–69, esp. 147–61.

114. *Nowiny,* 15 June 1907, 2; 9 June 1907, 2; 27 July 1907, 3.

115. *KK,* 9 August 1902, 2–3.

116. Ibid., 3–5.

117. *Nowiny,* 21 August 1903, 1; *Nowiny,* 8 December 1909, 1; *IKC,* 3 March 1911, 1; *Nowiny,* 15 June 1912, 1. For more on images of big cities, please see chap. 6.

118. *Nowiny,* 9 August 1910, 1, 3, shows the original report; the following two weeks carried front-page coverage of the murder.

119. See *Die Neue Zeitung,* 17 June 1912, 1–2; *Nowiny,* 21 June 1912, 1; or *IKC,* 21 June 1912, 1.

120. *Nowiny,* 20 June 1909, 1.

121. *IKC,* 4 February 1911, 4, had the first mention of the tango in the Cracovian popular press. The following *IKC* articles demonstrate its connection to the tango trend in other cities and countries: 1 January 1914, 1; 10 January 1914, 1; 29 January 1914, 7; 10 February 1914, 1; 15 February 1914, 1, 4; 21 February 1914, 1.

122. *IKC,* 6 July 1912, 4.

123. For more on Cracow's nineteenth-century coffeehouse and sweetshop culture, see Irena Homola-Skąpska, "Krakowskie cukiernie i kawiarnie w XIX wieku," *Annales Universitas Mariae Curie-Skłodowska Lublin-Polonia* 51, no. 5 (1996): 43–61.

124. For a particularly bad Cracovian Sherlock Holmes story, in which the protagonist attempts to disguise himself as "a Negro" when entering the city's most famous restaurant, see the Carnival Issue of *Nowiny,* 27 February 1911, 2–3. A murder reported in Cracow was accompanied by a sub-article, "A Home-Grown Sherlock," about a local amateur investigator. *IKC,* 21 May 1911, 3–5. The Polish term for Jack the Ripper is Kuba Rozpruwacz. Kuba is a nickname for Jakób, like Jake for Jacob, and *rozpruwacz* is the noun form of *rozpruwać,* to rip apart.

125. Judith Walkowitz, *City of Dreadful Delight: Narratives of Sexual Danger in Late Victorian London* (Chicago, 1992); L. Perry Curtis, Jr., *Jack the Ripper and the London Press* (New Haven, CT, 2001).

126. *Nowiny,* 3 August 1907, 3; 4 August 1907, 2; 16 February 1907, 1; 20 February 1909, 1; 24 December 1911, 5.

127. *Nowiny,* 8 August 1907, 1–2. The story was reported in novelistic tones, with dramatic turns and developments, including the detail that the victim died just before revealing the name of her assailant.

128. *Nowiny,* 27 August 1909, 1.

129. *Nowiny,* 30 March 1910, 2–3; 17 September 1911, 1, 6; 1 November 1913, 5.

130. *Nowiny,* 8 July 1903, 3, offered bit of commentary on an instance when Cracow's press was cited in the European press. In this case, *Nowiny* found it hilarious that the *Post* in Berlin misidentified the arch-conservative *Czas* as "a revolutionary-socialist publication."

131. *Nowiny,* 2 February 1910, 1. Archival copies include pre- and post-censored versions of the paper.

132. *Nowiny,* 6 February 1910, 2–3.

133. *KK,* 5 December 1902, 6.

134. *IKC,* 2 August 1913, 7.

135. *Nowiny,* 15 October 1908, 1; 6 July 1912, 4–5; *IKC,* 20 May 1911, 7. On more than one occasion, strollers on the A-B side of Market Square downtown said that they felt like they were in Paris, a clear indication that they felt a kinship between their city and the famous capital on the Seine.

136. See for example, *Nowiny,* 9 February 1911, 1.

137. *Nowiny,* 13 July 1906, 4–5; 30 December 1908, 1–2; 6 March 1910, 2–3; 21 March 1908, 2; 3 April 1908, 2. Readers of the last article learned that London consumed as much food as all other English cities combined and as much as half of Galicia.

138. *Nowiny,* 31 July 1910, 3.

139. *IKC,* 8 September 1911, 4-5

140. *Nowiny,* 1 September 1903, 1, 2. See also *IKC,* 12 March 1913, 3.

141. *Nowiny,* 2 August 1907, 2. The city was slated to replace some outmoded public toilets with "Viennese style" commodes.

142. *IKC,* 8 February 1913, 4-5.

143. *IKC,* 21 June 1912, 1.

144. *Nowiny,* 23 May 1912, 4. See also *IKC,* 15 January 1912, 5, "Kraków się 'europezuje'" (Cracow Europeanizes itself), a note that indicated two applications for new cinemas.

145. *IKC,* 19 November 1914, 4.

CHAPTER 3

1. *Nowiny,* 27 May 1903, 1.

2. Ibid.

3. *IKC,* 16 February 1911, 5. When *Nowa Reforma* pirated a story in *IKC* from the previous day, the latter paper lashed out at *Nowa Reforma* with the scathing image of its journalists composing a newspaper while perched in their "soft lounge chairs in front of green tables." I do not endorse this epithet as a statement of truth (I know that *Nowa Reforma* had reporters on the streets), but the basic distinction remains. Popular boulevard papers like *Nowiny* (and later *IKC*) would interview a smuggler, not *Nowa Reforma* or *Czas.*

4. "Community chief" is the literal translation of the term used to describe such a suburban leader (*naczelnik gminy*); it's not an attempt on my part to impose colonialist language.

5. Hohenberg and Lees, *The Making of Urban Europe,* 217.

6. Friedrich Engels, *The Condition of the Working Class in England* (original German edition, 1845; NY, 1987).

7. Maria Raluca Popa and Emily Gunzburger Makaš, "Bucharest," in *Capital Cities in the Aftermath of Empires: Planning in Central and Southeastern Europe,* ed. Emily Gunzburger Makaš and Tanja Damljanović Conley (London and NY: Routledge, 2010), 61-74.

8. Eve Blau, "The City as Protagonist: Architecture and the Cultures of Central Europe," in *Shaping the Great City: Modern Architecture in Central Europe, 1890-1937,* ed. Eve Blau and Monika Platzer (Munich and NY, 1999), 11-25.

9. Brian Ladd, *Urban Planning and Civic Order in Germany, 1860-1914* (Cambridge, MA, 1990), 7-35.

10. Gunter Düriegl, "Portrait of a City, Configuration and Change," in *Vienna, 1890-1920,* ed. Robert Waissenberger (NY, 1984), 18.

11. APK IT 1273 Teczka II; Magistrat stoł. król. m. Krakowa. *Studya do sprawy przyłączenia gmin sąsiednich do miasta Krakowa* (Cracow, 1905), 5.

12. APK IT 1272 Teczka I, doc. 74.

13. APK IT 1272 Teczka I, doc. 53, p. 313ff. Casimir III the Great (reigned 1333–1370) issued many substantial decrees regarding the development of Cracow and its surroundings. In 1335 he created the city of Kazimierz on the island between the Old Vistula and the new riverbed. The king created Garbary, or Czarna Wieś, as a suburban manufacturing area in 1361. *Kronika Krakowa*, ed. Marian B. Michalik (Warsaw, 1996), 35–45.

14. APK IT 1272 Teczka I, doc. 79; APK IT 1273 Teczka II, docs. 52 and 60.

15. Celina Bąk-Koczarska, *Juliusz Leo. Twórca Wielkiego Krakowa* (Wrocław, 1986), 94.

16. Alexander Gerschenkron, *An Economic Spurt that Failed* (Princeton, NJ, 1977), 25, 55. Purchla, "Miasto a rzeka," in his *Kraków. Prowincja czy metropolia?* 117–21.

17. Bąk-Koczarska, *Juliusz Leo*, 60–61.

18. Ibid., 61. One might recall that Mayor Szalwiński of Grzegórzki had been in favor of incorporation at the time of his interview with *Nowiny*. He was the community chief who submitted a well-formulated list of demands.

19. *Nowiny*, 27 May 1903, 1.

20. *Nowiny*, 28 May 1903, 1–2.

21. *Nowiny*, 6 June 1903, 1.

22. For an example of "greediness," see *Nowiny*, 15 April 1904, 2–3.

23. *Nowiny*, 30 May 1903, 2.

24. *Nowiny*, 18 June 1903, 3.

25. Ibid.

26. *Nowiny*, 2 July 1903, 2.

27. *Nowiny*, 21 February 1904, 2–3.

28. *Nowiny*, 19 March 1904, 3–4.

29. *Nowiny*, 4 June 1903, 2. As late as 26 July 1904, well after most other left-bank districts had consented, Zbroja and his fellow councilors continued to oppose joining Greater Cracow. A signed handwritten letter from Zbroja to the Cracovian Magistrate notes that of the 17 community councilors voting at a recent meeting, 16 had voted against incorporation (APK IT 1273).

30. The new fortifications were begun in 1905. At the same time the old ones were torn down and Cracow bought the land from the army. Frančić, *Kraków. Kalendarz dziejów*, 185.

31. *Nowiny*, 6 June 1903, 1.

32. *Nowiny*, 11 June 1903, 2. Because Dębniki was on the other side of the river, it was not part of the initial group slated for incorporation.

33. For readers of Polish, there is a great wordplay here: "Ale naszej wody bielańskiej możecie potrzebować!-rzuciłem na odlew" ("But you may need our Bielany water!" I cast back.)

34. *Nowiny*, 11 June 1903, 2.

35. *Nowiny*, 13 June 1903, 2.

36. *Nowiny,* 16 June 1903, 2–3.

37. *Nowiny,* 17 June 1903, 3. Bartoszewicz was the editor of *Kuryer Krakowski,* the paper *Nowiny* put out of business. Apparently, he was still on decent terms with his erstwhile rival, Ludwik Szczepański. He was a later collaborator and feuilletonist for *Nowiny.*

38. *Nowiny,* 6 February 1904, 3.

39. Ibid.

40. *Nowiny,* 17 February 1904, 5.

41. *Nowiny,* 20 February 1904, 2.

42. *Nowiny,* 21 February 1904, 2–3.

43. *Nowiny,* 23 February 1904, 1–2.

44. *Nowiny,* 5 April 1904, 3–4. Jacenty is a first name, not a surname. The paper likely referred to the writer of this letter as Mr. Jacenty in order to maintain a measure of anonymity.

45. *Nowiny,* 6 February 1904, 3, and 1 April 1904, 3, 5–6.

46. The reporter's parting shot had been: "I won't even talk about losing my galoshes, because they were old anyway. Besides, what of galoshes, when we're talking about the public good?" *Nowiny,* 20 February 1904, 2.

47. Gustaw Gershon Bazes, a wealthy lamp merchant and influential city councilor, had crossed *Nowiny's* path early on and was the constant butt of jokes for much of the paper's first year. Neither side's behavior was above reproach. The paper probably libeled him, but he was convicted of improprieties that year, so not all of the paper's attacks had been unfounded. At the conclusion of Mr. Jacenty's letter, *Nowiny's* editors added that incorporation would probably go a long way in actually solving the problem of "Bazes and Co." by changing the balance [of Poles to Jews] in the city. Ironically, in its last years, Bazes bought a large share of *Nowiny.*

48. *Nowiny,* 15 April 1904, 2–3.

49. Ibid.

50. *Nowiny,* 16 April 1904, 5; *Nowiny,* 18 April 1904, 3.

51. *Nowiny,* 18 April 1904, 3.

52. *Nowiny,* 29 April 1904, 1–2.

53. *Nowiny,* 1 September 1903, 1, 2.

54. *Nowiny,* 16 April 1904, 5.

55. *IKC,* 15 October 1911, 1, 4–5.

56. Indeed, in the protocols eventually signed between the City of Cracow and the various districts, the very terms discussed in the "Wielki Kraków" series are central. The protocols for the districts that united with Cracow after the first round of incorporation in 1910 are printed in *Kraków. Rozszerzenie Granic, 1909–1915,* 222–38.

CHAPTER 4

1. Bąk-Koczarska, *Juliusz Leo,* 36.

2. *Nowiny,* 13 September 1904, 5–6.

3. Ibid. "Minęła wielka przeszłość, smutna jest terazniejszość, ale nasza jest przyszłość, jeżeli rzetelnie, rozumnie i wytrwale dla niej pracować będziemy." For more on Józef Dietl and Mikołaj Zyblikiewicz, another of Cracow's nineteenth-century presidents, please see Irena Homola, *Józef Dietl i jego Kraków* (Cracow, 1993) and *Kraków za prezydentury Mikołaja Zyblikiewicza, 1874–1881* (Cracow, 1976).

4. *Nowiny,* 13 September 1904, 5–6. Emphasis original.

5. *Nowiny,* 7 October 1904, 5.

6. APK IT 1273 Teczka II: Magistrat stoł. król. m. Krakowa. *Studya do sprawy przyłączenia gmin sąsiednich do miasta Krakowa* (Cracow, 1905), 9.

7. Ibid., 10. In Prague, the process had begun in the 1860s, undergone a round in the 1880s, and was under way presently. The completion of Greater Prague did not occur until after the Great War. For the materials from other cities that Cracovian officials consulted, please see IT 1279 Teczka VIII: Materiały obce rozszerzenie miast (Praga, Wiedeń, Insbruck, Rzeszów, Ikole.)

8. *Studya do sprawy,* 20–21.

9. Ibid., 16.

10. Ibid., 22, For more on the canalization aspect of the Koerber Plan see Gerschenkron, *An Economic Spurt that Failed,* 73, 76–84, 125–26. See also David Good, *The Economic Rise of the Habsburg Empire, 1750–1914,* 182–83; and Purchla, "Miasto a rzeka," in his *Prowincja czy metropolia?* 117–21.

11. Daszyński, *Pamiętniki,* 191–92.

12. Gerschenkron, *An Economic Spurt that Failed,* 85–122; and David Good's review of Gerschenkron's book in *Journal of Economic History* 37 (1977), 1061–62.

13. Tadeusz Przeorski, "Przyczyny podjęcia starań o przyłączenie do Krakowa sąsiednich gmin i obszarów dworskich," in *Kraków. Rozszerzenie granic, 1909–1915,* 211.

14. Purchla, "Miasto a rzeka," 119.

15. The Kościuszko Mound was a large earthen memorial, modeled after some prehistoric mounds nearby, that was built up in the 1820s to commemorate national hero Tadeusz Kościuszko (1746–1817). In the 1850s, the Austrian military built fortifications on the mound because of its height and strategic location—and almost certainly as an affront to the subjugated Poles.

16. *Studya do sprawy,* 24–25.

17. Ibid., 25–26.

18. Ibid., 27.

19. Ibid., 69–91. The list comes from the headings in the table of contents.

20. Bąk-Koczarska, *Juliusz Leo,* 115–16.

21. *Czas,* 23 December 1905, 7–8.

22. Bąk-Koczarska, *Juliusz Leo,* 102.

23. *Ibid,* 64–65. According to Bąk-Koczarska, Leo subscribed to the ideas of the Bodenreformer movement in Germany, which called for acquiring as much land for the city as possible.

24. For more on the Third Bridge, please see Purchla, "Krakowskie mosty," 104–21.

25. Orton, "The Stańcyk Portfolio and the Politics of Galician Loyalism," 55–64.

26. *Nowiny,* 15 September 1907, 1, and 21 September 1907, 1.

27. For commentary on the constant criticism in *Czas* that winter, see *Nowiny,* 21 March 1908, 2.

28. *Nowiny,* 21 January 1908, 1.

29. *Nowiny,* 24 January 1908, 1–2.

30. *Nowiny,* 5 April 1908, 2.

31. Bąk-Koczarska, *Juliusz Leo,* 74–75. Mr. Grodyński and Dr. Sikorski, authors of the 1905 study, appear in the paper frequently regarding plans for Greater Cracow and the canal project.

32. *Nowiny,* 23 October 1908, 1.

33. *Nowiny,* 18 September 1908, 1.

34. *Nowiny,* 6 September 1908, 1. For earlier reference to Czecz, please see *Nowiny,* 16 April 1904, 5. Czecz's speech can be found in *Nowiny,* 2 October 1908, 1.

35. Bąk-Koczarska, *Juliusz Leo,* 77.

36. Ibid.

37. APK IT 1274, "Sprawozdanie Komisyi gminnej o sprawie Wydziału krajowego w przedmiocie przyłączenia sąsiednich gmin i obszarów dworskich do miasta Krakowa," 2.

38. *Nowiny,* 10 November 1908, 2–3.

39. Bąk-Koczarska., *Juliusz Leo,* 78–79; *Nowiny,* 10 December 1909, 2.

40. *Nowiny,* 14 April 1910, 3.

41. APK IT 1299, Uroczystosci w dniu 17 IV 1910.

42. Ibid.

43. *Nowiny,* 19 April 1910, 1–3.

44. Ibid. "Even though Lwów is the capital of the country," Ciuchciński said, "Cracow has not ceased to be that sacred city that causes every Pole's heart to beat whenever they think of it."

45. *Nowiny,* 30 March 1905, 5–6. Liban is the same man who painted the dark image of night guards being replaced by soldier-police in black shakos (see chap. 3).

46. *Nowiny,* 8 September 1910, 1.

47. *Nowiny,* 17 September 1910, 2–3, 18 September 1910, 2, and 20 September 1910, 1–2.

48. *Nowiny,* 20 September 1910, 1–2.

49. *Nowiny,* 25 April 1913, 3, and 4 April 1913, 4–5.

50. *IKC,* 24 December 1910, 6, reported the emperor's sanction and provided statistics on the land and the number of people Cracow would acquire from the deal.

51. Bąk-Koczarska, *Juliusz Leo,* 83.

52. For coverage in *Nowiny,* please see 26 October 1911, 3; and for 1912 the following: 3 January, 1; 9 January, 1; 15 May, 1; 9 June, 4–5; 25 October, 4; 10 November, 4; and 27 November, 4. In 1913, see 27 February, 4; 1 April, 1–2; 4 April, 4–5; 16 April,

1–2; and 17 April, 3–4. In *IKC,* please see 5 October 1911, 5; for 1912, 3 January, 2–3; 9 January, 1; 15 May, 4; for 1913, 18 February, 4; 20 April, 13; 22 April, 1, 3; 25 April, 4.

53. *IKC,* 9 January 1912, 1.

54. *Nowiny,* 17 April 1913, 3.

55. *IKC,* 20 April 1913, 13, and 22 April 1913, 1, 3.

56. *Nowiny,* 22 April 1913, *Tydzień Humorystyczy* (insert). The drawing, while symbolic, was hardly futurist, as its creator knew well.

57. Bąk-Koczarska, *Juliusz Leo,* 86–87.

58. Ibid., 87.

59. *IKC,* 25 November 1914, 2.

60. *IKC,* 1 July 1915, 2.

61. *IKC,* 6 July 1915, 1.

62. *IKC,* 8 July 1915, 2.

63. *IKC,* 6 July 1915, 2.

64. Boy-Żeleński, "Wielki Kraków," in *Boy o Krakowie,* 123–24.

65. Ibid. 123.

66. Ibid. 126.

67. *Nowiny,* 16 April 1910, 1. The "applied arts," in particular, drew his ire. Bąkowski poked fun at chairs designed for "middle-class families" that cost 2,000 crowns or were so poorly designed that only a "consumptive" could fit between their armrests.

68. "Wasz Wielki Kraków . . . Wasze miasteczko, drodzy citizens, to jest istotnie ostoja humanizmu, ale to jest przy tym stolica hipokryzji, kolebka tanich wariacji i wylęgarnia snobów." Cited in *Kronika Krakowa,* 286. For more of the play, see Adolf Nowaczyński, *Małpie Zwierczadło. Wybór pism satyrycznych* (Cracow, 1974), 2:223–63.

69. *IKC,* 26 February 1913, 5.

70. *IKC,* 9 July 1915, 2.

71. See especially *Nowiny,* 20 September 1910, 3, which reported that 90,000 crowns had been appropriated to provide gas lighting for the new districts within the year. The same article reported that cables were being installed for electric lighting in parts of town, to the cost of approximately 300,000 crowns. Another article indicated that the city was also entering negotiations to purchase a majority share of the tram company. See also 22 September 1910, 2, and 14 December 1910, 2.

72. *Nowiny,* 14 December 1910, 2.

73. *Nowiny,* 4 January 1911, 2–3. Many of the lanterns were kerosene lamps, temporarily put in place until more permanent gas or electric lines could be installed.

74. Wolfgang Schivelbusch, *Disenchanted Night: The Industrialization of Light in the Nineteenth Century,* trans. Angela Davies (Berkeley and Los Angeles, 1988), 97–114, esp. 98. Schivelbusch's analysis gives greater meaning to the expression "hang them from the lampposts."

75. Like Schivelbusch, I allow for the fact that destroying the lamps may have been pleasurable for a number of intrinsic reasons, and that the street urchins who commonly did so may not have held well-developed opinions about the deeper

meanings of their rebellion. All the same, given the fact that lantern smashing occurred independently in nearly all of the communities so soon after the lights were installed, I think it must have been an inescapable observation at the time that the lights represented Greater Cracow and Cracovian authority and that destroying them was an affront to that authority.

76. *IKC,* 19 May 1912, 5, and *Nowiny,* 29 June 1912, 3.

77. *IKC,* 19 May 1912, 5.

78. *IKC,* 11 January 1913, 3.

79. Bąk-Koczarska, *Juliusz Leo,* 116.

80. Ibid., 153.

81. *IKC,* 27 April 1912, 4.

CHAPTER 5

1. I thank Jacek Purchla for calling this to my attention. For more on the decision to fund the theater instead of installing city water lines, please see Jan Małecki, "The Cracow Municipal Government in the 19th and 20th Centuries"; Purchla, "Local Government and the Civilizational Space of Cracow in the 19th Century," 40, 259; and Kazimierz Nowacki, *Architektura krakowskich teatrów* (Cracow, 1982), 130–35.

2. *Djabeł,* 15 January 1901, 2–3; *Nowa Reforma,* 6 January 1901, 1.

3. Gajzlerowa, *Tamten Kraków, tamta Krynica,* 20.

4. Rydlówka is a national museum housed in the home where Wyspiański witnessed the wedding of Lucjan Rydel and Anna Mikołajczyk, on which his play was based. *Dziennik Polski,* 15 March 2001, features a four-page spread devoted to the centennial of the play (13–16).

5. To be sure, much less has been written about the premiere of the tram than the premiere of the play. For some of the commentary on the play's initial reception, please see Stanisław Wyspiański, *"Wesele" o "Weselu,"* ed. Anna Boska (Warsaw, 1998), 255–88, which includes first reviews and recollections by Tadeusz Boy-Żeleński, Józef Kotarbiński, Stanisław Estreicher, Lucyna Kotarbińska, Wanda Siemaszkowa, Karol Frycz, Adolf Nowaczyński, Rudolf Starzewski, Ignacy Daszyński, and Adolf Neuwert-Nowaczyński.

6. Broniewski, *Igraszki z czasem,* 66.

7. *Czas,* 16 March 1901, 2 (evening edition), *Nowa Reforma,* 16 March 1901, 2 (evening edition). See also Broniewski, *Igraszki z czasem,* 49, which seems to have been taken largely from the article in *Czas.*

8. *Nowa Reforma,* 17 March 1901, 1 (morning edition).

9. *Czas,* 17 March 1901, 1 (morning edition).

10. Broniewski recalls that the fares were cheaper (10 halers for a second-class ticket, and 14 for one in first class). See, *Igraszki z czasem,* 48. It's likely that prices indeed dropped over time, if anything because of the tremendous volume of passengers, which immediately numbered in the millions annually.

11. *Głos Narodu,* 18 March 1901, 3. Emphasis original.

12. *Głos Narodu,* 19 March 1901, 4. The lead-in to this article called *Czas* "the newspaper of boosters for the tram company."

13. John P. McKay, *Tramways and Trolleys: The Rise of Urban Mass Transport in Europe* (Princeton, NJ, 1976), 107-24, 243-45; James R. Scobie, *Buenos Aires: Plaza to Suburb, 1870-1910* (NY, 1974), 160-78; Anton Rosenthal, "The Arrival of the Electric Streetcar and the Conflict over Progress in Early Twentieth-Century Montevideo," *Journal of Latin American Studies* 27, no. 2 (May 1995), 319-41.

14. *Historia komunikacji w mieście Krakowie,* ed. Z. Gierdziewicz (Cracow, 1975), 4. During the years 1898-1901, the Belgian joint-stock company renegotiated its contract with the city for the introduction of electric streetcars.

15. *Czas,* 12 September 1900.

16. *Bocian,* 15 March 1901, 4. See also *Djabeł,* 15 April 1901, 2.

17. *Czas,* 9 February 1901, 1 (morning edition).

18. *Nowa Reforma,* 29 March 1901, 2, and *Nowa Reforma,* 24 April 1901, 2. Another article that year blamed the speed of the electric tram and the narrowness of Lubicz Street for an accident with a servant girl. *Nowa Reforma,* 4 August 1901, 2.

19. An accident report in *KK,* 2 April 1903, 3-4, stated that the tram was traveling "at full speed [for a city street], 10 kilometers an hour."

20. *Djabeł,* 15 April 1901, 2; *Bocian,* 15 March 1901, 4.

21. *Djabeł,* 1 April 1902, 2, and 15 October 1902, 2; Sylvester, *Tales of Old Odessa,* 194.

22. *KK,* 4 March 1903, 4, and 5 March 1903, 4. That one of the girls, a servant in charge of two young children, inadvertently placed her charges in grave danger and then leapt out of the way herself, elicited a great deal of condemnation in the report.

23. *KK,* 2 April 1903, 1, 3-4. Several days later the paper assessed the poor father's condition with a bit of dark humor, responding to a rumor that had spread around town that Herman Żabner was killed by a tram. "The rumor . . . turns out to be false, because Żabner, though he has not regained consciousness, still lives." *KK,* 11 April 1903, 4.

24. *KK,* 10 September 1902, 3.

25. *Nowiny,* 31 March 1905, 5-6.

26. Viviana A. Zelizer discusses campaigns in American cities to solve the problem of child mortality due to streetcar accidents, in an era when urban youth often played in the street. See Zelizer, *Pricing the Priceless Child: The Changing Social Value of Children* (NY, 1985), 20-33, 36-49, 146-53. See *Nowiny,* 20 September 1903, 3.

27. *KK,* 7 November 1902 1, 6. Amazingly, a half-page advertisement for the Tram Company's new lines and schedules was printed on the opposite page—in an issue with a front-page illustration of the young woman being hit by the electric streetcar!

28. Scott McCloud, *Understanding Comics: The Invisible Art* (Northampton, MA, 1993), 24-46.

29. *Nowiny,* 10 November 1903, 1.

30. *Nowiny,* 10 September 1905, 5. A similar report in *Nowiny* from 1908

simply mentions that a 39-year-old man was run over by a tram, without indulging in commentary. *Nowiny*, 6 May 1908, 3. See also *Nowiny*, 11 January 1912, 2–3; *IKC*, 6 December 1911, 5; *IKC*, 12 December 1911, 4; *IKC*, 13 February 1914, 6; *IKC*, 20 March 1914, 2.

31. *Nowiny*, 8 October 1903, 4.

32. Vignettes about conversations from inside a tram reflected the paper's internal perspective. See *Nowiny*, 31 January 1908, 2, for example. One journalist complained that Galicians were either illiterate or too lazy to read, observing that only 20% of tram passengers were reading newspapers, while "in foreign countries, even the shopkeeper's assistant can hardly wait to get on the tram before pulling out his paper to read." *Nowiny*, 4 March 1909, 1.

33. *Nowiny*, 29 August 1909, 3.

34. *IKC*, 10 May 1912, 5.

35. *Nowiny*, 24 December 1911, 8. Emphasis added.

36. *Nowiny*, 4 November 1909, 2–3. Emphasis added.

37. *Nowiny*, 20 April 1911, 3.

38. *IKC*, 26 November 1911, 6. Emphasis added.

39. APK ELEKTR 6. See also Mirosław Nalepa, *Rozwój krakowskiej komunikacji zbiorowej w aspekcie działań samorządu krakowskiego w latach 1866–1939*, Master's thesis (under the direction of Krzysztof Zamorski), Institute of History, Jagiellonian University, 2000, 114–16. Cited with permission.

40. Wolfgang Schivelbusch, *The Railway Journey: The Industrialization of Time and Space in the 19th Century* (Berkeley and Los Angeles, 1986), 129–30.

41. Ernst Bloch, *Spuren* (Frankfurt and Berlin, 1962), 208, as cited in Schivelbusch, *Railway Journey*, 130–31. For more on the trauma of railway accidents, see Ralph Harrington, "The Railway Accident: Trains, Trauma, and Technological Crises in Nineteenth-Century Britain"; and Marc Caplan, "Trains and Trauma in the American Gilded Age," both in *Traumatic Pasts: History, Psychiatry, and Trauma in the Modern Age, 1870–1930*, ed. Paul Lerner and Mark Micale (NY, 2001), 31–80.

42. *Nowiny*, 29 June 1906, 4. An article in *IKC* in 1914, however, cautioned against the practice, noting that in Vienna in the first three months of that year some 1,100 people had injured themselves leaping onto or off of the trams, with 200 suffering serious injury and one person losing his life. *IKC*, 23 April 1914, 4.

43. *Nowiny*, 27 July 1907, 3; *KK*, 28 March 1903, 4. In another instance, a tram's brakes "decided not to work." *KK*, 5 February 1903, 5.

44. *Nowiny*, 29 August 1909, 3.

45. Thus a 1926 book entitled *The Life History of Automobiles* makes more sense. C. E. Griffin, *The Life History of Automobiles* (Ann Arbor, MI, 1926).

46. Bartoszewicz, perhaps the most popular city councilor in Cracow, was a true populist regarding company accountability and public accessibility of the trams—well before he acquired the editorship of *Kuryerek Krakowski* in late 1902. In a city council meeting on 15 March 1901, he spoke out against the single rate tariff for using the trams in the city, which he pointed out, was more expensive than in Vienna, Berlin, or

Dresden, where services were better. *Czas,* 16 March 1901, 2 (evening edition).

47. *KK,* 13 January 1903, 4.

48. *KK,* 18 January 1903, 4; *KK,* 31 January 1903, 4–5. I do not claim any affinity other than linguistic, but it bears mentioning that the only context in which I encountered the expression "always they" in a newspaper, before this series, was in a complaint about a Jewish merchant's deceitful business practices in the antisemitic *Głos Narodu,* 20 March 1901, 4 (afternoon edition).

49. *KK,* 14 February 1903, 4.

50. *Nowiny,* 7 June 1903, 1.

51. There are 20 reports of accidents and 3 more of near accidents. Eleven reports could be characterized as curiosity pieces, including articles about electric sparks, socialization in trams, suggestions on using the trams, and so forth. These comments often reflected the preoccupations of the city in other arenas (cleanliness, hygiene, and gender issues). Most notable were the early reports of electrical sparks and explosions, which invariably "terrified people present, especially women." See, *Nowiny,* 1 August 1903, 2–3, and *Nowiny,* 9 August 1904, 6.

52. *KK,* 31 January 1903, 4–5; *KK,* 19 March 1903, 4.

53. *Nowiny,* 7 July 1907, 1–2. In another report, the tram company was likened to Turkey and its leadership to the sultanate, "ruling poorly and cruelly, without regard for the wishes of its subjects." *Nowiny,* 27 August 1908, 3.

54. The press, of course, followed and encouraged this development. See APK ELEKTR 6; and Nalepa, *Rozwój krakowskiej komunikacji zbiorowej,* 51–52.

55. *Nowiny,* 16 June 1903, 2–3.

56. *Nowiny,* 13 February 1904, 4; *Nowiny,* 25 February 1904, 5; *Nowiny,* 23 June 1905, 2.

57. *Liberum Veto,* 20 June 1903, 10.

58. Rosenthal, "The Arrival of the Electric Streetcar," 331.

59. Personal communication, 8/21/2008.

60. *IKC,* 17 June 1911, 1.

61. *Nowiny,* 28 July 1911, 1 and 3.

62. *Nowiny,* 12 August 1911, 1; *IKC,* 5 November 1911, 1.

63. *Nowiny,* 24 October 1907, 3.

64. *Nowiny,* 22 May 1907, 2.

65. *Nowiny,* 7 September 1909, 2.

66. Adolph Schmal, *Die Kunst des Fahrens. Praktische Winke ein Automobil oder Motorrad richtig zu lenken. Ergänzungen zum Handbuche "Ohne Chauffeur"* (Vienna, 1916).

67. *IKC,* 21 May 1911, 7.

68. *Nowiny,* 6 November 1912, 9.

69. *Nowiny,* 10 September 1909, 2–3; *IKC,* 8 February 1911, 4–5.

70. *IKC,* 12 April 1911, 5–6.

71. See, for example, *Nowiny,* 5 March 1907, 3; *Nowiny,* 24 October 1907, 3; *IKC,* 2 July 1911, 4; *IKC,* 31 August 1911, 1 and 4; *IKC,* 1 September 1911, 5.

72. *Nowości Illustrowane,* 8 September 1904, 9.

73. *IKC,* 27 August 1912, 1.

74. *Nowiny,* 20 December 1910, 3, and 25 November 1908, 2.

75. *IKC,* 2 July 1911, 4.

76. *IKC,* 24 August 1911, 5.

77. *IKC,* 31 August 1911, 6.

78. *IKC,* 19 September 1912, 1–2, 4

79. From its inception, *IKC* made much of its use of automobiles for delivery purposes. See *IKC,* 18 December 1910, 2. The same issue also brags about the paper's rotary press, the fastest in Galicia.

80. *IKC,* 22 September 1912, 7. It must be noted that *IKC* at this time was supported by Stapiński's Peasant Party and would therefore have made every effort to win sympathy for Polish villagers with their compatriots in Cracow (see chap. 2).

81. *IKC,* 23 June 1912, 9; *IKC,* 12 April 1911, 4–5. See also *IKC,* 9 March 1913, 9.

82. *IKC,* 7 August 1912, 3. The mishaps of most victims were due to automobiles (248); trams and local trains ran over 58 people; horse-drawn vehicles struck 135. (Interestingly, trams and trains were listed before horse-drawn vehicles, even though they caused considerably fewer accidents.)

83. *IKC,* 12 July 1912, 1. Quimby died at sea. The illustration, as always, showed the moment of impact, as the wing of the airplane broke the surface of the water and the whirring propeller was about to do so. There was an inset of the pilot in her goggles and leather hat.

84. *IKC,* 24 May 1911, 7.

85. Both *Nowiny* and *IKC* carried the illustration and story of Frank Morock, the pilot whose plane crashed a tea party. See *Nowiny,* 14 January 1911, 1; or *IKC,* 14 January 1911, 1. *IKC,* 28 July 1912, 4, shows the airplane striking the cyclist.

86. *Nowiny,* 13 October 1912, 9–10.

87. *Nowiny,* 17 November 1911; *IKC,* 26 November 1911, 1

88. *Nowiny,* 23 October 1912, 4.

89. Two articles in *IKC* (10 January 1914, 1 and 5, and 15 November 1914, 4) describe military aerial exercises over Cracow that were observed by large crowds. Several articles in *IKC* (2 December 1914, 4, and 12 December 1914, 4) report Russian planes sighted over the city and pursued by Austrian aircraft. Readers were informed that although the Austrian pilots executed several "lovely" maneuvers, they were unable to engage in an aerial battle because the Russian plane's engine failed, forcing a landing in Austrian territory. The Russian pilot was taken prisoner.

90. *IKC,* 11 September 1914, 1.

91. H. G. Wells, *War in the Air, and particularly how Mr. Bert Smallways fared while it lasted,* was written in 1907 and published in installment form and as a book in 1908. *King of the Air* ran in *Nowiny* from 3 May to 22 November 1908, with a break in mid-September while Szczepański was on holiday in Zakopane. The book version was published by the reputable Warsaw firm Gebethner and Wolff in 1910.

92. See especially the epilogue to the story, *Nowiny,* 22 November 1908, 1–2.

While Wells's tale is superior on artistic merits and less transparently written to please than Szczepański's story, its dark vision of a world reduced to localized non-industrial peasant economies is more outrageous than Szczepański's conception of a more conventional conflict that also made use of aerial weapons. Wells imagined that aerial bombardment would so disable existing economic, military, and governmental organization that ordinary people, formerly dependent on the complex interconnections of industrial capitalism and modern governments, would be forced to revert to scavenging and small-scale peasant economies. H. G. Wells, *War in the Air* (London, 1967).

93. *Nowiny*, 12 May 1908, 1. Czesław Lechicki writes that Silnicki's character was modeled after Jan Szczepanik, a Polish inventor in Vienna and much-admired friend of Szczepański, who actually helped him describe some of the technical aspects of the aeromobile for the story. Lechicki, "Kartka," 127–28. Szczepański had featured Szczepanik in articles in *Ilustracya Polska* years before. See also *Nowiny*, 1 April 1904.

94. *Nowiny*, 10 May 1908, 1.

95. Szczepański eventually published a story about the siege of Cracow, *Przewrót* (Upheaval), in 1909 (the book appeared in 1911). In it, Silnicki comes to defend the city from joint Russian and Prussian attack. His aeromobile decimates Russian ground forces outside of the city and helps sway the battle between the Austrian and Prussian armies. In the end the Austrians capture Warsaw, and a peace conference in Cracow discusses the creation of an independent Poland. (Summary taken from Lechicki, "Kartka," 128.)

96. *Nowiny*, 20 October 1908, 1, and 24 May 1908, 1.

97. *Nowiny*, 12 September 1908, 2, and 13 September 1908, 2–3.

98. *Nowiny*, 26 June 1908, 1.

99. *Nowiny*, 16 February 1912, 1–2.

100. *IKC*, 1 May 1912, 5.

101. *Nowiny*, 27 March 1910, 2; 10 April 1910, 2; and 13 April 1910, 1.

102. *Nowiny*, 23 May 1910, 2. Stanisław Broniewski, *Igraszki z czasem*, 76–77.

103. Broniewski, *Igraszki z czasem*, 104–5.

CHAPTER 6

1. *The Urbanization of European Society in the Nineteenth Century*, ed. Andrew Lees and Lynn Lees (Lexington, MA, 1976), viii.

2. Wilhelm Heinrich Riehl, *Die Naturgeschichte des Volkes als Grundlage einer deutschen Social-Politik*, vol. 1, *Land und Leute* (Stuttgart and Tübingen, 1854), translated and excerpted in *The Urbanization of European Society*, ed. and trans. Lees and Lees, 58–64.

3. Nathaniel D. Wood, "Not just the National: Modernity and the Myth of Europe in the Capital Cities of Central and Southeastern Europe," in *Capital Cities in the Aftermath of Empire: Planning in Central and Southeastern Europe*, ed. Emily Gunzburger Makaš and Tanja Damljanović Conley (London and NY, 2010), 258–69.

4. Popa, "Bucharest."

5. Winifred Gordon, *A Woman in the Balkans* (London, 1918), 152, 139, 141. I thank Shay Wood for these findings.

6. A reference to the city as the "seedplot" of juvenile crime appears in *The Times* (London), 22 December 1853.

7. Robert Vaughan, *Age of Great Cities*, 221–29, 254–55. Vaughan was clearly in the Enlightenment tradition of viewing the city as a site of virtue and, increasingly, intelligence, yet as with many other intellectuals who set out to assess the merits of the city, he found himself shuddering at its moral dangers.

8. Riehl, in *Urbanization of European Society*, ed. Lees and Lees, 58.

9. For more on Polish literary attitudes toward the city in the nineteenth century, please see Jerzy Jedlicki, *Świat zwyrodniały. Lęki i wyroki krytyków nowocześćności* (Warsaw, 2000), 83–113, esp. 111.

10. Wojciech Gutkowski, "Symbolika urbanistyczna w literaturze młodej polski," in *Miasto, kultura, literatura, wiek XIX*, ed. Jan Data (Gdańsk, 1993), 189.

11. Stefan Witwicki, as cited in Jerzy Jedlicki, *Świat zwyrodniały*, 72.

12. Piotr Wandycz, *Lands of Partitioned Poland, 1795–1918* (1974; reprint, Seattle, 1993), 5–6.

13. Adam Mickiewicz, *Pan Tadeusz*, trans. Kenneth R. MacKenzie (NY, 1992), 582.

14. Mickiewicz, *Pan Tadeusz*, 580. There, in "God's world," he claims, people were more authentic and life more real, ". . . where servants more for masters care/ Than wives do for their husbands otherwhere." In the "lands of childhood" everyone knew each other and mourned when any "one of them did fall," shedding more tears there "For a dead dog than for a hero here" (582).

15. Of course, Mickiewicz had in mind the political turmoil of revolutionary Europe when he penned these lines, but his desire for a more natural, free, and *rural* Poland is clear there as well.

16. Stanisław Blejwas, *Realism in Polish Politics: Warsaw Positivism and National Survival in Nineteenth-Century Poland* (New Haven, CT, 1984), esp. 67–146.

17. *Nowiny*, 16 February 1905, 27, and 2 February 1910. The inset of the picture of the ruined gentleman showed him and his dog in their prime, in front of a nice home, to illustrate the depth of his fall.

18. *Nowiny*, 20 October 1908, 1.

19. *IKC*, 19 May 1912, 9.

20. *IKC*, 17 August 1913, 9.

21. *IKC*, 24 August 1913, 11–12.

22. *IKC*, 6 December 1913, 7. Emphasis original.

23. For a brilliant exposition of gaslight in London and the ways it was described, see Nead, *Victorian Babylon*, 101–8.

24. Schivelbusch, *Disenchanted Night*, 14–20, 40–44, 114–15.

25. Nead, *Victorian Babylon*, 101–8. See also Baudelaire's "*Le Crépuscule de Matin,*" in Charles Baudelaire, *The Flowers of Evil and Paris Spleen*, trans. William H. Crosby (Brockport, NY, 1991), 197–98.

26. *IKC,* 17 August 1913, 9.

27. Ibid.

28. This is not to say that Cracovian readers could not recognize their own similarities with those of metropolitans abroad, a point I make most directly in chapter 2. And ultimately, in both instances, readers imagined the city via the text, whether or not they had ever been to the spots it described.

29. *Nowiny,* 8 April 1904, 1–2; *IKC,* 17 May 1913, 7: "Ohydny mord seksualny w Berlinie"; *IKC,* 6 May 1914, 7: "Morderca dziewcząt w Budapeszcie."

30. *Nowiny,* 8 April 1904, 2.

31. This was the original idea that motivated Edgar Allan Poe's highly influential short story, "The Man of the Crowd" (1840). Please see, *The Collected Works of Edgar Allan Poe,* vol. 2, ed. Thomas Ollive Mabbott (Cambridge, MA, 1978), 505–18.

32. *Nowiny,* 7 June 1904.

33. The fate of the poor family was reported in *Nowiny,* 9 April 1905. This article, one of many about a family down on their luck in the city, well illustrates *Nowiny*'s populist, progressive streak.

34. *Nowiny,* 15 August 1911, 3.

35. *Nowiny,* 8 June 1907.

36. *Nowiny,* 15 May 1906, and 29 May 1906.

37. *Nowiny,* 3 July 1912, 4–5.

38. Alain Corbin, *The Foul and the Fragrant: Odor and the French Social Imagination* (Cambridge, MA, 1986), 144; Peter Stallybrass and Allon White, "The City: The Sewer, the Gaze, and the Contaminating Touch," in *The Politics and Poetics of Transgression,* by Stallybrass and White (Ithaca, NY, 1986), 125–48.

39. After the passage of the contagious diseases acts in the 1860s, prostitution was regulated in Great Britain according to the rhetoric of contagion. Formerly, prostitution was indirectly controlled according to the ideal of public order. The Vagrancy Act of 1826 stipulated that prostitutes could be imprisoned for one month for "riotous" or "indecent" behavior in public. See Lynda Nead, *Myths of Sexuality: Representations of Women in Victorian Britain* (NY, 1988), 115.

40. *Nowiny,* 21 November 1903, 1; 27 November 1903, 1; 4 December 1903, 2–3; 24 December 1903, 4, 7.

41. *Nowiny,* 4 December 1903, 2–3.

42. Jacob Riis, *How the Other Half Lives: Studies among the Tenements of New York* (NY, 1891).

43. *Nowiny,* 23 February 1906, 5.

44. *Nowiny,* 30/31 May 1903, 2.

45. *Nowiny,* 5 June 1903, 1–2.

46. *Nowiny,* 28 September 1905; 12 November 1905; 28 February 1907; 24 May 1907.

47. *Nowiny,* 24 May 1907.

48. Ibid.

49. *Nowiny,* 14 July 1904, 4.

50. *Nowiny,* 6 January 1905, 5.

51. Ibid. Ellipsis original.

52. *Nowiny,* 18 April 1905, 3.

53. *Nowiny,* 30 March 1907, 8.

54. *Nowiny,* 14 April 1907, 2-3.

55. *Nowiny,* 21 April 1904, 2-3. See also *Nowiny,* 11 June 1905, 4-5.

56. "A testimony of the morality of Cracow and Podgórze in figures," in *Nowiny,* 6 January 1910, 4, asserted that there was "a bit too much big-city scum in this little Cracow."

57. Stanley Cohen, *Folk Devils and Moral Panics: The Creation of the Mods and Rockers* (London, 1972), 9.

58. *Nowiny,* 9 January 1908, 2-3.

59. *Nowiny,* 10 January 1908, 2-3. My emphasis.

60. *Nowiny,* 11 January 1908, 1-2.

61. Ibid., 2.

62. *IKC,* 22 December, 1910, 2: "Ile mieszkańców będzie liczył Wielki Kraków 31 Grudnia?" ("How Many Inhabitants Will Greater Cracow Have on December 31st?") informed its readers that it wanted to help them with the contest designed by the paper by telling them statistical figures for Cracow in the past, along with the population of other cities.

63. *IKC,* 28 December 1910, 3.

64. Fritzsche argues that the Berlin press also used match girls as stereotypical representatives of urban life, in *Reading Berlin,* 124.

65. *IKC,* 5 May 1911, 1-2.

66. See Judith Walkowitz, *City of Dreadful Delight,* 81ff.

67. Cited in Walkowitz, 81. Walkowitz reports that the "Maiden Tribute" was a huge sensation; in addition to the wildly popular original story, some 1.5 million illegal reprints appeared (82).

68. Lynda Nead, *Myths of Sexuality.* Nead points out that Victorians tended to picture prostitutes as "social victims" or "fallen women" whenever they sought sympathetic treatment for these women, as opposed to the more frightening images of prostitutes as sources of contagion and "social chaos" that were employed when they sought to isolate and control them.

69. *IKC,* 27 July 1913, 2-3. The article claimed that there were some 12,000 registered prostitutes in Warsaw and many more who practiced clandestinely.

70. *Nowiny,* 12 November 1909, 1-2. The article further asserted that Muslims were cleaner as a people than Poles and held out the example of England as a model of cleanliness to which Galicia could someday aspire, given the fact that the English were once known for their aversion to bathing but now lived in the "cleanest country in the world."

71. For more on these developments in Central Europe, please see *Vernacular Art in Central Europe,* ed. Jacek Purchla (Cracow, 2001).

72. *Nowiny,* 31 July 1910, 3. Emphasis original.

73. I thank my friend Alexander Maxwell for asking this pointed question the day we met at the Midwest Slavics Workshop at the University of Illinois, Urbana-Champaign in April 2000.

74. A humor piece in the first issue of *IKC* in 1911 joked that if any future "social researcher" were to undertake a study of "the character of an average Cracovian, . . . he would definitely define him as a hypochondriac, a person never satisfied and critical of everyone and everything." *IKC,* 1 January 1911, 4.

75. An article in *Nowiny,* 4 May 1908, 2, discusses the relative danger of kissing, given the exchange of bacteria that would take place; in *Nowiny,* 18 July 1913, 6, there is a piece that discusses trimming children's nails and the safety of conserved meat and vegetables; *Nowiny,* 30 August 1907, 3, and *Nowiny,* 27 August 1910, 2, present reports on cholera in the city, with detailed descriptions of how to avoid spreading it.

76. *Kuryer Krakowski,* 10 February 1903, 3.

77. *IKC,* 7 May 1911, 5.

78. *Nowiny,* 15 November 1903, 5; *Nowiny,* 8 July 1905, 5; *Nowiny,* 13 August 1911, 3; *IKC,* 17 April 1912, 5; and for the story of the "musical rat," please see *IKC,* 24 May 1912, 6.

79. *Nowiny,* 21 March 1907, 3.

80. *KK,* 26 November 1902, 5.

81. *Nowiny,* 19 June 1903, 3; 19 July 1913, 5. See also *IKC,* 21 June 1912, 1.

82. For more on Cracow's municipal government, please see Małecki, "The Cracow Municipal Government in the 19th and 20th Centuries," and Irena Homola-Skąpska, "Municipal Government and the First Three Presidents of Cracow during the Period of Galician Autonomy, 1866–1884," in *Mayors and City Halls* (Cracow, 1998), 35–44, 59–64.

83. *KK,* 31 March 1903, 4.

84. *Nowiny,* 23 June 1903, 3.

85. *Nowiny,* 5 April 1906, 4. "Jacenty" could be a fictional character. If he was real, it seems clear that the journalist made him as clever and lazy as he could.

86. *Nowiny,* 31 August 1907, 3; 2 September 1908, 2. Siploryt, which was being tested on Zyblikiewicz Street, was supposed to resist dust and mud as well as kill microbes, thus serving as a disinfectant.

87. *Nowiny,* 24 January 1907, 1–2.

88. Ibid., 2.

89. *Nowiny,* 19 May 1910.

90. *Nowiny,* 15 November 1912, 4.

91. *Nowiny,* 27 February 1913, 4.

92. *IKC,* 22 August 1913, 4.

93. *Nowiny,* 10 September 1909, 2.

94. Fritzsche, *Reading Berlin,* 10.

95. *Nowiny,* 21 April 1904, 2–3.

CHAPTER 7

1. *Krytyka* 12 (1910): 35.

2. Jedlicki, *A Suburb of Europe.* See also, Wood, "Not just the National," 258–69.

3. Jedlicki, Świat Zwyrodniały, 78–81.

4. Jan Słomka, *From Serfdom to Self-Government: Memoirs of a Polish Village Mayor,* trans. William Rose (London, 1941), 183.

5. *KK,* 5 March 1903, 4–5.

6. Gruszecki, *Cygarniczka,* 29.

7. Ibid., 35.

8. Ibid., 24–25.

9. Samozwaniec, *Maria i Magdalena,* 55.

10. *Nowiny,* 10 March 1911, 3, reported the first sighting of *jupe* culottes in Cracow. For the next month or so, there were almost daily articles about the new sensation, including a report from Vienna about women who were heckled by huge crowds for wearing them, and a comment about the pair of Cracovian women who were harassed for wearing them. See *Nowiny,* 25 April 1911, 3.

11. *Nowiny,* 13 February 1909, 1.

12. *IKC,* 29 March 1911, 1

13. Muzeum Historyczne Miasta Krakowa, MHK1584–MHK8302; see also, *Album fotografii dawnego Krakowa z atelier Ignacego Kriegera,* ed. Maria Bronowski and Sławomir J. Tabkowski (Cracow, 1989).

14. *IKC,* 29 January 1911, 1.

15. Zechenter, *Upływa szybko życie,* 30; Broniewski, *Igraszki z czasem,* 78.

16. Samozwaniec, *Maria i Magdalena,* 66–67. Magdalena Samozwaniec and her sister Maria were the daughters of the Cracovian artist Wojciech Kossak.

17. *Kalendarz krakowski Józefa Czecha na roku 1903,* 71–73, and *Kalendarz krakowski Józefa Czecha na roku 1912,* 185–87.

18. For example, see reports on these three teams in *Nowiny,* 13 June 1911, 2, and *Nowiny,* 15 June 1911, 2. For more on the birth of sport in Cracow, see Józef Lustgarten, "Narodziny krakowskiego sportu" (The Birth of Cracovian Sport), in Gintel, ed., *Kopiec Wspomnień* (Cracow, 1964), 365–420.

19. *Nowiny,* 1 June 1911, 3.

20. *Nowiny,* 8 April 1913, 4–5; 22 April 1913, 4.

21. *Nowiny,* 10 January 1911, 2.

22. *IKC,* 2 March 1913, 4.

23. *IKC,* 2 March 1913, 13, offered the following illustrated statistic on the number of cinemas in respective countries: United States, 25,680; France, 4,700; Germany, 4,080; England, 2,940; Austria, 2,310; and Russia, 1,960. For more on Cracow's skating rink, see *Nowiny,* 25 April 1911, 3, and 3 May 1911, 2.

24. The most dramatic of these was the murder of Marya Kolasówna, whose mutilated body was found by some children in a field in September 1905 (*Nowiny,* 28 September 1905, 1–2). Many other stories like this one followed. For more on the Kolasówna scandal, please see Nathaniel D. Wood, "Sex Scandals, Sexual Violence, and the Word on the Street: The Kolasówna Lustmord in Cracow's Popular Press, 1905–06," *The Journal of the History of Sexuality* (forthcoming).

25. *Nowiny,* 9 August 1910, 3.

26. *Nowiny,* 25 January 1907, 2.

27. *Nowiny,* 4 April 1907, 1–3.

28. *Nowiny,* 6 August 1907, 1.

29. *Nowiny,* 11 May 1910, 4.

30. *Nowiny,* 21 April 1904, 2–3.

31. *Nowiny,* 21 April 1906, 1–4. Note the complex process of community framing here. By referring to his fellow Cracovians as "brothers," the journalist affirmed their common identity, while deliberately excluding the villagers who lived outside the city. Of course, if they were brothers, this left little room for female Cracovians in the group.

32. Ibid. Hawełka's was a top-notch store, complete with a café and restaurant. Wentzel's was one of the city's most popular bars. See also Chapter 1.

33. Emil Brix has written that the vernacular style in art was derived in large part by nationalist artists who, recognizing the great differences between urban and rural life, made an effort "to create new emotional bonds between the city and the countryside (for example in the writings of Wyspiański or in the music of Janácek)." See Emil Brix, "Intellectuals and Vernacular Art: Reflections on the Late Habsburg Monarchy," in *Vernacular Art in Central Europe,* ed. Jacek Purchla (Cracow, 2001), 50.

34. Benedict Anderson, *Imagined Communities,* 9–46.

35. *IKC,* 9 March 1911, 1–2.

36. Alison Fleig Frank, *Oil Empire: Visions of Prosperity in Austrian Galicia* (Cambridge, MA, 2005); John Kulczycki, *The Polish Coal Miner's Union and the German Labor Movement in the Ruhr, 1902–1934: National and Social Solidarity* (NY, 1997).

EPILOGUE

1. Jalu Kurek, *Kim był Andrzej Panik? Andrzej Panik zamordował Amundsena* (Cracow, 1926), as cited in Karolina Grodziska, "Gdzie miasto zaczarowane," 130.

2. Paul Fussell, *The Great War and the Making of Modern Memory* (NY, 1975). Modris Eksteins, *Rites of Spring: The Great War and the Birth of the Modern Age* (Toronto, 1989).

3. Martin, *Jewish Life in Cracow,* 40–41.

4. Alfred Döblin, *Journey to Poland,* 152.

5. Ibid., 40.

6. Ibid., 201.

7. Ibid., 181–82.

8. Ibid., 200.

9. Ibid., 187.

10. Ibid., 186. The reference came from a medieval lecture found in the Jagiellonian University Library that began: "'God is the subject of theology. Theology is a single science. Theology is a practical science.'" Döblin called it "A splendid, splendid statement! We are gradually beginning to understand it again."

11. Ibid., 207.

12. Ibid., 201.

13. Ibid., 140.

14. Ibid., 193, 200–201, 208.

15. *IKC,* 13 November 1924, 6.

Bibliography

PRIMARY SOURCES

Periodicals

Bocian (1901–1903, 1910, 1912)
Czas (1900–1901, 1905, 1907, 1910)
Djabeł (1900–1903, 1910, 1912)
Głos Narodu (1901, 1903, 1905)
Ilustracja Polska (1902–1904)
Ilustrowany Kuryer Codzienny (1910–1915, 1918, 1924)
Kalendarz Krakowski Józefa Czecha (1901, 1903, 1908, 1912, 1917)
Krytyka (1910)
Kuryerek Krakowski (1902–1904)
Liberum Veto (1903)
Naprzód (1901, 1903, 1905, 1907)
Nowa Reforma (1899, 1900, 1901, 1903, 1905, 1907, 1908, 1910)
Nowiny dla wszystkich (1903–1914)
Nowości Illustrowane (1904–1905, 1908)
Słowo Polskie (1908)
Statystyka Miasta Krakowa (1903, 1904, 1905, 1906, 1907)
Wiek Nowy (1904)
Życie (1898–1900)

Archival Sources

Archiwum Państwowe w Krakowie (National Archive in Cracow)

Police Records:
DPKr 58   1904
DPKr 67   1909
DPKr 72   1910

Prostitute Registries:
DPKr 436   Dziennik zatrzymanych prostytutek i wyniki badań lek, 1885–1893
DPKr 437   Dziennik zatrzymanych prostytutek i wyniki badań lek, 1894–1906
DPKr 438   Indeks prostytutek jawnych, 1877–1912
DPKr 439   Rejestr prostytutek, 1891–1904
DPKr 440   Rejestr prostytutek, 1897–1901
DPKr 441   Rejestr prostytutek, 1901–1905
DPKr 442   Rejestr prostytutek, 1907–1913

Criminal Court Records:
SKKKr 1209

Urban Infrastructure:
TRAM 6   korespondencje i akcje, 1910–1917
ELEKTR 6

Juliusz Leo:
IT 740   e. akta prezydenta (Leo Juliusz)

Creation of Greater Cracow:
IT 1272 Teczka I: Akta od 28 II 1867 do 31 XII 1901
IT 1273 Teczka II: Akta od 28 I 1902 do 19 IX 1907
IT 1274 Teczka II: Akta od 20 IX 1907 do 31 III 1910
IT 1275 Teczka IV: Akta od 1910 (I plan gmin otaczających Krakowa)
IT 1276 Teczka V: Akta Dąbie i Ludwinów
IT 1277 Teczka VI: Akta Płaszow
IT 1278 Teczka VII: Sprawozdania ustawy i prasa
IT 1279 Teczka VIII: Materiały obce Rozszerzenie miast (Praga, Wiedeń, Innsbruck, Rzeszów, Ikole)
IT 1280 Teczka IX: A. Akta Podgorza od 1903 do 31 III 1910
IT 1281 Teczka IX: B. Akta Podgorza od 1 IV 1910 do 1911
IT 1282 Teczka IX: C. Akta Podgorza od uchwały Sejmu 25 IV 1913
IT 1283 Teczka IX: D. Akta Podgorza od 26 IV 1913 do uchwały Sejmu
IT 1284 Teczka X: Materiały do Księgi o Wielkim Krakowie (przewaz. Podgorze)
IT 1299 "Uroczystości w dniu 17 IV 1910" z okazji przyłączenia okolicznych gmin
IT 1318 "Sprawozdania z działalności Rady Miasta i Magistratu od 1866. Nowe referaty opracowane od 10/9 1913r."
IT 1319 "Sprawozdania z działalności Rady Miasta i Magistratu od 1866. Referaty i materiały zupełnie przerobione i wycofane."

Muzeum Historyczne Miasta Krakowa (Historical Museum of the City of Cracow)
Photography Collection, especially the Ignacy Krieger Collection

Memoirs

Akavia, Miriam. *Moja winnica*. Warsaw: Państwowy Instytut Wydawniczy, 1990.
Broniewski, Stanisław. *Igraszki z czasem, czyli miniona lata na cenzurowanym*. Cracow: Wydawnictwo Literackie, 1970.
Ciechanowska, Elżbieta. *Pamiętnik*. Manuscript in the collection of the Jagiellonian University Library.
Daszyński, Ignacy. *Pamiętniki*. Cracow: Proletarjat, 1925.

Estreicher, Karol. *Nie od razu Kraków zbudowano.* Cracow: Państwowy Instytut Wydawniczy, 1953.

Gajzlerowa z Cerchów, Eleonora. *Tamten Kraków, tamta Krynica.* 1972. Reprint, Cracow: Spes, 1995.

Goetel, Ferdynand. *Patrząc wstecz.* London: Nakład Polskiej Fundacji Kulturalnej, 1966.

Kietlińska, Maria z Mohrów. *Wspomnienia.* Edited by Irena Homola-Skąpska. Cracow: Krajowa Agencja Wydawnicza, 1986.

Krygowski, Władysław. *W moim Krakowie nad wczorajszą Wisłą.* Cracow: Wydawnictwo Literackie, 1980.

Kurek, Jalu. *Mój Kraków.* Kraków: Wydawnictwo Literackie, 1963.

Leśnodorski, Zygmunt. *Wspomnienia i zapiski.* Cracow: Wydawnictwo Literackie, 1963.

Morawski, Kazimierz Marian. *Kraków przed trzydziestu laty.* Warsaw: Odbitki Myśli Narodowej, 1932.

Muczkowska, Zofia. "Pod Krukiem." In *Kopiec wspomnień,* ed. Jan Gintel, 39–80. Cracow: Wydawnictwo Literackie, 1959.

Nowakowski, Zygmunt. *Mój Kraków i inne wspomnienia.* Warsaw: Oficyjne Wydawnicza Interim, 1994.

Pigoń, Stanisław. *Z komborni w świat.* 1957. Reprint, Warsaw: Ludowa Spółdzielnia Wydawnicza, 1984.

Przybyszewski, Stanisław. *Moi współcześni.* 1926. Reprint, Warsaw: Czytelnik, 1959.

Puttkamer-Żółtowska, Janina. *Inne czasy, inni ludzie.* London: Alma Book Co., 1959.

Samozwaniec, Magdalena. *Maria i Magdalena.* Cracow: Wydawnictwo Literackie, 1970.

Słapa, Aleksander. "Chłopięca pasja książek." In *Kopiec wspomnień,* ed. Zygmunt Gitel, 178–202. Cracow: Wydawnictwo Literackie, 1964.

Smolarski, Mieczysław. *Miasto starych dzwonów.* Cracow: Wydawnictwo Literackie, 1960.

Szancer, Jan Marcin. *Curriculum vitae.* Warsaw: Czytelnik, 1959.

Turski, Marian. "Czase gimnazjalne." In *Kopiec wspomnień,* ed. Jan Gintel, 81–104. Cracow: Wydawnictwo Literackie, 1959.

Wysocki, Alfred. *Sprzed pół wieku.* Cracow: Wydawnictwo Literackie, 1958.

Zechenter, Witold. *Upływa szybko życie.* Cracow: Wydawnictwo Literackie, 1975.

Zweig, Stefan. *The World of Yesterday.* 1943. Reprint, Lincoln: University of Nebraska Press, 1964.

Other Primary Sources

Baedeker, Karl. Österreich-Ungarn. *Handbuch fur reisende.* Leipzig: Verlag von Karl Baedeker, 1903.

Boy-Żeleński, Tadeusz. *Boy o Krakowie.* Edited by Henryk Markiewicz. Cracow: Wydawnictwo Literackie, 1967.

———. *Znaszli ten kraj? . . . (Cyganeria krakowska) oraz inne wspomnienia o Krakowie.* Edited by Tomasz Wiess. Wrocław: Zakład Narodowy im. Ossolińskich, 1983.

Bystroń, Jan Stanisław. "Pięćdziesięciolecie samorządu Krakowa, 1866–1916." In *Józefa Czecha kalendarz krakowski na r. 1917*. Cracow, 1916.

——. "Rozwój demograficzny dzielnic Krakowa (Tworzenie się Centrum wiel komiejskiego w Krakowie)." *Ekonimista* 15, nos. 1–2 (1915): 112–60.

Cole, Grenville A. J. *The Gypsy Road: A Journey from Krakow to Coblentz*. London and New York: Macmillan & Co., 1894.

Conrad, Joseph. *My Return to Cracow*. London: Printed for Private Circulation, 1919.

Daszyńska-Golińska, Zofia. "Robotnicy Młodociani w rzemiośle i rękodziełach w Krakowie." *Czasopisma Prawnicza-Ekonomiczna* 14 (1913), 28–139.

Döblin, Alfred. *Journey to Poland*. Translated by Joachim Neugroschel and edited by Heinz Graber. 1925. Reprint, New York: Paragon House, 1991.

Griffin, C. E. *The Life History of Automobiles*. Ann Arbor: University of Michigan, Bureau of Business Research, 1926.

Gruszecki, Artur. *Cygarniczka*. Warsaw: Jan Fischer, 1906.

Hamburgier, Mieczysław. "Śmiertelność z gruźlicy i zapalenia płuc w Krakowie od 1900 r. do 1913 r." *Gruźlica* 1–2 (1925/1926), issues 3, 4, and 5.

Krumłowski, Konstanty. *Królowa przedmieścia. Wodewil w 5 aktach*. 1898. Reprint, Cracow, 1991.

Kumaniecki, Kazimierz Władysław. *Tymczasowe wyniki spisu ludności w Krakowie z 31 grudnia 1910 roku*. Cracow: City of Cracow, 1912.

Mickiewicz, Adam. *Pan Tadeusz*. Translated by Kenneth R. MacKenzie. New York: Hippocrene Books, 1992.

Norman, Ménie Muriel (Dowie). *A Girl in the Karpathians*. 5th ed. London: George Philip and Son, 1892.

Nowaczyński, Adolf. *Małpie Zwierczadło. Wybór pism satyrycznych*. Vol. 2. Cracow: Wydawnictwo Literackie, 1974.

——. *Nowe Ateny. Satyra na Wielki Kraków*. 2nd ed. Warsaw: Gebethner i Wolff, 1914.

Nowotny, Juliusz. *Odpowiedzialność redaktora*. Cracow, 1906.

Orłowicz, Mieczysław, and Roman Kordys. *Illustrierter Führer durch Galizien mit einem Anhang. Ost-Schlesien von Dr. Johan Kotas und Prof. Josef Londzin*. Vienna and Leipzig: A. Hartelben's Verlag, 1914.

Polaczek-Kornecki, T. *Trzydziestolecie tramwaju elektrycznego w Krakowie, 1901–1931*. Cracow, 1932.

Przeorski, Tadeusz. "Przyczyny podjęcia starań o przyłączenie do Krakowa sąsiednich gmin i obszarów dworskich." In *Kraków. Rozszerzenie granic, 1909–1915*. Cracow: K. Rolle, 1931.

Rosenblatt, J. "Reforma prawa prasowego Austrii." *Czasopisma Prawnicze i Ekonomiczne* 1, issue 1.2 (1900), 72–104.

Scharf, Rafael F. *Poland: What Have I to Do with Thee . . . Essays without Prejudice*. London: Vallentine Mitchell, 1998.

Schmal, Adolph. *Die Kunst des Fahrens. Praktische Winke ein Automobil oder Motorrad richtig zu lenken. Ergänzungen zum Handbuche "Ohne Chauffeur."* Vienna: Beck, 1916.

Sikorski, Rudolf. "Kraków w roku 1900, oraz jego podział administracyjny w ciągu

XIX stulecia." *Kalendarz Józefa Czecha na roku 1903.* Cracow: Józef Czech, 1904.

Słomka, Jan. *From Serfdom to Self-Government: Memoirs of a Polish Village Mayor, 1842–1927.* Translated by William John Rose. London: Minerva, 1941.

Szczepański, Ludwik. *Przewrót. Powieść z najbliszej przyszłości.* Cracow: G. Gebethner i Spółka; Warsaw: Gebethner i Wolff, 1911.

———. *Srebne noce. Lunatica.* Vienna: Franciszek Bonde; Warsaw: Centnerszwer, 1897.

Tambor, Jan. *Trwanie życia ludzkiego w Krakowie w okresie od r. 1881–1925.* Cracow: Polska Akademia Umiętności, 1930.

Vaughan, Robert. *The Age of Great Cities; or, Modern society viewed in its relation to intelligence, morals, and religion.* 1843. Reprint, Shannon: Irish University Press, 1972.

Wells, H. G. *The War in the Air.* 1908. Reprint, London: Macmillan, 1967.

Wyspiański, Stanisław. *The Wedding.* Translated by Gerard T. Kapolka. Ann Arbor, MI: Ardis, 1990.

SECONDARY SOURCES

Adamczewski, Jan. *In Cracow.* Warsaw: Interpress Publishers, 1973.

Album fotografii dawnego Krakowa z atelier Ignacego Kriegera. Edited by Maria Bronowski and Sławomir J. Tabkowski. Cracow: Krajowa Agencja Wydawnicza, 1989.

Anderson, Benedict. *Imagined Communities: Reflections on the Origin and Spread of Nationalism.* New York: Verso, 1991.

Anderson, Perry. "Modernity and Revolution." *New Left Review* 144 (1984): 96–113.

Art around 1900 in Central Europe. Art Centres and Provinces. Edited by Jacek Purchla. Cracow: International Cultural Centre, 1999.

Bąk-Koczarska, Celina. *Juliusz Leo. Twórca Wielkiego Krakowa.* Wrocław and Warszawa: Zakład Narodowy imienia Ossolińskich, Wydawnictwo Polskiej Akademii Nauk, 1986.

Bańdo, Adam. *Nie tylko krew na pierwszej stronie. Problematyka kulturalna na łamach "Ilustrowanego Kuriera Codziennego" w latach 1918–1939.* Cracow: Wydawnictwo Naukowe Akademii Pedagogicznej, 2006.

Barth, Gunther. *City People: The Rise of Modern City Culture in Nineteenth-Century America.* New York: Oxford University Press, 1980.

Bęczkowska, Urszula. *Pałac Sztuki. Siedziba Towarzystwa Przyjaciół Sztuk Pięknych w Krakowie.* Cracow: Universitas, 2002.

Beiersdorf, Zbigniew, and Jacek Purchla. *Dom pod Globusem. Dawna siedziba krakowskiej Izby Handlowej i Prszemysłowej.* Cracow: Wydawnictwo Literackie, 1988.

Berman, Marshall. *All that Is Solid Melts into Air: The Experience of Modernity.* 1982. Reprint, New York: Viking Penguin, 1988.

Bienarzówna, Janina, and Jan M. Małecki, eds. *Dzieje Krakowa.* Vol. 3. *Kraków w latach, 1796–1918.* Cracow: Wydawnictwo Literackie, 1979.

Binder, Harald. "Making and Defending a Polish Town: 'Lwów' (Lemberg), 1848–

1914." *Austrian History Yearbook* 34 (2003): 57–81.

———. "Das polnische Pressewesen." In *Die Habsburgermonarchie 1848–1918*. Vol. 8/2. *Politische Öffenlichkeit und Zivilgesellschaft*. 2. Teilband. *Die Presse als Faktor der politischen Mobilisierung*, 2039–90. Vienna: Austrian Academy of Sciences, 2006.

———. "Urban Landscape and the Printed Press in Habsburg Lemberg: The Kotsko Memorial of 1912." *East Central Europe* 33, pts. 1–2 (2006): 53–70.

Blejwas, Stanisław. *Realism in Polish Politics: Warsaw Positivism and National Survival in Nineteenth-Century Poland*. New Haven, CT: Yale University Press, 1984.

Blobaum, Robert. *Rewolucja: Russian Poland, 1904–1907*. Ithaca, NY: Cornell University Press, 1995.

Bogdanowicz, Janusz. "Od miasta-twierdzy do miasta-ogrodu. Przemiany śródmieścia Krakowa." In *Kraków na przełomie XIX i XX wieku*, ed. Jan M. Małecki, 89–110. Cracow: Wydawnictwo Literackie, 1983.

Borowiec, Piotr. *"Jesteśmy głosem milionów." Dzieje krakowskiego wydawnictwa i koncernu prasowego Ilustrowany Kurier Codzienny (1910–1939)*. Cracow: Wydawnictwo Uniwersytetu Jagiellońskeigo, 2005.

Briggs, Asa. *Victorian Cities*. London: Oldham's Press, 1963.

Brooks, Jeffrey. *When Russia Learned to Read: Literacy and Popular Literature, 1861–1917*. Princeton, NJ: Princeton University Press, 1985.

Brower, Daniel. "The Penny Press and Its Readers." In *Cultures in Flux: Lower-Class Values, Practices, and Resistance in Late Imperial Russia*, ed. Stephen P. Frank and Mark D. Steinberg, 147–67. Princeton, NJ: Princeton University Press, 1984.

Brubaker, Rogers. *Ethnicity without Groups*. Cambridge: Harvard University Press, 2004.

———. *Nationalism Reframed: Nationhood and the National Question in the New Europe*. New York: Cambridge University Press, 1996.

Brubaker, Rogers, Margit Fieschmidt, Jon Fox, and Liana Grancea, eds. *Nationalist Politics and Everyday Ethnicity in a Transylvanian Town*. Princeton, NJ: Princeton University Press, 2006.

Burgess, Ernest W., and Roderick D. McKenzie. *The City*. 1925. Reprint, Chicago, IL: University of Chicago Press, 1967.

Buszko, Józef. "Kraków w dobie autonomii galicyjskiej (1866–1914)." In *Szkice z dziejów Krakowa od czasów najdawniejszych do pierwszej wojny światowej*, ed. Janina Bieniarzówna, 355–390. Cracow: Wydawnictwo Literackie, 1968.

———. *Od niewoli do niepodległości (1864–1918)*. Cracow: Fogra, 2000.

———. "Stanowisko galicyjskiego obszarnictwa polskiego i burżuazji wobec reformy wyborczej w latach 1905–07." *Przegląd Historyczny* 46, no. 3 (1955): 380–419.

Campbell, W. Joseph. *Yellow Journalism: Puncturing the Myths, Defining the Legacies*. Westport, CT: Praeger, 2001.

Chalaby, Jean. *The Invention of Journalism*. New York: St. Martin's Press, 1998.

Chartier, Roger. *The Cultural Uses of Print in Early Modern France*. Translated by Lydia

G. Cochrane. Princeton, NJ: Princeton University Press, 1987.

The City in Central Europe: Culture and Society from 1800 to the Present. Edited by Malcolm Gee, Tim Kirk, and Jill Steward. Brookfield, VT: Ashgate, 1999.

Classic Essays on the Culture of Cities. Edited by Richard Sennett. New York: Appleton-Century-Crofts, 1969.

Cohen, Gary. "Society and Culture in Prague, Vienna, and Budapest in the Late Nineteenth Century." *East European Quarterly* 20, no. 4 (1987): 469–79.

Corbain, Alain. *The Foul and the Fragrant: Odor and the French Social Imagination.* Cambridge: Harvard University Press, 1986.

Corrsin, Stephen D. *Warsaw before the First World War: Poles and Jews in the Third City of the Russian Empire, 1880–1914.* Boulder, CO: East European Monographs, 1989.

Cracow: The Dialogue of Traditions. Edited by Zbigniew Baran. English version edited by William Brand. Cracow: Znak, International Cultural Centre, 1991.

Crowley, David. "Castles, Cabarets, and Cartoons: Claims on Polishness in Krakow around 1905." In *The City in Central Europe,* ed. Malcolm Gee, Tim Kirk, and Jill Steward, 101–17. Brookfield, VT: Ashgate, 1999.

Curtis, L. Perry, Jr. *Jack the Ripper and the London Press.* New Haven, CT: Yale University Press, 2001.

Dabrowski, Patrice. *Commemorations and the Shaping of Modern Poland.* Bloomington: Indiana University Press, 2004.

David-Fox, Katherine. "Prague-Vienna, Prague-Berlin: The Hidden Geography of Czech Modernism." *Slavic Review* 59 (Winter 2000): 735–60.

Davies, Norman, and Roger Moorhouse. *Microcosm: Portrait of a Central European City.* London: Jonathan Cape, 2002.

Davis, Lennard. *Factual Fictions: The Origins of the English Novel.* New York: Columbia University Press, 1983.

Decadence and Innovation: Austro-Hungarian Life and Art at the Turn of the Century. Edited by Robert B. Pynsent. London: Weidenfeld and Nicolson, 1989.

Demetz, Peter. *The Air Show at Brescia, 1909.* New York: Farrar, Straus, and Giroux, 2002.

———. *Prague in Black and Gold: Scenes from the Life of a European City.* New York: Hill and Wang, 1997.

Donia, Robert J. "Fin-de-Siècle Sarajevo: The Habsburg Transformation of an Ottoman Town." *Austrian History Yearbook* 33 (2002): 43–75.

Dużyk, Józef. "Polskie Ateny." In *Kraków Stary i Nowy. Dzieje kultury,* ed. Janina Bieniarzówna, 303–44. Cracow: Państwowe Wydawnictwo Naukowe, 1968.

Eksteins, Modris. *Rites of Spring: The Great War and the Birth of the Modern Age.* Toronto: Lester and Orpen Dennys, 1989.

Engels, Friedrich. *The Condition of the Working Class in England.* German edition, 1845. New York: Penguin Classics, 1987.

Frančić, Mirosław. *Kraków. Kalendarz dziejów od prawieków do wybuchu I wojny światowej.* Cracow: Wydawnictwo Literackie, 1998.

Frank, Alison Fleig. *Oil Empire: Visions of Prosperity in Austrian Galicia.* Cambridge:

Harvard University Press, 2005.

Fras, Zbigniew. *Galicja.* Wrocław: Wydawnictwo Dolnośląskie, 2004.

Fritzsche, Peter. *Reading Berlin, 1900.* Cambridge: Harvard University Press, 1996.

Fussell, Paul. *The Great War and Modern Memory.* New York: Oxford University Press, 1975.

Garlicki, Andrzej. "Rodzaje konfiskat prasowych w Krakowie w latach 1900–1914." *Przegląd Historyczny* 54, no. 3 (1963): 457–72.

Gerschenkron, Alexander. *An Economic Spurt that Failed.* Princeton, NJ: Princeton University Press, 1977.

Godziny zwierzeń. Wspomnienia synów i córek o ich sławnych i zasłużonych rodziców. Edited by Stefan Henel. Warsaw: Iskry, 1983.

Good, David F. *The Economic Rise of the Habsburg Empire, 1750–1914.* Berkeley and Los Angeles: University of California Press, 1984.

Grodziska, Karolina. "Gdzie to miasto zaczarowane . . ." *Księga cytatów o Krakowie.* Cracow: Znak, 2003.

Gyáni, Gábor. *Identity and the Urban Experience: Fin-de-Siècle Budapest.* Translated by Thomas DeKornfield. Boulder, CO: Social Science Monographs, 2004.

———. *Parlor and Kitchen: Housing and Domestic Culture in Budapest, 1870–1940.* Budapest: Central European University Press, 2002.

———. *Women as Domestic Servants: The Case of Budapest, 1890–1940.* Translated by András Vitányi. Revised by Peter Bogard. New York: Institute on East Central Europe, Columbia University Press, 1989.

Habermas, Jürgen. *The Structural Transformation of the Public Sphere: An Inquiry into a Category of Bourgeois Society.* Translated by Thomas Burger with the assistance of Frederick Lawrence. Cambridge, MA: MIT Press, 1991.

Hadler, Simon. "Der urbane Raum Krakaus als Medium des städtischen Images?" (De) Konstruktionen Galiziens. Kommunikation—Transformation—kulturelles Gedächtnis, Universität Wien, Vienna, 28 Nov. 2008.

———. "Die Wahrnehmung der Stadt. Krakau um 1900 als Konstruktion und Lebenswelt." Diploma thesis. Graz, 2006.

Hall, Peter. *Cities in Civilization.* New York: Pantheon, 1998.

Halsey, Francis, ed. *Seeing Europe with Famous Authors.* Vol. 4, part 2, *Germany, Austria-Hungary, Switzerland.* 1914. Reprint, New York: BiblioBazaar, 2004.

Hanák, Péter. *The Garden and the Workshop: Essays on the Cultural History of Vienna and Budapest.* Princeton, NJ: Princeton University Press, 1998.

Herget, Beate. *Die Selbstverwaltung Krakaus, 1866–1915. Ein rechtshistorischer Beitrag zur Bedetung der Statutarstädte in der Habsburg Monarchie.* Regensburg: Sophia-Verlag, 2005.

Herman, Arthur. *The Idea of Decline in Western History.* New York: Free Press, 1997.

Himka, John-Paul. *Socialism in Galicia: The Emergence of Polish Social Democracy and Ukrainian Radicalism (1860–1890).* Cambridge: Harvard Ukrainian Research Institute, 1983.

Historia komunikacji w mieście Krakowie. Edited by Z. Gierdziewicz. Cracow, 1975.

Hohenberg, Paul, and Lynn Hollen Lees. *The Making of Urban Europe, 1000–1994.* Cambridge: Harvard University Press, 1995.

Holmgren, Beth. *Rewriting Capitalism: Literature and the Market in Imperial Russia and the Kingdom of Poland.* Pittsburgh, PA: University of Pittsburgh Press, 1998.

Holzer, Jerzy. "Enlightenment, Assimilation, and Modern Identity: The Jewish Élite in Galicia." In *Polin: Studies in Polish Jewry,* vol. 12, *Focusing on Galicia: Jews, Poles, and Ukrainians, 1772–1918,* ed. Israel Bartal and Antony Polonsky, 79–85. London: Littman Library of Jewish Civilization, 1999.

Homola, Irena. *Józef Dietl i jego Kraków.* Cracow: Wydawnictwo Literackie, 1993.

——. *Kraków za prezydentury Mikołaja Zyblikiewicza (1874–1881).* Cracow: Wydawnictwo Literackie, 1976.

——. "Kwiat Społeczeństwa . . ." (Struktura społeczna i zarys położenia inteligencji krakowskiej w latach 1860–1914). Cracow: Wydawnictwo Literackie, 1984.

Homola-Skąpska, Irena. "Krakowskie cukiernie i kawiarnie w XIX wieku." *Annales Universitas Mariae Curie-Skłodowska Lublin-Polonia* 51, no. 5 (1996): 43–61.

——. "'Mały Wiedeń' nad Wisłą." *Zeszyty naukowe Uniwersytetu Jagiellońskiego. Prace historyczne* 121 (1997): 409–26.

——. "Municipal Government and the First Three Presidents of Cracow during the Period of Galician Autonomy, 1866–1884." In *Mayors and City Halls,* ed. Jacek Purchla, 59–64. Cracow: International Cultural Centre, 1998.

Howard, Ebenezer. *Garden Cities of Tomorrow.* Edited by F. J. Osborn. London: Faber and Faber, 1945.

Hutnikiewicz, Artur. *Młoda Polska.* Warsaw: Wydawnictwo Naukowe, PWN, 1994.

Iser, Wolfgang. *The Implied Reader: Patterns of Communication in Prose Fiction.* Baltimore, MD: Johns Hopkins University Press, 1974.

Janowski, Maciej. *Inteligencja wobec wyzwań nowoczeszczności. Dylematy ideowe demokracji liberalnej w Galicji w latach 1889–1914.* Warsaw: Instytut Historii PAN, 1996.

Jedlicki, Jerzy. *A Suburb of Europe: Nineteenth-Century Polish Approaches to Western Civilization.* Budapest: Central European University Press, 1999.

——. *Świat zwyrodniały. Lęki i wyroki krytyków nowocześćności.* Warsaw: Wydawnictwo Sic! 2000.

Jędrzejczyk, Olgierd. *Niech Kraków zawsze Kraków znaczy.* Cracow: Krajowa Agencja Wydawnicza, 1981.

Jenkins, Jennifer. *Provincial Modernity: Local Culture and Politics in Fin-de-Siècle Hamburg.* Ithaca, NY: Cornell University Press, 2003.

Jones, Aled. *Powers of the Press: Newspapers, Power, and the Public in Nineteenth-Century England.* Aldershot, England, and Brookfield, VT: Ashgate, 1996.

Judson, Pieter. *Guardians of the Nation: Activists on the Language Frontiers of Imperial Austria.* Cambridge: Harvard University Press, 2006.

Karolczak, Kazimierz. *Właściciele domów w Krakowie na przełomie XIX i XX wieku. Z badań nad dziejami Krakowa.* Cracow: Wydawnictwo Naukowe WSP, 1987.

Kern, Stephen. *The Culture of Time and Space, 1880–1918.* Cambridge: Harvard

University Press, 2003.

King, Jeremy. *Budweisers into Czechs and Germans: A Local History of Bohemian Politics, 1848–1948*. Princeton, NJ: Princeton University Press, 2002.

———. "The Nationalization of East Central Europe." In *Staging the Past*, ed. Maria Bucur and Nancy Wingfield, 112–52. West Lafayette, IN: Purdue University Press, 2001.

Kopiec Wspomnień. Edited by Jan Gintel. Cracow: Wydawnictwo Literackie, 1959.

Kozińska-Witt, Hanna. *Krakau in Warschaus langem Schatten. Konkurrenzkämpf in der polnischen Städtelandschaft, 1900–1939*. Stuttgart: Franz Steiner Verlag, 2008.

———. "Stadträte und polnische Presse. Die Falle Warschau und Krakau, 1900–1939. Ein Versuch." In *Stadt un Öffentlichkeit in Ostmitteleuropa 1900–1939*, ed. Andreas R. Hoffmann and Anna Veronika Wendland. Stuttgart, 2002.

Kozioł, Andrzej. *Na krakowskim Rynku. Historia i obyczaje od lokacji do najnowszych czasów*. Cracow: Wydawnictwo WAM, 2007.

Kraków. Nowe studia nad rozwojem miasta. Edited by Jerzy Wyrozumski. Cracow: Towarzystwo Miłośników Historii i Zabytków Krakowa, 2007.

Kraków. Stolica Kresów Południowo-Zachodnich. Studia nad nowym podziałem administracyjnym państwa. Cracow: Izba Przemysłowo-Handlowa w Krakowie, 1930.

Krakowianie. Wybitni Żydzi krakowscy XIV–XX wieku. Edited by Agnieszka Kutylak. Cracow: Muzeum Historyczne Miasta Krakowa, 2006.

Kraków-Małopolska w Europie środka. Studia ku czci Jana M. Małeckiego w siedemdziesiątą rocznicę urodzin. Edited by Krzysztof Broński, Jacek Purchla, and Jan Szpak. Cracow: Universitas, 1996.

Krakowski, Piotr. "Cracow Artistic Milieu around 1900." In *Art around 1900 in Central Europe: Art Centres and Provinces*, ed. Piotr Krakowski and Jacek Purchla, 71–79. Cracow: International Cultural Centre, 1999.

Kronika Krakowa. Edited by Marian Michalik. Warsaw: Kronika, 1996.

Kulczycki, John. *The Polish Coal Miners' Union and the German Labor Movement in the Ruhr, 1902–1934: National and Social Solidarity*. Oxford and New York: Berg, 1997.

Ladd, Brian. *Urban Planning and Civic Order in Germany, 1860–1914*. Cambridge: Harvard University Press, 1990.

Lechicki, Czesław. "Kartka z dziejów prasy krakowskiej XX wieku." *Małopolskie Studia Historyczne* 8, nos. 1/2 (28/29) (1965): 119–33.

Lees, Andrew, and Lynn Lees, eds. *The Urbanization of European Society in the Nineteenth Century*. Lexington, MA: D. C. Heath, 1976.

Le Rider, Jacques. *Modernity and Crises of Identity: Culture and Society in Fin-de-Siècle Vienna*. Translated by Rosemary Morris. New York: Continuum, 1993.

Lichtenberger, Elisabeth. *Vienna: Bridge between Cultures*. Translated by Dietlinde Mühlgassner and Craig Reisser. London: Belhaven Press, 1993.

Lukacs, John. *Budapest 1900: A Historical Portrait of a City and Its Culture*. New York:

Weidenfeld and Nicolson, 1988.

Lustgarten, Józef. "Narodziny krakowskiego sportu." In *Kopiec Wspomnień*. Cracow: Wydawnictwo Literackie, 1964.

Magocsi, Paul Robert. *Historical Atlas of Central Europe*. Revised and expanded edition. Toronto: University of Toronto Press, 2002.

Małecki, Jan M. "Cracow Jews in the Nineteenth Century: Leaving the Ghetto." *Acta Poloniae Historica* 76 (1997): 87–88.

———. "The Cracow Municipal Government in the 19th and 20th Centuries." In *Mayors and City Halls*, ed. Jacek Purchla, 35–43. Cracow: International Cultural Centre 1998.

———. "Kraków na przełomie XIX i XX wieku." *Nasza Przeszłość* 67 (1987): 5–25.

———. "Lemberg und Krakau—zwei Hauptstädte Galiziens." In *Festschrift Othmar Pickl zum 60. Geburtstag*, ed. Herwig Ebner et al., 409–15. Graz, 1987.

———. "Lwów i Kraków—Dwie Stolice Galicji." *Roczniki dziejów społecznych i gospodarczych* 50 (1989): 119–31.

Manoulien, Edward. "Invented Traditions: Primitivist Narrative and Design in the Polish Fin de Siècle." *Slavic Review* 59 (Summer 2000): 391–405.

Martin, Sean. *Jewish Life in Cracow, 1918–1939*. Portland, OR: Vallentine Mitchell, 2004.

Marzoff, Marion T. "American New Journalism Takes Root in Europe." *Journalism Quarterly* 61 (Autumn 1984): 529–36, 691.

Mayors and City Halls: Local Government and the Cultural Space of the Late Habsburg Monarchy. Edited by Jacek Purchla. Cracow: International Cultural Centre, 1998.

McCloud, Scott. *Understanding Comics: The Invisible Art*. Northampton, MA: Kitchen Sink Press, 1993.

McKay, John P. *Tramways and Trolleys: The Rise of Urban Mass Transport in Europe*. Princeton, NJ: Princeton University Press, 1976.

McReynolds, Louise. *The News under Russia's Old Regime: The Development of a Mass-Circulation Press*. Princeton, NJ: Princeton University Press, 1991.

Metropolis: Centre and Symbol of Our Times. Edited by Phillip Kasinitz. London: Macmillan, 1995.

Miłosz, Czesław. *The History of Polish Literature*. Berkeley and Los Angeles: University of California Press, 1983.

———. *A Treatise on Poetry*. Translated by the author and Robert Haas. 1956. Reprint, New York: Ecco, 2001.

Mossakowska, Wanda, and Anna Zeńczak. *Kraków na starej fotografii*. Cracow: Wydawnictwo Literackie, 1984.

Myśliński, Jerzy. "Nakłady prasy społeczno-politycznej w Galicyi w latach 1881–1913." *Rocznik historyczne czasopismennictwa polskiego* (*RHCzP*) 4, nos. 1, 2 (1965).

———. "Prasa polska w Galicji w dobie autonomicznej (1867–1918)." In *Historia prasy polskiej w latach 1864–1918*, ed. Zenon Kmiecik et al., 2:125–27. Warsaw: Państwowe Wydawnictwo Naukowe, 1976.

——. "Strona finansowa wydawnictwa 'Krytyka,' 1910–1913." *RHCzP* 5, no. 1 (1966).

——. *Studia nad prasą polską społeczno-polityczną w zachodniej Galicji, 1905–1914.* Warsaw: Państwowe Wydawnictwo Naukowe, 1970.

——. "Z dziejów prasy konserwatywnej w Krakowie przed I wojną światowną. Sprawy finansownie i wydawnictwa." *RHCzP* 5, no. 1 (1966).

Nalepa, Mirosław. *Rozwój krakowskiej komunikacji zbiorowej w aspekcie działań samorządu krakowskiego w latach 1866–1939.* Master's thesis (under the direction of Krzysztof Zamorski), Institute of History, Jagiellonian University, 2000.

Nead, Lynda. *Myths of Sexuality: Representations of Women in Victorian Britain.* New York: B. Blackwell, 1988.

——. *Victorian Babylon: People, Streets, and Images in Nineteenth-Century London.* New Haven, CT: Yale University Press, 2000.

Nemes, Robert. *The Once and Future Budapest.* DeKalb: Northern Illinois University Press, 2005.

Neuberger, Joan. *Hooliganism: Crime, Culture, and Power in St. Petersburg, 1900–1914.* Berkeley and Los Angeles: University of California Press, 1993.

Nowacki, Kazimierz. *Architektura krakowskich teatrów.* Cracow: Wydawnictwo Literackie, 1982.

Orton, Lawrence. "The Formation of Modern Cracow, 1866–1914." *Austrian History Yearbook* 19–20 (1983–1984): 105–17.

——. "The Stańczyk Portfolio and the Politics of Galician Loyalism." *Polish Review* 27, nos. 1 /2 (1982): 55–64.

Osborne, Peter. "Modernity Is a Qualitative, not a Chronological Category." *New Left Review* 192 (1992): 65–84.

Park, Robert E. "The Natural History of the Newspaper." *American Journal of Sociology* 29 (November 1923): 273–89.

Pijaj, Stanisław. *Między polskim patriotyzmem a habsburgskim lojalizmem. Polacy wobec przemian ustrojowych.* Cracow: Towarzystwo Wydawnicze "Historia Iagellonica," 2003.

Popa, Maria Raluca, and Emily Gunzburger Makaš. "Bucharest." In *Capital Cities in the Aftermath of Empires: Planning in Central and Southeastern Europe,* ed. Emily Gunzburger Makaš and Tanja Damljanović Conley, 61–74. London and New York: Routledge, 2010.

Porter, Brian. *When Nationalism Began to Hate: Imagining Politics in Nineteenth-Century Poland.* New York: Oxford University Press, 2000.

Próchnik, Adam. *Ignacy Daszyński. Życie—praca—walka.* Radom and Warsawa: Polska Partia Socjalistyczna, Towarzystwo Uniwersytetu Robotniczego, 1996.

Prokopovych, Markian. *Habsburg Lemberg: Architecture, Public Space, and Politics in the Galician Capital, 1772–1914.* West Lafayette, IN: Purdue University Press, 2009.

Przygrodzki Robert L. "Tsar Vasilii Shuiskii, the Staszic Palace, and Nineteenth-Century Russian Politics in Warsaw." In *Polish Encounters, Russian Identity,* ed. Bozena Shallcross and David L. Ransel, 144–59. Bloomington: Indiana University Press, 2005.

Purchla, Jacek. *Cracow in the European Core.* Cracow: International Cultural Centre, 2000.

———. *Jak powstał nowoczesny Kraków.* Cracow: Wydawnictwo Literackie, 1990.

———. *Krakau unter Österreichischer Herrschaft, 1846–1918. Faktoren seiner Entwick lung.* Vienna: Böhlau, 1993.

———. *Kraków. Prowincja czy metropolia?* Cracow: Universitas, 1996.

———. "Liberalyzm i symbolika a powstanie nowoczesnego Krakowa." In *Kraków na przełomie XIX i XX wieku,* ed. Jan M. Małecki, 115–23. Cracow: Wydawnictwo Literackie, 1983.

———. "Local Government and the Civilizational Space of Cracow in the Nineteenth Century." In *Mayors and City Halls,* ed. Jacek Purchla, 253–74. Cracow: International Culture Centre, 1998.

———. *Matecznik polski. Pozaekonomiczne czynniki rozwoju Krakowa w okresie autonomii galicyjskiej.* Cracow: Znak, 1992.

———. "Z dziejów mieszczaństwa krakowskiego w XIX i XX wieku." *Znak* 37 (September–October 1985): 109–125.

Riis, Jacob. *How the Other Half Lives: Studies among the Tenements of New York.* 1891, 1901. Reprint, New York: Dover, 1971.

Rosenthal, Anton. "The Arrival of the Electric Streetcar and the Conflict over Progress in Early Twentieth-Century Montevideo." *Journal of Latin American Studies* 27, no. 2 (May 1995): 319–41.

Rotenberg, Robert. *Time and Order in Metropolitan Vienna.* Washington, D.C.: Smithsonian Institution, 1992.

Różek, Michał. *Kraków.* Wrocław: Wydawnictwo Dolnośląskie, 1997.

Rusinow, Dennison. "Ethnic Politics in the Habsburg Monarchy and Successor States: Three Answers to the National Question." In *Nationalism and Empire: The Habsburg Empire and the Soviet Union,* ed. Richard L. Rudolph and David F. Good, 243–67. New York: St. Martin's Press, 1992.

Salmonowicz, Stanisław, Janusz Szwaja, and Stanisław Waltoś. *Pitaval krakowski.* Cracow: Wydawnictwo Literackie, 1974.

Schivelbusch, Wolfgang. *Disenchanted Night: The Industrialization of Light in the Nineteenth Century.* Translated by Angela Davies. Berkeley and Los Angeles: University of California Press, 1988.

———. *The Railway Journey: The Industrialization of Time and Space in the Nineteenth Century.* Berkeley and Los Angeles: University of California Press, 1986.

Schneider, Wolf. *Babylon Is Everywhere: The City as Man's Fate.* Translated by Ingeborg Sammet and John Oldenburg. New York: McGraw-Hill, 1963.

Schorske, Carl. *Fin-de-Siècle Vienna: Politics and Culture.* New York: Knopf, 1980.

———. "The Idea of the City in European Thought: Voltaire to Spengler." In *The Historian and the City,* ed. Oscar Handlin and John Burchard, 95–114. Boston: M.I.T. Press and Harvard University Press, 1963.

Schudson, Michael. "News, Public, Nation." *American Historical Review* 107, no. 2 (April 2002): 481–96.

Schwartz, Vanessa R. *Spectacular Realities: Early Mass Culture in Fin-de-Siècle Paris.* Berkeley and Los Angeles: University of California Press, 1998.

Scobie, James R. *Buenos Aires: Plaza to Suburb, 1870–1910.* New York: Oxford University Press, 1974.

Segel, Harold. *Turn-of-the-Century Cabaret: Paris, Barcelona, Berlin, Munich, Vienna, Cracow, Moscow, St. Petersburg, Zurich.* New York: Columbia University Press, 1987.

Sennett, Richard. *Flesh and Stone: The Body and the City in Western Civilization.* New York: W. W. Norton, 1994.

Shaping the Great City: Modern Architecture in Central Europe, 1890–1937. Edited by Eve Blau and Monika Platzer. Munich and New York: Prestel, 1999.

Short, John Rennie. *Urban Theory: A Critical Assessment.* New York: Palgrave, 2006.

Simmel, Georg. "The Metropolis and Mental Life." In *The Sociology of George Simmel,* ed. Kurt H. Wolf, 409–24. New York: Free Press, 1950.

Sommerville, C. John. *The News Revolution in England: Cultural Dynamics of Daily Information.* Oxford: Oxford University Press, 1996.

Staging the Past: The Politics of Commemoration in Habsburg Central Europe, 1848 to the Present. Edited by Maria Bucur and Nancy Wingfield. West Lafayette, IN: Purdue University Press, 2001.

Stallybrass, Peter, and Allon White. *The Politics and Poetics of Transgression.* Ithaca, NY: Cornell University Press, 1986.

Statystyka Miasta Krakowa za lata 1903, 1904, i 1905. Cracow: City of Cracow, 1908.

Stauter-Halsted, Keely. "Moral Panic and the Prostitute in Partitioned Poland: Middle-Class Respectability in Defense of the Modern Nation." *Slavic Review* 68, no. 3 (Fall 2009): 557–81.

———. *The Nation in the Village: The Genesis of Peasant National Identity in Austrian Poland, 1848–1914.* Ithaca, NY: Cornell University Press, 2001.

Steed, Henry Wickham, Walter Alison Phillips, and David Hannay. *A Short History of Austria-Hungary and Poland.* London: The Encyclopedia Britannica Company, 1914.

Stoddard, John L. *John L. Stoddard's Lectures.* Vol. 6. *Berlin, Vienna, St. Petersburg, Moscow.* Boston: Bach Brothers, 1903.

Supranowicz, Elżbieta. *Nazwy ulic Krakowa.* Cracow: Instytut Języka Polskiego PAN, 1995.

Sylvester, Roshanna. "Making an Appearance: Urban 'Types' and the Creation of Respectability in Odessa's Popular Press, 1912–1914." *Slavic Review* 59, no. 4 (Winter 2000): 802–25.

———. *Tales of Old Odessa: Crime and Civility in a City of Thieves.* DeKalb: Northern Illinois University Press, 2005.

Traumatic Pasts: History, Psychiatry, and Trauma in the Modern Age, 1870–1930. Edited by Paul Lerner and Mark Micale. New York: Cambridge University Press, 2001.

Tyrowicz, Marian. "Prasa Krakowa w dziejach polskiego dziennikarstwa." *Zeszyty Prasoznawcze* 1 (1968).

Unowsky, Daniel L. *The Pomp and Politics of Patriotism: Imperial Celebrations in Habsburg Austria, 1848–1916.* West Lafayette, IN: Purdue University Press, 2005.

The Urbanization of European Society in the Nineteenth Century. Edited by Andrew Lees and Lynn Lees. Lexington, MA: D. C. Heath, 1976.

Vernacular Art in Central Europe. Edited by Jacek Purchla. Cracow: International Cultural Centre, 2001.

Visions of the Modern City. Edited by William Sharpe and Leonard Wallock. Proceedings of the Heyman Center for the Humanities. New York: Columbia University, 1984.

Vošahlíková, Pavla. *Jak se žilo za časů Františka Josefa I.* Prague: Nakladeství Svoboda, 1996.

Vyleta, Daniel M. *Crime, Jews, and News: Vienna, 1895–1914.* New York: Berghan Books, 2007.

Walkowitz, Judith. *City of Dreadful Delight: Narratives of Sexual Danger in Late Victorian London.* Chicago, 1992.

Wandycz, Piotr. *The Lands of Partitioned Poland, 1795–1918.* 1974. Reprint, Seattle: University of Washington, 1993.

Wapiński, Roman. "Transformations of Customs and Behaviour in Poland during the First Decades of the Twentieth Century: A Survey of Research Problems." *Acta Poloniae Historica* 94 (2006): 189–205.

Weber, Eugen. *Peasants into Frenchmen: The Modernization of Rural France, 1870–1914.* Stanford, CA: Stanford University Press, 1976.

Wierzbicki, Robert. *Wodociągi Krakowa do roku 1939.* Cracow: Miejskie Przedsiębiorstwo Wodociągów i Kanalizacji, 1999.

Wilk, Bernadeta. *W 'Małym Wiedniu nad Wisłą.'* Cracow: Wydawnictwo Naukowe Papieskiej Akademii Teologicznej, 2008.

Williams, Rosalind H. *Dream Worlds: Mass Consumption in Late Nineteenth-Century France.* Berkeley and Los Angeles: University of California Press, 1982.

Witzmann, Reingard. "The Two Faces of Vienna." In *Vienna, 1890–1920,* ed. Robert Waissenberger, 65–98. New York: Rizzoli, 1984.

Władyka, Władysław. *Krew na pierwszej stronie. Sensacyjne dzienniki Drugiej Rzeczypospolitej.* Warsaw: Czytelnik, 1982.

Wolff, Larry. *Child Abuse in Freud's Vienna: Postcards from the End of the World.* New York: New York University Press, 1995.

——. "Dynastic Conservatism and Poetic Violence in Fin-de-Siècle Cracow: The Habsburg Matrix of Polish Modernism." *American Historical Review* 106, no. 2 (June 2001): 735–64.

Wood, Nathaniel D. "Becoming a 'Great City': Metropolitan Imaginations and Apprehensions in Cracow's Popular Press, 1900–1914." *Austrian History Yearbook* 33 (2002): 105–29.

——. "Becoming Metropolitan: Cracow's Popular Press and the Representation of

Modern Urban Life, 1900–1915." Ph.D. diss., Indiana University, 2004.

———. "Not just the National: Modernity and the Myth of Europe in the Capital Cities of Central and Southeastern Europe." In *Capital Cities in the Aftermath of Empires: Planning in Central and Southeastern Europe*, ed. Emily Gunzburger Makaš and Tanja Damljanović Conley, 258–69. London and New York: Routledge, 2010.

———. "Sex Scandals, Sexual Violence, and the Word on the Street: The Kolasówna *Lustmord* in Cracow's Popular Press, 1905–06." *The Journal of the History of Sexuality* (forthcoming).

———. "Urban Self-Identification in East Central Europe before the Great War: The Case of Cracow." *East Central Europe* 33, pts. 1–2 (2006): 11–31.

Woźniakowski, Jacek. "Old City, Modern Art." In *Cracow: Dialogue of Traditions*, ed. Zbigniew Baran, trans. William Brand, 77–94. Cracow: Znak, 1991.

Wyka, Kazimierz. "Kraków stolicą Młodej Polski." In *Kraków i Małopolska przez dzieje*, ed. Celina Bobińska, 339–52. Cracow: Wydawnictwo Literackie, 1970.

Wynne, Deborah. *The Sensation Novel and the Victorian Family Magazine*. London: Palgrave, 2001.

Wyspiański, Stanisław. *"Wesele" o "Weselu."* Edited by Anna Boska. Warsaw: Phillip Wilson, 1998.

Zamorski, Krzysztof. "Kraków-przestrzeń społeczna." In *Kraków. Dziedzictwo wieków*, ed. Jan Małecki, 74–101. Cracow: Muzeum Historyczne Miasta, 2006.

———. "Rozwój demograficzny Krakowa w ciągu wieków." In *Kraków. Nowe studia nad rozwojem miasta*, ed. Jerzy Wyrozumski, 841–87. Cracow, 2007.

Zbijewska, Krystyna. "Saga rodu Szczepańskich." *Kraków—magazyn kulturalny* 4 (1991): 45–46.

———. "Z dziejów słynnego romansu. Nieznane listy Gabrieli Zapolskiej." *Przekrój* 24 (8 September 1991): 8–9.

Żbikowski, Andrzej. *Żydzi krakowscy i ich gmina w latach 1869–1919*. Warsaw: Wydawnictwo DiG, 1994.

Żeleński, Tadeusz. *See* Boy-Żeleński, Tadeusz, under the heading Other Primary Sources.

Zelizer, Viviana A. *Pricing the Priceless Child: The Changing Social Value of Children*. New York: Basic Books, 1985.

Zyblikiewicz, Lidia. "Education and Social Structure according to the Cracow Census of 1880." In *L'enseignement des Élites en Europe Centrale (19e–20e siècles)*, ed. Victor Krady and Mariusz Kulczykowski, 111–20. Cracow: Instytut Historii Uniwersytetu Jagiellońskiego, 1999.

———. *Kobieta w Krakowie w 1880 r. Studium demograficzne*. Cracow: Historia Iagellonica, 1999.

Index

*Bold page numbers indicate illustrations.